3DS MAX 4 MEDIA ANIMATION

BY
John P. Chismar

New Riders

201 West 103rd Street, Indianapolis, Indiana 46290

Project 1   Funhouse

Project 2   2002 Vote Machine

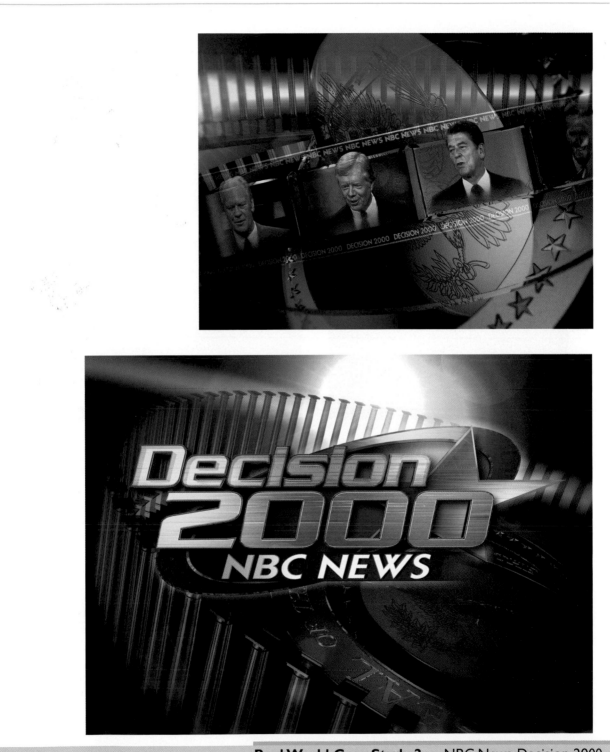

3DS MAX 4 MEDIA ANIMATION

BY

John P. Chismar

201 West 103rd Street, Indianapolis, Indiana 46290

3ds max 4 Media Animation

International Standard Book Number: 0-7357-1059-7

Library of Congress Catalog Card Number: 00-108084

Printed in the United States of America

First Printing: June 2001

05 04 03 02 01   7 6 5 4 3 2 1

Interpretation of the printing code: The rightmost double-digit number is the year of the book's printing; the rightmost single-digit number is the number of the book's printing. For example, the printing code 01-1 shows that the first printing of the book occurred in 2001.

Trademarks

Warning and Disclaimer

Publisher
David Dwyer

Associate Publisher
Al Valvano

Executive Editor
Steve Weiss

Product Marketing Manager
Kathy Malmloff

Managing Editor
Sarah Kearns

Acquisitions Editor
Linda Anne Bump

Development Editor
Barb Terry

Project Editors
Sean Monkhouse
Jake McFarland

Copy Editor
Audra McFarland

Technical Editor
Larry Minton

Cover Designer
Aren Howell

Interior Designers
Wil Cruz
Suzanne Pettypiece

Compositors
Kim Scott
Ron Wise

Proofreader
Marcia Deboy

Indexer
Lisa Stumpf

Media Developer
Jay Payne

Contents at a Glance

Introduction..XV

Part 1   Funhouse

1   Erecting the Simple Billboard Objects.........................2

2   Finishing the Billboard..................................50

3   Creating the Funhouse Environment and Special Effects........106

4   Finishing the Funhouse Animation.......................146

Part 2   2002 Vote Machine

5   Building the Vote Machine..............................182

6   Assembling the 2002 Vote Machine.....................214

7   Adding Materials to the Vote Machine and
     Creating the Environment.............................281

8   Animating and Rendering the 2002 Vote Machine........315

Part 3   TV 3 News Open

9   Creating the Globe Environment........................366

10   Animating the Globe Environment......................406

11   Finishing the TV 3 News Open Project..................436

Part 4   Real World Case Studies

Real World Case Study 1: The Millennium..................480

Real World Case Study 2: NBC News Decision 2000..........508

Real World Case Study 3: Newsfront......................534

Appendix What's on the CD-ROM   559

Table of Contents

Introduction   **XV**

Part I Funhouse

1 Erecting the Simple Billboard Objects   **2**

  Creating the Shapes 5
    Setting Up the Flaming Billboard Backdrop 5
    Working with the Clown's Body 27
    Creating the Clown Hands 35
    Building the Clown's Head 45
  In Conclusion 49

2 Finishing the Billboard   **50**

  Building the Funhouse Type 52
    Creating the Type Objects 52
    Painting the Funhouse Type Objects 64
  Finishing the Billboard 69
    Working with the Billboard 69
    Creating the Lighting Fixtures and the Billboard Post and
    Applying the Lighting 81
  In Conclusion 105

3 Creating the Funhouse Environment and Special Effects   **106**

  Setting Up the Funhouse Environment 108
    Creating the Camera Animation 108
    Creating the Background Environment 119
    Adding Special Effects 126
  Tweaking the Scene 142
    Brightening the Colors of the Billboard 142
    Illuminating the Funhouse Type 144
  In Conclusion 145

4 Finishing the Funhouse Animation   **146**

  Animating the Head Object 148
  Animating the Hands 152
  Animating the Lights 162
  Smashing the Bulb 165
  Adding Lightning 174
  Rendering the Animation 178
  In Conclusion 179

Part 2 2002 Vote Machine

5 Building the Vote Machine   **182**

Using an Adobe Illustrator File to Create the
2002 Vote Machine 185
Correcting Problems That Occur in Imported Files 186
    Scaling and Neatening the Imported Shape 186
    Improving the Screen 195
    Adjusting the Vertices in the Body 199
    Working on the Back Foot 203
    Fixing the Legs, Keyboard, and Remaining Feet 209
In Conclusion 213

6 Assembling the 2002 Vote Machine   **214**

Putting the Objects Together 216
    The Body Object 217
    The Legs 222
    The Keyboard 242
    The Monitor 244
    The Armature 250
    Attaching the Keyboard to the Body 256
    Attaching the Monitor to the Body 267
    Creating the Monitor Armature Hierarchy 275
In Conclusion 280

**7 Adding Materials to the Vote Machine and Creating
the Environment**   **281**

Adding Materials to the Vote Machine 283
    Creating the Metal Material for the Body of the
    Vote Machine 283
    Creating the Material for the Faceplate of the
    Vote Machine 286
    Creating the Material for the Monitor Screen 293
Creating the 2002 VOTE Environment 300
    Finishing the Hierarchy 301
    Instancing the Vote Machine 302
    Creating the Circle Star Ceiling 304
    Adding Lights and Creating the Floor 310
In Conclusion 314

8 Animating and Rendering the 2002 Vote Machine   **315**

Adding the Musical Score 316
Animating the Scene 317
    Planning the Animation to the Storyboard and Music ...317
    Animating Shot One 319

Animating Shot Two 330

Animating Shot Three 341

Animating Shot Four 346

Animating Shot Five 355

Putting the Rendered Images to the Music 359

In Conclusion 364

Part 3   TV 3 News Open

9   Creating the Globe Environment   366

Creating the Objects 369

   Setting Up the Wireframe-Like Object 369

   Adding the Globe and Its Rings 377

   Shedding Light on the Scene 381

   Applying a Material to the Globe Object 384

   Applying a Material to the Ring Objects 392

Adding the Environment 394

Adding the Type Elements 396

In Conclusion 405

10   Animating the Globe Environment   406

Adding Sound to the Scene 408

Animating the Camera 410

Bringing the Scene to Life 412

Checking the Lighting in the Scene 418

Adding the Lens Flare 423

In Conclusion 435

11   Finishing the TV 3 News Open Project   436

Creating the TV 3 Logo Scene 438

   Building the TV 3 Logo 441

   Creating Animatable Venetian Blinds 451

   Animating the Environment Background 456

   Adding a Strip of Text 461

Animating the TV 3 Logo 465

Setting Up the Lens Flare 469

In Conclusion 477

Part 4   Real World Case Studies

Real World Case Study 1: The Millennium   480

Ready, Set, Go! 482

Creating the Animation 483

   Shot 1: The Clocks 484

   The Clock-Map01 Object 486

   The Clock-Glass01 Object 487

Shot 2: The NBC Peacock 490
   The Cross-Section 491
   The Ring of Light 493
   The Peacock Feathers 494
   The Peacock Particle Effect 495
Shot 3: The Globe and the Clock 497
   The Clock Face 498
   The Globe's Volumetric Beams 500
   The Camera 500
Shot 4: The Millennium Logo 501
   Building the Logo 503
   The MSNBC Type 503
   The Millennium Particles 505
Rendering the Final Composite 507

Real World Case Study 2: NBC News Decision 2000   508
Making the Preliminary Studies 511
   RingsA01.max 511
   RingsB01.max 513
Working with the Storyboard 514
Creating Shot 1 515
   The Presidential Seal 516
   The Colonnade and NBC NEWS Type 520
   The Environment 520
   The NBC NEWS Shooters 523
   A Few Extra Thoughts 524
Creating Shot 2 524
   The Ring 524
   The Presidents' Heads 526
   Finishing the Scene 526
Creating Shot 3 527
   The NBC Peacock 528
   The U.S. Capitol Dome 528
   The Presidential Seal 529
Creating Shot 4 530
   The Logo Resolve 530
   The Materials 531
Viewing the Final Animation 533

Real World Case Study 3: Newsfront   534
Working Through the Pre-Production Phase 537
   The First Attempt at a Flythrough 537
   The Second Attempt at a Flythrough 538
   The Successful Flythrough 539
   The Final Camera Animation 541

Creating the NBC Peacock Section 542

Putting Together the Environment 543

The Barcode 543

The Mosaic Lester Headshot 544

The Shooters 544

Finishing the Peacock 546

The Textures of the Peacock 546

The Peacock Composite..548

The Monitors 549

Other Miscellaneous Layers 552

Creating the Newsfront Logo Section 552

Creating the Streaking Animation 553

Building the Vortex 555

Building the Newsfront Logo 557

Appendix   What's on the CD-ROM   559

System Requirements 560

Loading the CD Files 560

Exercise Files 560

Read This Before Opening the Software 560

About the Author

John Chismar, Senior 3d Animator at MSNBC, has been working in 3D animation since 1991 and in media animation since 1993. Using 3ds max, Chismar has garnered several awards for his work: 1997 and 1998 Emmy Awards; *3D Design* magazine Big Kahuna Awards in 1998, 1999, and 2000; three Broadcast Design Association International Bronze Awards; and a 1995–96 Emmy nomination. How did he reach that point?

After John graduated from high school, he enrolled in a two-year Broadcast Communications program at Luzerne County Community College (LCCC) in Pennsylvania. In his second semester, the school acquired Video Toaster, which ran on a Commodore Amiga 2000. The "toaster," as everyone called it, included a new 3D software program called LightWave 3D.

Up to that point in his life, John had never really touched a computer. But there was something about the 3D world that enticed him. He asked the professor for a copy of the LightWave manual, took it home, and read it from start to finish, without even touching the computer. Soon he was working at the college as a teacher's assistant, tending to the television studio, adjusting equipment, using LightWave, and figuring out new things to teach the professor, who was too busy to learn the software. John's love for 3D snowballed.

In 1991, John worked weekends for WVIA (PBS), in Pittston, PA, operating studio camera and soundboard part-time for minimum wage. There he made a contact at the local ABC affiliate, WNEP, in Montage, PA. The WNEP staff let John volunteer during the night shift for a few months, and he learned many tricks of the trade. John says the people at WNEP are still making some of the most impressive locally produced graphics he's ever seen.

In June of 1992, a friend of John's informed him that the small company for which he worked, Audio/Video Concepts, had an opening for a camera guy. It turned out that the boss was away on vacation for a week, so John's friend just decided to take John in and show him the ropes. A few days later, a man John had never seen before entered the room, looked him up and down, and said, "Who are you?" John quickly replied, "I'm John, the new camera guy. Who are you?" With authority, the stranger replied, "I am Juan, the boss, and *I* didn't hire *you*!" After a half hour or so, Juan calmed down and hired John, and he remained with Audio/Video Concepts until May 1993.

Then John was offered a part-time job at WYOU, the CBS affiliate in Scranton, PA. The hours conflicted with the hours he was working at A/V Concepts, so he quit the company. When he notified Juan that he was leaving, Juan said, "Tell me what they are giving you, and I will beat it." John smiled and said, "Juan, it's part-time, and it's paying $4.75 an hour." He almost had a heart attack and said, "I'm already paying you almost double that, and it's full-time! Why do you want to go?" John's answer was simple. "It will look better on my resume."

While John was working for WYOU, the station bought a new PC and 3D Studio DOS version 2. The art director was far too busy working on his larger projects and creating animation on the Art Star to learn the program. John took it upon himself to learn it. He found that the PC was faster than the Amiga he was using to run LightWave, so he abandoned LightWave and spent all his time working in 3D Studio.

In November of 1994, a reporter friend of John's tipped him off that the NBC affiliate, WBRE Wilkes-Barre, PA, was looking to start an art department. One month later, John was the new Art Director at WBRE, where he was basically a one-man show, creating graphics for both the 6 and 11 o'clock news. His responsibilities also included making all the on-air animations for news, promotions, and commercial production. John worked primarily with 3D Studio DOS versions 3 and 4, Photoshop, and the Grass Valley Video Designer (a 2D paint device). While working this job, he was one of three entrants nominated for the regional Emmy Award for graphics. The winner was the Art Director at the ABC affiliate that had showed him the ropes just a few years back.

While he was at WBRE, a few of John's friends left to live in New Jersey and work for CNBC, a new start-up station that focused on business. In late 1995, John decided to fax his resume to CNBC and take his chances. Several weeks later, he saw one of the secretaries in the office using the fax machine. He asked her, "You're supposed to put the pages in *face down*?" She smiled and replied with a nod. Later that night, he sent his resume off to CNBC again—this time with the pages face down in the fax machine.

A few weeks later, John started working at MSNBC, a new cable station that was just starting. The company didn't even have any 3D equipment. While he worked designing graphics for the News with Brian Williams and waited for a 3D machine at MSNBC, John bought a computer of his own and a copy of 3D Studio Max. Every night he would spend a few hours teaching himself the software and creating pretend animations. By the time a machine was in place at MSNBC, John was ready to crank out award-winning animations.

In the summer of 1998, John was so thoroughly disappointed with the 3D Studio Max books on the market that he emailed New Riders Publishing to explore the possibility of writing a book on 3D Studio Max. He felt that a book that walked the reader step by step through a project would be far better than any short tutorial. New Riders agreed. The result was his first book, *3D Studio Max 3 Media Animation*.

Acknowledgments

I want to say "Thank you" to the following people for their advice and support:

Vince Diga: For a job well done designing the Funhouse billboard and environment.

Victor Newman: For finding the time in your crazy schedule to storyboard the 2002 Vote project.

John Hudson: For stepping up to bat late in the game and storyboarding the TV3 animation.

Gordon Miller: For composing such delicious soundtracks for all three projects.

Larry Minton: For taking on the daunting task of technical editing the book.

Amy Beth Jackson: For always standing by me and offering unconditional support.

Barb Terry, Linda Bump, and the rest of the New Riders crew: For putting up with me and working so hard to create another great book!

NBC and MSNBC: For encouraging this project.

Frank Delise, Jo-Ann Palmer, David Marks, and the rest of the discreet crew: For always being there when I need a helping hand.

Dr. Smedley: For hypnotizing me into a smoke-free life. It's been over a year!

Jason Bube: For listen to me whine about how busy I am.

Marian Traistaru: For keeping me posted on his animations in Romania.

Mom and Dad: For bringing me up right and always being there for me. I love yas!

I also want to say thanks to you, the reader, for your support, enthusiasm, and dedication.

—John Chismar

A Message from New Riders

As the reader of this book, you are our most important critic and commentator. We value your opinion and want to know what we're doing right, what we could do better, in what areas you'd like to see us publish, and any other words of wisdom you're willing to pass our way.

As Executive Editor at New Riders, I welcome your comments. You can fax, email, or write me directly to let me know what you did or didn't like about this book—as well as what we can do to make our books better. When you write, please be sure to include this book's title, ISBN, and author, as well as your name and phone or fax number. I will carefully review your comments and share them with the authors and editors who worked on the book.

Please note that I cannot help you with technical problems related to the topic of this book, and that due to the high volume of email I receive, I might not be able to reply to every message. Thanks.

Email: steve.weiss@newriders.com

Mail: Steve Weiss
         Executive Editor
         New Riders Publishing
         201 West 103rd Street
         Indianapolis, IN 46290 USA

Visit Our Web Site: www.newriders.com

On our Web site, you'll find information about our other books, the authors we partner with, book updates and file downloads, promotions, discussion boards for online interaction with other users and with technology experts, and a calendar of trade shows and other professional events with which we'll be involved. We hope to see you around.

Email Us from Our Web Site

Go to www.newriders.com and click on the Contact link if you

- Have comments or questions about this book.
- Want to report errors that you have found in this book.
- Have a book proposal or are interested in writing for New Riders.
- Would like us to send you one of our author kits.
- Are an expert in a computer topic or technology and are interested in being a reviewer or technical editor.
- Want to find a distributor for our titles in your area.
- Are an educator/instructor who wants to preview New Riders books for classroom use. In the body/comments area, include your name, school, department, address, phone number, office days/hours, text currently in use, and enrollment in your department, along with your request for either desk/examination copies or additional information.

Call Us or Fax Us

You can reach us toll-free at (800) 571-5840 + 9 + 3567 (ask for New Riders). If outside the U.S., please call 1-317-581-3500 and ask for New Riders. If you prefer, you can fax us at 1-317-581-4663, Attention: New Riders.

 Note

Technical Support for This Book Although we encourage entry-level users to get as much as they can out of our books, keep in mind that our books are written assuming a non-beginner level of user-knowledge of the technology. This assumption is reflected in the brevity and shorthand nature of some of the tutorials.

New Riders will continually work to create clearly written, thoroughly tested and reviewed technology books of the highest educational caliber and creative design. We value our customers more than anything—that's why we're in this business— but we cannot guarantee to each of the thousands of you who buy and use our books that we will be able to work individually with you through tutorials or content with which you may have questions. We urge readers who need help in working through exercises or other material in our books—and who need this assistance immediately— to use as many of the resources that our technology and technical communities can provide, especially the many online user groups and list servers available.

Introduction

Just a few years back, I was a young animator

willing to do anything to get a job in the field

of 3D animation. I worked for minimum

wage, and I even worked for free—anything

to get my portfolio and professional working

experience started.

In my thirst for knowledge, I bought magazines, books, and training videos, hoping to get more information to develop my style and skill. It didn't take long to figure out that these materials weren't providing me with the information necessary to launch a successful career. My determination forced me to explore and experiment with the available software in an effort to re-create the beautiful animations the pros were making. After more than nine years of experimentation, wandering through the vast capabilities of 3D, I have learned a great deal about the best ways to create animation.

Welcome to my second book, *3ds max 4 Media Animation*. For those of you familiar with my first book, you can expect the same quality of projects, more techniques, and practical workflows. With this book, I am continuing the tradition of providing projects from start to finish, explaining every step along the way. And in my pursuit to continuously improve the quality of tutorials, I have added audio to each project in the book.

While learning inside tricks and techniques, you will also learn how to correctly plan your projects to streamline the production process and make them "edit-friendly." You will gain insight about the pre-production and post-production processes. I am going to share with you the experience I have gained, my insight into successful design in 3D, and the working style that enables me to produce high-quality animations.

What Is Media Animation?

Media animation is the rapidly growing industry that provides graphic content for television, film, print, Internet, and every other multimedia format imaginable. The industry demands original content under tight deadlines. In this fast-paced industry where the speed of the technology pushes your skills to the edge, people working in the field need a deep understanding of the tools available to them, and they must know how to create cutting-edge effects on-the-fly.

Many animators in the corporate world complain that the "powers that be" think the animator clicks a "Make Animation" button and a wonderful animation manifests itself. It's true that those in management often misunderstand the term *computer animation*; they don't understand the amount of work that is actually involved. Because of this misunderstanding, the animator must be prepared, must have the ability to create any type of animation or effect that is expected of them, and must be able to edit and change their work quickly.

Who Needs This Book?

Many computer graphics students learn just enough of 3ds max 4 to make bare-bones animation and are then left feeling dissatisfied with their end products. Not anymore.

This industry has many one-person graphics departments, and (believe me) I know what that's like. When no resources are available to help the lonely animators, they are forced to load pre-made scenes or geometry. Not anymore.

An inexperienced animator who manages to land a job in a big-name design company has hope of learning from the pros on the staff. Unfortunately, the pros that know the tricks don't have time to share their expertise with new employees; they are too busy working on their projects.

In this book, however, a pro is going to take the time to share what he knows so that you can quickly create sophisticated, fascinating animations on your own.

What Does This Book Offer?

3ds max 4 Media Animation is unique because it provides 3ds max animators with the working knowledge to better perform their jobs. You don't just walk blindly through steps to make prefab effects that have only one specific use. This book helps you create compelling animations with predictable rendering results in a very short amount of production time. As you read this book, complete the exercises, and examine the sample files, you will learn how to think more creatively, plan your animations, and effectively build your projects.

The collection of sample files on the accompanying CD and the scenes you will create during the exercises are valuable reference resources. Simply refer to the samples when you later need to determine what sort of effects or moves you want to use in your animations. Then refresh your mind with the techniques you used to create them, and you're off and running. You'll probably even find yourself adding your own new discoveries and cool sample files, and you'll end up with quite a resource library as your experience grows and your career progresses.

How Is This Book Organized?

3ds max 4 Media Animation is organized into four parts:

> Part 1: Funhouse
>
> Part 2: 2002 Vote Machine
>
> Part 3: TV 3 News Open
>
> Part 4: Real World Case Studies

Part 1, "Funhouse," has a moderate level of outside artistic direction. A designer carefully designed the logo, and we received a sound track to sync the animation to. Extra attention is necessary to ensure that the animation moves correctly to the audio.

Part 2, "2002 Vote Machine," is storyboarded in full color. In this project, we choreograph multiple cameras to the audio, with straight cut transitions from camera to camera.

Part 3, "TV 3 News Open," is loosely storyboarded in full color. This project requires us to use our artistic judgment to take the storyboard to the next creative level. The animation will flow to a musical score.

In Part 4: "Real World Case Studies," we take a behind-the-scenes look at how I created three 3D animations for the cable news channel MSNBC.

This book structures the projects so you are placed into the mind of an animator. Approaches to modeling, animating, effects, rendering, and compositing are described in full detail, along with choreography, composition, and color. The purpose of these projects is to help you create your own animation and to develop your own style without spending years in independent study.

What Are the Goals of the Exercises?

The trick to accurate and streamlined completion of projects is the development of good working habits. Along with sharing technical knowledge, I've written the exercises to expose you to the time-tested processes, which organize everything from creating geometry to final renderings. By working through the exercises, you learn these basic principles:

- *Economize.* Create your objects using the fewest polygons necessary to produce the desired rendered output. Keep your scenes uncluttered. Use lights wisely. Organize your track editor and your hierarchies.

- *Use logical naming conventions.* Give all the elements in your scene unique descriptive names so they can be easily located for adjustments. This applies to everything including materials, modifiers, geometry, lights, and cameras.

- *Save files.* Save your work frequently! Apply a unique name each time you reach a satisfactory point in your progress. This applies when enough has changed in the scene and you are happy with the results. Having the progression of a project at different stages is very handy when changes are necessary.

- *Test.* Create test renders frequently during setup to cut down on rework time. This also decreases the time it takes to locate a problem that occurs in the final stages of a project.

- *Identify problems.* When viewing a test render, study it carefully. Examine it frame by frame. Check the way the light hits the objects, and make sure that the motion is smooth. Look for anomalies in the output, and make sure the materials are applied correctly.

How Should You Work with the Files on the CD?

To organize your work while working on the projects, I highly recommend that you create an organized directory structure on your hard drive.

Example: Drive:\3ds4-ma\

Before starting a project, you should create a subfolder for the project.

Example: Drive:\3ds4-ma\project1\

Copy the Maps and Sounds folders from the respective project folder on the CD into the project folder on your hard drive.

Example: Drive:\3ds4-ma\project1\maps
Drive:\3ds4-ma\project1\sounds

As you are prompted to save your work within 3ds max 4, you should save it in the respective project folder.

Example: Drive:\3ds4-ma\project1\example.max

Note

> **Important note about working with 3ds max 4:** It is assumed that you are working
> with a default installation of 3ds max 4. This means that if you have changed any of your
> preferences or customized any settings in 3ds max 4, you may encounter unexpected
> problems while working on the projects. This is especially the case when working with
> 3ds max 4 units of measurement. It is assumed that you are working in Generic Units,
> configured in the Customize, Units Setup dialog.

Personal Statement

In keeping with the spirit of my first book, *3D Studio Max 3 Media Animation*, the
projects in this book are completely new. It is my strong opinion that learning materials must be completely rewritten and developed with every iteration of the software. Not only does this ensure that the information is fresh, but it also keeps the
design principles current with the industry. This book is my way of sharing my real-
world knowledge with you. We need to share ideas and information to push 3D
design further. Our combined knowledge will take the world of 3D animation to
new levels. Thank you for joining me in this pursuit!

Part 1

Funhouse

The first project of this book gives you an opportunity to approach media animation from a little different angle, as the animator involved in an advertising campaign. Here's the scenario: Because of the popularity of thrill rides, the amusement park industry has become very competitive, and most major parks claim to have the biggest, fastest, most frightening chills. Even though roller coasters are getting taller and faster, die-hard fans are (unfortunately) becoming desensitized to the experience. Thrill-ride designers are constantly brainstorming new ideas or figuring new ways to combine the old thrills into new concepts.

Lynch Family Amusement Park has decided to spend millions of dollars on a new ride they hope will boost their proceeds next year. The concept is simple, "Make the greatest 'dark ride' ever!" The Lynch family is keeping a tight upper lip on the details of the ride, but what is publicly known about this ride is that it's going to be fast, scary, and hi-tech.

Because the summer season is right around the corner, they have decided to roll out their media blitz and get the buzz started. They hired a production company to put together a commercial for them, and luckily it's the one you're working for right now.

Chapters 1 through 4 step you through the animation of that commercial.

Chapter 1

Erecting the Simple Billboard Objects

As you return to your workstation from your morning coffee with Mr. Boss, he begins to fill you in on the details. "Oh, those crazy guys over at Lynch Family Amusement Park are at it again.

They are building some new thrill ride and it's supposed to be really scary, with loads of deranged clowns on the prowl. The ride is currently under construction, and they are ready to start the media buzz."

"What I want you to do is animate the logo. Vince is finishing up the illustration right now, and when it's complete, he will deliver it to you with any associated textures. I'm sure you can handle it. That's why we pay you the *big* bucks." Mr. Boss chuckles as he strides away to another big meeting.

You sit down in your comfy computer chair, press Ctrl+Alt+Delete, and log in to your workstation. Just as you find yourself getting comfortable, Vince sneaks up on you from behind and shoves a beautifully crafted illustration in front of your face (see Figure 1.1). "Here you go," Vince quietly says. "Oh, and you will find the associated files on this disk as well." "Thanks!" you reply as you watch Vince toss a hipshot with his yo-yo. He nods in your direction and walks away wearing a toothy smile.

Figure 1.1
The Funhouse project illustration.

You say to yourself, "Hey, I gotta get me one of those yo-yos. When's payday?" You look down at your desk, and Vince's illustration reminds you that you have work to do. "Ah, before I start, I'm getting something with loads of caffeine."

In this chapter, you gain experience in the following areas:

- Working with Viewport Background images
- Creating shapes for the purpose of extruding Spline sub-object level Boolean operations

- Using the Extrude modifier
- Applying planar UVW Map modifiers
- Working with Material IDs
- Creating multi/sub-object materials

Creating the Shapes

As you study Vince's illustration, one thing becomes quite obvious: You have a lot of shapes to create and extrude. At first it may seem like an overwhelming amount of work, but the more you examine the illustration, the more you see that it isn't going to be so bad.

When it comes to being a 3D media animator, it is important to learn as much about working with shapes as possible. As you extrude, bevel, lathe, or loft shapes, they become the foundation of the objects in your scene. Therefore, you must pay close attention to the quality of the shapes you create, because later down the road, you could run into problems caused by the smallest of errors. Throughout this book, you will examine these problems and their various solutions.

However, as you work on this project, remember the importance of the shapes you are creating, because you certainly don't want to have to re-create them. You have very little time to spare, so you should get started.

Setting Up the Flaming Billboard Backdrop

Because the flaming backdrop is the back-most layer on the billboard, it would be appropriate to create it first. Not only is it the backing of the billboard, but after it is built, the backdrop will determine the scale of all the other objects in the scene. If you add parametric primitives to the scene, you may be forced to work with fractions of values or four-digit values if the billboard is too large or too small.

Exercise 1.1   Setting Up the Viewport Background: Creating the Billboard

Enough chitchat, get working! To create a billboard backdrop that matches Vince's artwork precisely, you will add a Viewport Background to your workspace.

1. Choose File > Reset to reset 3ds max 4.
2. Select the Top view and maximize it (by pressing the W key or clicking the Min/Max toggle button).
3. To add the flaming billboard backdrop image, choose Views > Viewport Background (Alt+B). The Viewport Background dialog opens (see Figure 1.2).

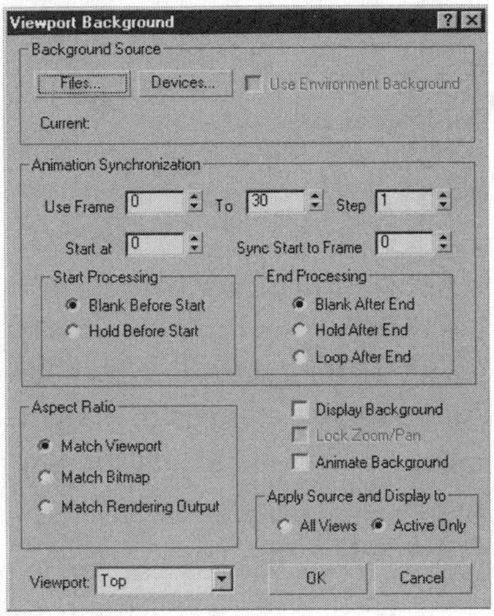

Figure 1.2
The Viewport
Background dialog.

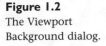

4. Click the Files button in the Background Source group to open the Select Background Image dialog.

5. From the 3ds4-ma\project1\Images folder on the included CD, choose tmpl-fire.jpg and click Open.

6. In the Aspect Ratio group of the Viewport Background dialog, select Match Bitmap, and then check Lock Zoom/Pan (see Figure 1.3). Then click OK to close the dialog.

   Choosing Match Bitmap instructs the Viewport Background dialog to use the raster images image aspect when displayed in the viewport. Checking Lock Zoom/Pan allows you to pan and zoom the bitmap along with the view as you work.

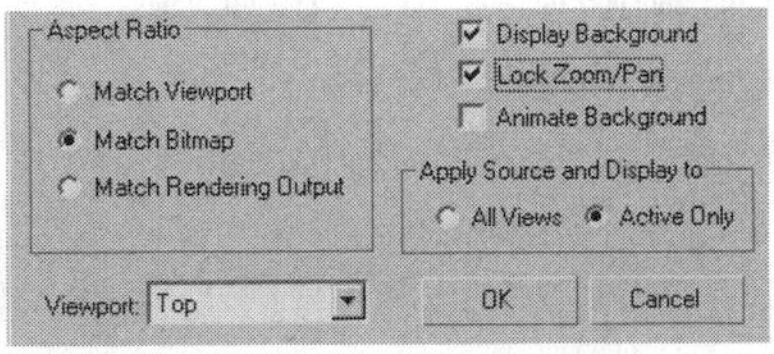

Figure 1.3
The Match Bitmap
and Lock Zoom/Pan
options are selected.

Note

If you are zooming in extremely close to examine your splines, you may want to turn off the Viewport Background by right-clicking the Top view's label and deselecting Show Background. When you zoom in close, the default 3ds max 4 Software Z-Buffer resizes the background image, sometimes to an unrealistically large size—which eats up a lot of memory and makes you wait a long time.

The fire backdrop should now occupy the Top view (Figure 1.4). You can easily trace around the edge to create the shape you will extrude to create the backdrop. Before you do so, however, get rid of the view's grid to clean up the view.

Figure 1.4
The fire template is now the background in the Top view.

7. Right-click the Top view label in the upper-left corner of the Top view and remove the check from Show Grid. The grid is no longer superimposed over the fire template.

Exercise 1.2   Using 3ds max Standard Shapes

With Vince's beautiful fire background template visible in the Top view, you can start to trace its edges. You will *not* go immediately to the Create Panel and use Line to trace everything by hand. Instead, to make life a little easier, you will create as much of it as you can by using the standard shapes from 3ds max. You'll start by creating the basic rectangle shape.

1. From the Create Panel, choose Create > Shapes > Rectangle and place the pointer at the upper-left corner of the artwork. Click and drag the mouse to the lower-right corner of the billboard and release the mouse to draw a rectangle.

   Um, something isn't so good here. The white background of the fire template matches the white color of the rectangle you just created (see Figure 1.5).

   To avoid spending a weekend reconfiguring the color preferences of 3ds max 4 and dealing with the consequences of doing so, you can just change the white background of the image to a more neutral gray color in PhotoShop and reload it. So pretend you opened PhotoShop and replaced the white with gray, and now you are ready to reload it into the scene. Make a mental note of this: Never create another template image with a white background.

2. Open the Viewport Background (Alt+B) dialog again. From the included CD, choose 3ds4-ma\project1\images**tmpl-fire2.jpg**, click Open to close the Select Background Image dialog, and click OK to close the Viewport Background dialog.

It's much better now, as you can see in Figure 1.6. Now that you can actually see what you are doing, you can continue creating the fire backdrop for the billboard.

Figure 1.5
The white background matches the white line of the rectangle.

Figure 1.6
The white lines of the rectangle don't get lost over the gray background.

3. With the rectangle selected, click the Modify tab. Notice the size of the rectangle you just created. It should be approximately 242 × 344 (see Figure 1.7).

These shapes are perfectly sized for this scene. They aren't too small, and they aren't so large that it would take a 1,000-unit Extrude to create the appropriate depth so you can continue. You will use circle shapes to create the outlines for the rolling flames that protrude from the sides of the billboard.

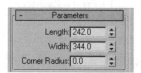

Figure 1.7
The Parameters rollout of the rectangle you created.

4. Make sure the rectangle is still selected, click Create > Circle, and uncheck Start New Shape so the circle will be added to the rectangle shape.

5. Place the cursor in the center of the upper-left swirl of fire and click and drag to create a circle as shown in Figure 1.8.

Figure 1.8
The circle shape created in the Top view.

It's okay if the circle doesn't line up correctly right now, but you need the shape to get started. Now you can line it up and make it nice.

6. With the rectangle-circle shape selected, click the Modify tab and rename the object **bil-back**.

7. In the Selection rollout, choose the Spline sub-object mode (see Figure 1.9).

8. Activate the Select and Move tool (using the view's XY-axis) and select the circle shape you created. Move the circle to create a clean outline of the protrusion of the upper-left curling flame (see Figure 1.10). You might have to use the Select and Uniform Scale tool (using the View's XY-axis) to adjust the size.

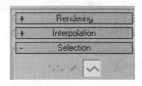

Figure 1.9
The Selection rollout of the Modify panel with the Spline sub-object mode active.

Figure 1.10
The circle shape is positioned in the correct place (it is not selected for the sake of clarity).

Exercise 1.3   Working with Sub-Objects

Now that you have drawn the rectangle shape and the first circle, the rest should be a cakewalk. You can continue to work in the sub-object levels of the bil-back object to create everything else you need.

1. Activate the Select and Move tool and Shift-drag the circle spline to the right, to produce two circle splines in the shape, as shown in Figure 1.11.

2. Using the Select and Move and the Select and Uniform Scale tools, adjust the new circle spline to conform to the edge of the top-middle fire tendril (see Figure 1.12).

Figure 1.11
Now there are two circle splines in the shape.

Figure 1.12
The second circle shape in its correct position and scale.

Tip

To switch between the Select and Move, and Select and Uniform Scale tools more easily, you can use the right-click quad menu. Simply right-click and choose the desired tool.

The circle doesn't have to be absolutely perfect, just close. Remember, however, to err on the inside of the artwork, not the outside. Otherwise, when the artwork is mapped to the object, the edge of the texture will be visible, and that's an undesirable effect. Now you're ready to create the rest of the rolling tendrils.

3. From the toolbar, select Views > Save Active Top View. This saves the top view to memory. Now if you need to pan or zoom around the view, you can return to the view exactly the way it is now by choosing Views > Restore Active Top View.

4. Using the Select and Move, and the Select and Uniform Scale tools, create the rest of the outlines for the rolling tendrils as in Figure 1.13.

Remember that to copy an object, you must hold down the Shift key while moving or scaling the object. Feel free to use the Pan or Zoom tool to aid your view.

Now it's time to take care of those pesky pointy fire tongues that protrude from the billboard. At first this might seem tricky, but you'll quickly figure out the best way to do it. All you have to do is Boolean circle shapes together to create the points.

5. Zoom in to the upper-left corner of the billboard, as shown in Figure 1.14.

Figure 1.13
All the rolling fire tendrils are outlined.

Figure 1.14
The upper-left corner of the billboard.

6. Copy a circle shape and match it to the left side of the fire tongue (see Figure 1.15).

7. Next, copy the circle and match it to the right side of the protruding tongue, as shown in Figure 1.16.

Figure 1.15
The circle traces the left side of the fire tongue.

Figure 1.16
Circles now enclose both sides of the fire tongue.

Now we will use Boolean to subtract one circle spline from the other, resulting in a spline the shape of the tongue.

8. Select the leftmost tongue circle, open the Geometry rollout, and activate Boolean Subtraction (see Figure 1.17).

9. Click the rightmost tongue circle, and 3ds max subtracts the second circle from the first circle, creating a crescent shape (see Figure 1.18). Temporarily save your work as **01FH01.max**.

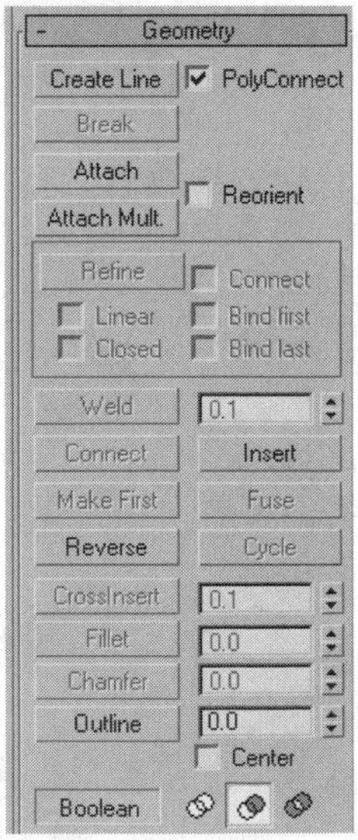

Figure 1.18
The crescent shape is left behind as a result of the Boolean operation.

Figure 1.17
The Geometry rollout with Boolean Subtraction active.

The Interpolation Rollout

If you look closely at the top tip of the fire tongue, you will see that three vertices create the point. This is completely unnecessary; you should actually delete two of the vertices. If you do not delete the extra vertices, extraneous faces will be created due to the Step Interpolation that occurs when the shape is extruded. The Steps: value, which is assigned in the Interpolation rollout of a Line, designates how many straight lines will be created between two consecutive vertices.

Consider, for example, the file \3ds4-ma\project1\scenes\StepInterpolation.max that's shown in the accompanying figure. (If you are going to load this file, make sure you saved your work at the end of the previous exercise.) This scene contains three identical line shapes. The only difference between these three shapes is the Step Interpolation value. Notice that the first (selected) shape has Bézier vertex types, but the line is not curved. This is because the Steps: value in the Interpolation rollout is 0. The shape in the middle has a Steps: value of 1, and the shape on the right has a Steps: value of 2. The Steps: value, once again, determines how many straight lines are created between vertices.

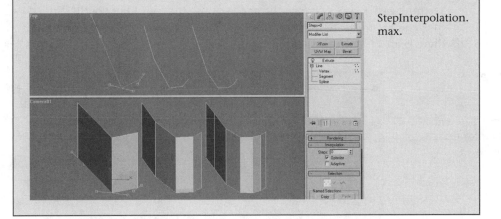

StepInterpolation. max.

Exercise 1.4   Removing Extra Vertices and Uniting the Splines

The sidebar "The Interpolation Rollout" discusses Step Interpolation and shows the troubles that can result from having too many vertices too close together. You need to remove some of those unwanted vertices in your bil-back object. Deleting them probably won't change the appearance of the object in a rendering. However, in my opinion, it is sloppy to leave unnecessary vertices in a shape.

To delete the vertices, you need to be in Vertex sub-object level.

1. If you loaded the example file, reload **01FH01.max** now. Select the bil-back object and activate Vertex sub-object level.

Note

You can easily change sub-object levels by using the right-click quad menu and choosing Sub-objects > Vertex.

2. Select the two vertices that are not at the point of the tongue (see Figure 1.19).

3. Press the Delete key to delete the two vertices. The curvature of the tongue is lost because you deleted the two vertices that defined the curves. Therefore, you need to adjust the remaining vertex to re-create the curve.

4. Using the Select and Move tool, select the tip vertex. Because the Bézier handles are very tiny, it might be tricky to adjust the handles. Here's an easy trick to make them more manageable.

5. Select and right-click the vertex. From the Tools 1 quad menu, choose Corner to change the vertex's type to Corner. Select and right-click the vertex once more and choose Bézier Corner, which makes the handles longer and easier to adjust.

6. Adjust the Bézier handles to create the desired tongue shape, as shown in Figure 1.20.

See how easy it was to create the shape of the tongue? I bet you're thrilled that you get to create three more! Now that you have created one, maybe there is an easier way.

Figure 1.19
Select the two vertices indicated. Viewport Background is turned off for the sake of clarity.

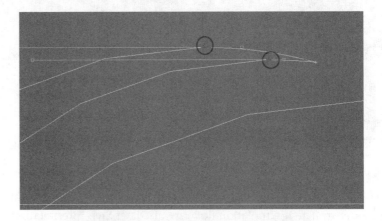

Figure 1.20
The finished tongue shape.

7. Copy the original tongue by holding down the Shift key while performing a transform on the tongue in spline sub-object mode. You will have to rotate the tongue spline and then adjust the vertices to conform to the correct shape. Remember, all that matters is what the shape looks like outside the rectangle; you are going to unite all these shapes in a Boolean operation in a little bit.

Figure 1.21 shows the resulting image.

Figure 1.21
The fire backdrop with all necessary splines.

8. Save your work as **01FH01.max**.

Now for the fun part, the Boolean operations that will unite all of our splines into one unified spline.

9. Make sure the bil-back object is still selected, activate Spline sub-object mode, select the rectangle spline, and then open the Geometry rollout and choose Boolean Union (see Figure 1.22).

10. With Boolean Union still active, click the remaining splines to unite them with the rectangle shape. I started with the one in the lowest-left corner and worked my way around clockwise (see Figure 1.23).

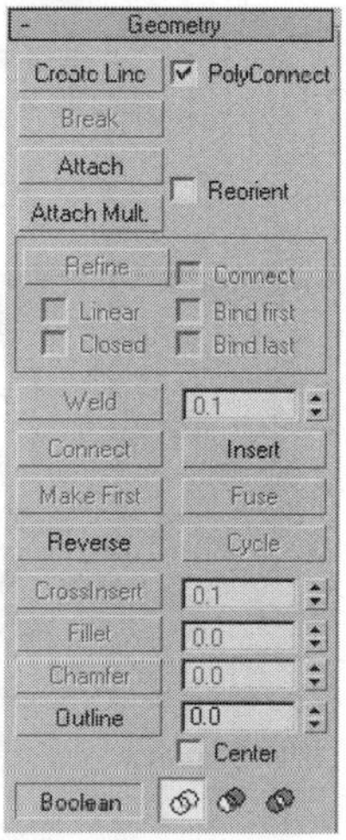

Figure 1.22
The Geometry rollout with Boolean Union active.

Figure 1.23
The billboard back
shape with all the
tendrils and tongues
united.

Exercise 1.5   Adding a Vertex Using Refine

Think you're finished? Well, you are—almost. But take a close look at the lower-left
corner: Sneaky Vince made one of the roots of the fire protrude from the base.
Adding this root to the billboard is a snap using the Refine tool.

1. Enter sub-object Vertex mode, open the Geometry rollout, and activate Refine.

2. Place the cursor where the top of the root intersects the side of the image,
   and then click to create a vertex (as shown in Figure 1.24). Right-click to exit
   Refine mode.

3. Right-click the new vertex and make sure its type is Bézier Corner. Adjust its
   handles and the handles of the vertex below it to create the correct shape
   (see Figure 1.25).

Figure 1.24
A new vertex is added to the shape,
thanks to the Refine tool.

Figure 1.25
The vertices of the tendril root
adjusted correctly.

The bil-back shape is now complete. Good job. All the others will be a breeze compared to this one.

4. Save your work as **01FH02.max**.

Exercise 1.6   Extruding an Object

Now that you have the beautiful bil-back shape you created using a little ingenuity and Boolean operations, you can extrude it.

1. With **01FH02.max** still open, minimize the Top view with the Min/Max toggle button or by pressing the W key.

2. Activate the Perspective view, and then adjust it to look like Figure 1.26 by using the Zoom tool and the Arc Rotate tool.

Figure 1.26
The Perspective view is adjusted correctly.

When you can see the bil-back object clearly in the Perspective view, you can start to do your magic to it. And by that, of course, I mean you can extrude it.

3. Select the bil-back object and activate the Modify panel. Deactivate any sub-object modification level so you can add the Extrude modifier.

4. From the Mesh Editing group of the Modifier list, choose Extrude so that the bil-back object becomes a solid object in the shaded Perspective view (see Figure 1.27).

Figure 1.27
The bil-back object is now a solid in the shaded Perspective view.

5. In the Parameters rollout, change the Amount value to **5** and deselect Cap Start (as shown in Figure 1.28). If you deselect Cap Start, the Extrude modifier will not create capping faces on the back of the object. Feel free to use Arc Rotate on the shaded Perspective view to see the missing backside.

   Now you can add the material. This should be relatively easy because Vince already did all the hard work by giving you a clean illustration of each layer.

6. Open the Material Editor and, with the upper-left sample slot active, change the name to **bil-back.** Click the Assign Material to Selection button. The color of the bil-back object turns gray.

   Now you have to add the flaming tendril texture to the object.

7. In the Material Editor, expand the Maps rollout and click None next to Diffuse so that the Material/Map Browser opens (see Figure 1.29). Choose Bitmap and click OK to open the Select Bitmap Image File dialog. Choose 3ds4-ma\ project1\maps\bil-back.jpg and click Open to close the dialog. Name this map **bil-back-dif.**

   The fire tendril image shows on the sample sphere in the Material Editor. Now see how it looks on the object.

Figure 1.28
The Parameters rollout of the Extrude modifier with correct settings.

Figure 1.29
The Material/Map Browser.

8. Click the Show Map in Viewport button to place the map on the object in the shaded Perspective view, as shown in Figure 1.30.

Remember that you're using two different files: The flames you see in the Top view are from the Viewport Background image file, and the flames you see in the Perspective view are from the map file. You used two different image files for these two different purposes. The image in the Top view came from the image folder on the CD, and the map in the Perspective view is from the maps folder on the CD.

Figure 1.30
The flame diffuse map on the bil-back object.

9. To verify that this is correct, click the View Image button in the Material Editor, and then examine the map.

You will see that the map version is on an orange background and is cropped to the edge of the flames. It is on an orange background because it's your safety net in case you didn't stay in the lines when you were tracing the edge of the flames. Pretty smart, eh?

Now, I suppose, is a good time to render a test frame, to make sure it looks okay.

10. Before you render the frame, change the background color so you can see the edges of the object. From the toolbar, choose Rendering > Environment, click the Color: swatch, and change it to RGB: **125, 125, 125**. Close the Environment dialog.

11. With the Perspective view active, click the Quick Render button to render a frame (see Figure 1.31).

In this case, it doesn't look too bad; however, I can see orange down the straight edge of the right side, and that's an undesirable effect (see Figure 1.32).

In Figure 1.32, you see the close-up of the lower-right corner of the bil-back object. You can plainly see that the black backdrop is not extending far enough right to the edge. Also, notice that the mapping on the extrusion needs a little work as well; right now, it is stretched and mangled-looking. This is because when the Extrude modifier generates mapping coordinates on those extruded sides, it basically wraps the texture once all the way around the object. This makes the texture look stretched around the object and squashed from top to bottom as it is applied to the height.

Figure 1.31
The rendered
Perspective view.

Figure 1.32
A close-up of the
lower-right corner of
the bil-back object.

Exercise 1.7   Changing Mapping Coordinates

It seems the mapping coordinates that the Extrusion modifier added to the object are not suitable in this case. Therefore, you will need to do it by hand.

1. Close the Material Editor and make sure the bil-back object is still selected.

2. From the Modifier list, choose UVW Map in the UV Coordinate Modifiers group.

3. Right-click the Top view's label and deselect Show Background. Right-click the Top view's label again and check Smooth Highlights so you can see the flame texture map in the Top view.

4. Maximize the Top view (see Figure 1.33).

Figure 1.33
The Top view, displaying the fire map on the bil-back object.

5. Click the Quick Render button again to view the resulting image.

   Now that you can see the image directly from the top, you can better align the UVW Map Gizmo. If you created your trace as cleanly as possible, the map shouldn't be misaligned, and simply increasing the Length and Width settings of the UVW Mapping modifier should do the trick. However, if the map is off-center, you might have to enter Gizmo sub-object level and move the Gizmo to the desired position.

6. Adjust the Length and Width values of the UVW Mapping modifier until the map fills the object. To get the best results, try changing the values at .5 intervals. Render the object in the Top view after each value change to see the results. In my scene, I needed to increase each value by only 1.5.

7. After the map fills the screen, minimize the Top view, select the Perspective view, and render another sample (see Figure 1.34).

Figure 1.34
A close-up of the bottom right corner of the bil-back object.

Notice that the map now fits the object correctly, and thanks to the planar UVW Mapping modifier, the map is stretched along the extruded edges of the object, which gives a much cleaner look.

8. Change the Top view back to Wireframe and activate the Top view's background image again.

9. Save your work as **01FH03.max**.

If you view the comp that Vince drew up (see the file 3ds4-ma\project1\images\ finalclown.jpg), you will see that each extrusion on every piece of the billboard displays a wood texture. Right now, the bil-back object has the flames textured on the extrusion. You really should add that wood texture to it.

For this project, you are going to collapse the bil-back object into an editable mesh, in order to make modifications to its sub-object level. You could add an Edit Mesh instead, but because you really don't need to modify the shape in the stack, there is no need to leave superfluous modifiers in the modifier stack.

Exercise 1.8   Adding Texture to an Extrusion

1. Make sure you are completely satisfied with the UVW Mapping you applied, and then select and right-click the bil-back object.

   If you are a stickler for detail and you think there should be more faces on the side of the bil-back object, add them now. To do so, simply select Editable Spline in the stack, open the Interpolation rollout, and increase the Step: value. In my scene, the default of 6 works fine, so I will leave it set to that.

2. From the Transform quad menu, choose Convert To > Convert to Editable Mesh. The stack collapses and results with an Editable Mesh object type. To change the extruded side of the bil-back object, you need to change the Material ID of those polygons and create a wood material to apply to the object.

3. Make sure the bil-back object is selected and activate Polygon sub-object level.

4. Right-click the Perspective view's label and choose Edged Faces to superimpose the edges of the polygons over the shaded object. Maximize the Perspective view (see Figure 1.35).

Figure 1.35
The polygonal edges of the bil-back object are superimposed over the shaded object.

5. From the toolbar, choose Edit > Select All to select all the polygons of the bil-back object.

6. Expand the Surface Properties rollout and change the Material ID: to **1**, as shown in Figure 1.36.

    Now every polygon of the bil-back object has a Material ID value of 1. Ultimately, the Material ID 1 will be the wood grain texture, and Material ID 2 will be the fire tendril material. You better change the front of the bil-back object to Material ID 2 before you forget.

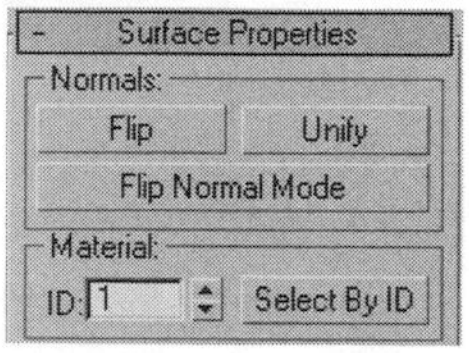

Figure 1.36
Change the Material ID value to 1.

7. Using the Select Object tool, click on the front of the bil-back object to select only the front surface, and then deselect all the other polygons.

8. In the Surface Properties rollout, change the Material ID to **2**, exit sub-object mode, and return to the top level.

Exercise 1.9   Organizing Materials and Sub-Materials

The object is now ready for the wood grain material. Go into the Material Editor and create it now.

1. Open the Material Editor and click Go To Parent to return to the root of the bil-back material.

    Because the object now has two material IDs, you need to create a multi/sub-object material in order to apply a different sub-material to each ID.

2. With the bil-back material still active, click the Standard button to open the Material/Map Browser shown in Figure 1.37.

3. Choose Multi/Sub-Object and click OK to close the browser. In the Replace Material dialog, leave Keep Old Material As Sub-Material? selected and click OK to keep the flame material as a sub-material.

4. Rename this material **Billboard** (see Figure 1.38).

    The multi/sub-object material now has 10 slots; the bil-back object only has 2 Material IDs so we can adjust the material to only have two sub-materials.

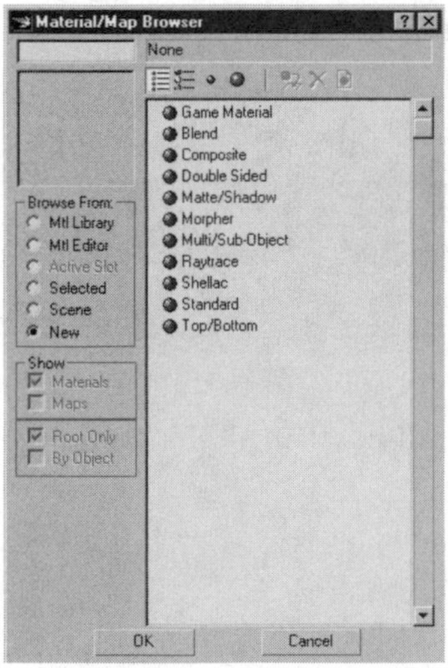

Figure 1.37
The Material/Map Browser.

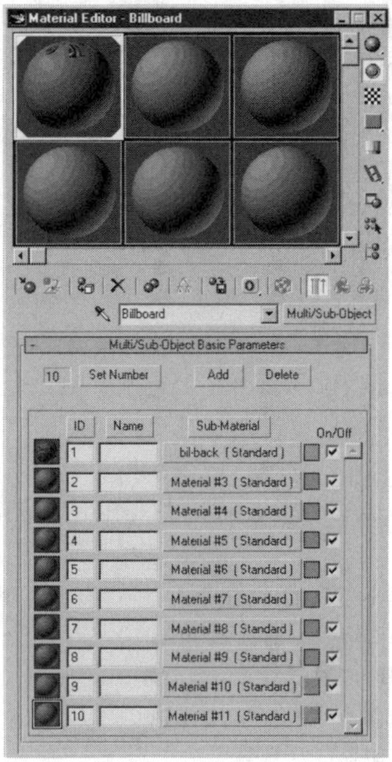

Figure 1.38
The Material Editor with the new Billboard Multi/Sub-Object material.

5. Click the Set Number button to open the Set Number of Materials dialog and change the number to **2** (see Figure 1.39). Click OK to close the dialog.

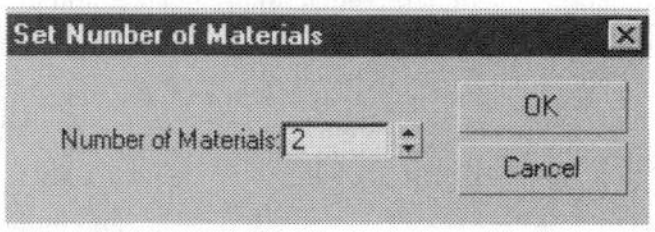

Figure 1.39
The Set Number of Materials dialog with the correct value of 2.

There are now only two sub-material slots in the Billboard material. When you gave polygons of the bil-back object their Material IDs, you assigned the extruded polygons (wood material) a Material ID of 1 and the front polygons (fire background material) a Material ID of 2. Currently, the sub-material with the Material ID of 1 is the fire; it needs to be swapped with the second sub-material.

6. Drag the bil-back button over the sub-material ID 2 button and release the mouse button. In the Instance (Copy) Material dialog, choose Swap (as shown in Figure 1.40), and click OK to close the dialog.

The two materials have changed position. You could have simply changed the number next to each slot, and that would have worked just as well. The materials would not have switched position, but the result would be the same. When you changed the material from a Standard type to the Multi-Sub Object type, you lost the fire map in the shaded Perspective view. Now you should go back and activate it.

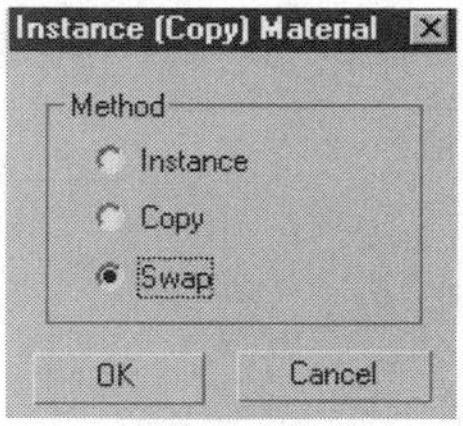

Figure 1.40
The Instance (Copy) Material dialog with Swap selected.

7. In the Material Editor, click the bil-back (Standard) button. Then click the Show Map in Viewport button so the fire map returns to the view. Click Go to Parent to return to the root of the material.

8. Now click the Material #3 (Standard) button to enter its settings. To add a dull highlight to the material, change Specular Level to **5** and Glossiness to **25.** Name this material **bil-wood.** Expand the Maps rollout and click the Diffuse None button to open the Material/Map Browser.

9. Choose Bitmap and click OK to open the Select Bitmap Image File dialog. From the included CD, choose 3ds4-ma\project1\maps\bil-wood.jpg and click Open. Name this map **bil-wood-dif** and click Show Map in Viewport**.**

10. Render a test frame from the Perspective view (see Figure 1.41).

Well, maybe the wood doesn't look very real, because it is stretched from the planar mapping gizmo, but it almost looks like what Vince illustrated in his design. However, the streaks could be a tad smaller. You can accomplish that easily by tiling the wood map.

11. In the Coordinates rollout of the bil-wood-dif map, change the U: and V: Tiling values to **2** (see Figure 1.42).

12. Render the Perspective view again (Figure 1.43).

Figure 1.41
The rendered
Perspective view of
the bil-back object.

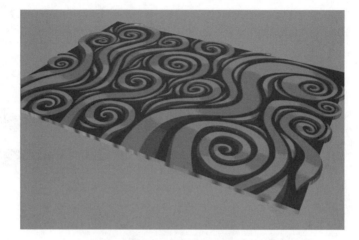

Figure 1.42
The U and V tiling has
been changed to 2.

Figure 1.43
The rendered
Perspective view.

The grain is a little bit tighter now. It's acceptable for what you need it to do. You will never really see it enough to make it worth spending more time on adjusting it. It looks like your work here is finished.

13. Close the Material Editor and save your work as **01FH04.max**.

Working with the Clown's Body

The flaming backdrop of the billboard is now complete. Don't worry about it laying down in world space. You will build the whole billboard in this fashion and stand it up when it's finished. The next step in completing the billboard is to create the clown's body. In the illustration Vince gave you, you can discern that the next layer of the billboard will be the clown's wings, body, neck, and arms (minus the hands). Because Vince gave you the individual layers, you can use them as a template to trace the shapes. It's time to start tracing again.

Exercise 1.10   Tracing the Body Template

To create the object accurately to the texture Vince provided, you will load the matching template as you did for the fire backdrop. When you have the template in the Top view, you can start to trace out the shape.

1. With **01FH04.max** loaded, minimize the Perspective view and select and maximize the Top view. In the maximized Top view, you should see the fire image you loaded as a Viewport Background and the object you created by tracing it (as shown in Figure 1.44).

Figure 1.44
The maximized Top view.

2. From the toolbar, select Views > Viewport Background to open the Viewport Background dialog. Click the Files button, choose \3ds4-ma\project1\images\ tmpl-body.jpg, and click Open to close the Select Background Image dialog. Click OK to close the Viewport Background dialog. The fire background is replaced with the clown's body (see Figure 1.45).

Notice the extra thick black edge around most of the clown. Once again, Vince provided a safety net—this time in case you didn't trace perfectly around the edge of the body. Although this is not the actual map file you will be applying to the object, it is the same artwork. If you want to examine the map, it is \3ds4-ma\project1\maps\bil-body.jpg. The only difference between this template and the map is the color of the background and the way the bitmap is cropped.

3. You are now ready to start tracing the body. If you desire, pan and zoom the view until the clown body template fills the view (see Figure 1.46).

Figure 1.45
The tmpl-body.jpg is now the Viewport Background image.

Figure 1.46
The body template image fills the Top view.

4. Click Create > Shapes/Line and click in the middle of the black edge on the lower-left corner of the body template to create your first vertex. Continue creating vertices clockwise around the clown, keeping in mind that a click will create a Corner type vertex and a drag will create a Bézier type vertex. When you have made your way all the way around the outer edge of the clown's body, click the first vertex you created and click Yes when prompted to close the spline.

Place vertices in all the positions indicated in Figure 1.47.

Note

Throughout this exercise, as you trace the templates, make sure you close all your splines. Although they will still extrude, no caps will appear at the front or back of the extruded object unless the spline is closed.

Figure 1.47
The vertices of the clown body shape.

5. Click the Modify tab and enter sub-object vertex mode. Using the Select and Move tool, edit the positions of each vertex and the tangent handles of the Bézier vertices. Your modified shape should look like Figure 1.48.

Remember, you can change the vertex type by selecting a vertex, right-clicking it, and then choosing the desired type from the quad menu. When you want to change a Bézier vertex type to a Bézier Corner vertex type, hold down the Shift key and move a tangent handle. The vertex type automatically changes. If you desire a Bézier vertex type with two different-length handles, hold down the Shift key and adjust the handles, and then right-click the vertex and choose Bézier from the quad menu. The vertex will change back to Bézier, and the handles will be the desired lengths.

If you need to add more vertices, simply click the Refine button in the Geometry rollout and click at the desired location along the spline. If you need to remove a vertex, select it and press the Delete key.

Figure 1.48
The finished clown
body shape.

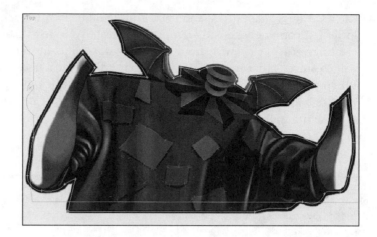

Notice in Figure 1.48 that the body shape I created is drawn in the middle of
the black outline surrounding the clown's body. If you examine Vince's complete image again, you can see that these objects have a black outline around
them, almost in comic book fashion. So don't be too concerned with getting
too precise on either edge.

6. Name this shape **bil-body** and save your work as **01FH05.max**.

   Now that you have finished tracing the clown's body template, you are
   ready to extrude and texture it.

Exercise 1.11   Extruding the Shape and Transform Type-In

The hard part of creating the clown's body is behind you. All that's left is to apply
an Extrude and UVW Map modifier and add the material. Piece of cake.

1. With 01FH05.max open, minimize the Top view.

2. Make sure the bil-body object is selected. From the Modify panel, apply an
   Extrude modifier. In the Parameters rollout, enter an Amount of **5** and deselect
   Cap Start (as shown in Figure 1.49).

Note

If you are working straight through this chapter, you might not have to re-enter these
parameters. This is because these values are "sticky," which means the modifiers remember
the values previously assigned to other objects during the session.

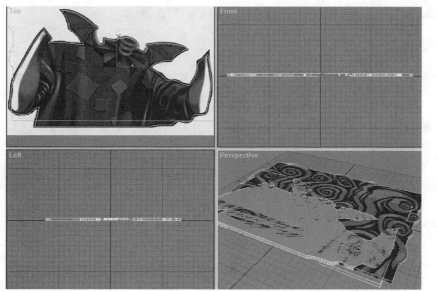

Figure 1.49
The extruded bil-body object in the four views.

Notice that the bil-back and bil-body objects occupy the same height space in the views. This is because both shapes were created on the home grid and were extruded the same amount. You will move the bil-body object forward in just a second. Because you know planar mapping coordinates must be applied to this object, let's add a planar mapping gizmo now.

3. From the Modify panel, apply a UVW Map (from the UV Coordinate Modifiers list). The UVW Mapping gizmo is applied to the object and precisely fit to its boundaries. To move the bil-body object forward, you will use the Transform Type-In that's built into the Status Panel of 3ds max 4 (or you could open the floater by right-clicking the Select and Move, Rotate, or Scale button).

Looking down on your object in the Top view, the local axis is Y: up and down; X: right to left; Z: front to back. You need to move the bil-back object along its local Z-axis.

4. With the bil-body object still selected, activate the Select and Move tool and enter a value of **5** next to the Z: parameter on the Status panel.

You moved the bil-body object 5 units forward because the bil-back object is 5 units deep. Now the bil-body object appears to be resting on the bil-back object (see Figure 1.50).

Figure 1.50
The bil-body object now rests on top of the bil-back object.

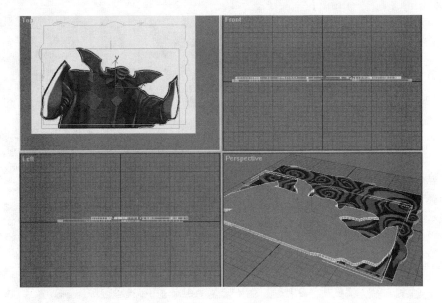

Exercise 1.12   Adding a Sub-Material

To finish the bil-body object, you must apply the material.

1. Open the Material Editor and make sure the bil-body object is still selected.

2. Click the Assign Material to Selection button to apply the Billboard (Multi/Sub-object) material to the bil-body object (see Figure 1.51).

   Houston, we have a problem. It looks like the bil-body object needs to be painted over that wood grain texture. The bil-wood material is applied to the bil-body object because by default the Extrude modifier applies a Material ID of 1 to the end cap of the object. Before you can apply the bil-body sub-material to the object, you have to create it.

Figure 1.51
The bil-wood sub-material is applied to the bil-body object.

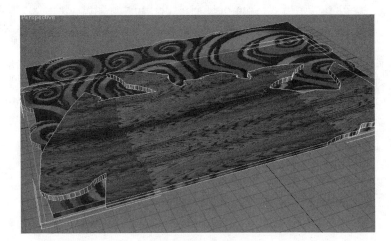

3. In the Material Editor, with the Billboard material selected, click Set Number in the Multi/Sub-Object Basic Parameters rollout, and then change the Number of Materials: value to **3** (as shown in Figure 1.52). Click OK to close the dialog.

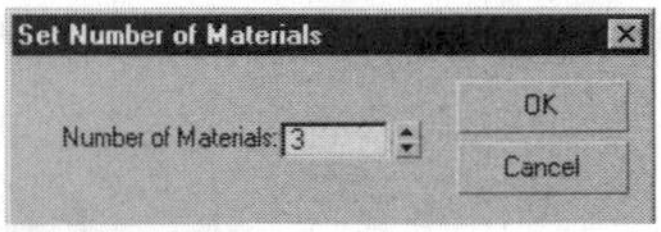

Figure 1.52

The Set Number of Materials dialog with the correct value of 3.

4. Drag the bil-back sub-material over the third sub-material button and release the mouse. In the Instance (Copy) Material dialog, choose Copy and click OK to close the dialog.

Although the name of the sub-material in the third slot did not change, its settings are now identical to those of the bil-back object. All you need to do now is change the Diffuse map to finish the bil-body sub-material.

5. Click the Material #1 (Standard) button to open its settings. Rename this sub-material **bil-body** and click the Diffuse map button (currently named bil-back-dif [bil-back.jpg]) to open the Diffuse Color map parameters.

6. In the Bitmap Parameters rollout, click the Bitmap: button, choose 3ds4-ma\project1\maps\bil-body.jpg, and click Open to close the Select Bitmap Image File dialog. Rename this map **bil-body-dif** and click the Show Map in Viewport button. Close the Material Editor.

You still don't see the bil-body sub-material in the shaded Perspective view. That's because you never applied the Material ID of 3 to the front of the bil-body object. Collapse the stack on the object and change the ID now.

Note

In my scene, the default interpolation of six steps creates plenty of faces around the bil-body object. If you feel your scene needs more (or fewer), adjust the Steps: value in the Interpolation rollout of the Line object in the Modify stack. Remember, to see the changes you are making to the Steps: value, you must activate the Show End Result toggle switch in the Modify panel.

7. If you are happy with the number of polygons surrounding the bil-body object, select it, right-click it, and choose Convert To > Convert to Editable Mesh.

This collapses the modify stack, and you can no longer increase the Steps: value of the line because it is now a mesh. Now you need to change the Material IDs.

8. With the bil-body object selected, enter Polygon sub-object level and click to select the front of the bil-body object (see Figure 1.53).

Figure 1.53
The front face of the bil-body object is selected. It is a solid color for the sake of clarity.

9. In the Material group of the Surface Properties dialog, change the ID: value to **3** (as shown in Figure 1.54).

   The bil-body object is almost finished. Next you render a test frame to see how it looks.

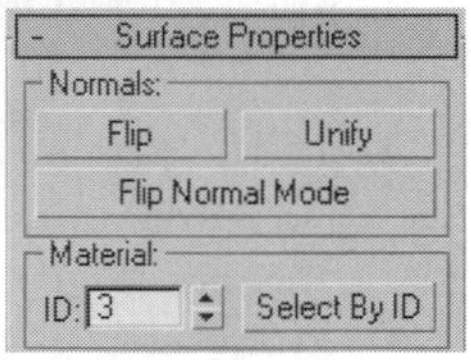

10. Select the Perspective view, click the Quick Render button, and the billboard you've created so far appears (see Figure 1.55).

    It seems like you lost the wood texture on the extrusion as well. By default, when an Extrude modifier is applied to a shape, it applies Material ID 1 to the Cap End, Material ID 2 to the Cap Start, and Material 3 to the extruded sides. When there are only two sub-materials, they alternate, meaning Material ID 1 is 1, 2 is 2, 1 is 3, 2 is 4, and so on.

Figure 1.54
The Material ID with the correct value of 3.

Figure 1.55
The rendered Perspective view.

That is why, when you added the Billboard material to the bil-body object, the wood material was correctly applied to the object. The extruded side had a Material ID of 3, which was generated automatically from the Extrude modifier. Because the Billboard material had only two sub-materials at the time, they alternated, and the wood texture (ID1) became (ID3) as well. When you added the third sub-material for the bil-body, it was correctly applied to the extrusion of the object. However, that wasn't the desired result. To place the correct material on the extrusion, you need to change the Material ID of those polygons.

11. Make sure the front face of the bil-body object is selected. From the toolbar, choose Edit > Select Invert to select the extruded faces.

12. Now in the Material: group of the Surface Properties rollout, change the ID: to **1**, which is the bil-wood sub-material ID.

13. Click the Render Last button to see the updated scene (see Figure 1.56)

Figure 1.56
The rendered
Perspective view.

14. Deactivate Polygon sub-object level and save your scene as **01FH06.max**.

You are finished with the bil-body object. Just think, we only have to make the heads, hands, and text using this method. It's going to be a breeze. I am sure you're getting the hang of this now.

Creating the Clown Hands

Let's take one more look at the final image Vince illustrated. From the toolbar, choose File > View Image File, and then choose \3ds4-ma\project1\images\finalclown.jpg. Take a close look at the hands. Vince was doing a favor either for you or for himself, because those hands are simply mirrored. That will surely make your life twice as easy.

Exercise 1.13   Tracing the Hand

All you have to do is make one hand and mirror it to create the second one. Cool.

1. With 01FH06.max open, select and maximize the Top view.

2. Open the Viewport Background dialog (Alt+B) and click the Files button to open the Select Background Image dialog. Choose 3ds4-ma\project1\images\ tmpl-hands.jpg and click Open to close the dialog. Click OK to close the Viewport Background dialog.

   The clown's hands now appear as the Top view background, as shown in Figure 1.57. Next you'll adjust your view to maximize the clown's right hand (yeah, that's the one on the left) so you can trace it.

3. With the Top view maximized, use Region Zoom to drag a region around the clown's right hand to fill the Top view with the clown's right hand, as shown in Figure 1.58.

Figure 1.57
The clown's hands in the Top view.

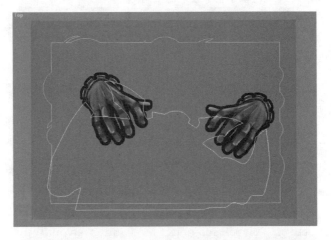

Figure 1.58
The clown's right hand is maximized in the Top view.

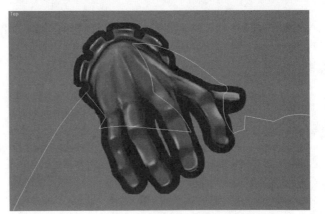

Before you start tracing the hand, hide the other objects from the scene. This will make your workspace a little more organized.

4. Click the Display tab and check Geometry in the Hide by Category rollout (see Figure 1.59).

Both objects you created are hidden from the view. You can uncheck the Geometry category at any time if you want to view them. Now, to get back to tracing that hand.

5. Choose Create > Shapes > Line. Pick a good starting point on the outline of the hand and trace the outline around it (keeping your spline in the center of the black outline). Don't forget to trace between the index, middle, and ring fingers. Remember, it doesn't have to be perfect; you can make adjustments to the shape using the same techniques you used to create the body.

Figure 1.59
On the Hide by Category rollout of the Display tab, Geometry is checked.

6. To make adjustments to your hand shape, click the Modify tab and enter sub-object vertex level. When the hand is the desired shape, name it **bil-handr** (see Figure 1.60).

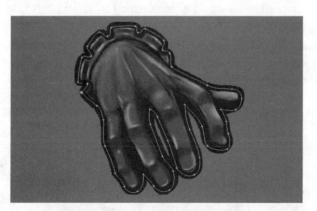

Figure 1.60
The finished bil-handr shape.

You should always remember the importance of working with shapes. Generally, they are the basis of your objects, and you want them to be as perfect as possible. Experiment with the different vertex types by right-clicking the vertices. Each type serves a different purpose. For example, most of the vertices in my bil-handr shape are Bézier. However, the vertices that create hard corners in the seams where the fingers meet are Corner vertex types.

7. Save your work as **01FH07.max**. (If you are currently working with the 01FH06.max file, you can click the + button in the Save File As dialog to save the file as the next numeric increment.)

Exercise 1.14   Using the Modify Stack

Now that we have a clean trace of the right hand, we will employ the same techniques we used earlier to create the preceding objects to finish the hand.

1. With 01FH07.max open, minimize the Top view so all four views are visible again.

2. Open the Modify tab and add an Extrude modifier to the bil-handr shape. The bil-handr shape immediately changes into an object, and the hidden objects automatically are displayed. Take note of those sticky Parameter roll-out settings again. The Amount should be 5, and Cap Start should not be checked.

    To see what you're doing, you need to hide the billboard object you are finished with.

3. Make sure the bil-handr object is still selected and right-click in the Perspective view. From the Display quad menu, choose Hide Unselected. The unselected bil-back and bil-body objects are hidden again (until you unhide them the next time). You no longer need the background image in the Top view, so get rid of that now.

4. Right-click the Top view label and deselect Show Background so the background is no longer visible in the view.

5. Maximize the Perspective view and examine the bil-handr object (see Figure 1.61).

    Because you added a vertex for practically each knuckle of the hand, there are probably more faces than you actually need. You can change this by using the technique I described before.

Figure 1.61
The bil-handr object in the Perspective view.

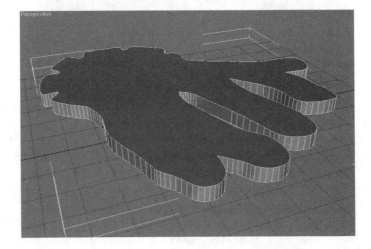

6. In the Modify panel, select the Line object from the stack. Activate the Show End Result on/off toggle, and in the Interpolation rollout, change the Steps: value to **3** (as shown in Figure 1.62).

   That's about right for my scene. I know the camera won't be getting too close to the hand objects, so there isn't much point in wasting polygons on them.

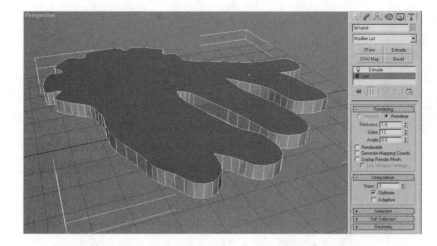

Figure 1.62
Notice that fewer faces are shown on the hand as a result of the lower Steps: value.

Exercise 1.15   Adding a UVW Map Modifer

When you're happy with the object, you will add the UVW Map modifier.

1. Make sure that the bil-handr object is selected and the Extrude modifier is active in the Modify panel. Add a UVW Map modifier. Once again, by default the UVW Map Gizmo is planar, and it is automatically sized to fit the object.

   Now that the object is essentially finished, you can collapse it.

2. Select and right-click the bil-handr object, and then choose Convert To: > Convert to Editable Mesh. The modifier stack collapses, and a single Editable Mesh object appears in the stack (see Figure 1.63).

3. To apply the material, open the Material Editor and move to the root of the Billboard material by clicking Go to Parent twice. Then click Assign Material to Selection (see Figure 1.64).

   The wood texture appearing on the front of the objects is getting to be a familiar problem. It's not too hard to adjust. All you have to do is change the object's Material IDs.

Figure 1.63
The Modify stack, showing the Editable Mesh object.

4. To adjust the Material IDs, activate Polygon sub-object level and click the top of the hand object (see Figure 1.65).

5. In the Surface Properties rollout, click the up arrow next to the Material ID value once. Now the Material ID value is 2, and you can see the bil-back material on the object.

6. Click the up arrow to increase the Material ID value to **3**. You can see the bil-body material mapped on the top of the hand.

7. Change the Material ID to **4**.

The Material ID of 4 is the correct ID for this surface, but why is the bil-wood material back on it? Because of what we discussed earlier when you were working on the bil-back object. The materials alternate if they don't exist. Because there is no sub-material 4 yet, it has applied sub-material 1 (the next number after the last number—3).

Figure 1.64
The bil-handr object with the Billboard material applied.

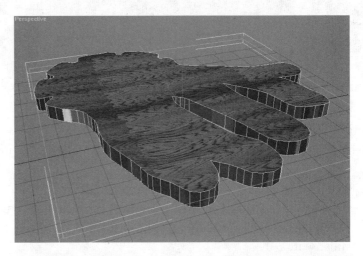

Figure 1.65
The bil-handr object with the top polygon selected (it's solid color for clarity in the figure).

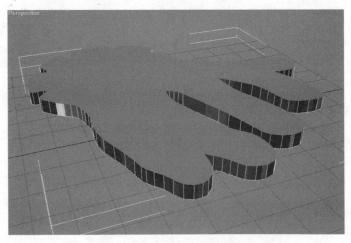

Now you'll create the fourth sub-material for the hand object right.

8. Open the Material Editor. From the root of the Billboard object, click Set Number to open the Set Number of Materials dialog. Change the Number of Materials: to **4** and click OK to close the dialog. The top of the hand changes to a gray color.

9. Now simply copy the third material to the fourth material slot. Drag the third material button over the fourth material button and release the mouse. From the Instance (Copy) Material dialog (shown in Figure 1.66), choose Copy and click OK to close the dialog.

10. Click the fourth sub-material button to open its settings. Name this sub-material **bil-hand**, and in the Maps rollout, click the Diffuse Color button (currently named bil-body-dif [bil-body.jpg]). Name this map **bil-hand-dif**.

11. In the Bitmap Parameters rollout, click the Bitmap: button, choose the hand map \3ds4-ma\project1\maps\ bil-hands.jpg, and click Open to close the dialog. Click Go to Parent twice to return to the root of the Billboard material and close the dialog. The hand material is now applied to the bil-handr object (see Figure 1.67).

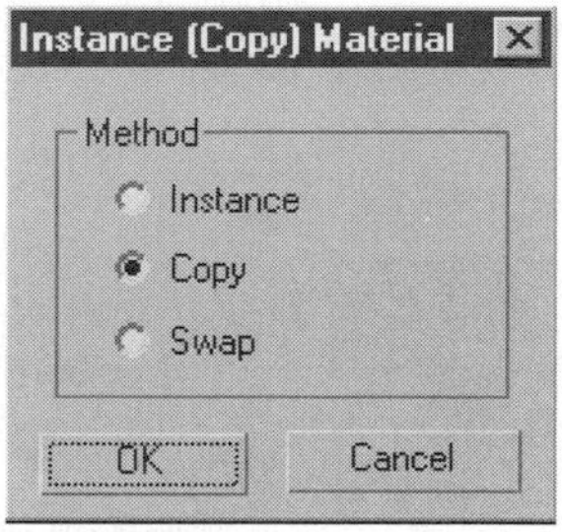

Figure 1.66
The Instance (Copy) Material dialog with Copy selected.

The only other thing you have to do to finish the hand is to change the extruded sides of the bil-handr object to Material ID: 1.

12. The bil-handr object should still be selected and in Polygon sub-object mode. From the toolbar, choose Edit > Select Invert. The unselected faces become selected, and the selected face becomes unselected.

13. In the Surface Properties rollout, change the Material ID: to **1** to apply the bil-wood material to the extruded sides of the hand, as shown in Figure 1.68. Deactivate Polygon sub-object mode.

14. Save your work as **01FH08.max**.

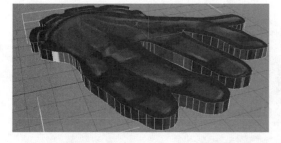

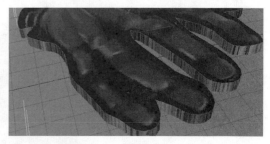

Figure 1.67
The bil-hand sub-material is applied to the front face of the bil-handr object.

Figure 1.68
The bil-handr object is now complete.

Exercise 1.16   Mirroring Objects

The bil-handr object is finished. Feel free to render a test frame to make sure everything is okay.

Now you will create the easiest object in this project: the second hand. Remember that Vince did you a big favor by making the second hand a mirror copy of the first. So making the second hand is going to be a snap.

1. With 01FH08.max loaded, minimize the Perspective view.

2. Select and maximize the Top view, right-click the Top view label, and check Show Background. Zoom out and pan left until both hands in the Background Image are visible.

3. Make sure the bil-handr object is selected, and then click the Mirror Selected Objects button on the toolbar to open the Mirror: Screen Coordinates dialog. In the Clone Selection: group, choose Copy (see Figure 1.69). Then click OK to close the dialog.

   You now have two hand objects in the scene: one facing right and the other facing left (as shown in Figure 1.70). Before you forget, you'd better name the new hand object correctly.

4. Make sure the new hand object is selected, and then change its name from bil-handr01 to **bil-handl**.

5. Activate the Select and Move tool and move the hand over the left hand of the Background Image (see Figure 1.71).

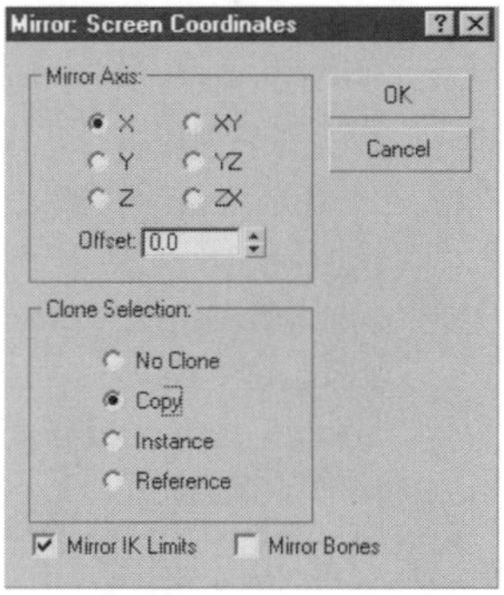

   It looks like the object needs to be rotated. But before you rotate it with the Select and Rotate tool, consider one thing. If we simply use the Select and Rotate tool on the bil-handl object, not only will the object rotate, but so will

Figure 1.69
The Mirror: Screen Coordinates dialog with the correct settings.

Figure 1.70
There are now two hand objects in the scene.

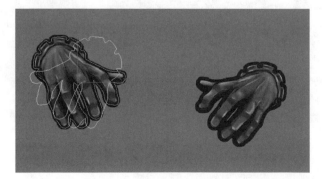

its local axis. In this case, that shouldn't be a problem. However, during the modeling phase of a project, you generally should not change the local axis orientation of an object. To get around this, you will use an XForm modifier. By using an XForm modifier, you can rotate the object but not its local axis.

To see what this actually means, activate the Select and Rotate tool, change your Reference Coordinate System to Local, and rotate the hand about its Z-axis. Note that the axis rotates as well (see Figure 1.72). Now click Undo to revert to the original orientation.

Now use the XForm modifier to rotate the object without changing its local axis orientation.

6. Open the Modify panel. With the bil-handl object selected, apply an XForm modifier (from the Parametric Modifier list) so that a yellow gizmo surrounds the hand object.

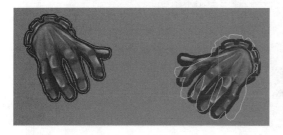

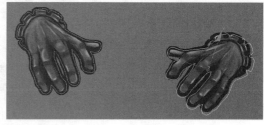

Figure 1.71
The bil-handl object is placed over its place on the Background Image in the Top view.

Figure 1.72
The axis rotates along with the object when you use the Select and Rotate tool.

7. Click the + next to the XForm modifier in the stack to expand its subtree (see Figure 1.73).

The yellow bar highlighting the Gizmo indicates that the Gizmo is active and that any transform changes applied at this point are applied at the Gizmo level not the object level. Now you can rotate the hand object without changing its local axis orientation.

8. Activate the Select and Rotate tool with the Z-axis of the View Reference Coordinate System, and then rotate the Gizmo approximately 18 degrees as shown in Figure 1.74.

9. Click the yellow-highlighted Gizmo bar in the Modifier list to deactivate it.

Figure 1.73
The sub-tree of the XForm modifier is expanded with Gizmo selected.

The bar turns gray and highlights the XForm modifier. With the Select and Rotate tool still active and Local Reference Coordinate System still active, you can see that you rotated the hand but not the local axis. Great! Now that you are finished with the XForm modifier, you can collapse the stack again.

10. Right-click the XForm modifier in the Modifier List and choose Collapse To. The Warning dialog shown in Figure 1.75 appears. Click Yes, and the stack collapses (as if you right-clicked the object and chose Convert to Editable Mesh).

    Now there is only an Editable Mesh object in the Modifier List.

11. Using the Select and Move tool in the Top view, match the bil-handl object as closely to the Background Image as possible (see Figure 1.76).

    The hands are good for now; however, you still have to build the Funhouse type to fit under the hands, so there really isn't any need to place them any more accurately on the billboard just yet. You will do that in the next chapter.

12. Save your work as **01FH09.max**.

Figure 1.74
The bil-handl object is rotated into its correct orientation.

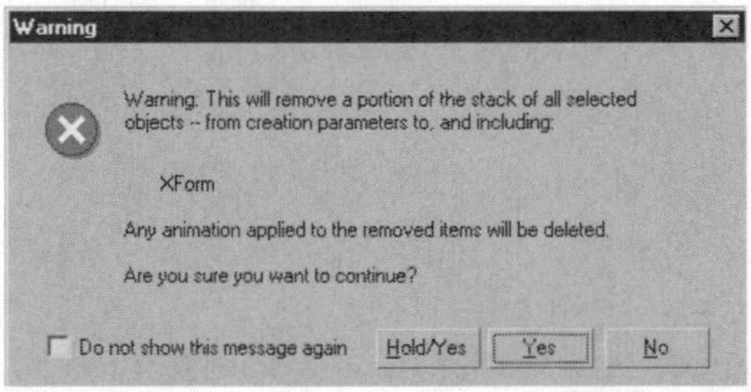

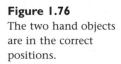

Figure 1.75
The Collapse To warning.

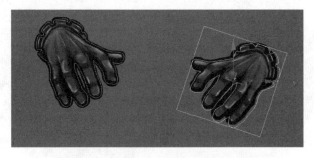

Figure 1.76
The two hand objects are in the correct positions.

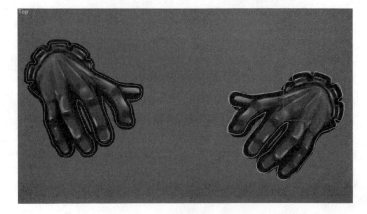

You are chipping away at the objects you need for this scene. You're probably halfway there at this point. One thing you know for sure is that the more you work with shapes, the more easily and quickly you can create and manipulate them.

Building the Clown's Head

Only one object remains to be built using the trace and extrude technique in its simplest form, and that's the head. However, you will use the trace and extrude technique to create the Funhouse type for the billboard, which gives this a creative twist. So here's your last chance to master this technique before going one step up on it.

Exercise 1.17   Working with Shapes

You know the drill by now: You have to hide those hand objects and change the Viewport Background image.

1. With 01FH09.max open, deselect both hand objects and right-click any-where in the Top view. From the Display quad menu, choose Hide Unselected so that both hand objects are hidden.

2. Open the Viewport Background dialog (Alt+B) and click the Files button to open the Select Background Image dialog. Choose \3ds4-ma\project1\ images\tmpl-head.jpg and click Open to close the dialog. Click OK to close the Viewport Background dialog.

   The evil clown head appears in the Top view. I sure hope none of you fine folks are skived out by clowns (who isn't a little bit?).

3. Adjust the maximized Top view to make the clown head fill the view as much as possible (see Figure 1.77).

Figure 1.77
The clown head image fills the Top view.

You can see that the head is made up of primitive shapes, so you can use the same Boolean technique you used on the flaming bil-back object. If you want to apply this technique, feel free—it should work out well. If you do so, pick up this exercise at Step 7. For the sake of practice, however, this tutorial has you create the shape manually.

4. Choose Create > Shapes > Line and click to create the first vertex in the black outline where the clown's right ear meets his head.

5. Continue clicking clockwise around the clown's head, creating points where necessary (see Figure 1.78).

Tip

You might notice that all the vertices I created are of the Corner type. I often create them all this way, but I am very used to right-clicking them and changing the type as needed. Using this technique, I can plot out where I need the vertices and then go back and adjust them after the shape is closed.

6. Click the Modify tab and enter Vertex sub-object level to edit the spline. Adjust all the vertices as needed to have the shape follow through the middle of the thick black outline (see Figure 1.79).

   You might need to add vertices to or delete vertices from your shape, depending on how you created the shape. In my shape (and it is obvious in Figure 1.78 and Figure 1.79), I had to delete a vertex from the tassel on the clown's hat to form the desired shape.

7. When you finish adjusting your shape, deactivate Vertex sub-object and turn off the Viewport Background. Name the object **bil-head**.

8. Minimize the Top view, and with the bil-head object still active, apply an Extrude modifier.

Figure 1.78
The vertices created for the clown head.

Figure 1.79
The clown head with the vertices in the correct configuration.

9. In the Parameters rollout, make sure that the Amount is **5** and Cap Start is not checked.

10. Apply a UVW Map modifier. By default, the UVW Map gizmo is Planar and is automatically sized to fit the object. That's precisely what you need, as you can see in Figure 1.80.

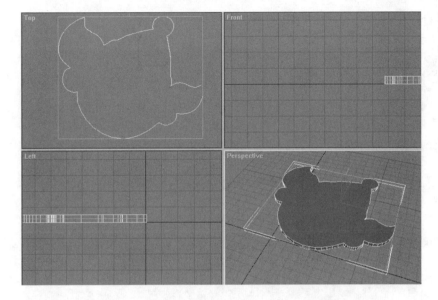

Figure 1.80
The bil-head object is extruded with a UVW Map modifier applied.

Exercise 1.18   Adding the Materials to the Head

Now you can add the material to the object.

1. Open the Material Editor, and with the Billboard material active, click the Set Number button and change the value to **5**.

2. Drag the fourth material button over the fifth material button and release the mouse. In the Instance (Copy) Material dialog, choose Copy and click OK to copy the material and close the dialog.

3. Click the fifth material button and rename the material **bil-head**. In the Maps rollout, click the Diffuse Color Map button and rename this map **bil-head-dif.**

4. In the Bitmap Parameters rollout, click the Bitmap: button, choose \3ds4-ma\ project1\maps\bil-head.jpg, and click Open to load the bitmap and close the dialog. Click Go to Parent twice to go to the root of the material.

5. Click the Assign Material to Selection button to assign the material to the bil-head object.

Once again, you are faced with that whole wrong Material ID problem. Of course, you are a pro by now; you know exactly what to do. The first thing you should do is collapse the stack. So if you are happy with the number of faces along the extrusion (adjusted by the Steps: value in the Interpolation rollout of the Line), you can go ahead and collapse the stack now. As for me, I changed my Steps: value to 8 (see Figure 1.81).

6. Right-click the bil-head object. From the Transform quad menu, choose Convert To > Convert to Editable Mesh.

7. Activate Polygon sub-object mode and select the top front of the bil-head object, as shown in Figure 1.82.

Figure 1.81
The bil-head object with the Steps: value changed to 8.

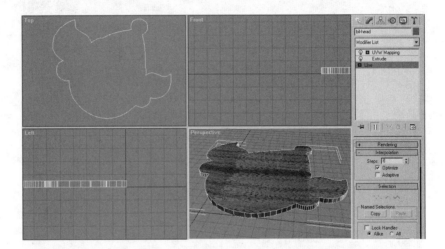

Figure 1.82
The front polygon of the bil-head object (the solid color is used for the sake of clarity).

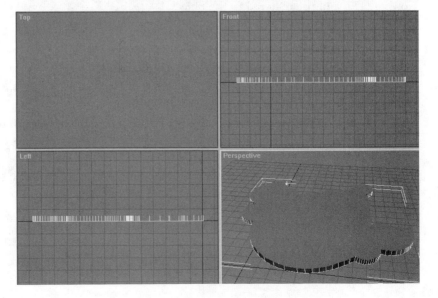

8. In the Surface Properties rollout, change the Material ID to **5** so the clown head image appears on the object.

9. From the toolbar, choose Edit > Select Invert to select the extruded faces of the bil-head object. Change the Material ID to 1 so the bil-wood material appears on the extrusion.

10. Render a test frame to make sure everything is okay (see Figure 1.83). The bil-head object is complete.

11. Save your work as **01FH10.max**.

Figure 1.83
The rendered bil-head object.

In Conclusion

As of now, you have created the billboard backdrop and the clown's body, hands, and head and their associated materials. You have learned how to use the basic trace and extrude modeling technique with the Viewport Background as a template. While creating these objects, you learned the importance of shapes, the Steps Interpolation value, and the types of vertices. When these shapes were turned into objects, you learned how to apply planar mapping coordinates and how to change a polygon's Material ID. In the Material Editor, you began to create a complex multi/sub-object material and applied it to the objects in your scene.

Chapter 2

Finishing the Billboard

A few hours have passed since you started

this project, and Mr. Boss has already

stopped by to visit and inquire on your

progress. It's not like he's snooping on

you or breathing down your neck to get it done. He's just being social. Mr. Boss enjoys stopping by periodically to chat about vintage cult movies and comic books. I suppose everyone likes to get out of working every now and then.

As for you, you really need to dig in your heels and continue your work on this project. The progress you have made with this project is exciting, and you're anxious to finish the objects so you can start to finesse the scene and animate it. Then you hear that Gordon Miller is currently downstairs working on the audio for the animation. When it comes to making great audio, Gordon always brings home the goods.

In this chapter, you gain experience in the following:

- Using the Refine and Outline sub-object tools
- Detaching splines from a shape
- Creating a simple beveled object
- Using a single modifier on multiple objects
- Applying and editing the Lathe modifier
- Using the Bend modifier
- Creating spotlights
- Using the Align tool

Building the Funhouse Type

In the previous chapter, you created and added materials to the flaming billboard background and the clown's body, head, and hands using the simple trace and extrude technique. To complete the geometry in the scene, you need to create the "Funhouse" type object, the light fixtures, and most importantly the post for the billboard. Because the Funhouse type will be created using the same trace and extrude technique you used to create the other objects in this scene, you should build it next.

Creating the Type Objects

As you sit back in your chair to get busy with the project, you suddenly realize this will be the last object in this scene that you need to trace and extrude. You look at the illustration Vince provided you with, and you realize that the type has two edges. This means that for each letter, you will need to create two splines. Hopefully the Outline will expedite that process. For now, just trace the outside of the letters.

Exercise 2.1   Tracing Type

Get ready to do some tracing! You'll begin by tracing the outside of the letters.

1. Load 01FH10.max. The clown head object you created is looking at you (see Figure 2.1)

Figure 2.1
01FH10.max—the scene you created in the previous chapter.

2. Maximize the Top view and right-click in it. Make sure the bil-head object is not selected. From the Display quad-menu, choose Hide Unselected to hide the bil-head object.

3. Right-click the Top view label and check Show Background.

   Vince's clown head illustration appears. You need to change the template to the Funhouse image template.

4. From the toolbar, choose Views > Viewport Background to open the Viewport Background dialog. Click the Files button, choose \3ds4-ma\ project1\images\tmpl-type.jpg, and click Open to close the Select Background Image dialog. Click OK to close the Viewport Background dialog.

5. Using the Pan and Zoom tools, adjust the Top view to the point that you can see the letters FUNH filling the view (as shown in Figure 2.2).

   Now before you start to trace the letters of this type, take a look at Vince's illustration again.

6. From the toolbar, choose File > View Image File... and view the image \3ds4-ma\project1\images\finalclown.jpg.

Figure 2.2
The Funhouse type
template image is
cropped so that
"FUNH" is in the Top
view.

As you can see, you will need a pair of shapes for the Funhouse type, one to
create the yellow outline object and one to create the green interior of the
type. Maybe there is some way you could get out of tracing this type twice.
Trace the outside of the letters first.

7. Open the Create/Shapes panel and click the Line button. Click to create the
   first corner vertex on the upper-left outermost corner of the blue line.
   Continue clicking around the exterior of the "F" creating corner vertices
   until you close the shape (see Figure 2.3).

   If you need to tweak the vertices a little, don't hesitate to go to the Modify
   panel and use Vertex sub-object level transforms on the vertices to get them
   perfect. I did.

8. Trace the U. From the Create/Shapes menu, click the Line button and deselect Start New Shape. Click the outmost edge of the upper-left corner of
   the blue line around the U and continue to create vertices around the object
   until you close the shape. Remember: Simply clicking creates a corner
   vertex, whereas dragging the mouse creates a Bézier vertex type (to create
   the round bottom of the U (see Figure 2.4).

   Because you deselected Start New Shape, the U you just created is attached
   to the F shape. Notice the placement of the Bézier vertices in Figure 2.4. I
   created three vertices on the exterior of the U and only two on the interior.
   This is because Step Interpolation occurs when you extrude this shape.
   Because I didn't want unnecessary polygons to be created on the inside
   curve, I used only two vertices. On the outside curve, however, I used three
   because I want to see more polygons on that extruded surface.

9. If you want to make final adjustments to the U shape, enter Vertex sub-
   object mode and make those adjustments.

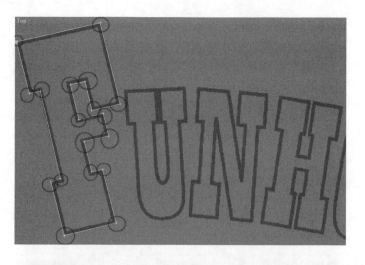

Figure 2.3
The "F" shape you
just created by tracing
the outer edge of the
blue line.

Figure 2.4
The finished U shape
in the Top view.

Because there is another letter U in the shape, you should copy the one you just created.

10. Zoom out the view in order to see both U's simultaneously. Enter Spline sub-object level, activate the Select and Move tool (View XY-axis), and Shift+move the U spline to the right to create a copy.

11. Using the Select and Rotate tool (View Z-axis), rotate the new U to the correct angle. Use the Select and Move tool to move it into closer position if necessary (see Figure 2.5).

Instead of going back to the Create panel to finish tracing the Funhouse type, you can finish it more efficiently by staying within the sub-object mode of the Funhouse type.

Figure 2.5
The two U's in the Funhouse type are complete.

12. Expand the Geometry rollout and click Create Line. Click on the outermost edge of the upper-left corner of the "N" and continue tracing it around until you close the spline.

13. Continue to trace the remaining letters. Right-click to exit Create Line mode. (Remember: Clicking creates a corner vertex, and dragging creates a Bézier vertex.) Once again, feel free to enter Vertex sub-object mode to tweak the vertices.

14. Name the new shape **bil-type-out** and save your work as **02FH01.max**. That wasn't so bad, was it?

Figure 2.6
The outer tracing of Funhouse is complete.

Exercise 2.2   Using the Outline Tool

Because you already traced the outside of the Funhouse type, there has to be an easy way to create the inside trace. Lucky for you, 3D Studio Max has provided a tool exactly for that use.

1. With 02FH01.max open and the bil-type-out shape selected, activate Spline sub-object level. Adjust your maximized Top view so the letters "FUNH" fill it (see Figure 2.7).

Figure 2.7
The letters "FUNH" are filling the maximized Top view.

Now you will create the inside trace for the letter "F."

2. Select the F shape, and in the Geometry rollout, enter Outline: –2 (see Figure 2.8) and press Enter.

The Outline: value returns to 0, and a new shape is created two units inside the original letter F spline as shown in Figure 2.9.

3. Select the letter U shape and enter an Outline value of –2 to it also.

4. Select the letter N shape and apply the Outline value of –2. View the results (see Figure 2.10).

On the new shape that was created for the interior N, notice that the points on the tight corners are long and pointy as compared to the Viewport Background image. You will fix that next. It's a snap.

Figure 2.8
The Modify panel displays the Outline –2 value applied in the Geometry rollout.

Figure 2.9
Introducing the new, smaller letter F spline created from the Outline function.

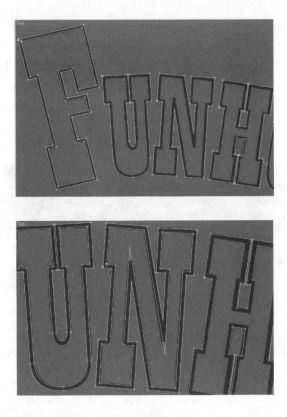

Figure 2.10
The two splines creating the letter N.

5. Enter Vertex sub-object mode, and in the Geometry rollout, click the Refine button. Click on the interior spline to create new points where the spline travels off the blue outline (see Figure 2.11).

   Now all we need to do is get rid of the old pointy vertices.

6. Select the two vertices, one on each interior point (see Figure 2.12), and press the Delete key to permanently delete them from the shape.

7. Select all four of the new vertices you added with the Refine tool, right-click them, and change their Vertex type to Corner.

   With the N finished, you can continue making the interior letter shapes using the Outline tool.

8. Activate Spline sub-object level and select the H shape. In the Geometry roll-out, enter an Outline value of **–2**. The new interior H shape is perfect.

9. Select the outer O shape and assign an Outline value of **–2** to it (see Figure 2.13).

   You don't want to give the shape that designates the hole of the O a negative outline value; that would make the hole smaller. So you have to select it and apply a positive value.

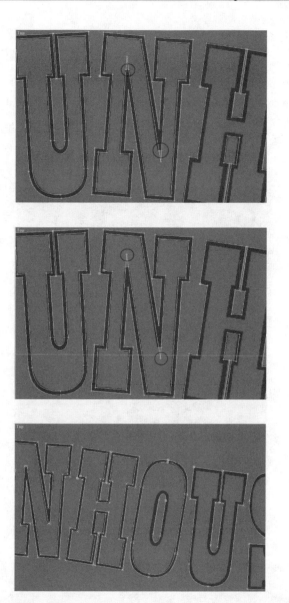

Figure 2.11
The four new vertices are added to the interior N shape.

Figure 2.12
Delete these two vertices.

Figure 2.13
The Funhouse type that you've created to this point.

10. Select the hole spline of the letter O and apply an Outline value of **2**. The line grows outward and creates the new shape in the correct position, as shown in Figure 2.14.

    The finished O shape in the correct position.

11. Select the remaining three letters: U, S, and E. To do so, either drag a Rectangular Selection Region around them or CTRL+click them. Then apply an Outline value of **–2** (see Figure 2.15).

    Cool, we were able to apply the Outline operation to multiple shapes at once.

Hmmm, that letter S doesn't quite look perfect. You can use the Refine technique you learned while working on the letter N to fix the sharp points that occurred on the serifs. And while you're at it, adjust the vertices a little to make the interior of the S look better.

12. If you need to make any final adjustments to your shapes, do so at this time.

Because you will be creating two separate objects from these shapes, you need to detach the inside traces from this shape.

13. Adjust the Top view to see all the Funhouse type (see Figure 2.16).

Figure 2.14
The finished O shape in the correct position.

Figure 2.15
The letters USE with the –2 Outline applied.

Figure 2.16
The Funhouse type in the Top view.

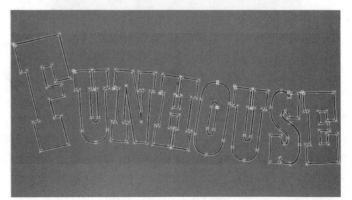

14. While working in Spline sub-object mode, select all the interior traces of the letters by Ctrl+clicking them. Remember to select the correct splines of the letter O (not the innermost circle).

15. Near the bottom of the Geometry rollout, click the Detach button. In the Detach dialog (shown in Figure 2.17), enter the name **bil-type-in** and click OK to close the dialog and detach the selected shapes (see Figure 2.18).

    The Funhouse type tracing is now complete. See, it wasn't that bad. You learned how to use some sub-object level tools to make your life much easier.

16. Save your work as **02FH02.max**.

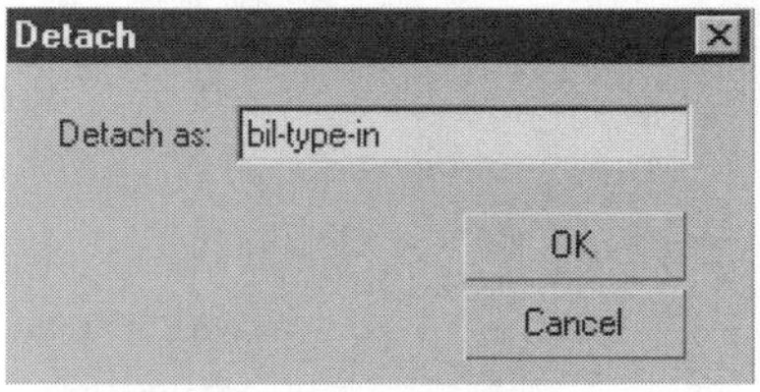

Figure 2.17
The Detach dialog that appears when you click the Detach button.

Figure 2.18
The interior splines you selected are now detached.

Exercise 2.3   Converting Shapes into Objects

Now that you have carefully traced all the letters of the Funhouse type, it's time to put the Funhouse type shapes into action. Because you took the time to create the double outline using the outline tool around the text shapes, you can use them to the fullest by adding different levels to the front surface of the type objects.

1. Open **02FH02.max**.

2. Take one more look at the original illustration Vince provided: \3ds4-ma\ project1\images\finalclown.jpg. In that image, you can see that you should simply extrude the outer shape of the letters, and maybe you can place a small bevel on the interior shapes of the letters.

3. Minimize the Top view and click Zoom Extents All to center the Funhouse type in all the views. Zoom and Arc Rotate the Perspective view to get a good view of the Funhouse type. Then right-click the Perspective view's label and deselect Show Grid, as shown in Figure 2.19.

4. If it isn't already selected, select the bil-type-out object. Exit from sub-object mode if necessary.

5. In the Modify panel, apply an Extrude modifier with an Amount: of **10** and deselect Cap Start (see Figure 2.20).

   That was so easy you should just go ahead and make the bil-type-in object now as well.

Figure 2.19
The four viewports show the Funhouse type centered.

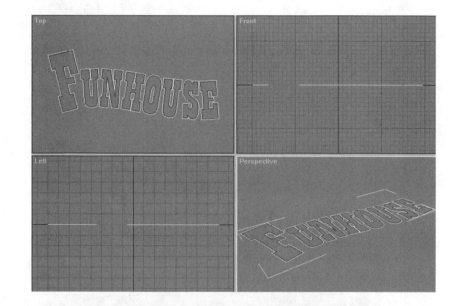

Figure 2.20
The bil-type-out object shows an Extrude of 10 applied.

6. Open the Select Objects dialog either by clicking the Select by Name button on the toolbar or by pressing the H key. Select bil-type-in (as shown in Figure 2.21) and click Select to select the object and close the dialog.

The bil-type-in object was created on the home grid along with the bil-type-out object. To see what you are doing to it in the shaded Perspective view, move it forward into its permanent placement.

7. Activate the Select and Move tool. In the Transform Type-In on the status bar, enter a value of Z: **10** to move the bil-type-in object forward 10 units (the height of the extruded bil-type-out object).

Instead of simply extruding this shape, go crazy and put a Bevel modifier on it. Actually, it looks like that's what Vince intended in his illustration anyway.

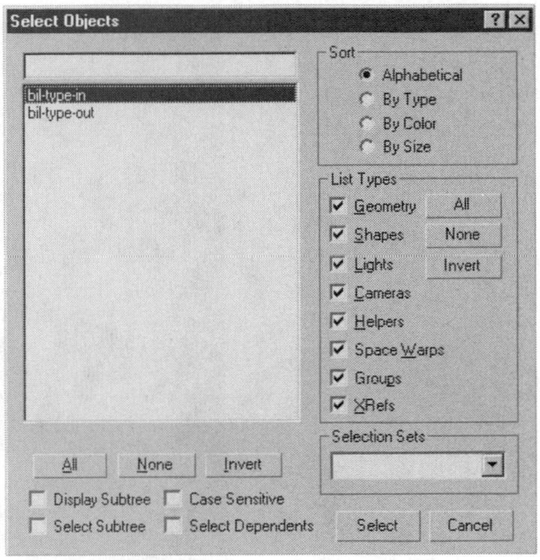

Figure 2.21
The Select Objects dialog shows the bil-type-in object selected.

8. With the bil-type-in object still selected, open the Modify panel and apply a Bevel modifier (from the Mesh Editing group).

You will never see the back of this object, so you might as well deselect Start in the Capping group of the Parameters rollout. And to apply the bevel, enter a Height: of **2** and an Outline: of **–2** for Level 1 in the Bevel Values rollout (see Figure 2.22).

The bil-type-in object is now beveled. The Height value acts like the Extrude modifier and simply extrudes the shape and adds the sides. The Outline: value works like the Outline sub-object tool you used to create the bil-type-in object. It tells the Bevel modifier how far to offset the distance of the original outline.

Note

If any of the End caps fail to appear when you bevel the shape, it is because the shape is intersecting itself at one point or another. To fix this, you need to determine where the intersection is and enter the sub-object level of the shape.

9. Save your work as **02FH03.max**.

Figure 2.22
The finished Funhouse type objects in the four views.

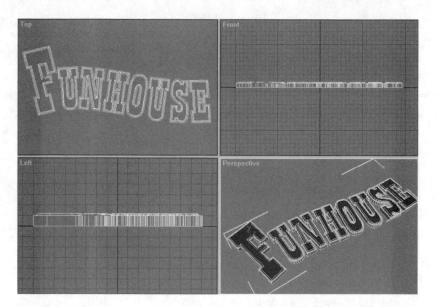

Painting the Funhouse Type Objects

Now that you have created the Funhouse type objects, you can start to apply the materials to them. It shouldn't be long before the scene will really start to take form.

Exercise 2.4   Adding the Materials

Because you have already created the Billboard Multi\sub-object material, you might as well just add two more sub-materials to it.

1. Make sure 02FH03.max is open, and then open the Material Editor. Confirm that the Billboard material is selected and its root is showing (as shown in Figure 2.23). If you aren't at the root of the material, click the Go to Parent button until it is deactivated.

   Because each of the two Funhouse type objects will have its own unique sub-material, you should just add two more sub-materials to the Billboard material.

2. Click the Set Number button and change the Number of Materials: to **7**.

3. Click the Material 6 button to open its settings. Name this material **bil-type-out.** Click the Go Forward to Sibling button to move to sub-material 7. Name this material **bil-type-in.** Click Go To Parent (see Figure 2.24). You now have the two extra sub-materials you need for the type objects.

   Next you'll apply the Material ID of each sub-material to the appropriate Funhouse type object.

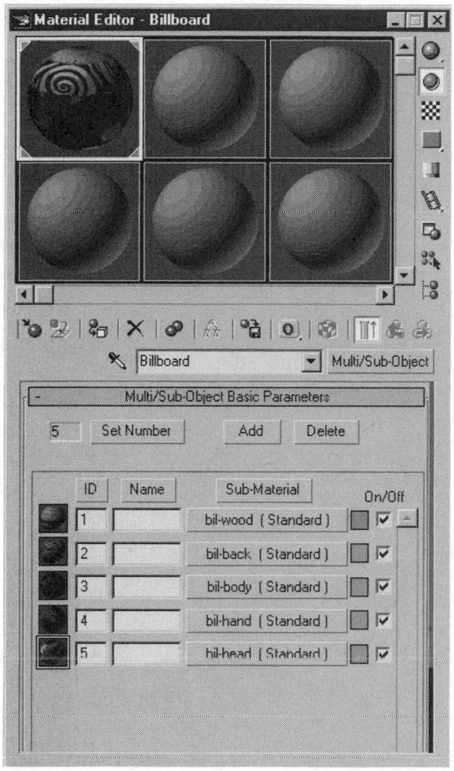

Figure 2.23
The Material Editor shows the Billboard material selected.

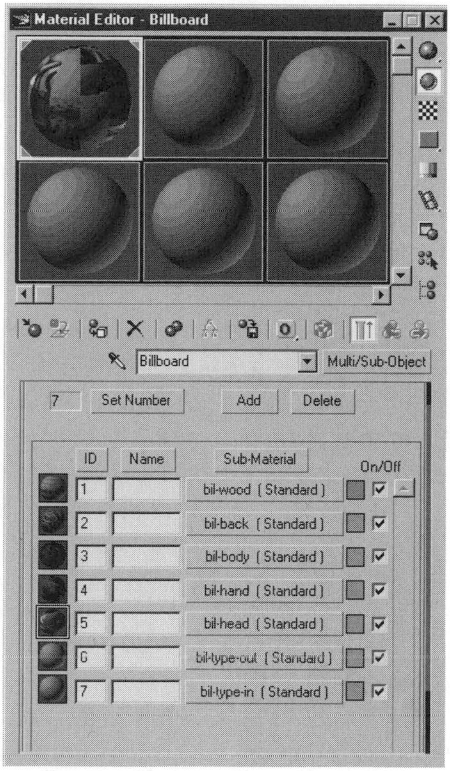

Figure 2.24
The Billboard material shows correctly named sub-materials.

4. Select the bil-type-out object and open the Modify panel. Apply a Material modifier (from the Surface Modifiers list) and assign the value that matches its sub-material number, **6** (see Figure 2.25).

   Now you need to apply the Material ID of **7** to the bil-type-in object. It's the same process.

5. While the bil-type-out object is still selected, right-click the Material modifier in the stack and choose Copy. Select the bil-type-in object, right-click its Bevel modifier in the stack, and choose Paste to apply the Material modifier above the Bevel modifier on the stack. Change the Material ID: to **7**.

   Next you'll apply the Billboard material to the objects.

6. Drag the Billboard material sample Sphere over each object and release the mouse. When you release the mouse, the objects should turn gray (the default Diffuse color of the sub-materials).

Figure 2.25
The Material modifier in the Modify panel with a Material ID of 6.

Exercise 2.5   Creating Sub-Materials

The sub-materials are all correctly applied to the Funhouse type objects. All that's left to do is to create the sub-materials.

1. Click the bil-type-out material button (sub-material 6) to open its parameters. You need to see what type of material to create for this object. To do so, load Vince's illustration again.

2. From the toolbar, choose Files > View Image File, and view \3ds4-ma\ project1\images\finalclown.jpg. Leave the image open.

    From Vince's illustration, you can see that the bil-type-in object's color should be a yellowish color. But how can you match that color precisely?

3. Right-click and drag on the image, and a color dropper appears with the pixel information (see Figure 2.26).

    However, this not only shows you the pixel information, it also copies the current pixel color to the little box on the image's toolbar. This color swatch could be dragged and copied into the Material Editor or onto any other color swatch in 3ds max.

Image	
Width: 818	Aspect: 1.00
Height: 614	Gamma: 1.00
Type: 24 Bits (RGB)	

Pixel (232,391)		
Red:	255	100.0 %
Green:	231	90.6 %
Blue:	94	36.9 %
Alpha:	255	100.0 %
Mono:	194	75.8 %

Figure 2.26
The right-click pixel information is displayed when you right-click over an image in 3ds max.

4. Locate a bright yellow pixel on the Funhouse type edge and drag the color swatch to the Diffuse channel of the bil-type-out sub-material (The yellow pixel color I chose was RGB: **255**, **231**, **94**).

    Because the Ambient and Diffuse channels are locked (as signified by the clamp button to the left of the swatches), both swatches change color. The bil-type-in object is now yellow in the shaded Perspective view.

5. Close Vince's illustration.

    Only one sub-material to go!

6. Click the Go Forward to Sibling button in the Material Editor to move to the bil-type-in sub-material.

7. Click the blank square to the right of the Diffuse color swatch to open the Material/Map Browser. Choose Bitmap and click OK to close the browser.

8. In the Select Bitmap Image File dialog, choose \3ds4-ma\project1\maps\ bil-typemesh.jpg and click Open to close the dialog. Name this map **bil-type-in-dif** and click the Show Map in Viewport button. Click Go to Parent twice to return to the root of the Billboard material and close the Material Editor.

The bil-typemesh.jpg is now applied as a Diffuse map to the bil-type-in object. However, you don't know if it is mapped correctly on the object. To ensure that it is, apply a Planar UVW Map to it.

9. Select the Perspective view and click the Quick Render button.

   You can see the green honeycomb pattern on the Funhouse image using the UVW Coordinates generated by its Bevel modifier (see Figure 2.27).

   Now add the UVW Map modifier.

10. With the bil-type-in object selected, activate the Modify panel and apply a UVW Map modifier. Render the Perspective view again.

   Very little changes. However, you want to ensure that the texture is applied using the intended aspect ratio from Vince's texture image. You can easily resize the UVW Map Gizmo to match the aspect of the bitmap.

11. In the Alignment: group of the Parameters rollout of the UVW Map modifier, click the Bitmap Fit button to open the Select Image dialog. Choose \3ds4-ma\project1\maps\bil-typemesh.jpg and click View to see the image (Figure 2.28).

Figure 2.27
The honeycomb pattern in the rendered Perspective view.

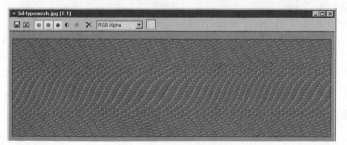

Figure 2.28
Bil-typemesh.jpg is the green honeycomb texture map.

Notice the aspect of the image; it is much longer than it is high. That is the way Vince intended the texture to appear on the objects, so you should respect his wishes and use the images aspect ratio.

12. Close the bil-typemesh.jpg image and click Open to close the Select Image dialog.

The UVW Map Gizmo is automatically resized to match the aspect of the bil-typemesh.jpg image (see Figure 2.29).

Figure 2.29
The UVW Map Gizmo
is resized.

Exercise 2.6   Linking Objects in a Hierarchy

Your work here is almost finished. Because you know that the bil-type-in object will always be attached to the bil-type-out object, you should link them together in a hierarchy.

1. With the bil-type-in object selected, click the Select and Link button on the toolbar and press H to open the Select Parent dialog. Choose bil-type-out as the parent (as shown in Figure 2.30) and click Link to close the dialog.

Now you need to make sure you've linked them together correctly. To do so, examine the sub-tree in the Select Object dialog.

2. Activate the Select Object tool and press the H key to open the Select Objects dialog. Check Display Subtree, and the object list should update, showing the bil-type-in object is a child of the bil-type-out object (see Figure 2.31). Click Cancel to exit the dialog.

Looks like you're finished building the Funhouse type objects.

3. Save your work as **02FH04.max** and continue.

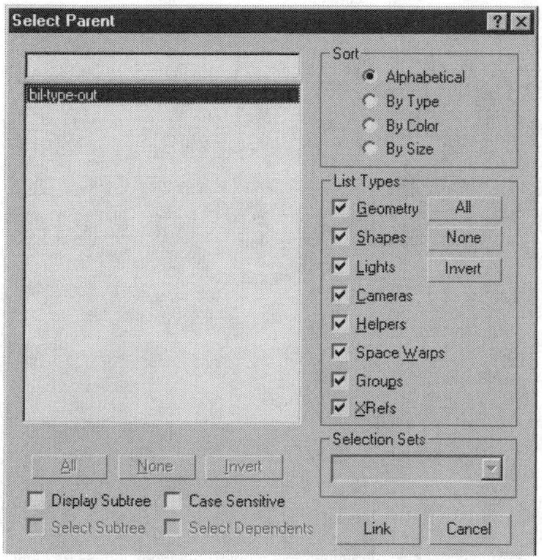

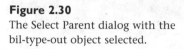

Figure 2.30
The Select Parent dialog with the
bil-type-out object selected.

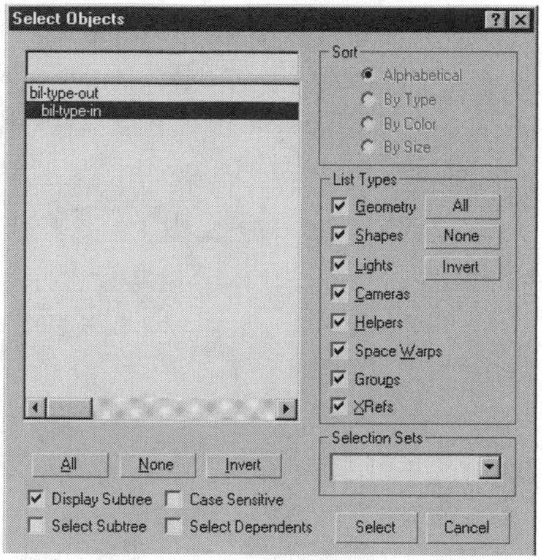

Figure 2.31
The Select Objects dialog shows Display
Subtree active.

Finishing the Billboard

The artwork of the billboard is now complete, so you can stand it up in world space
and erect the rest of the surrounding objects such as the post and light fixtures. You
will also have to adjust the placement of the individual artwork elements of the billboard, putting them into their final, most appealing, locations. You will also add a
camera and a few lights to illuminate the scene.

Working with the Billboard

You need to arrange the individual pieces of the clown artwork into their correct
positions. You also need to stand the billboard up in the scene. When the billboard
is upright, you will add a camera to the scene and adjust the camera to view the
objects and make sure they match those in Vince's original illustration as closely as
possible.

Exercise 2.7   Standing Objects Up in World Space

Now most of the objects you need for this scene are complete, so it's time to stand
them up in world space. The first thing you need to do is unhide all the other
objects you've created.

  1. With 02FH04.max loaded, right-click in any view and choose Unhide All
     from the Display Quad Menu (see Figure 2.32).

Figure 2.32
All the billboard objects you've created are unhidden.

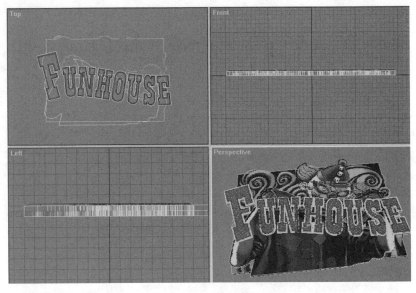

It's not quite the beautiful billboard it could be just yet. You will need to move some things around to make it more appealing. First, move the bil-type-out object into a better position.

2. Select the bil-type-out object and activate the Select and Move tool. With the Perspective view active, use the Status Bar Transform Type-In and drag the arrow to the right of the Y: value downward to lower the type on the Y-axis. You want the type to almost touch the bottom of the billboard (see Figure 2.33).

Figure 2.33
The funhouse type is lower on the billboard.

3. Make sure the Perspective view is still selected and activate Offset Mode Transform Type-In. (It's the little crosshair button to the left of the XYZ transforms on the Status Bar—it allows you to simply offset the object *x* amount of units as opposed to moving an object to a specific (absolute) location.) Drag the Z: value arrow upward to enter a value of **10**.

The funhouse type now rests on top of the bil-body object. Now place the head in its correct position.

4. Select the bil-head object. With the Perspective view still selected, move the bil-head object 10 units forward on its Z-axis until it rests on the neck of the bil-body object as shown in Figure 2.34.

5. To place the hand objects in the correct position, select the two bil-hand objects. With the Perspective view selected, use the Transform Type-In to move the hands forward 22 units on the Z-axis so that the hands are on top of the Funhouse type (see Figure 2.35).

Figure 2.34
The bil-head object is resting on the bil-body object.

Figure 2.35
All the objects are in the correct layered positions.

Before you stand the billboard up in world space, you should link all the objects to the bil-back object. Then all you will have to do is rotate the bil-back object to stand everything up.

6. Open the Select Objects dialog. Notice that the two bil-hand objects are still selected. (If they are not selected, select them now.) Click Cancel to close the dialog. Activate the Select and Link tool and link the hands to the bil-body object.

7. Activate the Select Object tool and open the Select Objects dialog. Select the bil-head object and, using the Select and Link tool, link it to the bil-body object.

8. Activate the Select Object tool again and open the Select Objects dialog. Select the bil-body object and the bil-type-out object and, using the Select and Link tool, link them to the bil-back object.

The subtree should now look like Figure 2.36.

Now any transform that you apply to the bil-back object will also be applied to the rest of the children objects. It's time to stand up the billboard up in world space.

Figure 2.36
The correct hierarchy subtree in the Select Objects dialog.

9. Select the bil-back object and activate the Select and Rotate tool. With the Perspective view active, enter a value of X: **90** in the Transform Type-In. Click Zoom Extents All to view the billboard standing up in world space (as shown in Figure 2.37).

10. Save your work as **02FH05.max**.

Figure 2.37
The billboard objects are now standing in world space.

Exercise 2.8   Creating a Camera

With the objects you've created so far standing up in world space, you can create the light fixtures and add the billboard post. However, before you get involved with that, you should try to match your objects up to the illustration Vince created. To match the objects to the illustration, you need a camera. So create one now.

1. With 02FH05.max loaded, open the Create/Cameras panel. Click the Target button and click in the lower area of the Top view (to create the camera). Then drag the mouse to position the camera's target in the center of the billboard and release the mouse (see Figure 2.38).

   Now view the scene through the camera.

2. Select the Perspective view and press the C key to change it into the Camera01 view.

Figure 2.38
The target camera created in the Top view.

3. Use the Dolly Camera tool in the Camera01 view to view the entire billboard. Click Zoom Extents All (see Figure 2.39).

   Now put Vince's illustration in the Camera01 view so you can align your objects to it.

4. With the Camera01 view selected, choose Views > Viewport Background... from the toolbar to open the Viewport Background dialog. Click the Files button, choose \3ds4-ma\project1\images\finalclown.jpg, and click OK to close the Viewport Background dialog.

Figure 2.39
The billboard is visible in all four views.

5. Right-click the Camera01 view's label and check Show Safe Frame.

   Show Safe Frame locks the background image to the renderer's aspect. It's kind of hard to discern where your objects and Vince's illustration begin and end at this point. You should clean up your workspace a little.

6. Right-click the Camera01 view's label and check Wireframe so that the Camera01 view is no longer shaded.

7. Select the bil-back object and right-click to open the quad menu. Choose Hide Unselected from the Display menu.

Exercise 2.9   Matching an Object to an Illustration

Now you can concentrate on making the bil-back object to match the illustration.

1. Maximize the Camera01 view. Using the viewport navigation controls (Dolly Camera, Perspective, Roll Camera, and so on), try to match the bil-back object to the perspective in Vince's illustration (as shown in Figure 2.40).

Figure 2.40
The Camera01 view shows the bil-back object aligned to Vince's illustration.

Not as easy at it seems? The closest I matched the bil-back object to the background is visible in Figure 2.40. At least I have the top and bottom of the billboard lined up. My current camera settings are listed here:

Camera01 position XYZ: –223, –427, –223

> Dolly: 519.224
>
> Roll: –5
>
> Lens: 33.358mm

Camera01.Target position XYZ: –32, 16, –31

Note

If you want to use my settings for the camera, you will have to unhide the camera. To do so, click the Display tab and click the Unhide by Name button. Then unhide Camera01 and Camera01.Target. All the values can be entered in the Move Transform Type-In dialog (accessible by right-clicking the Select and Move tool), except for the Lens: value. You will have to enter the Lens: value in the Modify panel with Camera01 selected.

With the camera in this position, you can see that the bil-back object needs to be wider. Adjust that right now.

2. Make sure the Camera01 view is maximized. Select the bil-back object and open the Modify panel.

To scale this object without modifying the local axis, you use an XForm modifier.

3. Apply an XForm modifier to the bil-back object and open the XForm modifier's subtree by clicking the + next to it in the modifier stack (see Figure 2.41) to access the XForm Gizmo.

Notice that a yellow bar highlights the XForm Gizmo. This means that any transforms applied at this time will be applied to the Gizmo and not at the object's local axis level.

4. To scale the bil-back object, activate the Select and Non-Uniform Scale tool (Local X-axis). Scale the bil-back object approximately X: **135%** until the sides roughly match (as shown in Figure 2.42).

Figure 2.41
The modifier stack with the XForm subtree expanded.

Now you can see how poorly your perspective really matches Vince's illustration. This isn't entirely your fault. In the 2D illustration world, there is a technique called Pinning. *Pinning* allows the 2D artist to simply grab any of the four corners and move it to a desired location. It is often possible for the 2D artist to pin a perspective that is nearly impossible to match in the 3D world without distorting the model unrealistically. The problem you are experiencing right now results from the fact that Vince used pinning to simulate a 3D image when he drew his illustration.

Because you will be creating a different camera to animate with, it doesn't make much sense to fret over this. Later, when you are animating, the camera will be in constant motion, so it won't be very important for you to capture this precise angle.

Now that the bil-back is as perfect as it's going to get, you can line up the rest of the objects.

5. In the Display tab click Unhide by Name and unhide the bil-body object. Looks like you have the same scaling issues here. Luckily you know what to do.

6. Select the bil-body object and, in the Modify panel, apply an XForm modifier. Scale (local axis) the Xform Gizmo to approximately X: **130%**. You might also have to move the Gizmo (local axis) approximately X: **10** units (see Figure 2.43).

Figure 2.42
The scaled bil-back object in the Camera01 view.

Figure 2.43
The bil-body object moved to the correct position.

Exercise 2.10   Using a Modifier on Multiple Objects

The Funhouse type is next. You need to scale the Funhouse type in order for it to be the correct proportion to the billboard. And once again, instead of applying the scale to the object, you will apply the scale transform to an XForm Gizmo in the modifier stack. Because you will be applying the same scale transform to both objects that create the type, you will use the same XForm modifier to scale them simultaneously.

1. Open the Display tab and click Unhide by Name. Unhide both the bil-type-in and bil-type-out objects.

2. Open the Select Objects dialog and select both of the Funhouse type objects you just unhid (see Figure 2.44).

Figure 2.44
The Funhouse type objects are no longer hidden and are selected.

3. With both objects selected, activate the Modify panel and apply an XForm modifier.

   It's pretty cool that you can apply the same modifier to more than one object at once!

4. Click the + next to the XForm modifier to open its subtree and activate the Gizmo.

5. Use the Select and Non-Uniform Scale tool (Local X-axis) to scale the Gizmo to approximately X: **130%** (as shown in Figure 2.45).

   The Funhouse type objects are about the right size now, but they need to be lower and rotated counterclockwise a little.

6. With the XForm Gizmo still active, use the Select and Move tool (Local Z-axis) to move the type down approximately Z: **–35** units.

7. Activate the Select and Rotate tool (Local Y-axis) and rotate the gizmo approximately Y: **–4** degrees (see Figure 2.46).

Although the type is now oriented correctly on the billboard, it seems a little too tall. Fix that while you still have the Gizmo active.

8. Activate the Select and Non-Uniform Scale tool (Local Z-axis) and scale the Gizmo approximately Z: **85%** (as shown in Figure 2.47).

Figure 2.45
The Funhouse type
scaled on its X-axis.

Figure 2.46
The Funhouse type is
now in the correct
position.

Figure 2.47
The Finished
Funhouse type is
scaled to the correct
proportion.

Exercise 2.11   Aligning the Remaining Objects

That looks much better. The Funhouse type is as good as it's going to get. Do the
head next. Instead of clicking the Display tab to choose Unhide by Name, you can
use the keyboard shortcut.

   1. Press the 5 key to open the Unhide Objects dialog. Choose the bil-head object
      and click Unhide to unhide the clown's head (as shown in Figure 2.48).

      Hmm, it looks like it needs to be adjusted a little to match Vince's illustration.

Figure 2.48
The bil-head object is
no longer hidden.

2. Select the bil-head object and apply an XForm modifier to it. Make adjust-ments to the XForm Gizmo by using the Select and Move tool (Local XY-axis), Select and Rotate tool (Local-Z axis), and Select and Non-Uniform Scale (Local XY-axis) to match the comp as closely as possible (see Figure 2.49).

Now all that's left is the hands. So unhide them and start lining them up.

Figure 2.49
The bil-head object now matches the illustration.

3. Press the 5 key to open the Unhide Objects dialog and unhide both hand objects. Each needs to be scaled slightly on its local X-axis and moved into position. Because you are now a pro at using the XForm Gizmo, I am going to leave you on your own for this one. Just remember, you will have to mod-ify each hand separately, using the technique described in the following step.

4. Select one hand object, apply an XForm modifier, and match the hand to the billboard as closely as possible using the Select and Move tool (Local XY-axis) and the Select and Non-Uniform Scale (Local X-axis) (see Figure 2.50). Try to scale both hands the same amount; you wouldn't want one to be bigger than the other.

Cool. Now turn off the Viewport Background and activate the shaded Camera01 view again.

5. Right-click the Camera01 view's label and deselect Show Background. Then right-click the Camera01 view's label and check Smooth+Highlights.

The shaded Camera01 view is back (see Figure 2.51), and we are ready to render a test frame.

6. Click the Quick Render button.

The test frame looks pretty good, except the clown's head is not quite on his neck (see Figure 2.52). That's okay, you can fix that a little later. For now, sit back and appreciate all the hard work you've done so far.

7. Save your work as **02FH06.max**.

Figure 2.50
Both hand objects are
in the correct orienta-
tion on the billboard.

Figure 2.51
The billboard in the
shaded Camera01
view.

Figure 2.52
The billboard in the
rendered Camera01
view.

Creating the Lighting Fixtures and the Billboard Post and Applying the Lighting

Now you can add the light fixtures, give the billboard a post, and light the scene. You should be happy that you won't have to extrude any more traced shapes. That's all behind you now—and you thought it would never end! As you already know, for us Media Animators, a good portion of our modeling time is spent tracing and beveling. It's all part of the job.

Looking at Vince's illustration, you see that two lighting fixtures are attached to the billboard. You examine the lighting fixtures and find it apparent that you can easily create them by lathing a cross-section of the lamp and then placing it on the end of a bent cylinder. So that's what you are going to do. This shouldn't take too long.

Exercise 2.12   Lathing to Create a Lamp

The term "lathing" is borrowed from the world of woodworking. Usually a piece of wood is placed in a rapidly spinning vice. The woodworker, in turn, uses tools to chisel a uniform groove or shape into the spinning piece of wood. You will use this technique to create the light fixture for the billboard, but in 3ds max, it is much simpler and not nearly as messy. In short, you will draw a shape that represents one half of the cross-section, and then you will lathe it about itself a full 360 degrees.

1. With 02FH06.max open, minimize the Camera01 view. Use the Hide Cameras toggle (Shift+C) to hide the camera, and then click Zoom Extents All.

    Then create the cross-section you will lathe to create the lamp.

2. Maximize the Front view and pan the billboard objects to the top of the view.

    In Vince's illustration, you can see that the height of the lamp is approximately half the height of the "FUNHOUSE" letters. Draw your cross-section roughly to that scale.

3. Activate the Create/Shapes panel and click the Line button. In the Front view, draw a shape that's similar in shape and scale to the one in Figures 2.53 and 2.54. Name the shape **lamp01**.

    You will probably have to enter Vertex sub-object mode and make some adjustments to the shape to get it just right. When you acquire the desired shape, you can lathe it.

4. Select the lamp01 object and click Zoom Extents Selected (from the Zoom Extents flyout).

5. Minimize the Front view and apply a Lathe modifier to the lamp01 object (see Figure 2.55).

    The lamp looks more like a chalice than a lamp because it has been lathed around its center.

Figure 2.53
The correct shape and scale of the lamp cross-section.

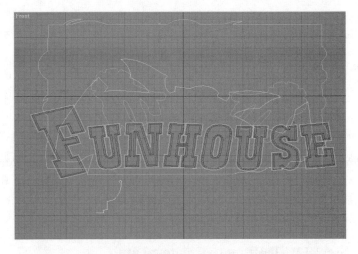

Figure 2.54
The correct lamp cross-section shape up close.

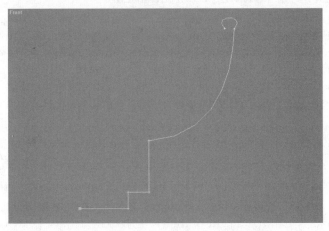

Figure 2.55
The lathed Lamp01 object in the four views.

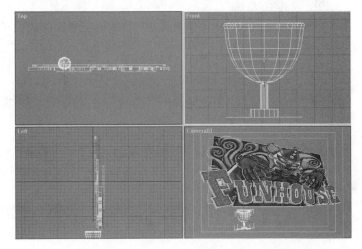

6. In the Align group of the Parameters rollout, click the Min button to lathe the lamp01 shape around its minimum extents. Click Zoom Extents Selected. Figure 2.56 shows the result.

Great, now the lamp looks more like a punchbowl than it does a lamp. It's a good thing 3ds max allows you to easily—and visually—edit this type of thing.

7. In the Modifier stack, click the + next to the Line object. Click the Vertex sub-object level to activate it. The lathe disappears, and you can edit the loft shape again.

Wouldn't it be great if you could see the finished loft as you were modifying this shape? Today is your lucky day!

8. Click the Show End Result on/off toggle to see the view shown in Figure 2.57.

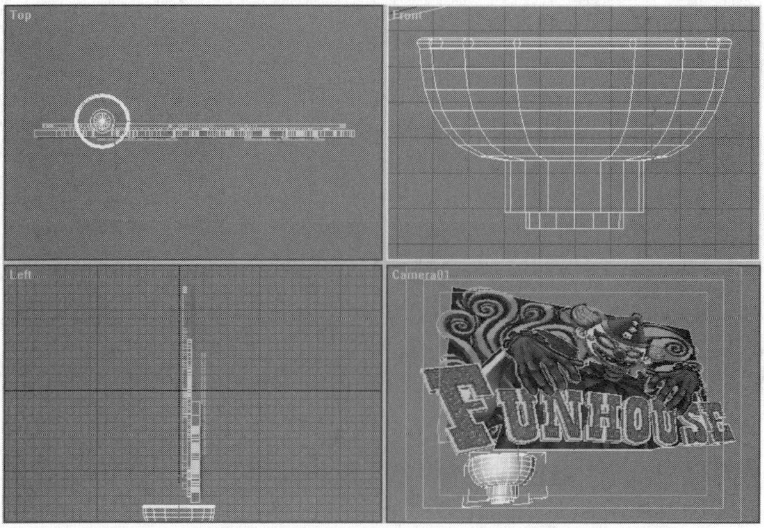

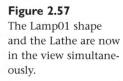

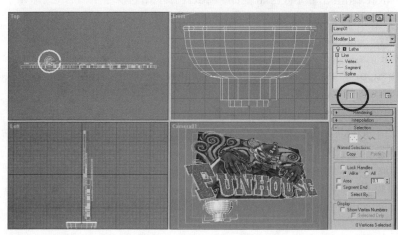

Figure 2.56
The lamp shape is now lathed on its minimum extents.

Figure 2.57
The Lamp01 shape and the Lathe are now in the view simultaneously.

Now you can see the shape and the loft in the views simultaneously! As you edit the Lamp01 shape in the Front view, you can watch as each viewport interactively updates the Lamp01 lathe.

9. Adjust the Lamp01 shape to create a more realistic lamp object (see Figure 2.58). You will have to return to the Lathe modifier and click the Min button to ensure the correct lathe (otherwise the lamp might get a hole in the bottom—otherwise known as the core).

Figure 2.58
The finished Lamp01 object in the four views.

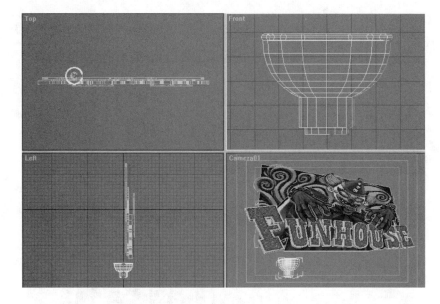

Exercise 2.13   Using the Bend Modifier

Now you can create the arm that will attach the light to the billboard. To do so, you won't do any more work than necessary. The easiest way to create the arm is to link a cylinder to the lamp object.

1. Open the Create/Geometry panel and click the Cylinder button. In the Front view, click in the center of the base of the Lamp01 object and drag to create a Radius: of approximately **4**. Then drag downward to create a negative Height: value (as shown in Figure 2.59); you are going to change them anyway.

   Now you need to adjust the cylinder's parameters to better suit your needs.

2. You don't need all those sides on the cylinder, so change the Sides: value to **8**. Name the object **lamp-arm01**.

   Before you change the rest of the parameters of the lamp-arm01 object, move the light into the desired orientation.

3. Right-click the Camera01 view label and check Show Background. Then right-click the Camera01 label again and check Wireframe.

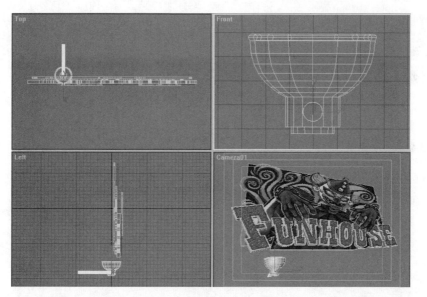

Figure 2.59
The cylinder object you just created with a radius of roughly 4.

This is your last chance to easily fix the shape of the Lamp01 object. So compare your lamp to the one in Vince's illustration to see if you want to make adjustments. In my scene, I needed to make the lamp just a little smaller.

When you are happy with your Lamp01 object, you can move it into position. You need to link the lamp-arm01 object to the lamp01 object first.

4. Activate the Select and Link tool, select the lamp-arm01 object, drag the pointer over the lamp01 object, and release the mouse. The lamp01 object should blink, indicating that it is now the parent.

5. Activate the Select and Move tool (View XY-axis) and move the lamp01 object in the orthographic Top, Front, and Left views into its rough position (see Figure 2.60).

The lamp is in front of the billboard in its approximate location, but it needs to be rotated in order for the lamp arm object to match Vince's illustration. Before you rotate the Lamp01 object, you must adjust its pivot point. Right now the pivot is off center, which would make it hard to rotate the object subtly. You want the lamp to rotate about its bottom center as if it were attached to the lamp arm. If you rotated the object right now, it would not rotate from its center.

6. With the lamp01 object selected, click the Hierarchy tab. In the Move/Rotate/ Scale group, activate the Affect Pivot Only button, and in the Alignment group, click Center to Object. The lamp's local axis is now centered to the lamp object. Now lower the axis to be centered with its base.

7. Activate the Front view and click Zoom Extents Selected. Activate the Select and Move tool (View Y-axis) and move the pivot down to center it on the base (as shown in Figure 2.61). Deactivate Affect Pivot Only.

Now you can rotate the lamp01 object with ease.

8. Activate the Select and Rotate tool (Local Y-axis) and rotate the lamp01 object Y: **–25** degrees (see Figure 2.62).

Now you need to rotate the lamp on its local Z-axis in order to better simulate Vince's illustration.

Figure 2.60
The lamp is in its rough position.

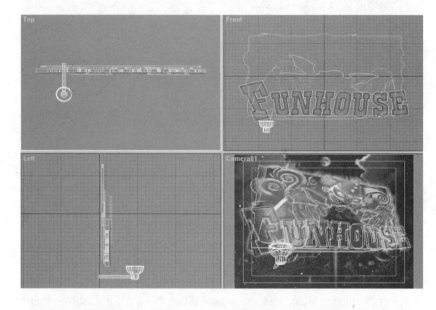

Figure 2.61
The pivot is now centered to the base of the lamp01 object.

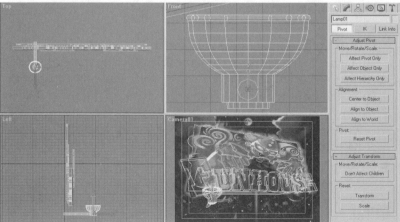

9. Activate the Select and Rotate tool (Local Z-axis) and rotate the lamp 01 object
   Z: **–15** degrees to position the lamp one step closer to its correct orientation.

   The lamp01 object is now rotated slightly clockwise in the Camera01 view.
   You need to point the light at the billboard now.

10. Activate the Select and Rotate tool (Local X-axis) and rotate the lamp01
    object X: **–20** degrees (see Figure 2.63).

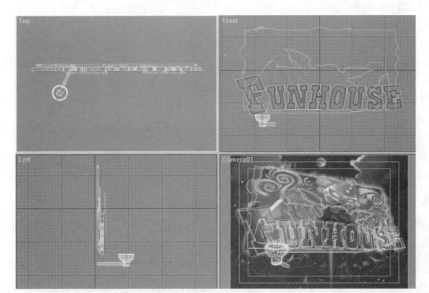

Figure 2.62
The lamp01 object is rotated to Y:–25 degrees.

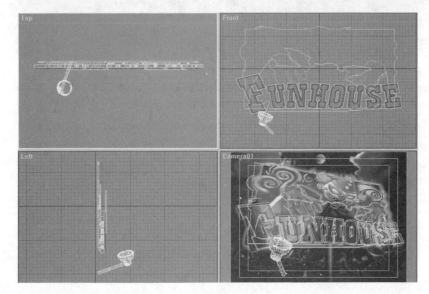

Figure 2.63
The correct orientation of the lamp01 object in the four views.

The lamp01 object looks like it's in the right place, but the lamp-arm01 object certainly isn't doing what it should. It's not bent the way it was in Vince's illustration. Turn your attention to that.

11. Select the lamp-arm01 object and open the Modify panel. Apply a Bend modifier to the lamp-arm01 object. In the Parameters rollout, enter these settings:

   Angle: **60**

   Direction: **–90**

   Bend Axis: **Z**

   Figure 2.64 shows what the arm looks like with the Bend modifier applied.

   I don't know what yours looks like, but my lamp-arm01 is much too short to make it behind the billboard. Luckily 3ds max lets you change the parameters of objects after they are created.

Figure 2.64
The lamp-arm01 object with the Bend modifier applied.

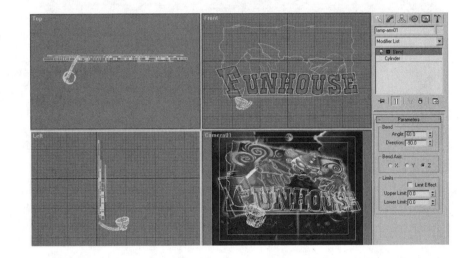

12. In the Modify stack, click the Cylinder object to open the Cylinder's Parameters rollout. Change the Height: to **–200** (as shown in Figure 2.65).

   The lamp-arm01 object is long enough now, but it doesn't curve behind the billboard. To fix that, tweak the Bend modifier's settings.

13. Click the Bend modifier in the Modify stack to open its settings. Change the Angle: value to **90** (see Figure 2.66).

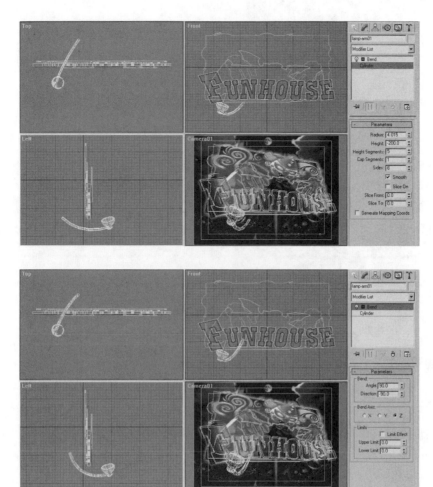

Figure 2.65
The lamp-arm01 object shows a Height of –200.

Figure 2.66
The finished lamp-arm01 object in the four views.

Exercise 2.14   Finessing the Lamp

The lamp-arm01 object now bends behind the billboard. It doesn't have to be attached to anything because you will never see behind the billboard. Render a frame to see your progress.

I. Select the Camera01 view and click the Quick Render button (see Figure 2.67).

This doesn't look too bad! However, two glaring things could use a little help: the pinching of the faces at the core of the lamp01 lathe and the lack of smoothness to the lamp-arm01 object. Smooth out the lamp-arm01 object first.

Figure 2.67
The rendered
Camera01 view dis-
plays your progress.

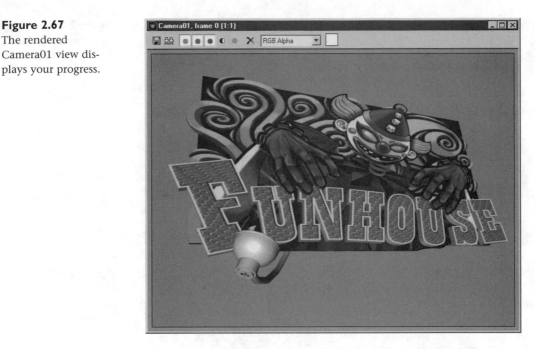

2. Make sure the lamp-arm01 object is selected. In the Modify stack, click the Cylinder object, and in the Parameters rollout, change the Height Segments: to **15**. Click Render Last to render the frame again.

   That's much better. There are now enough height segments for the lamp-arm01 object to bend smoothly. Next, take a look at the lamp01 object.

   If you have a mess of pinched faces on the base of the lamp01 object, you did well. If you have a hole in the bottom of your lamp01 object, you didn't do as well. If you have a hole, you didn't return and click the Min button in the lathe modifier as you were instructed in Step 9 of Exercise 2.12. You can, however, still make sub-object changes to the lamp01 object. Just remember to use the Local XY-axis because the shape needs to remain planar. If the shape isn't planar, the lathe may create undesired and unpredictable results.

   Now you can fix the pinched faces on the base of the lamp01 object.

3. Select the lamp01 object and in the Modify stack, select the Lathe modifier. In the Parameters rollout, check Weld Core. Weld Core instructs the lathe modifier to weld together vertices that lie on the axis of revolution. This results in a much cleaner model.

4. Render the Camera01 view again. Figure 2.68 shows the result.

   The core of the lamp01 object looks much better, but you should add more segments to the lathe to create a smoother lamp.

5. In the Parameters rollout of the Lathe modifier, change the Segments: to **30**.
Then render the Camera01 view again (see Figure 2.69).

By almost doubling the segments of the lathe, you created a much smoother
lathe. It looks great! Save your work and take a break.

6. Save your work as **02FH07.max**.

Figure 2.68
The core of the
lamp01 object is
much cleaner.

Figure 2.69
The rendered
Camera01 view,
displaying your
billboard.

Exercise 2.15   Creating a Spotlight

So far the lighting fixture looks great. Of course, because it *is* a lighting fixture, light should come from it (and because Vince illustrated it that way).

I. Make sure 02FH07.max is open. Go to the Create/Lights panel and click the Free Spot button, and then click to create a spotlight in the Top view (as shown in Figure 2.70). The name **Fspot01** is perfect for this scene.

Figure 2.70
The Free Spot is created in the Top view.

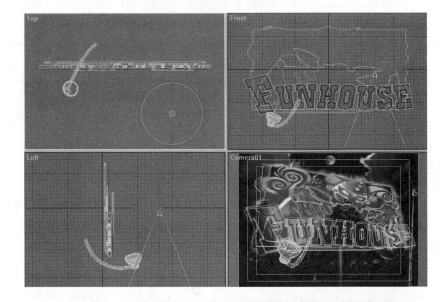

The spotlight doesn't seem to be pointing in the correct direction. That's okay though because you are going to use the Align tool to place the Spot in a snap.

2. With the Fspot01 object still selected, click the Align button on the toolbar, and then click the lamp01 object. The Align Selection (Lamp01) dialog opens (see Figure 2.71).

    You need to move the Fspot01 light to the position of the Lamp01 object.

3. In the Align Position (Screen): group, check X-Position, Y-Position, and Z-Position.

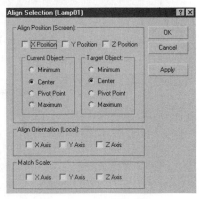

Figure 2.71
The Align Selection (Lamp01) dialog.

As you check each box, you will see the light interactively move in the view-ports. To create a realistic result, you want the pivot point of the spotlight to be placed precisely on the pivot of the lamp object.

4. In the Current Object: group, choose Pivot Point. In the Target Object group, choose Pivot Point. The pivot points are in the same position. Now you need to rotate the Fspot01 light to match the lamp01 object.

5. In the Align Orientation (Local): group, check X Axis, Y Axis, and Z Axis (as in Figure 2.72). Click OK to close the dialog.

   The Align tool almost worked great. The light is 90 degrees off because of the direction of the local axis. Although the local axes of both objects match, because of the various ways you created the objects, the local axes are oriented in different ways. At least now you know that all you have to do is rotate the Fspot01 light 90 degrees.

6. Activate the Select and Rotate tool (Local X-axis) and Rotate the Fspot01 light X: **90** degrees (see Figure 2.73).

7. With the light in place, go ahead and render a frame. Activate the Camera01 view and click the Quick Render button (see Figure 2.74).

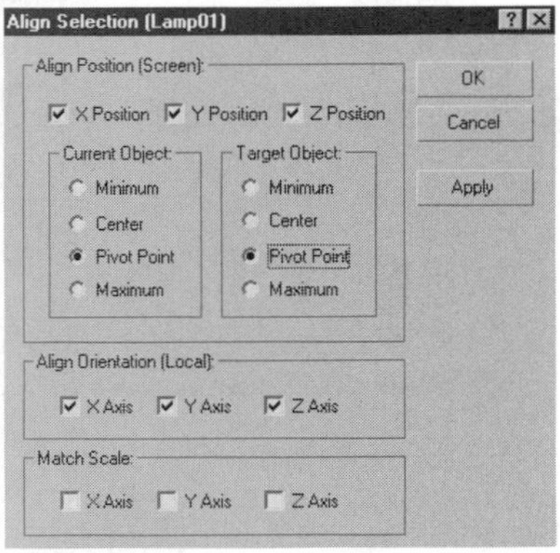

Figure 2.72
The Align Selection (Lamp01) dialog with the correct settings.

Figure 2.73
The Fspot01 light is rotated 90 degrees.

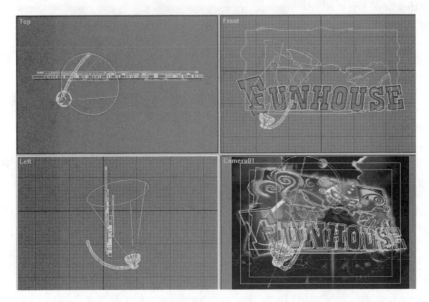

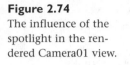

Figure 2.74

The influence of the spotlight in the rendered Camera01 view.

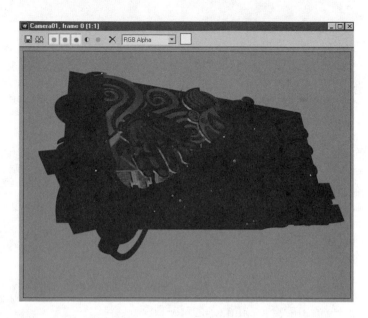

This might not be quite as spectacular as you were hoping for, but it is a great first try. The light seems to light the extrusion of the billboard objects more than it does the important parts of the billboard objects. Maybe having the Fspot01 light directly inside the lamp01 object isn't the best idea. Move it a little more forward and orient it a little differently.

8. Activate the Select and Move tool (View XY-axis) and move the Fspot01 object slightly lower and to the right of its current location (see Figure 2.75).

   You can render another frame from the Camera01 view if you want to; however, it probably looks worse than it did before you moved it. The reason I asked you to move it further away from the billboard was so the light wouldn't have such a harsh angle meeting the billboard. Now you

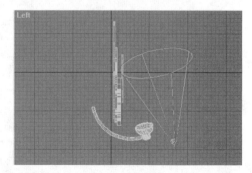

Figure 2.75

The Fspot01 light is moved to the lower-right of its origin in the Left view.

have to rotate the Fspot01 light a little to cast more desired light.

9. Activate the Select and Rotate tool (Local X-axis) and rotate the Fspot01 light to X: **–25**. Then change to the Local Y-axis and rotate the Fspot01 light Y: **15**. Render another frame from the Camera01 view (see Figure 2.76).

Figure 2.76
The spotlight creates a more realistic light cone in the rendered Camera01 view.

Doesn't that look more like what you were expecting the first time around? However, the Fspot01 object casts light on the lamp01 object. You most certainly don't want that to happen because the lamp01 object is supposed to be creating that light.

10. With the Fspot01 light active, open the Modify panel. In the General Parameters rollout, click the Exclude... button to open the Exclude/Include dialog (shown in Figure 2.77). Select all the "bil-" objects, click the arrow pointing to the right, and click Include. Click OK to close the dialog.

   You just instructed the light to illuminate only the "bil-" objects. Now if you render another frame, the Fspot01 light will no longer illuminate the lamp01 object.

   Now fine-tune the light's properties and make it look more like Vince's illustration. The first thing you need to do is give the light a little bit of a yellow hue.

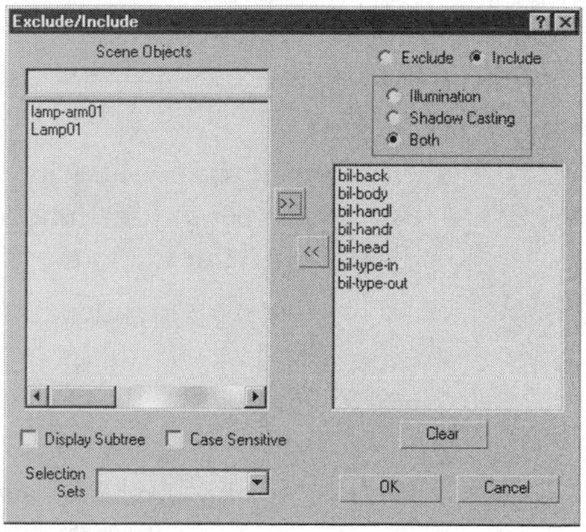

Figure 2.77
The Exclude/Include dialog shows the correct settings.

11. In the General Parameters rollout of the Fspot01 light, enter the color RGB: **255, 255, 180**. The color swatch now has a slight yellow tint to it. Soften the edges of the light a little.

12. In the Spotlight Parameters rollout, enter a Hotspot: value of **40** and a Falloff: value of **60**. Then render the Camera01 view (see Figure 2.78).

   That is just about perfect.

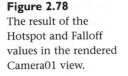

Figure 2.78
The result of the Hotspot and Falloff values in the rendered Camera01 view.

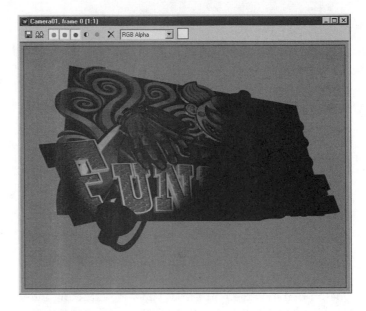

Exercise 2.16   Adding More Light

Now you're going to add more lights to the scene before you add materials to the light objects. This will allow you to achieve a more realistic look. First you will add a backlight to the scene so the lamp arm objects will catch a highlight. Then you will create a fill light to soften the harsh shadows in the scene, simulating ambient light.

1. Open the Create/Lights panel, click the Omni button, and click the Top view behind the billboard to create an omni light. Name the light **OmniBack** and move it to XYZ: **0**, **40**, **–250** (see Figure 2.79).

   Now if you render an image from the Camera01 view, you will see that the new OmniBack light casts great highlights on the light objects. The OmniBack light also lights the extrusions of the billboard objects. It looks kind of cool though, so just tone the light down a little.

2. With the OmniBack light selected, enter the Modify panel and change its color to RGB: **180, 180, 180**.

   While you are playing with the settings of the OmniBack object, you should attenuate the light so it dies down by the time it reaches the clown's head.

3. In the OmniBack light's Far Attenuation: group of the Attenuation Parameters dialog, enter Start: **190** and End: **330**. Then check Use.

   Now the light diminishes as it travels away from the OmniBack light. If you render an image from the Camera01 view, you should be happy with the results (shown in Figure 2.80).

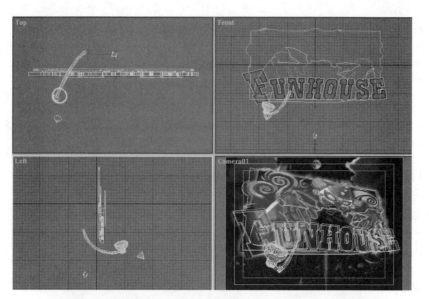

Figure 2.79
The OmniBack light is now in the correct position.

Figure 2.80
A rendered image from Camera01 shows the influence of the Attenuation settings.

You certainly don't want the parts of the billboard that aren't hit by target light to be in total darkness. So to brighten everything up a little, you can add a fill light in the foreground. This will simulate ambient light in the scene.

4. Open the Create/Lights panel and click the Omni button. Create a light at XYZ: **0, –650, 0** with RGB: **40, 40, 50**. Name the light **OmniFill** and save your work as **02FH08.max**.

Now all the black areas of the billboard have a little detail.

Exercise 2.17   Adding Materials to the Lights

With ample light on your light objects, you can create the materials for them. Start with the Lamp01 object. Because you have been building on your Billboard Multi/sub-object material, just add these materials to that.

1. Make sure 02FH08.max is open.

2. Open the Material Editor and make sure the Billboard material is selected. In the root of the Billboard material, click the Set number and change the Number of Materials: to **9**—yes, 9. You have two more sub-materials. Apply the Billboard Material to the two light objects (lamp01 and lamp-arm01).

   Now you need to tell the light objects which sub-materials to use. This should be a breeze; you've done it before.

3. Select the lamp01 object and open the Modify panel. Apply a Material modifier and change the Material ID to **8**.

4. Select the lamp-arm01 object and apply a Material Modifier. Change the Material ID to **9**.

   Now you can concentrate on making the materials.

5. Click the sub-material 8 button to open its material settings. Name this sub-material **bil-lamp**.

   The Material for the light fixtures needs to appear to be old, yet shiny, mottled metal. See if you can easily create this look.

6. In the Shader Basic Parameters rollout, change the shader from Blinn to **Metal**. In the Specular Highlights group of the Metal Basic Parameters rollout, change the Specular Level to **120** and Glossiness: to **50** (as shown in Figure 2.81).

   If you were to render the Camera01 view, you would see something pretty pleasing. However, you still need to add the mottled metal look.

7. Open the Maps rollout of the bil-lamp sub-material. Click the Diffuse Color button to open the Material/Map Browser. Then choose Dent and click OK to close the dialog. Name this map **bil-lamp-dif**.

8. In the Dent Parameters dialog, change the Size: to **150**, change Color #1 to RGB: **130, 130, 130**, and change Color #2 to RGB: **200, 200, 200**.

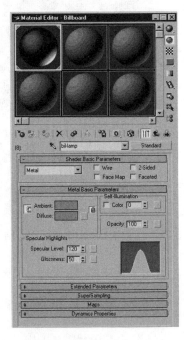

Figure 2.81
The Material Editor displays the current bil-lamp settings.

If you rendered the Camera01 view now, you would see a slight mottled effect on the lamp01 object. It's subtle, yes, but that's all it really needs. To make the material for the lamp arm objects, you will simply copy the lamp material and change a few of the parameters.

9. Click Go to Parent twice to return to the root of the Billboard material.

10. Drag the bil-lamp sub-material button over the sub-material 9 button and release the mouse. In the Instance (Copy) Material dialog, choose Copy and click OK to close the dialog. Click the sub-material 9 button to open its settings and name it **bil-lamp-arm**.

Exercise 2.18   Creating a Bump Map

If you were to render a frame from Camera01, you would see the same mottled metallic material applied to the bil-lamp-arm object. If you were to examine Vince's illustration, however, you would see ribs around the lamp-arm01 object. You can accomplish the same thing with a bump map.

1. In the Maps rollout of the bil-lamp-arm material, click the Bump button to open the Material/Map Browser. Choose Gradient Ramp and click OK to close the browser. Name this map **bil-lamp-arm-bmp**.

   Now you are going to create a striped image to be mapped on the lamp-arm01 object to create the bump effect.

2. Deactivate the Show End Result button to view the map in the material preview slot (see Figure 2.82).

3. In the Gradient Ramp Parameters rollout, change the Interpolation: to **Solid**. The colors no longer gradate to one another. They abruptly change with each flag.

   Now you have to create the image for the ribs.

4. Change the first color flag to RGB: **0, 0, 0** so the first half of the gradient is black.

5. Change the middle color flag to RGB: **150, 150, 150** so the second half of the gradient is gray.

6. Move the middle flag to Pos: **70** (see Figure 2.83).

   If you render a frame from the Camera01 view, you will see the influence your Bump map has on the lamp-arm01 object. However, the rut runs lengthwise down the bar, not across. You need to rotate that.

7. In the Coordinates rollout of the Bump: map, change the W: Angle to **90**. You will see the gradient rotate 90 degrees in the material preview window.

   Now there is one rib on the lamp-arm01 object, but you need to add many more. Instead of adding more flags to the gradient, just tile the map to itself.

8. In the Coordinates rollout, change the U: Tiling to **10**. Then render a frame from the Camera01 view. Figure 2.84 shows the result.

There, in the highlight of the lamp-arm object, you can see the bump mapped ribs. Cool.

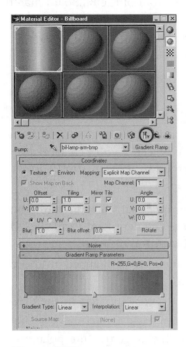

Figure 2.82
The Show End Result button is off.

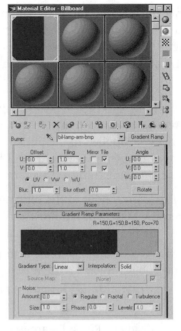

Figure 2.83
The Material Editor shows the bil-lamp-arm-bmp map so far.

Figure 2.84
The tiled ribs in the rendered Camera01 view.

Exercise 2.19   The Second Light Fixture

Now that you have created the perfect light fixture, you can copy it to create the second one.

1. Select lamp-arm01 and lamp01.

2. Click the Mirror Selected Objects button on the toolbar to open the Mirror: Screen Coordinates dialog. In the Clone Selection: group, choose Instance (see Figure 2.85), and then click OK to close the dialog and to instance the light fixture.

   You now have a mirrored copy of the selected objects. You just need to move them into position.

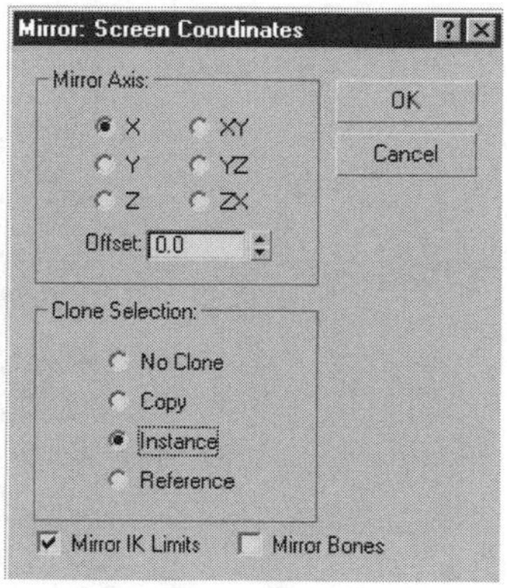

3. Make sure the instanced objects are selected. Activate the Select and Move tool (View X-axis) and move them approximately **330** units to the right in the Top view.

   The second light fixture objects are in the correct position now, but you need to create another spotlight to illuminate.

4. Select Fspot01 and from the toolbar, choose Edit > Clone, and in the Clone Options dialog, choose Instance (see Figure 2.86). Then click OK to close the dialog and instance the light.

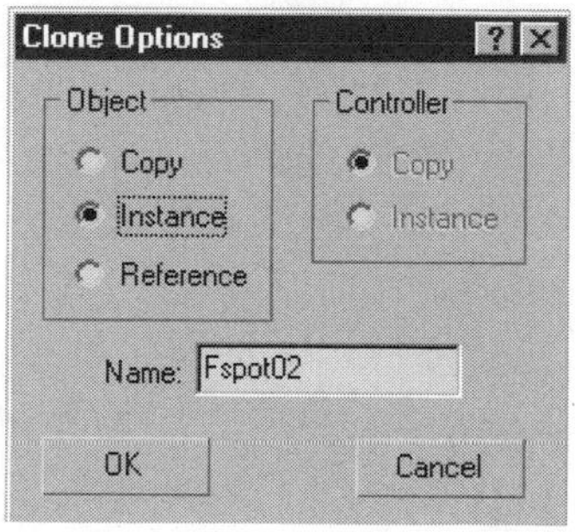

5. In the Modify panel's Spotlight Parameters rollout, check Show Cone so you can see the cone of both Fspot lights.

   The Fspot01 cone appears, even though it's deselected, because it is an instance of Fspot02.

   You chose Instance so both lights would have identical settings. Now when the settings of one are changed, the settings of the other will change automatically.

6. Open the Rotate Transform Type-In and in the Absolute: World group, delete the – from the Z: value and add a – to the Y: value.

   In my scene, for example, I changed Y: 4.199 and Z: –14.426 to Y: –4.199 and Z: 14.426. The light is now mirrored as well (see Figure 2.87).

   Now that the Fspot02 light is oriented correctly, you can move it into its correct position.

7. Activate the Select and Move tool (View X-axis) and move the light approximately X: **360** in the Top view (as shown in Figure 2.88).

8. Render a frame from the Camera01 view (see Figure 2.89).

Figure 2.85
The Mirror: Screen Coordinates dialog shows the correct settings.

Figure 2.86
The Clone Options dialog shows the correct settings.

Figure 2.87
The Fspot02 object was manually "mirrored."

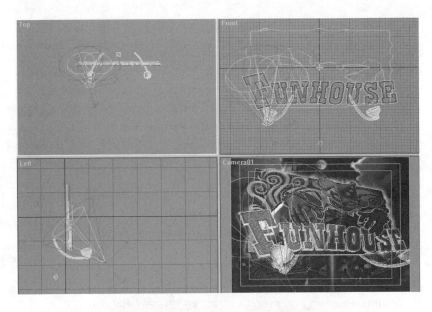

Figure 2.88
The Fspot02 light is in the correct position.

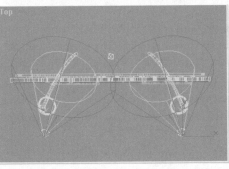

Figure 2.89
The effect of the new spotlight in the rendered Camera01 view.

Everything looks great, but the light fixture on the right doesn't match Vince's illustration perfectly. That's okay, I am sure he won't mind.

9. Save your work as **02FH09.max**.

Exercise 2.20   Creating a Cylinder

Now you're ready to create a very important part of the billboard: the post. Without it, the billboard has nothing to stand on.

1. With 02FH09.max open, open the Create/Geometry panel and click the Cylinder button. Drag the mouse in the Top view to create a Radius of about 20 and a height of 400.

2. Using the Transform Type-In, move the cylinder you just created to (Absolute World) XYZ: **0, 40, −400** (as shown in Figure 2.90). Adjust the object's parameters a bit to make it more suitable for your needs.

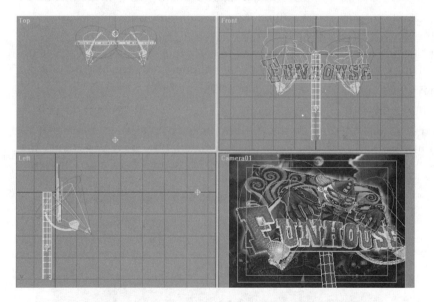

Figure 2.90
The Cylinder post we just created.

3. Open the Modify panel and rename the Cylinder01 object **bil-post.** Change the Height Segments: to **1** and Sides: to **16.**

   You won't be bending the bil-post object, so you don't need all the Height Segments. One will do just fine. Now you can add the material to the bil-post object. I think you can squeeze one more material into your Billboard Multi\sub-object material. (Actually, you could squeeze in a total of 1,000!)

4. Open the Material Editor and click the Go to Parent button twice to return to the root of the Billboard material. Assign the Billboard material to the bil-post object.

5. Click the Set Number button and change the Number of Materials: to **10**. Drag the bil-lamp sub-material over the sub-material 10 button and release the mouse. In the Instance (Copy) Material dialog, choose Copy and click OK to close. Close the Material Editor.

Now you have to assign a Material ID of 10 to the bil-post object. You certainly know how to do that!

6. Select the bil-post object and open the Modify panel. Apply a Material modifier and change the Material ID to **10**. Render the Camera01 view.

Exercise 2.21   Highlighting an Object

There don't seem to be any lights creating a highlight on the bil-post object. Go ahead and add one.

1. From the Create/Lights panel, click Omni and create an Omni light at XYZ: **0, –500, –150** and RGB: **180, 180, 180**. Name this light **OmniPost.**

You have to instruct the OmniPost light to illuminate only the pole.

2. Click the Exclude button to open the Exclude/Include dialog. Select bil-post and click the arrow pointing to the right. Click Include and click OK to close the dialog. Now the OmniPost light will illuminate only the bil-post object.

3. Render the Camera01 view (see Figure 2.91).

The highlight on the pole is a slightly too large and dull. Liven it up a bit.

4. Open the Material Editor. In the Billboard material, click the sub-material 10 button to open its settings. Name this sub-material **bil-post** and change the Specular Level: to **60** and the Glossiness: to **77**. Render the Camera01 view.

Figure 2.91
The lighted post in the rendered Camera01 view.

That is a better highlight, but it is far too bright. You need to decrease the light's intensity a tad.

5. Close the Material Editor and make sure the OmniPost light is selected. Change its color to RGB: **50, 50, 65**, a dark blue tint. Render the Camera01 view again (see Figure 2.92).

The billboard is really shaping up. You might want to come back to it and tweak some things as you progress with the project, but all in all, it looks pretty good.

6. Save your work as **02FH10.max**.

Figure 2.92
The reduced light's effect on the post, as shown in the rendered Camera01 view.

In Conclusion

Good work. I am very proud of you for digging in your heels and working through this modeling stage. It takes a special kind of person to enjoy this kind of work, and you should pat yourself on the back for being one of them.

Coming up next is some of the fun stuff. You get to create the environment and add some special effects. If you thought these first two chapters were fun, just wait!

Chapter 3

Creating the Funhouse Environment and Special Effects

With the billboard complete, your heart

starts to race excitedly knowing you will

be polishing the scene and adding all the

embellishments.

Periodically, your co-workers stop by your workstation, and you proudly show them the billboard you created. Everyone seems anxious to see it completed, including you. It seems like this project is shaping up nicely.

Setting Up the Funhouse Environment

Vince did a great job designing the environment for this animation. I am sure you will be able to duplicate it reasonably. Before you start creating the environment, however, you should create the camera animation for the scene. Then you can create the environment around the camera's motion.

Creating the Camera Animation

The camera animation you will employ in this scene is somewhat complicated. Take a look at the billboard: The camera starts on the left with a close-up of the clown's right hand and head. The camera will then slowly pull backward and orbit to the right. These complicated sweeping moves could be very hard to create, but if you know how to do it, it's quite simple.

Exercise 3.1   Building a Jib

You will create a virtual crane arm, or *jib*, for the camera. This will allow you to move the camera the way they do in the real world to achieve a type of sweeping move. Now all you have to do to create this jib is make two dummy helpers. Follow these steps:

1. Open **02FH10.max**. You don't need to see all the lights at this time, so hide them.

2. Use the Hide Lights Toggle [Shift+L] to hide the lights in the scene.

3. Right-click the Top view's label and check Show Grid.

    You will see the Home Grid in the Top view again.

4. Activate the Create/Helpers panel and click the Dummy button. Activate the 3D Snap toggle, and then click and drag in the Top view at the intersection of the dark black lines (XYZ: 0, 0, 0 World Space) to create a dummy object (see Figure 3.1). Name this dummy helper **Dummy-updown**.

5. Make sure the Dummy button is still active and click and drag at the intersection of the dark black lines once more to create another Dummy helper slightly larger than the first (as shown in Figure 3.2). Name this dummy helper **Dummy-rightleft**.

    You have created your virtual jib. Now you have to attach a camera to it.

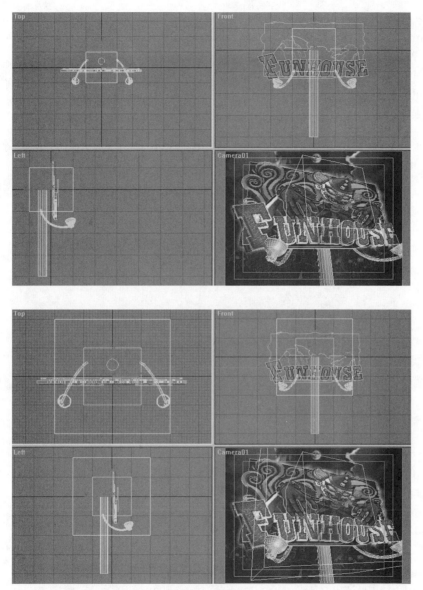

Figure 3.1
The Dummy helper created in the Top view.

Figure 3.2
There are now two dummy helpers in the scene.

6. Open the Create/Cameras panel and click the Free button. With 3D Snap still active, click in the Front view to create a camera at XYZ: **0, 0, 0** (the intersection of the black lines). Name the camera **Camera-jib** and change its Stock Lens to 35mm.

You have everything you need to create the camera animation. Before you can use your virtual jib, however, you need to create the hierarchy.

7. Move the camera to XYZ: **0**, **–500**, **0** (Absolute World) and click Zoom Extents All. Select the Camera01 view and press the C key to change the view to the Camera-jib view.

8. Activate that Select and Link tool and link the Camera-jib object to the Dummy-updown helper. Then link the Dummy-updown helper to the Dummy-rightleft helper.

9. Activate the Select Object tool and open the Select Objects dialog [press H]. Check Display Subtree and double-check to make sure the hierarchy is correct (see Figure 3.3). Click Cancel to exit the dialog.

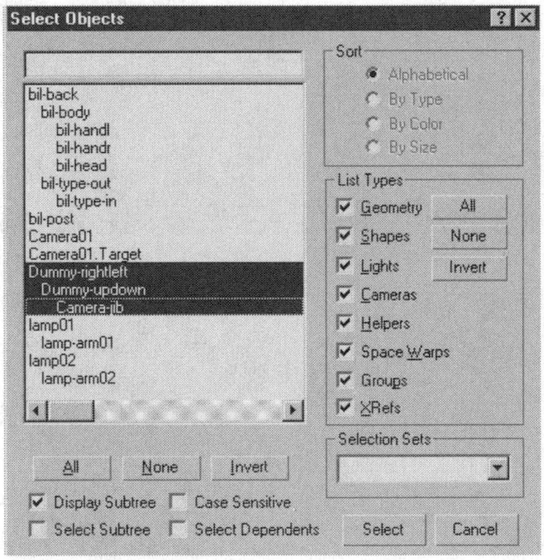

Figure 3.3
The Select Objects dialog displays the current subtree.

Exercise 3.2   Adding a Music Track

Gordon Miller, the music guy, has such perfect timing. He just stopped by with the music base for this animation. According to Gordon, he has more work to do, and he is going to add sound effects and such, but this music will give you an idea how long the animation needs to be. Don't hesitate. You'll want to put it in your scene.

I. Open the Track View and click the + next to the Sound Track to open its tracks. Click the Sound track label to select it (it will turn orange), and then right-click it. Choose Properties from the list to open the Sound Options dialog (shown in Figure 3.4).

2. Click Choose Sound to open the Open Sound dialog. Find and select \3ds4-ma\project1\sounds\ FH-Music.wav (see Figure 3.5).

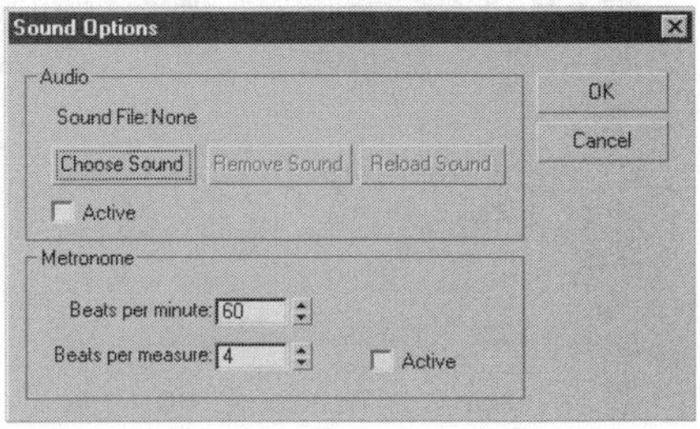

Figure 3.4
The Sound Options dialog.

Notice under the preview play button that the track is 12 seconds long. Click the preview play button to hear the music. You will hear the eerie ballroom waltz music. Click OK to close the Open Sound dialog, and click OK to close the Sound Options dialog.

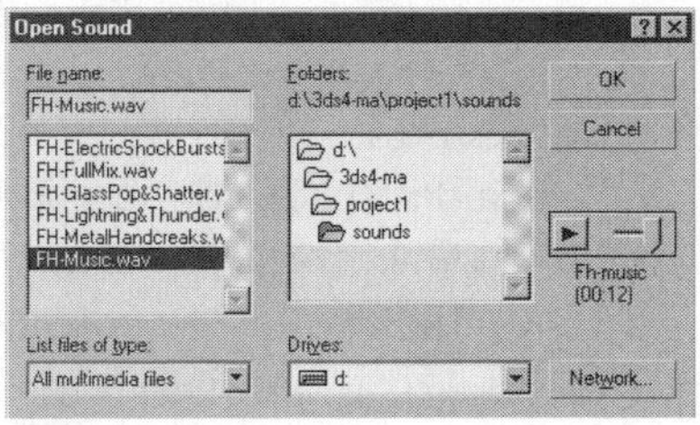

Figure 3.5
In the Open Sound dialog, select FH-Music.wav.

You can now see the audio's waveform graph in the Track View (as shown in Figure 3.6). This enables you to visualize the music quickly and helps you accurately sync keys to the track.

You need to adjust the length of your animation to accommodate the music. The music is 12 seconds long, but notice that it starts right at frame zero. In the production world, it is always smart to create pre-roll and pad. *Pre-roll* is at least an extra second of animation before the actual animation starts; *pad* is at least one second of animation after the animation ends.

This gives the production people some leeway when adding dissolves or transitions to and from the animation. Luckily in 3ds max 4, you can offset the music track in the Track View.

3. In Track View, use the Zoom tool until the frame units change to intervals of 10 (10, 20, 30, and so on). Right-click to exit the Zoom tool and slide the black bar to the right of the Sound track label to start at frame 30 (see Figure 3.7).

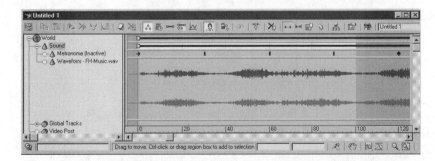

Figure 3.6
The Track view with the waveform graph of the FH-Music.wav file.

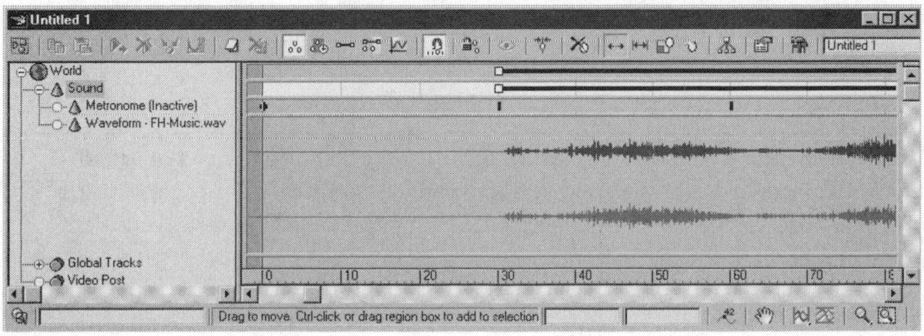

Figure 3.7
The FH-Music.wav file is offset by 30 frames in the Track View.

Essentially, you moved the music forward in time, adding one second of time to the overall animation. Gordon included a second of blank audio at the end of his music, so the pad is built in. So if the original music was 12 seconds (including pad), and you added one second to it, the audio is now 13 seconds long. Ooh, creepy. Change the length of your animation to match.

4. Click the Time Configuration button to open its dialog. In the Time Display group, click SMPTE to show the time in a Minutes:Seconds:Frames fashion. In the Animation group, change the Length: to **0:13:0** (as shown in Figure 3.8).

Note

SMPTE (Society of Motion Picture and Television Engineers) is the standard way time is displayed for broadcast animation work. The SMPTE format displays minutes, seconds, and frames, separated by colons.

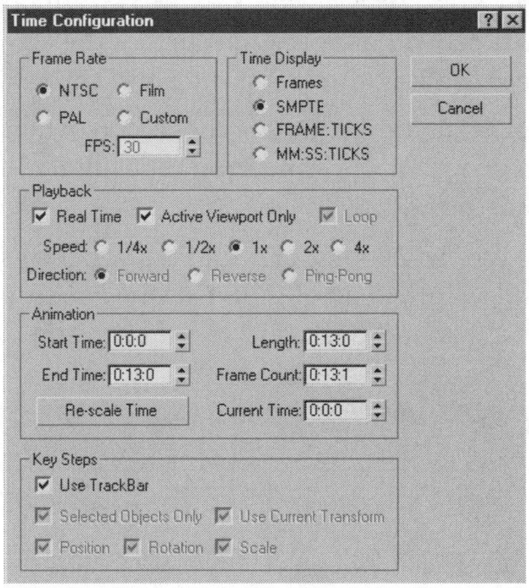

Figure 3.8
The Time Configuration dialog with the correct settings.

You know the animation is 13 seconds long, so you can change the Time Display back to Frames.

5. In the Time Display group of the Time Configuration dialog, click Frames. The Length: is now 390 frames—and at NTSC 30 Frames Per Second (FPS), that's 13 seconds. Click OK to close the dialog.

Note

NTSC (National Television Standards Committee) is the video standard used in North America, most of Central and South America, and Japan. The frame rate is 30 frames per second or 60 fields per second, with each field accounting for half the interleaved scan lines on a television screen.

You should arrange the Track View to double-check the length of the music.

6. In the Track View, click the Zoom Horizontal Extents button (see Figure 3.9).

   You can see the entire music track in the Track view. If you click the Play button, you will see a line marking the current location in the Track View. If you go to Frame 330, you will see that the music has almost faded by then. It seems like the music actually trails away by frame 335. Right now you have almost two seconds of pad at the end of the animation. That's okay; the client can get rid of it if it's not needed. It's always better to have too much than too little.

   The camera jib is all set up, and the animation is the correct length, so you can start animating your scene. Before you do, though, save your work.

7. Save your work as **03FH01.max**.

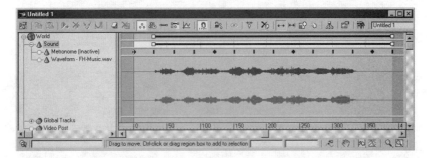

Figure 3.9
The Track View now displays the full FH-Music.wav waveform.

Exercise 3.3   Animating the Camera Jib

It seems like all your hard work to this point is finally going to start paying off. Now you get to add a little motion to the scene!

1. With 03FH01.max open, right-click the Camera-jib view's label and deselect Show Background. The background image will just confuse you visually at this point.

2. With the Camera-jib view active, use the Dolly Camera tool to move the Camera-jib object to XYZ: **0, –160, 0** (as shown in Figure 3.10). You can see the position in the Status Bar Transform Type-In.

   Get a close-up of the clown's right hand.

3. Deactivate the 3D Snap tool if it is still active. Activate the Select and Rotate tool (Local Z-axis) and rotate the Dummy-rightleft object, offsetting Z by **–45** degrees.

   The Dummy-rightleft object and its children should rotate, rotating the Camera-jib view as well (see Figure 3.11).

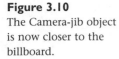

Figure 3.10
The Camera-jib object is now closer to the billboard.

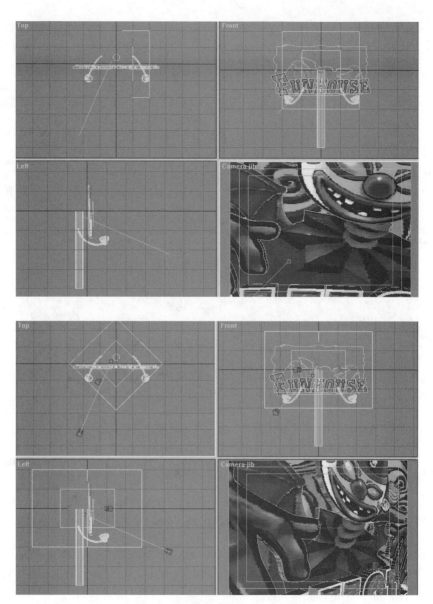

Figure 3.11
The Dummy-rightleft object is rotated, off-setting Z by –45 degrees.

The shot will be more dramatic if you place the camera higher in the shot. That should be pretty easy using the jib helpers.

4. Activate the Select and Rotate tool (Local X-axis) and rotate the Dummy-updown helper, offsetting X about **–15** degrees (as shown in Figure 3.12).

You can see the billboard from a little higher angle now. Move the jib to make the shot a little more attractive.

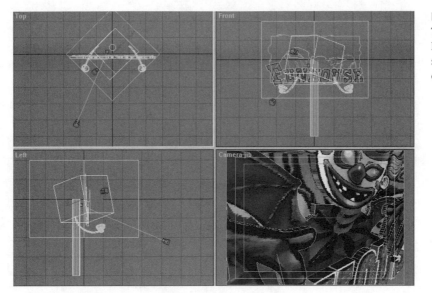

Figure 3.12
The Camera-updown helper is rotated, offsetting X about –15 degrees.

5. Activate the Select and Move tool (View X-axis) and move the Dummy-rightleft helper to (Absolute: World) XYZ: **–70, 0, 0**. The Camera-jib now captures a close-up of the clown's right hand.

    It's time to add a little camera animation to the scene.

6. In the Time Controls, click Go To End to go to frame 390. Activate the Animate button. Then activate the Select and Rotate tool (Local Z-axis) and rotate the Dummy-rightleft object Z: **90** degrees. When you release the mouse, the Transform Type-In will display Z: 45 because you rotated the object 90 degrees, from –45 to 45.

    The Dummy-rightleft object must be moved back to its origin, XYZ: 0, 0, 0.

7. With the Animate button still active, activate the Select and Move tool and in the Transform Type-In, change X to **0**. The Dummy-rightleft object moves back to XYZ: **0, 0, 0**.

    The camera should view the billboard from a low angle at the end of the animation. You can easily make that happen.

8. Activate the Select and Rotate tool (Local X-axis) and rotate the Dummy-updown object, offsetting X: **40** degrees (as shown in Figure 3.13). When you release the mouse, the X: value changes to 25 degrees.

    The camera needs to be dollied back in order for you to view the whole billboard.

9. Using the Dolly Camera tool in the Camera-jib view, dolly the camera back until the billboard fits comfortably in the Camera-jib view (see Figure 3.14).

Figure 3.13
The current orientation of the objects at frame 390.

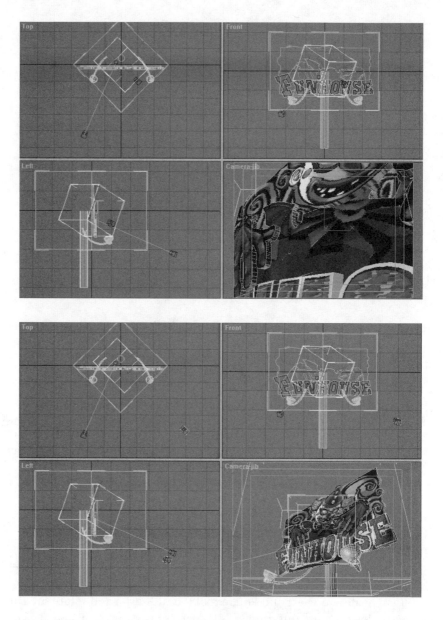

Figure 3.14
The billboard fits comfortably in the Camera-jib view.

You are finished roughing out the camera animation. If you play the animation, you can see that it still needs work, but most of the animation you need is there.

If the animation appears choppy during playback, you can change the Camera-jib view to Wireframe by right-clicking the Camera-jib view's label and choosing Wireframe. The playback will improve considerably.

10. Deactivate the Animate button and save your work as **03FH02.max**.

Exercise 3.4   Adjusting the Camera Animation

You now have the basic camera move roughed out in your scene, so with some minor adjustments, you should be just fine. The most obvious aspect of the camera animation that needs to be fixed is the speed at which it dollies away from the billboard.

Before you continue, delete the old camera.

1. Select Camera01 and press the Delete key to delete it from the scene.
2. Select the Camera-jib camera.

    In the Track Bar, you can see two red tics signifying the Camera-jib's keys (see Figure 3.15). The blue time indicator will hide the red tics if it is on the tics frame.

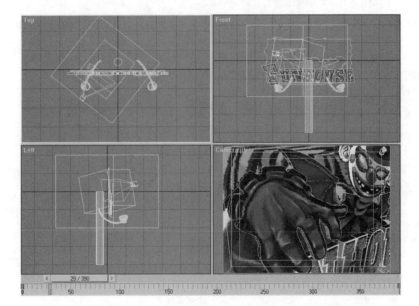

Figure 3.15
The Camera-jib's keys in the Track Bar.

The Track Bar provides an incredibly easy way to edit the keys in the scene. It only shows the selected objects' keys, so if you are editing only one object at a time, you might consider changing the keys on the Track Bar instead of the Track View.

3. Right click the Camera-jib's key at frame 390 and choose Camera-jib: Position to open its dialog (shown in Figure 3.16).

    You can edit this key's parameters now.

4. Change the Time: to **150**. You can see the key; it's white because it's selected. Move to frame 150 on the Track Bar.

Figure 3.16
The Camera-jib: Position dialog at frame 390.

5. Change the In: Tangent Type to **Slow** (see Figure 3.17) so that the dolly of the camera will ease into frame 150.

Play the animation again from the Camera-jib view. It looks better. However, you need to fix the animation of the Dummy-rightleft's position. Right now it is animating from left to center over the course of the 390 frames. You should animate it to match the camera dolly so the billboard is centered by frame 150.

6. Select the Dummy-rightleft helper. Then right-click the key at frame 390 in the Track Bar and choose Dummy-rightleft: Position (not Rotation). Change its Time: to **150** and change Slow In: to **Tangent Type** (see Figure 3.18).

Play the animation again in the Camera-jib view. The animation is really starting to look great. However, the billboard is a little too low in the view. You need to drop the camera a tad.

7. Go to frame 150, open the Dummy-rightleft: Position dialog, and change the Z Value: to **–20** (see Figure 3.19). Close the dialog.

 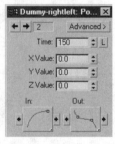 

Figure 3.17
The Camera-jib:
Position dialog now
has the correct
settings.

Figure 3.18
The Dummy-
rightleft: Position
dialog now has the
correct settings.

Figure 3.19
The Z Value: is
changed to –20.

The Dummy-rightleft object is lowered –20 units in World Space. Pretty neat, huh? And you didn't even have to use the Select and Move tool. Play the animation in the Camera-jib view again. It looks much better.

8. The only thing you might change is to pull the camera back just a little more because the billboard is dangerously outside the Title Safe area (the orange Safe Frame guide). To fix it, activate the Animate button, go to frame 150 (because the Camera-jib's Position key is there), and use the Dolly Camera tool to dolly the camera-jib camera back a little more.

Play the animation again. If you aren't happy with the Dolly amount, change it (at frame 150) until you are satisfied.

9. Deactivate the Animate button and save your work as **03FH03.max**.

Creating the Background Environment

Now that the camera animation is complete, you can begin to build the environment. You will concentrate on the background environment first, and then you will turn your attention to the special effects in the scene.

Examining the background, you can see the moon, the clouds, and the circus tent scene. You will add these elements to the scene in that order. Start with the moon.

Exercise 3.5   Creating a Composite Environment Map

Adding the moon to the scene is going to be as easy as adding the post to the billboard. All we are going to do is load a moon image into the Material editor, adjust its tiling and voilà. First, we need to create Environment map.

1. With 03FH03.max loaded, choose Rendering/Environment from the toolbar to open the Environment dialog (see Figure 3.20).

2. In the Background group, click the Environment Map button to open the Material/Map Browser. Choose Composite and click OK to close the Browser.

3. Open the Material Editor. Drag the Environment Map: button from the Environment dialog into the second preview slot in the Material Editor and release the mouse. In the Instance (Copy) Map dialog, choose Instance and click OK. Then close the Environment dialog; you are finished with it now.

   You assigned a Composite map to the Environment Map and then you instanced it into the Material Editor in order to apply the individual layers. Now you can add the moon map.

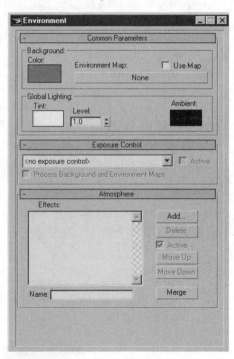

Figure 3.20
The Environment dialog.

4. Name the root of the Composite map **env** and click the Map 1: button to open the Material/Map Browser. Choose Bitmap and click OK to close the browser. In the Select Bitmap Image File dialog, choose \3ds4-ma\project1\maps\back-moon.jpg and click Open to open the map. Name this map **env-moon** (see Figure 3.21).

By default, the image is applied using Environment Screen mapping in the Coordinates rollout. This means that the image will stay locked to the view, no matter where the camera moves. That's precisely what you want. However, right now the moon is too big. You need to make it much smaller.

5. In the Coordinates rollout of the env-moon map, change U: Tiling to **9** and V: Tiling to **7**. You will see a grid of moon images in the sample view.

It's a little hard to determine how the moon is going to look based on the sample swatch. One of the major problems with the sample swatch is its square 1:1 image aspect. You need to see the environment rendered in the same image aspect with which you will be rendering the animation—in other words, in 4:3.

6. Right-click the sample swatch and choose Render Map from the list. In the Dimensions group of the Render Map dialog, change the Width: to **320** and Height: to **240** and click the Render button to close the dialog and render the map. Figure 3.22 shows the result.

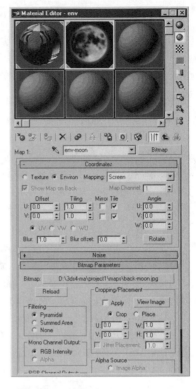

Figure 3.21
Back-moon.jpg is loaded into the Material Editor.

Figure 3.22
The rendered env-moon map.

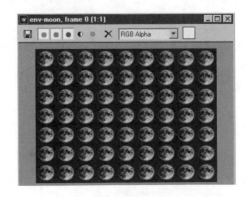

Very cool. Now you don't have to render the whole scene with the billboard and everything to see your environment. Looking at the rendered env-moon map, you see nine moons across the U(X): axis and seven moons down the V(Y): axis.

Note

UVW is how 3ds max refers to the coordinates for materials and textures. They named them UVW to differentiate them from the XYZ coordinates.

Now the moon of the moon is smaller, but you don't need 63 of them, just one.

7. In the Coordinates rollout, deselect U and V Tile. Now only one moon appears in the preview slot.

   By the way, the rendered env-moon map will not automatically be updated; you must right-click the sample slot again and choose Render Map.

   Now you only have one moon, but it's smack dab in the middle of the screen. You can raise it up a little higher, like the way Vince illustrated it.

8. In the Coordinates rollout of the env-moon map, change the V: Offset to **.4** and choose Render Map again. The moon is now higher in the screen, but it is still a little too big.

9. Change U: Tiling to **16** and V: Tiling to **12**. Choose Render Map again.

   That looks much better. You don't want it to stick out like a sore thumb; it's more of an accent. Maybe you should just push it a tad higher.

10. Change the V: Offset to **.43** and choose Render Map again. Now you've nailed it. It's going to look great peeking out above the billboard.

11. Save your work as **03FH04.max**.

Exercise 3.6 Adding Another Layer to the Composite Map

No eerie night sky is complete without some creepy clouds. Lucky for you, Vince was gracious enough to save all his elements as layers for you. So you have his wonderful cloud artwork, complete with Alpha channel to composite them right into your scene.

1. With 03FH04.max open, click the Go to Parent button once to return to the env map in the Material Editor.

2. To add the clouds, click the Map 2: button to open the Material/Map Browser. Choose Bitmap and click OK to close the browser. In the Select Bitmap Image File dialog, choose \3ds4-ma\project1\maps\back-clouds.tga and click Open to close the dialog. Name this map **env-clouds**.

If the Show End Result toggle is on, you will see the clouds automatically composited over the env-moon image. The Material Editor uses the Alpha channel that is included in the TGA file. If you click the View Image button in the Bitmap Parameters rollout, the Specify Cropping/Placement dialog will open, and you can see the image in its actual resolution. In the upper-left corner of the image's window, you can click the circle that is half black and half white to see the image's alpha (see Figure 3.23).

Figure 3.23
The Specify Cropping/Placement dialog displays the back-clouds.tga alpha channel.

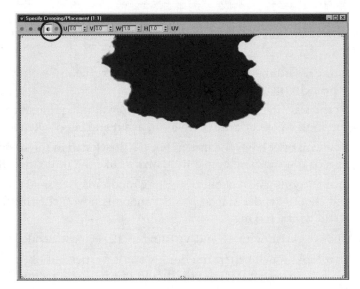

In the Bitmap Parameters rollout, you will see in the Alpha Source group that Image Alpha is active. This is why the back-clouds.tga image is being composited over the env-moon map.

The env-clouds map is Environment Screen mapped as well, so it's locked to the view. Because the moon is a static element throughout the animation, you should animate the clouds to add a little drama to the scene.

3. In the Coordinates rollout of the env-clouds map, change the V: offset to **.3** and render the map (see Figure 3.24).

The map moves upward, but it is tiling on the bottom. You need to get rid of the tiling.

4. Deselect V: Tiling, and the tiling of the back-clouds.tga image is removed.

Now it's time to add some animation keys to the map.

5. Go to Frame 390 and activate the Animate button. Change the V: Offset to **0** and deactivate the Animate button.

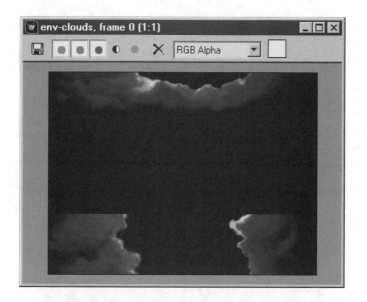

Figure 3.24
The env-clouds map rendered.

If you scrub the time slider through the animation, you will see that the clouds in the material preview slot get lower over the course of 390 frames. It looks good so far. Keep going!

6. Save your work as **03FH05.max**.

Exercise 3.7   Adding Another Layer to the Composite Map

Now you'll add the coolest part of the environment: the circus silhouette. Vince's overactive imagination really paid off this time. He did a great job illustrating a backdrop for the billboard. Because he made your life so much easier by creating such great maps, you'll have to take him out for a Coke sometime.

1. With 03FH05.max open, click the Go to Parent button once to return to the root of the env map. You need to add another map to your composite.

2. Click the Set Number button and change the Number of Maps: to **3**. Click the Map 3: button to open its settings. Choose Bitmap and open \3ds4-ma\ project1\maps\back-circus.tga. Name this map **env-circus**.

   This map may be a little hard to see in the preview slot, as well as in the Render Map feature. It is the circus scene silhouetted by the purple fire. The image's aspect is a little strange (much taller than it is wide) because the map is intended to be a tiled Spherical Environment. Let's set its parameters and then render a few test frames from the Camera-jib view.

3. In the Coordinates rollout, change the Mapping: to **Spherical**. The map is now mapped on an imaginary sphere surrounding the scene. Hide your objects and render some frames through the Camera-jib view.

4. With the 3ds max interface selected (not the Material Editor), press Shift+C to hide the camera. Press Shift+H (the Hide Helpers toggle) to hide the dummy helpers. Press Shift+O (the Hide Objects toggle) to hide the objects in your scene.

   Everything you've created is now hidden from all the views.

5. Go to Frame 180 and render the Camera-jib view (see Figure 3.25).

   You can see a very large and distorted circus scene in the view. The reason it is so stretched along its U (horizontal) axis is because the bitmap is very narrow and was meant to be tiled along its U-axis.

6. In the Coordinates rollout, change the U: Tiling to **6** and render the Camera-jib view at frame 180 again (see Figure 3.26).

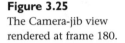

Figure 3.25
The Camera-jib view
rendered at frame 180.

Figure 3.26
The tiled env-circus
map.

Now remember, because this tiled map uses a Spherical Environment, it will react to the camera motion. That means that as your camera orbits through the scene, the circus silhouette will move as well.

Right now the silhouette looks pretty darn good, but it needs to play a little lower in the screen to better match what Vince illustrated.

7. Change the V: Offset to **–.05**, and the silhouette drops slightly.

8. Now unhide the billboard and render a few test frames. Press Shift+O to unhide the billboard objects. Then render the Camera-jib view at frames 180, 240, and 300 to see how the silhouette reacts to the camera motion (see Figures 3.27, 3.28, and 3.29).

Figure 3.27
The rendered Camera-jib view at frame 180.

Figure 3.28
The rendered Camera-jib view at frame 240.

It looks great. Notice that the billboard silhouette, which is in constant motion thanks to the camera, starts to move out of view by frame 300. This allows the person viewing the animation to really focus on the billboard one last time. Now save your work and head on to some special effects.

9. Save your work as **03FH06.max**.

Adding Special Effects

It's time to add the final atmospheric touches to your renderings. As of now the environment looks great and the billboard is dead-on, but you really need to add some of the nuances Vince accomplished in his illustration.

These effects include the fire around the perimeter of the billboard and the volume light from the billboard lamps. You will add both to the scene.

Exercise 3.8   Creating a Volume Light

You will start with the volume light first.

1. Load **03FH06.max**. From the toolbar, choose Rendering/Environment to open the Environment dialog.

2. In the Atmosphere rollout, click the Add button to open the Add Atmospheric Effect dialog. Choose Volume Light (as shown in Figure 3.30) and click OK to close the dialog.

Figure 3.30
The Add Atmospheric Effect dialog shows Volume Light selected.

3. Close the Common Parameters, Exposure Control, and Atmosphere rollouts.

4. You will need to tell the Volume light which lights to use as its source, so unhide your lights. Press Shift+L to unhide the lights.

5. In the Volume Light Parameters rollout, click Pick Light and press the H key to open the Pick Object dialog. Choose Fspot01 and Fspot02 (see Figure 3.31), and then click Pick to choose those lights and close the dialog.

   The two Fspot lights are now added to the Volume light effect.

6. Render frame 180 from the Camera-jib view. Figure 3.32 shows the result.

   That certainly is volume light, but you should probably tame it down a little. Start by attenuating the light.

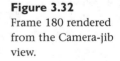

Figure 3.31
The Pick Object dialog with Fspot01 and Fspot02 selected.

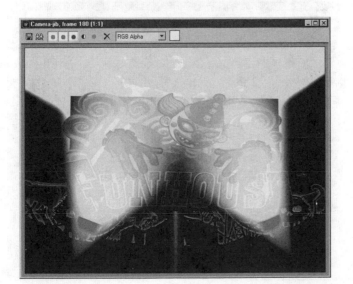

Figure 3.32
Frame 180 rendered from the Camera-jib view.

7. Select Fspot01 and enter the Modify panel. In the Far Attenuation group of the Attenuation Parameters rollout, check Use and set Start: to **200** and End: to **400** (as shown in Figure 3.33). Click Render Last to render frame 180 again (see Figure 3.34).

The settings of both Fspot lights changed although you changed the settings of only the Fspot01 object. That's because you created the two Fspot lights to be instances of one another.

That looks much closer to what it should look like. The strange thing right now is the point the volume light creates below the lamp objects. That's not very realistic, but you should be able to fix that.

8. In the Near Attenuation group of the Attenuation Parameters rollout, check Use and change Start to **60** and End to **100**. Render frame 180 again (see Figure 3.35).

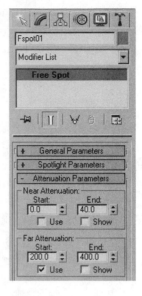

Figure 3.33
The Far Attenuation is set to Use, Start: 200 and End: 400.

That looks great, but you have to keep one important thing in mind. If you were to see the billboard from an extreme side angle, you would see that the volume light doesn't match the lamp object because you moved the Fspot lights forward from the billboard so they would cast more desirable light on the billboard.

Figure 3.34
The volume light is attenuated.

9. Render the Camera-jib view at frame 90 (see Figure 3.36).

From this angle, you can see that the volume light really doesn't match the lamp object correctly, but you will be lessening the visibility of the volume light, and no one will know better.

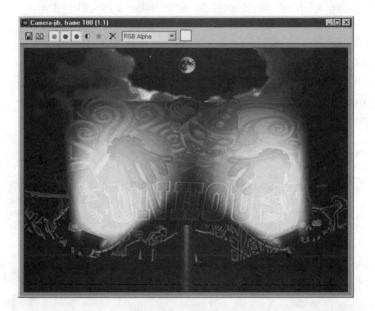

Figure 3.35
The rendered Camera-jib view at frame 180.

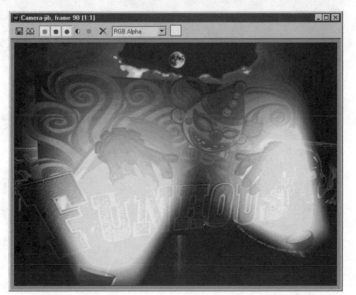

Figure 3.36
The rendered Camera-jib view at frame 90.

However, look at the lamp objects. You can see through their insides! When you created the loft shape for the lamp objects, you only created a spline for the outside and the lip. You didn't create an inside. But you can fix that easily with a sub-material modification.

10. Open the Material Editor. Select the Billboard material and click the sub-material 8 button bil-lamp (Standard) to open its settings.

This is the bil-lamp sub-material. Let's make the material two-sided.

11. In the Shader Basic Parameters dialog, check 2-Sided and render frame 90 again (see Figure 3.37).

The lamps have an inside now, but they certainly don't look like light is emitting from them. Take care of that now.

Figure 3.37
The rendered Camera-jib view at frame 90.

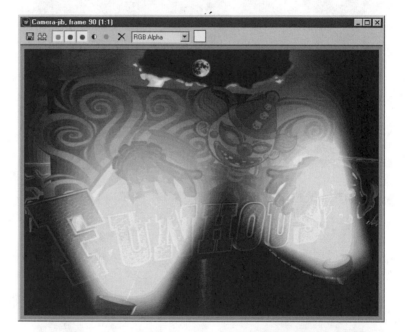

12. Deselect 2-Sided. Click the Standard button to open the Material/Map Browser. Choose Double Sided from the list and click OK to close the browser. In the Replace Material dialog, choose Keep old material as sub-material? (see Figure 3.38), and click OK to close the dialog.

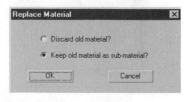

Figure 3.38
The Replace Material dialog.

Now you see the Double Sided Basic Parameters in the Material Editor (see Figure 3.39).

Our bil-lamp material is now the Facing Material: sub-material. The Back Material has the default gray material applied. You'll need to change that.

13. Click the Back Material button to open its settings. Name this sub-material **bil-lampin**. Select one of the Fspot lights and from the Modify panel, drag the yellow-colored swatch to the Diffuse color swatch of the bil-lampin sub-material. In the Copy or Swap Colors dialog, choose Copy. The yellow color is now in the Diffuse and Ambient color swatches (because they are locked).

14. Change the value of Self-Illumination to **80** and render frame 90 again from the Camera-jib view (see Figure 3.40).

The lamps look like they are creating some light now. The time has come to soften the volume light effect.

15. From the toolbar, choose Rendering/Environment to open the Environment dialog. In the Volume group of the Volume Light Parameters rollout, change the Density: to **2.5** (as shown in Figure 3.41). Then render frame 90 again (see Figure 3.42).

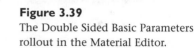
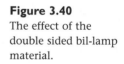

Figure 3.39
The Double Sided Basic Parameters rollout in the Material Editor.

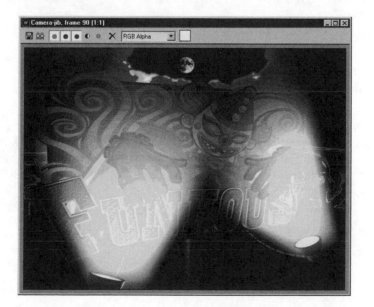

Figure 3.40
The effect of the double sided bil-lamp material.

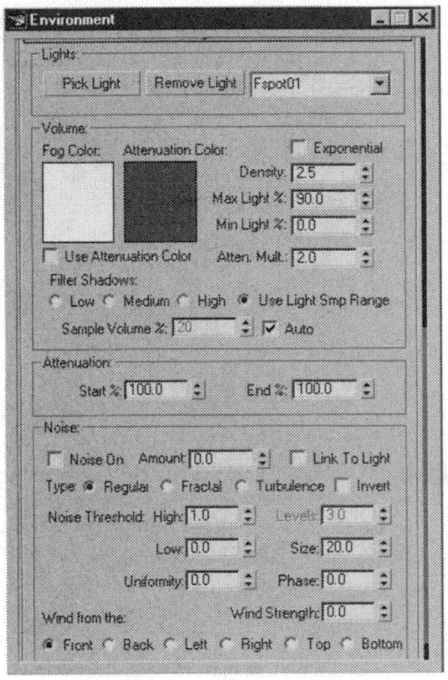

Figure 3.41
The Density setting has been
changed to 2.5 in the Volume
group of the Volume Light
Parameters rollout.

Figure 3.42
The rendered Camera-jib view at frame 90.

That's an appropriate Density setting for the volume
light. When you look at the rendering, however, you
see that the light needs to be a little more saturated
with color in order to match Vince's illustration.

16. Select the Fspot01 light and in the Modify panel,
change its color to RGB: **255, 210, 89** (see Figure
3.43). Open the Material Editor, click the sub-material
8 button, click the Back Material: button (bil-lampin),
and copy the Fspot01 light's color to the Diffuse
swatch.

17. Change the bil-lampin Material Effects Channel (it's
the flyout to the left of the Show Map in Viewport
button) to **1**. This might come in handy when you
add post effects. Close the Material Editor and render
frame 90 again.

This looks a little better. However, the added hue saturation to the volume light kind of washes out all the
color of the billboard, making it an orange color. That's
okay. You will come back to the billboard's appearance
when you add the final touches. You should decrease
the density of the volume light a few notches though.

Figure 3.43
The color of the
Fspot01 light has
been changed to
RGB: 255, 210, 89.

18. Open the Environment dialog and in the Volume Light Parameters rollout, change the Density: value to **2**. Render frame 90 again (see Figure 3.44).

The volume effect looks nicer now. As animators, we must live with the constant back-and-forth of tweaking the parameters in our scenes. That's why it's important to know what 3ds max 4 is capable of. With this project, you're giving the interface a pretty good workout, and it's not over yet.

19. Save your work as **03FH07.max**.

Figure 3.44
Frame 90 rendered from the Camera-jib view.

Exercise 3.9   Adding an Effects Glow

Remember when you changed the bil-lampin sub-material's Material Effects ID to 1? You are going to utilize that right now and add a soft glow to the inside of the lamp.

1. With 03FH07.max open, choose Rendering/Effects from the toolbar. In the Effects rollout, click Add to open the Add Effect dialog. Choose Lens Effects (see Figure 3.45) and click OK to close the dialog.

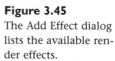

Figure 3.45
The Add Effect dialog lists the available render effects.

2. In the Lens Effects Parameters rollout, choose Glow and click the arrow pointing to the right (see Figure 3.46).

   You have just added a Glow effect to your scene. Now you have to specify how it should be applied to the rendering.

3. In the Glow Element rollout, click the Options tab. Check Effects ID: 1 (as shown in Figure 3.47).

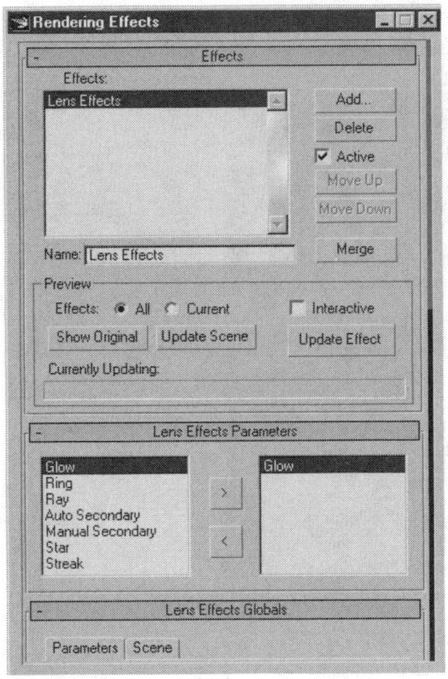

Figure 3.46
The Lens Effects Parameters rollout displays the newly added Glow effect.

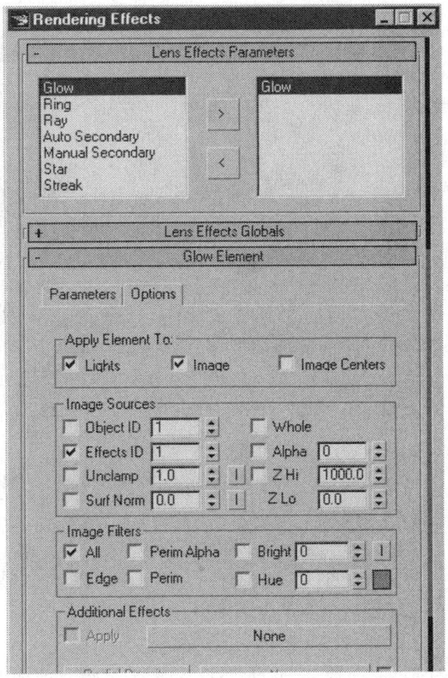

Figure 3.47
The Effects ID: 1 is now active in the Image Sources group.

The term Effects ID: refers to the Material Effects ID: in the Material Editor. This is not the Material ID number you used to apply the sub-materials to the objects, but the Material Effects ID that is stored in each material (and sub-material).

In this case, you are instructing that the Glow be applied to the Material Effects ID: of 1, which you applied to the bil-lampin material when you changed its color a few steps ago.

4. Select the Camera-jib view, go to Frame 90, and in the Effects rollout of the Rendering Effects dialog, check Interactive.

   The Camera-jib view renders, and when it finishes, a subtle post glow is added to the lamp objects. Don't close the rendered Camera-jib view; it will change interactively when you adjust the Glow's parameters.

   You can collapse the Lens Effects Globals and Lens Effects Parameters rollouts for now.

5. In the Glow Element rollout, click the Parameters tab and enter a Size of **1.5** (see Figure 3.48).

The Glow effect is reapplied with its new settings to the rendered Camera-jib image. Currently, it applies the white color from the Radial Color group. It looks kind of nice, but it would look better if you mixed some of the yellow lamp color as well.

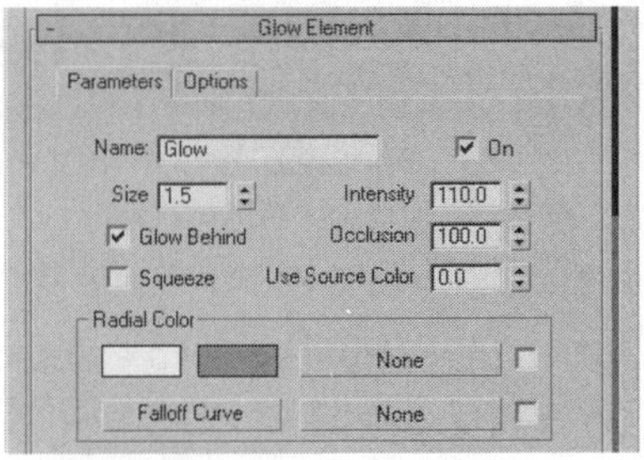

6. Change the Use Source Color value to **50**, as shown in Figure 3.49.

Now the glow uses the white Radial Color and the yellow color from the lamp's pixels (see Figure 3.50). Pretty cool. The glow actually looks great. Leave it like that.

7. In the Effects rollout of the Rendering Effects dialog, deselect Interactive and close the dialog.

You deselected Interactive in case you ever go back into the Rendering Effects dialog to work again. If you leave it on accidentally, you might be freaked out when Max starts rendering all on its own.

8. Save your work as **03FH08.max**.

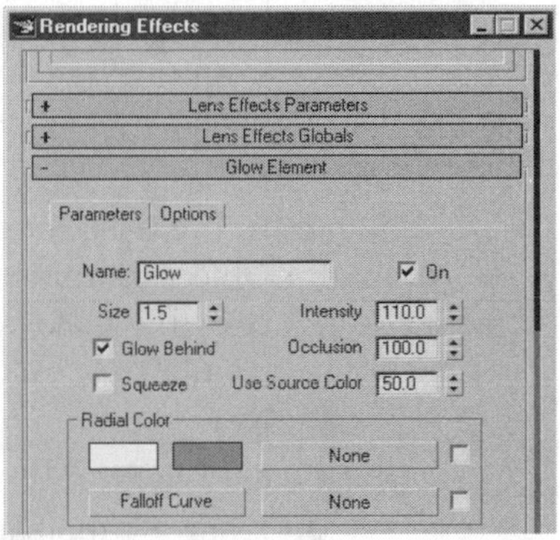

You just learned how to create a Render Effects Glow and apply it to a Material Effects ID in your rendering. It's a fairly easy technique to master, and it can be used to soften up just about any scene.

Figure 3.48
The Size of the glow has been changed to 1.5.

Figure 3.49
The Use Source Color has been changed to 50.

Figure 3.50
The finished Render Effects glow on the lamps.

Exercise 3.10   Adding a Video Post Lens Effects Glow

You are now going to add the fiery glow around the edge of the billboard. To do so, you will use a different technique than you used before. You will use the Lens Effects Glow that is in Video Post. Why? Because it has a few more features that you can use to achieve the fiery glow.

Before you can add the glow, you need to apply a unique Object ID to the billboard object in order for the glow to be applied to it.

1. Open **03FH08.max**. Open the Select Objects dialog and select the following objects: bil-back, bil-body, bil-handl, bil-handr, bil-head, bil-type-in, and bil-type-out. Right-click on the selected billboard objects and choose Properties from the Transform quad menu. The Object Properties dialog opens (see Figure 3.51).

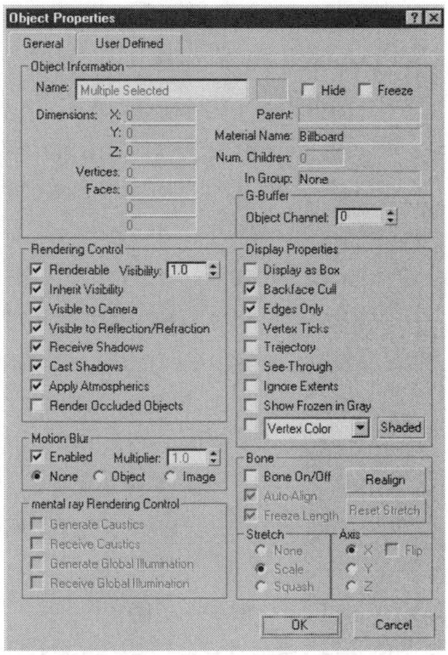

2. In the G-Buffer group, change the Object Channel: to **1** and click OK to close the dialog. All the selected object should have an Object Channel: of 1. Now you can use that value to apply a glow around the objects collectively.

3. From the toolbar, choose Rendering/ Video Post. The Video Post dialog opens.

4. Click the Add Scene Event button, and the Add Scene Event dialog opens. Click OK to accept its default settings.

5. Click the Add Image Filter Event button, and the Add Image Filter Event dialog opens. Choose Lens Effects Glow from the Filter Plug-In group (as shown in Figure 3.52) and click OK to close the dialog.

    The Video Post queue, shown in Figure 3.53, now has two events in it: the Camera-jib event and the Lens Effects Glow event.

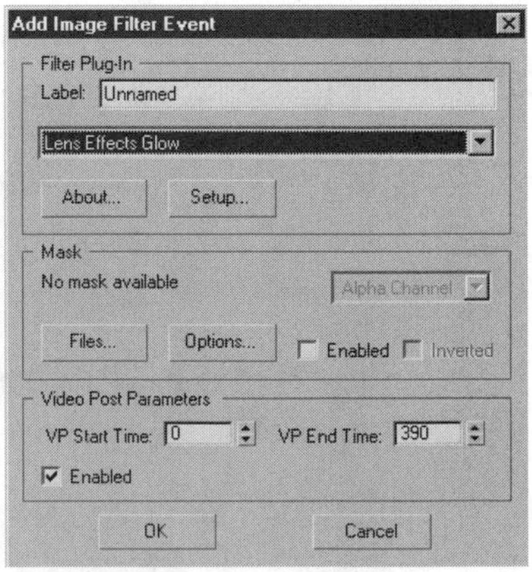

Figure 3.51
The Object Properties dialog.

Figure 3.52
The Add Image Filter Event dialog with Lens Effects Glow active.

You can now use the Lens Effects Glow filter to add the fiery glow around the billboard objects.

6. Advance the time slider to frame 90. Then, in the Video Post dialog, double-click the Lens Effects Glow effect to open the Edit Filter Event dialog. Click the Setup button to enter the Lens Effects Glow settings.

7. Click the VP Queue button (this allows you to use the Camera-jib view in the preview window), and then click Preview.

The Lens Effects Glow in progress dialog appears briefly while the scene is rendered. When it's finished rendering, the image with the glow applied appears in the Preview window (see Figure 3.54).

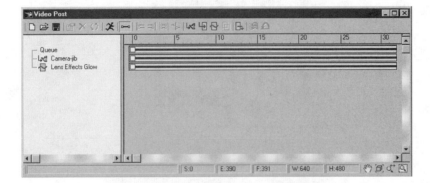

Figure 3.53
The Video Post queue to this point.

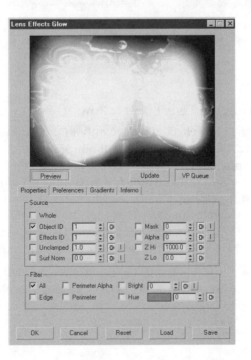

Figure 3.54
The Lens Effects Glow dialog shows a pre-view of the rendered glow effect.

That's an awfully bright glow. But don't fret; you can adjust the settings. Notice in the Properties tab that Object ID 1 is checked. It must be your lucky day! That's the Object ID you just assigned to the billboard objects. In the Filter group, All is checked. That means the Glow effect is being applied to all the pixels with an Object ID of 1. However, you want the effect to be applied only around the edges of the billboard, so you need to change the filter.

8. In the Filter group, deselect All, and then check Perimeter Alpha (see Figure 3.55).

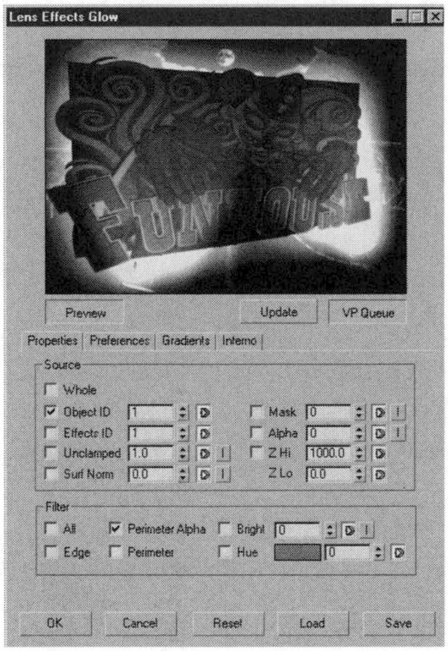

Figure 3.55

The Lens Effects Glow dialog with the Perimeter Alpha filter active

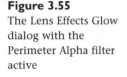

Exercise 3.11   Adjusting the Lens Effects Glow

That looks much better. The glow effect is applied only to the perimeter of the billboard objects. If you look closely, however, you will notice some anti-aliasing problems, especially where the billboard overlaps its post. This is an inherent problem of the Glow filter because there isn't really an alpha edge to apply the effect to (because the post object is generating alpha as well). So where there is no alpha on the perimeter, the Glow filter generates an edge. That edge, however does not anti-alias smoothly. There isn't any easy way around this problem, but it is so subtle you can probably get away with it. Now you need to make the glow appear to be fiery.

1. Click the Preferences tab and in the Color group, choose Gradient. The Glow filter uses the gradients in the Gradients tab to generate the color of the glow.

2. Click the Gradients tab to open its settings (shown in Figure 3.56).

   Here you can see how the gradient affects the color of the gradient. Notice that the Radial Color gradient goes from left to right, white to blue. Now in the preview window, you see that the glow is white where it meets the billboard, and it turns blue as it is applied outward. This color change is directly associated with the Radial Color.

   If you look at Vince's illustration one more time, you will see that the fiery glow changes from an orange color (where it's closest to the billboard) to a red color (as it is applied outward). Change the Radial Color gradient's colors to match those of Vince's illustrated glow.

3. Double-click the leftmost color flag of the Radial Color gradient to open its Color Selector: Color dialog, and then enter the color RGB: **243, 190, 74**. Close the dialog.

4. Double-click the rightmost color flag of the Radial Color gradient to open its Color Selector: Color dialog, and then enter the color RGB: **217, 71, 71** and close the dialog.

5. Click in the middle of the Radial Color gradient to create a new flag and move it to Pos=35. Change its color to RGB: **218, 77, 71**. The glow now is similar in color application to that of Vince's (see Figure 3.57).

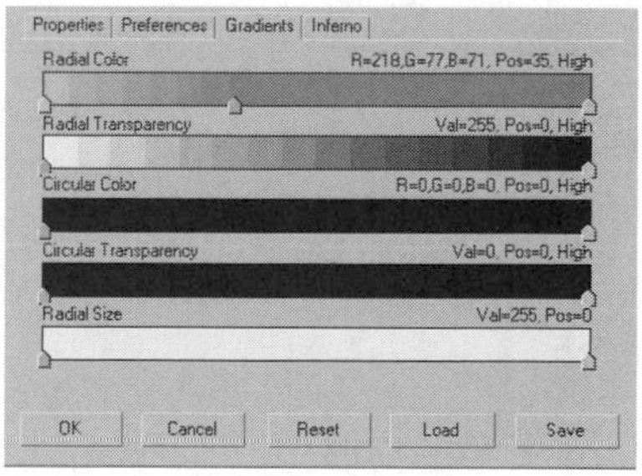

   The color looks great, but the glow is a little large and still doesn't look like tongues of fire. Before you make the glow look fiery, make it smaller.

6. Click the Preferences tab and in the Effect group, change the Size to **2.5**. The glow effect is about half its original size. Now that the glow is the right color and the right size, you can add the fiery effect.

   You will use some of the Lens Effects Glow features that the Render Effects Glow doesn't have. Most of these features are found on the Inferno tab.

7. Click the Inferno tab. Check the Red, Green, and Blue boxes to activate the effect.

   That doesn't look too bad! Leave the Gaseous type active; it looks perfect. However, you will need to change a few of the values.

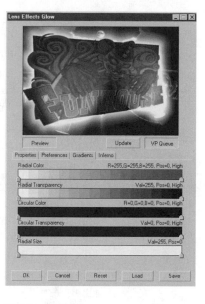

Figure 3.56
The Lens Effects Glow dialog with the Gradients tab selected.

Figure 3.57
The Lens Effects Glow Gradients tab with the correct gradient settings.

The Motion: value indicates how quickly the inferno effect pans through the view. A setting of 0 will prevent any panning from occurring, the larger the number the faster it pans.

The Direction: value indicates the direction in which the inferno effect pans. A value of 0 means it will travel toward the 12 o'clock position. A value of 90 (degrees) will make it pan toward 3 o'clock, and so on.

The Direction value is good, but the default Motion value of 10 is too fast; you need to change that.

8. Change the Motion: value to **3**.

Not much changes in the preview window, but the effect now pans more slowly when you render the animation. One other value needs to be adjusted: the Speed value. The Speed value indicates how quickly the noise effect undulates. The default value of 1 will make your flames undulate too quickly, so you need to decrease the value.

9. In the Parameters group, change the Speed: value to **.25** (as shown in Figure 3.58).

A Speed: value of .25 will create a nice churning fire effect that's not too fast but not too slow.

There is only one thing left to adjust before you call this Glow "done," and that's the Radial Density of the effect. Currently the Inferno effect is applied evenly to the glow. It would be more dramatic if the glow was solid on the

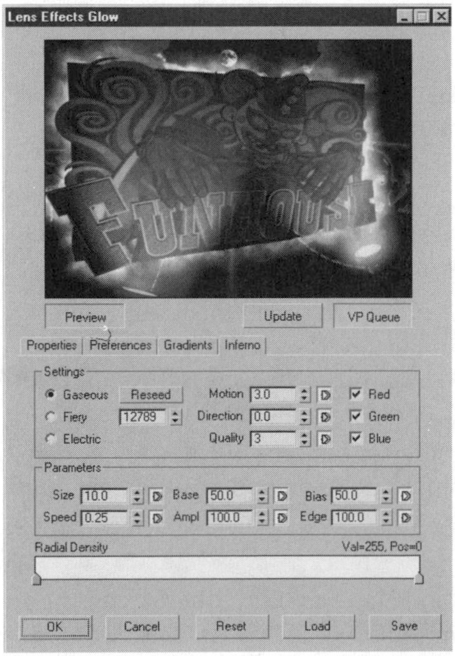

Figure 3.58
The Lens Effects Glow dialog with the correct settings so far.

billboard's perimeter and gradually turned into the Inferno effect as it was applied outward.

10. Double-click the leftmost flag of the Radial Density gradient and change its color to RGB: **0, 0, 0**.

By changing the leftmost flag to black, you instructed Inferno to not apply any inferno effect at the beginning but to apply it as the gradient turns to white more inferno effect is applied to the glow. This gradient, however, has removed too much of the Inferno effect so you need to add more flags to the Radial Density gradient.

11. Click in the middle of the Radial Gradient to create a new flag. Change its color to RGB: **255, 255, 255** and move it to Pos **20** (as shown in Figure 3.59).

The effect is solid on the perimeter of the billboard, and the Inferno effect is gradually applied to the glow as the glow is generated outward.

12. Click OK to close the Lens Effects Glow dialog.

13. Save your work as **03FH09.max**.

If you are ready for a break (I know I am), and you want to render the animation to see what you have so far, here are the instructions for how to do it.

14. In the Video Post dialog, click the Add Image Output Event button. In the Add Image Output Event dialog, click the Files button. Enter a path and file-name (I used \3ds3-ma\proeject1\images\FH-LEglow1.avi) and click Save to

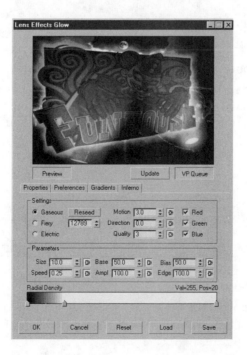

Figure 3.59
The Lens Effects Glow Inferno dialog with the correct settings.

close the Select Image File for Video Post Output dialog. Choose a Video Compressor (I chose Microsoft Video 1) and a Compression Quality (I chose 90). When you are finished in the Add Image Output Event dialog, click OK to close it, and then click the Execute Sequence button.

15. When the Execute Video Post dialog opens, choose Range 0 To 390, and an Output Size (I chose 320 × 240). Click Render, and Video Post will start to render the queue. When it finishes, you can view your file. It's a pretty good start! Please remember that you do not want to save your scene again with the Image Output Event in the queue.

Tweaking the Scene

Because you had an opportunity to test render the animation, you can now examine the full rendered result and see what needs to be adjusted. Really only two things desperately need some attention: the brightness of the colors and the visibility of the Funhouse type.

Brightening the Colors of the Billboard

If you examine Vince's illustration again and compare his image to yours, you will immediately notice that your billboard looks muddied (by the orange light) as compared to the clean and bright colors of Vince's illustration.

Exercise 3.12   Brightening Colors

Follow these steps to brighten up the clown's colors:

1. With 03FH09.max open, go to frame 90 and render the Camera-jib view.

   Notice that the flame glow around the billboard does not appear. The Flame glow will appear around the edge of the billboard only if you render the frame from Video Post. For now, however, you can live without it.

   Now you are going to use the Ram Player to view the changes you are making in the scene.

Note

The RAM Player, which has a channel A and a channel B, loads a frame sequence into RAM and plays it back at selected frame rates. Two different sequences can be loaded into the channels to play back together, which enables you to compare them.

2. From the toolbar, choose Rendering, RAM Player. The RAM Player opens.

3. In the Channel A: group, click the Open Last Rendered Image in Channel A button (the green teapot). Click OK to accept the RAM Player Configuration

default settings. The last rendered image loads into the RAM Player (see Figure 3.60).

The RAM Player enables you to view two images at once for comparison.

4. Minimize the RAM Player for the time being.

5. Create an Omni light at XYZ: (Absolute World) **0, –100, 20** and RGB: **180, 180, 180**. Name the light **OmniClown**. Then render frame 90 again.

6. Maximize the RAM Player and in the Channel B: group, click the Open Last Rendered Image in Channel B button. Click OK to accept the default settings. Both images are loaded into the RAM Player (as shown in Figure 3.61).

Figure 3.60
The RAM Player with the Last Rendered Image loaded in Channel A.

Figure 3.61
The RAM Player with two images loaded.

On the left side of the RAM Player, you can see the old rendering you loaded into Channel A; on the right side is the new image you rendered with the OmniClown light. The difference is quite dramatic. In the RAM Player, you click and drag on the image to reposition the wipe. Also, you can click the A|B Horizontal/Vertical Split Screen button to change the axis of the wipe to horizontal.

The color of the billboard is certainly brighter now. Go ahead and attenuate the OmniClown light to soften its effect a little.

7. Minimize the RAM Player. With The OmniClown light selected, enter the Modify panel. In the Attenuation Parameters rollout, change the Far Attenuation Start value to **120** and the Far Attenuation End value to **200**, and then click Use (see Figure 3.62). Render frame 90 again.

8. Maximize the RAM Player and in the Channel B group, click the Open Last Rendered Image in Channel B button. The new rendered image loads into channel B.

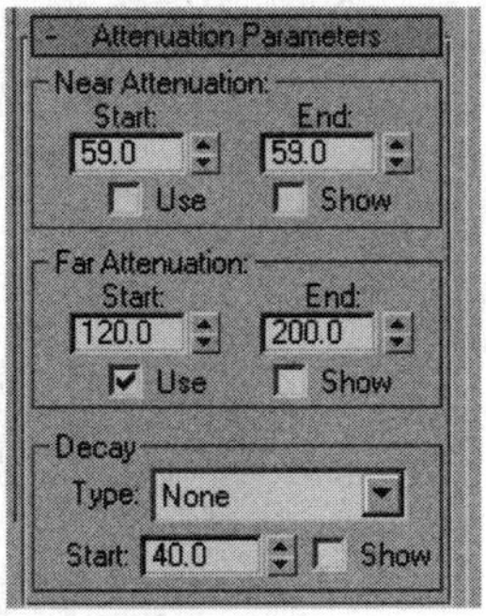

Figure 3.62
The OmniClown light's Attenuation Parameters rollout.

Move the wipe through the two images again. The colors of the edge of the billboard match the colors of the original image in channel A. By attenuating the light, you light only the center of the billboard. The colors of the billboard look great.

Now move on to the Funhouse type.

9. Minimize the RAM Player when you finish examining the images.

Illuminating the Funhouse Type

The final detail to be tweaked is that the Funhouse type isn't very visible when it is in the shadows. You have to remember that the most important part of this animation is the Funhouse type because that is the name of the product you are trying to sell.

Exercise 3.13   Adding Self-Illumination to a Sub-Material

The letters of the funhouse type look as thought they are light boxes, which would backlight them. You can accomplish this backlit look by adding a little self-illumination to its sub-material.

1. Open the Material Editor. Select the Billboard material and click the sub-material 7 bil-type-in (Standard) button to open its settings. In the Blinn Basic Parameters rollout, change the Self-Illumination value to **50**. Render the Camera-jib view at frame 90 again.

2. Maximize the RAM Player and in the Channel A: group:, click the Open Last Rendered Image in Channel A button (to replace the old image you first loaded into the RAM Player). Click OK to accept the default settings.

   By scrubbing the wipe between the two images, you can see that the Funhouse type is slightly brighter. I think that's all it needed to make it legible. You're finished tweaking the image—for now at least.

3. Close the RAM Player and click OK to unload all files. Close the Material Editor and save your work as **03FH10.max**.

In Conclusion

The scene is complete. You have erected the billboard, created the environment, and added the special effects. In the next chapter, you will animate the billboard and add a few more visual bells and whistles. This animation appears to be shaping up. Cheers!

Chapter 4

Finishing the Funhouse Animation

You ease back in your chair feeling satisfied about your progress so far. Seeing the test rendering you created with the music builds your excitement about completing the scene.

Anxious to show someone your progress, you give Vince a call, "Dude, stop over when you get a chance…" When the conversation ends Vince starts to head toward your workstation.

"Nice job!" Vince excitedly says. "I really like the fire glow around the billboard." As you both watch the animation looping on the monitor over and over, you almost become hypnotized. When you realize your attention has drifted off to La La Land, you snap back to reality and prepare to get your hands dirty again.

In this chapter, you gain experience in the following areas:

- Adjusting keys in the Track View
- Working with Bézier controller tangent types
- Applying parameter curve out-of-range types to animation
- Synchronizing animation to an audio track
- Assigning Track View filters
- Using the Super Spray particle system
- Adding a Reflection Map to materials
- Creating an IFL

Animating the Head Object

With the scene fully constructed, you can start to animate the individual elements of the billboard. The first object you will animate is the clown's head. You can make sure the clown's head is placed on his neck correctly and animate his head to spring up and down.

Exercise 4.1   Creating a Controlled Ping-Pong Animation

You'll use a ping-pong animation to make the clown's head spring up and down without jerking.

I. Open **03FH10.max**, the file you created in the last chapter, and hide the lights (Shift+L). Maximize the Front view, right-click its label, and check Smooth+Highlights. Zoom in on the billboard objects (see Figure 4.1).

In this scene, the clown's head isn't quite centered on the neck of the body. But before you fix it, collapse the bil-head object's stack. You don't want to mistakenly make any changes to the XForm modifier you added.

2. Select the **bil-head** object and collapse it into an Editable Mesh.

3. Activate the Select and Move tool (View XY-axis) and move the bil-head object until it rests correctly on the body's neck (as shown in Figure 4.2).

   It's okay if the head is a little close to the left hand; you will be moving the hand object later when you animate it. Now that the bil-head object is correctly positioned, you can animate its looping up and down motion.

Figure 4.1
The Front view displays the billboard objects.

Figure 4.2
The bil-head object fits correctly on the clown's neck.

4. With the Select and Move tool (View Y-axis) active, lower the bil-head object to its lowest point in the animation (shown in Figure 4.3). The head should cover the second coil of the neck.

5. Go to frame 40 and click the Animate button. Move the bil-head object up (View Y-axis) in the maximized Front view until it is as high up as it realistically can go before lifting above the neck (see Figure 4.4). Deactivate the Animate button.

6. Change from Front view back to Wireframe to improve the real-time playback, play the animation, and then stop it when you finish watching.

Figure 4.3
The bil-head object at its lowest point.

Figure 4.4
The bil-head object at its highest point at frame 40.

The bil-head object moves linearly from its low position at frame 0 to its higher position at frame 40. Believe it or not, you've created all the keys you need to finish the bil-head's motion.

7. Open the Track View and expand the tracks until the bil-head Transform tracks are expanded (see Figure 4.5).

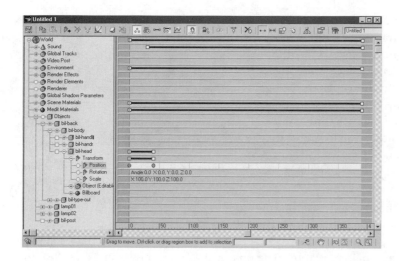

Figure 4.5
The Track View with the bil-head's Transform track expanded.

In the bil-head's Transform Position track, you see the two keys you created. The key at frame 0 is the bil-head low position, and the key at frame 40 is the bil-head high position. We now want to create a smooth, slide up, slide down motion. To smooth the motion of the bil-head's position, we will adjust the Bezier Tangent Types of the keys.

8. Right-click the Position key at frame 0 to open the bil-head\Position dialog and change its Out: Tangent Type to Slow (as shown in Figure 4.6).

As you learned earlier, when you're animating the camera, the Slow Tangent Type eases the motion out of the key. You now need to ease the motion into the key at frame 40.

9. With the bil-head\Position dialog still open, click the right arrow in the top left of the dialog to move to the next key (2). Change the In: Tangent Type to Slow (see Figure 4.7). Close the dialog.

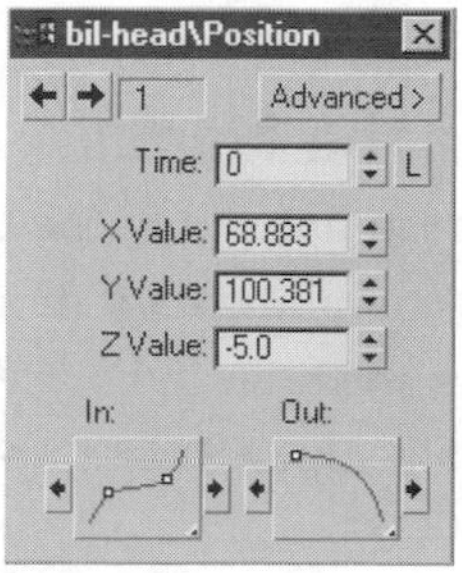

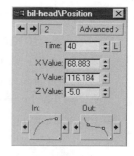

Figure 4.6
The bil-head\Position dialog.

Figure 4.7
The In: tangent for the key at frame 40 is changed to Slow.

If you play the animation now, you will see that the clown's head smoothly begins its journey upward, speeds up through the middle of the move, and gently decelerates into the key at frame 40. After frame 40, the bil-head object just stays in its high position. You can ping pong the head's motion now to reverse the animation back to its start position and then continue to loop that motion.

10. In the Track View, click the bil-head's Transform Position label (it will turn orange). Click the Parameter Curve Out-of-Range Types button to open its dialog. Click the Ping Pong graph image, and both the backward and forward buttons will look as if they're pressed in (as shown in Figure 4.8). Click OK to close the dialog. Play the animation again.

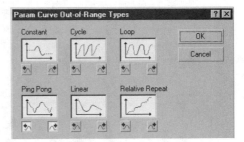

Figure 4.8
The Param Curve Out-of-Range Types dialog with Ping Pong active.

The bil-head object is smoothly bobbing up and down now. The Ping Pong Parameter Curve Out-of-Range Type instructs the track's keys to ping-pong their animation. The up-down motion, however, is too fast and seems to be too pronounced for the size of the billboard. You'd better slow it down.

11. In the Track view, move the bil-head's Position key from frame 40 to 75. Play the animation again.

That looks believable. It almost dances to the music as well. You'll keep it.

12. Save your work as **04FH01.max**.

Animating the Hands

Just as you finish animating the bil-head object, Gordon, the sound guy, stops by. He shares his complimentary thoughts about your progress so far and informs you that he has finished the audio. He hands you the disc, and you put it in your workstation. "Thanks, Dude. I can't wait to hear it. I was just about ready to animate the hands objects."

Gordon replies with, "Great. Well, you know I saved out all the individual sound effects in place for you to sync your animations with them." "Really?" you ask with a raised brow. "Gee, thanks Gordon. You know how to make my life easy." Go ahead and give the final audio a listen.

Exercise 4.2   Setting Up a Sound Track

Setting up a sound track is a simple process when you have really good individual sound effects available.

1. With **04FH01.max** loaded, open the Track View (if it isn't already open). Expand the Sound tracks and select the **Waveform – FH-Music.wav track** (see Figure 4.9).

2. Right-click the Waveform – FH-Music.wav track and choose Properties to open the Sound Options dialog. Click the Choose Sound button to open the Open Sound dialog. Select the **FH-FullMix.wav** file (you should already be in the \3ds4-ma\project1\sounds\ folder) and click the Play Preview button in the dialog. Leave the dialog open.

   Because you are going to animate the hand object next, you should load that sound track and animate to it.

3. In the Open Sound dialog, choose **FH-MetalHandcreaks.wav** and click OK to close the Open Sound dialog. Click OK to close the Sound Options dialog. Then play the animation.

   You hear the sound effect for the metal creaking hands. But do you remember that you shifted the music in the animation to add pre-roll? Because of that, you need to offset this sound effect as well.

4. In the Track View, use the Zoom tool until time intervals of 30 frames are displayed on the Time Ruler. Drag the black bar in the Sound track to the right 30 frames (as shown in Figure 4.10).

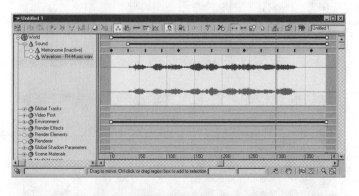

Figure 4.9
The Track View with Waveform – FH-Music.wav selected.

Figure 4.10
In the Track View, offset the Sound track 30 frames forward.

Now the sound file is in the correct position, allowing for pre-roll. But you're going to prepare the hand object for animation, so you won't need the Track View for a while.

5. Close the Track View.

Exercise 4.3   Synchronizing Animation to a Sound Track

When you animate the hand object, the hands will rotate at the wrists. In the Wireframe display Front view, you can see that the hands don't match up to the wrists of the bil-body object (see Figure 4.11). In these steps, you will fix that.

1. Activate the Select and Move tool (View XY-axis) and place the hands better on their wrists in the maximized Front view (as shown in Figure 4.12).

If you select the bil-hand objects individually, you will see their local axis displayed. In the scene shown in the figure, the pivot axis for the hand objects is far from the wrists. Adjust the pivot now.

Figure 4.11
The hands aren't anatomically placed on the wrists.

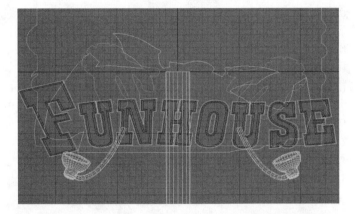

Figure 4.12
The bil-hand objects in the correct position.

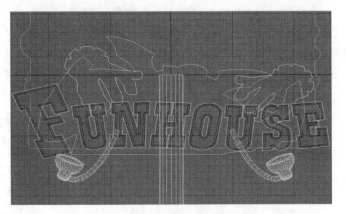

2. Click the Hierarchy tab and in the Adjust Pivot rollout, activate the Affect Pivot Only button. In the maximized Front view, select each bil-hand object individually and use the Select and Move tool (View XY-axis) to position the pivot correctly (see Figure 4.13).

3. Deactivate the Affect Pivot Only button.

   The hands are ready to be animated. Before you begin working though, remove some of the distractions from the workspace.

4. Open the Track View, make sure the Sound track is expanded, and expand the tracks for the two bil-hand objects (see Figure 4.14).

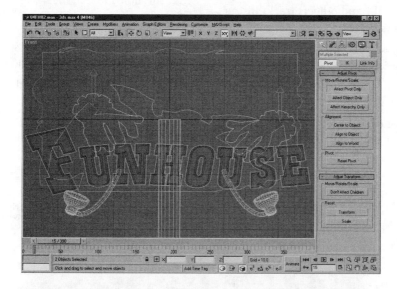

Figure 4.13
The pivot's of the bil-hand objects are in the correct position. Both hands are selected for clarity of the figure.

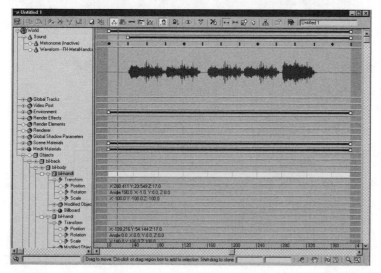

Figure 4.14
The Track View with Sound and both bil-hand objects' tracks expanded.

You might wish there was a way to get the bil-hand tracks closer to the Sound track, especially since you will be adding your keys to sync to the sound. Well, consider that wish granted.

Notch

5. In the Track View, drag the notch that is above the vertical scroll bar on the right (see Figure 4.15), down to split the Track view window. Adjust the views so you can see the sound's waveform on top and the bil-hand objects tracks in the bottom (see Figure 4.16).

Figure 4.15
Drag this notch to split the Track View.

That's great, but if you will only be animating rotation, why do you need to see the Position and Scale tracks as well? You don't; you could get rid of those too.

6. Click the Filters button (the first one on the Track View toolbar) to open the Filters dialog (shown in Figure 4.17).

7. In the Show group of the Filters dialog, deselect Position and Scale. While you're at it, deselect Modified Objects, Materials/Maps, and Material/ Parameters too. Click OK to close the Filters dialog.

Figure 4.16
The split view Track View.

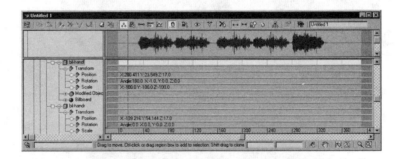

Figure 4.17
The Filters dialog.

The Track View is much easier to work in now (see Figure 4.18). As you've just seen, you can use the Track View Filters dialog to help tidy the Track View by hiding parameters you are not animating.

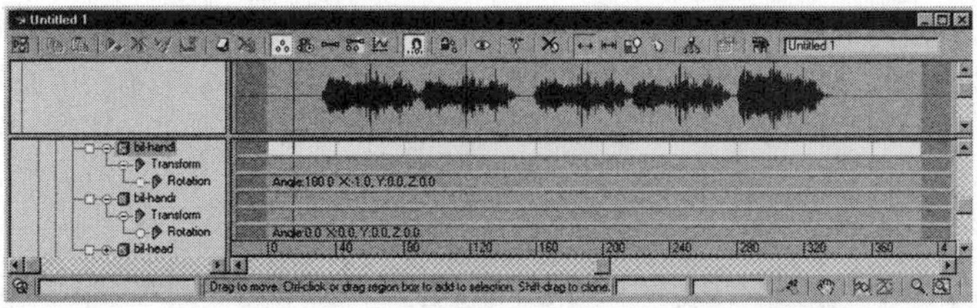

Figure 4.18
The Track View is easier to work with after unnecessary filters have been deselected.

Note

The Filters dialog is both a blessing and a curse. Remember which options you deselected (and that you did deselect them!) so you can return them to normal later. I often find myself in a panic looking for something, only to find out a few minutes later that the track was hidden because I deselected a particular filter.

The hands are in the correct orientation, so you are ready to animate them.

8. Scrub the time slider through the audio and listen for the first squeak. Watch the Waveform in the Track view as well.

You start to hear the audio playing loudly around frame 32, so the hands have to be moving by then. You will start rotating the hands at frame 30. (Why not wait until frame 32? Well, you could, but I am a strong believer in using motion first, and letting sound follow, just as you see lightning before you hear it.)

9. In the Track View, activate the Add Keys button on the toolbar. Click in both bil-hand Rotation tracks at frame 30 to create a key for each (see Figure 4.19). If you click and drag when you create the key, it will drag with the pointer, and the status bar will show you the key's location.

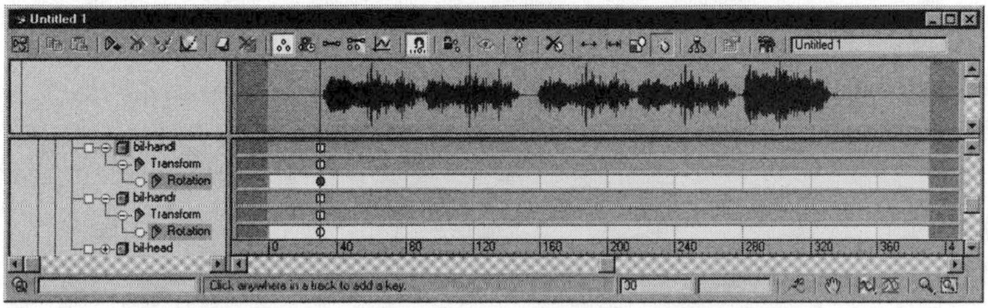

Figure 4.19
The Track View, with newly added Rotation keys at frame 30.

10. Click the Play button and listen to the audio to find out what frame the hands should stop rotating.

Even though the sound continues through two rotations back to back, the animation would look better if there was a brief pause before the hands rotated back to their original orientation. You should make the rotation end by frame 80.

11. Go to frame 80, minimize the Track View, and activate the Animate button. Activate the Select and Rotate tool (View Z-axis) and in the maximized Front view, rotate the bil-handr object Z: **–30** degrees. Then play the animation.

The hand sure does look like it's rotating with the audio. Now do the other hand.

12. Return to frame 80. Rotate the bil-handl object Z: **30** degrees. Then play the animation again and deactivate the Animate button.

It's lookin' good. Now, using the keys you just created, you will create the return rotation in the Track View.

13. Restore the Track View. Drag a rectangular selection region around the two Rotation keys at frame 80. Shift+drag them to create copies at frame 90 (see Figure 4.20).

You have copied the rotation keys from frame 80 to frame 90 to insert a pause before the hands rotate back to their origins. Now you will copy the rotation keys from frame 30 to frame 145.

14. In the Track View, drag a rectangular selection region around the two bil-hand objects' Rotation keys at frame 30. Shift+drag them to frame 145 (as shown in Figure 4.21). Then minimize the Track View and play the animation.

Figure 4.20
In Track View, create copied keys at frame 90.

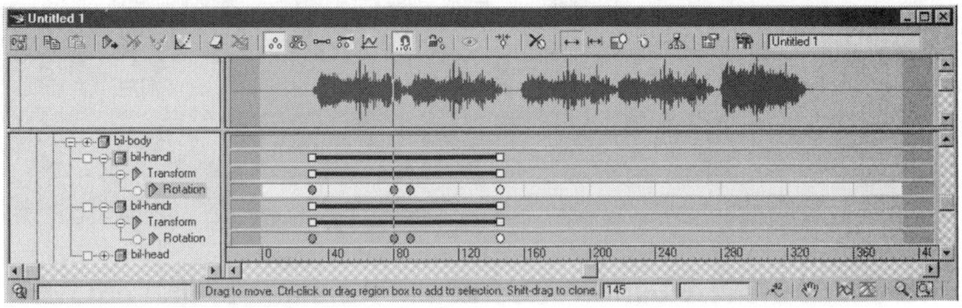

Figure 4.21
In Track View, create copied keys at frame 145.

Exercise 4.4   Adjusting Interpolation

There doesn't seem to be a pause between frames 80 and 90 even though you put the keys in to create one. The reason the hands are not pausing is that the keys are interpolating the rotation to create a smooth rotation. Therefore, you need to adjust the keys for a more mechanical result. Start by adjusting the left hand.

1. Restore the Track View. In the bil-handl's Rotation track, right-click the key at frame 30 to open the bil-handl\Rotation dialog (shown in Figure 4.22).

   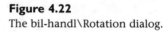

   Notice how the graph is rounded in the middle? That's the smooth interpolation of the rotation. You need to remove that from all the keys in the track.

2. Change the Continuity value to **0** so that the rotation is linear in and out of the key at frame 30. Keep the dialog open.

   You've changed only the settings of the key at frame 30. You need to fix the other three now as well. Before you do, you need to consider the desired behavior of the rotation you created. A linear rotation out of frame 30 is good, but what if the rotation gradually slows down as it reaches its destination? That sounds like a great idea!

3. In the top-left of the bil-handl\Rotation dialog, click the arrow pointing to the right to move to key 2, the one at frame 80. Change the Continuity value to **0** and the Ease To value to **25** (as shown in Figure 4.23). Keep the dialog open.

   Now that you've increased the Ease To value to **25**, you can see the +'s on the graph bunch up around the red key in the graph. This means the rotation is easing into the key. Notice, however, that to the right of the red key, the +'s are evenly spaced. The move out is linear and that's what you want (it's the beginning of the pause). So adjust the next key.

4. Click the arrow pointing right to view key 3 at Time: **90**. Change the Continuity to **0**.

   The key at frame 90 is the key coming out of the brief pause. The linear key ensures that there will be no interpolation before the key and an abrupt and even rotation out of the key. That's what you want. Now ease the rotation into the next key.

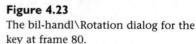

Figure 4.22
The bil-handl\Rotation dialog.

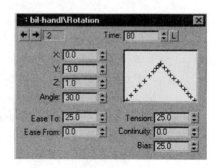

Figure 4.23
The bil-handl\Rotation dialog for the key at frame 80.

5. Click the arrow pointing right to view key 4 at Time: 145. Change the Continuity to **0** and the Ease To to **25** (as shown in Figure 4.24). Then close the dialog.

   Play the animation and watch the left hand as compared to the right hand. The changes you made to the left hand make its rotation much more realistic. Now you have to make the same adjustments to the bil-handr rotation.

6. Right-click the key at frame 30 in the bil-handr Rotation track to open its settings. Use the following settings:

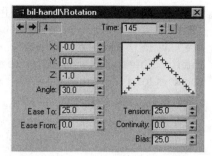

Figure 4.24
The bil-handl\Rotation dialog for the fourth key.

Key 1	Continuity: **0**
Key 2	Ease To: **25**
	Continuity: **0**
Key 3	Continuity: **0**
Key 4	Ease To: **25**
	Continuity: **0**

7. Close the dialog, minimize the Track View, and play the animation.

   Both hands animate correctly now through frame 145. In the next section, you will manipulate the keys to finish the hand rotation.

Exercise 4.5   Matching Keys to a Sound Track

Finishing the hands' rotation now will be a cinch because you have already created the keys for rotating the hands outward and returning them to their origin. All you have to do is copy the keys and match them to the audio.

1. Scrub the time slider, and notice that the next hand rotation cycle starts at 159. You will copy the rotation keys to have the next cycle precede the audio by 1 frame, thus starting at frame 158.

2. In the Track View, drag a rectangular selection region around all eight rotation keys for the two bil-hand objects (as shown in Figure 4.25).

   Now you will copy all the keys to the next cycle, starting at frame 158.

Figure 4.25
All eight rotation keys are selected in the Track View.

3. Go to frame 158 so you can use the time indicator as a reference. Shift+drag one of the keys at frame 30 to copy all eight keys. Match the yellow line that drags with the key to the time indicator line at frame 158 and release the mouse to copy the frames (see Figure 4.26).

4. Play the animation and scrub the time slider. Listening to the audio and examining the waveform shows that the final rotation starts at frame 280. You want to start the rotation at 278.

   It looks like everything is perfect. All you need to do is copy the keys to create the last half cycle.

5. Go to frame 278. In the Track View, select only the first two rotation keys from each rotation track (see Figure 4.27).

6. Shift+drag either key at frame 30 and match it up to the time indicator at frame 278. Release the mouse to copy the keys. Close the Track View.

   When you play the animation, you should be delighted by the results. The hands rotate in perfect sync with the audio. However, at its highest state, the left hand obscures the "SE" of the funhouse type too much. You'd better adjust that before Mr. Boss says, "I can't read that."

Figure 4.26
The Track View with the copied keys.

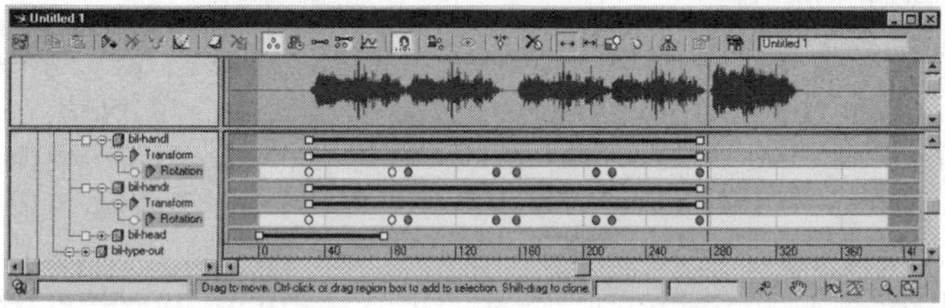

Figure 4.27
The first two keys of both rotation tracks are selected.

7. In the maximized Front view, activate the Select and Rotate tool (View Z-axis) and rotate the bil-handl object about Z: **–17** degrees (see Figure 4.28).

Figure 4.28
Rotate the bil-handl object Z: –17 degrees.

There. That's much better. The left hand no longer obscures the type completely.

8. Save your work as **04FH02.max**.

Next you will add a little animation to the lights in the scene.

Animating the Lights

To add more realism and drama to the billboard, you will animate the virtual bulbs of the billboard to blink intermittently. Gordon already has added the electric shock sound effects to the final music mix. He was also kind enough to save the electric shock sound effects into a separate file for you to animate with. You're ready to animate some more!

Exercise 4.6   Creating a Flickering Effect

In this exercise, you will set the Fspot01 light to blink on and off in conjunction with the electric shock sounds.

1. With **04FH02.max** loaded, open the Track View. Select the Sound track's label, right-click it, and choose Properties to open the Sound Options dialog. Click the Choose Sound button, choose **\3ds4-ma\project1\sounds\ FH-ElectricShockBursts.wav**, and click OK to close the dialog.

2. In the Track View, use the Zoom tool until the Time Ruler displays time in 30-frame intervals. Drag the Sound track's bar to the right and offset it to start on frame 30 (see Figure 4.29).

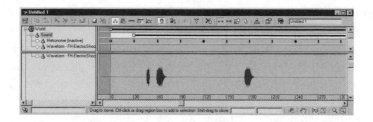

Figure 4.29
The Sound track is offset to frame 30 in the Track View.

If you play the animation and watch the waveform in the Track View, you see basically two clumps of sound. The first clump is two shock sounds; the second has one shock sound. You will be animating the Fspot01 light to flicker with the shock sounds.

You must remember that the Fspot01 and Fspot02 lights are instances of one another. If you animate the parameters of one, the other will be animated as well. That is not what you want, though, so you have to make the Fspot01 light unique.

3. Minimize the Track View, unhide the lights (Shift+L), and select the Fspot01 light. Open the Modify panel.

   Because you no longer need to see the Fspot light's cones, you can deactivate that.

4. In the Spotlight Parameters dialog, uncheck Show Cone.

   Now you can make the Fspot01 lights unique.

5. Click the Make Unique button (it's under the Modify stack) so you can animate the Fspot01 light independently of the Fspot02 light.

   You want the Fspot01 light to dim when the electric shock sounds occur. Because you already have the electric shock sounds file, you should be able to use that sound file to animate the light automatically.

6. Restore the Track View and adjust it so the Sound track's waveform in the top split and in the lower half expand the Fspot01's Multiplier track (as shown in Figure 4.30).

   You will now apply an Audio controller to the Multiplier track. Before you do though, adjust the Modify panel so you can see the Multiplier settings.

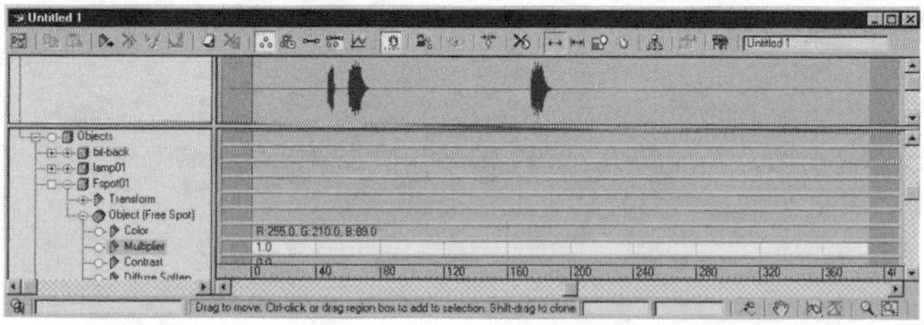

Figure 4.30
The Track View with the Sound track's waveform in the top half and the Fspot01 Multiplier track in the lower half.

7. With the Fspot01 light selected, open the Modify panel. Notice that the Multiplier value is 1.

The Multiplier value of a light allows you to increase the intensity of the light beyond its standard range. So, for example, a Multiplier value of 2 would make the light twice as bright. A Multiplier value of 0 would essentially turn the light off. The Multiplier value could also fall into the negative numbers, in which case it would remove light from the scene.

For all intents and purposes, you only want to animate the Multiplier value to flicker the light between the values of 0 and 1.

8. Adjust your workspace so you can see the Fspot01's Multiplier value in the Modify panel and the Track View.

9. In the Track View, select the Multiplier track. On the Track View toolbar, click the Assign Controller button to open the Assign Float Controller dialog, and then choose AudioFloat (see Figure 4.31). Click OK to close the dialog, and the Audio Controller dialog opens (see Figure 4.32).

10. In the Audio Controller dialog, click the Choose Sound button and choose the file **\3ds4-ma\project1\sounds\ FH-ElectricShockBursts.wav**. Keep the Audio Controller dialog open.

The waveform appears in the Track View, but the audio starts at frame 0. It needs to start at frame 30.

11. In the Track View, drag the Object (Free Spot) bar to the right and place its start position at frame 30 (as shown in Figure 4.33). As you drag the bar, the waveform offsets as well.

Now the two waveforms match in the Track View. Notice that (at frame 0) in the Modify panel, the Multiplier value is 0. That is because no sound occurs at frame 0. In the Controller Range group of the Audio Controller, notice the Min value is 0. That means when there is no sound, the value is 0. You should adjust that.

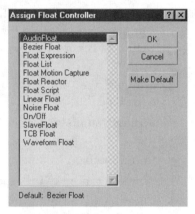

Figure 4.31
The Assign Float Controller dialog with AudioFloat selected.

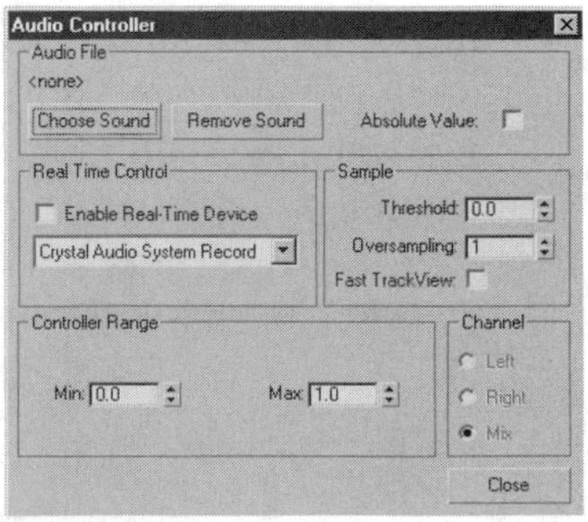

Figure 4.32
The Audio Controller dialog.

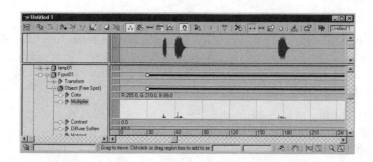

Figure 4.33
In Track View, offset the Multiplier track offset.

12. In the Audio Controller dialog, change the Min value to **1**.

The Multiplier value in the Modify panel changes back to one. All that is left is to instruct how low to take the Multiplier when there is sound. That's what the Max value is for. By changing the Max value to a lower number, you tell the controller to lower the Multiplier value when there is audio. Give it a try.

13. In the Audio Controller dialog, change the Min value to **0** (see Figure 4.34). Leave the Audio Controller dialog open.

Now if you scrub the time slider through the animation and watch the Multiplier value, you will see that the Multiplier value dips down when the shock sounds occur. However, it dips down only to a value of approximately .85 because the audio is not as loud as it could be. You need to decrease the Max setting in order for the Multiplier value to dip lower.

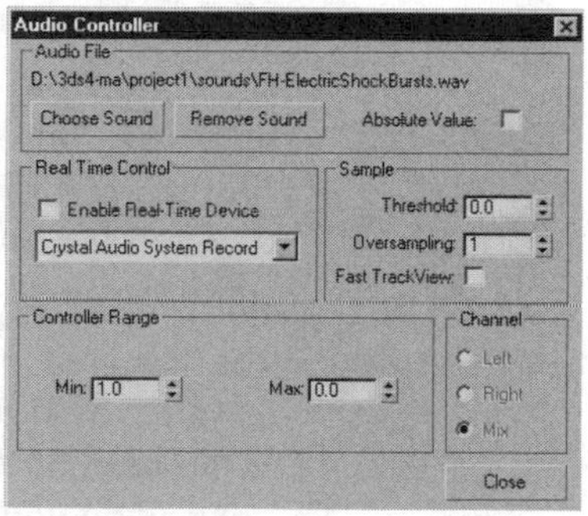

14. In the Audio Controller dialog, change the Max value to **–5.5**.

Figure 4.34
The Audio Controller dialog with the correct settings to this point.

Now scrub the time slider through the animation, and you will see a more dramatic dip in the Multiplier's value. You don't want the value to go into the negative values, and it seems like a value of –5.5 is pushing that envelope as far as it can go.

15. Click Close to close the Audio Controller dialog and save your work as **04FH03.max**.

Smashing the Bulb

In the previous section, you animated an electrical short into the Fspot01 light. It should consider itself lucky. The Fspot02 light bulb isn't going to make it to the end of the animation: It is about to burst.

Exercise 4.7   Creating a Shattering Effect

Have you ever been around a light bulb when it bursts or just burns out? Usually, the bulb makes an extraordinary flash as if to give a last "Hoorah." You're going to animate that type of burst into the Fspot02 light. You'll begin by animating the Fspot02 light bulb.

1. With **04FH03.max** loaded, open the Track View. Right-click the Sound track's label and choose Properties from the resulting list. In the Sound Options dialog, click the Choose Sound button and choose **\3ds4-ma\ project1\sounds\FH-GlassPop&Shatter.wav**. Click OK to close the two dialogs.

2. In the Track View, offset the Sound track's bar to frame 30, and then close the Track View. Minimize the Front view and play the animation.

   While the animation is playing, you hear the glass pop and shatter sound effect between the frames of 230 and 300. Adjust your workspace so you can work only in this area of the animation (with a little pre-roll and pad).

3. Click the Time Configuration button to open the Time Configuration dialog. In the Animation group, change the Start Time to **220** and the End Time to **310** (as shown in Figure 4.35). Click OK to close the dialog.

   The active time segment is now 90 frames. So now you don't have to watch the first 220 frames of the animation when you are previewing your effect.

   Since you know the bulb is going to pop, animate the Fspot02 light to turn off when the pop sound occurs.

4. Open the Track View and expand the Fspot02 light's Multiplier track (see Figure 4.36).

Figure 4.35
The Time Configuration dialog with the correct settings.

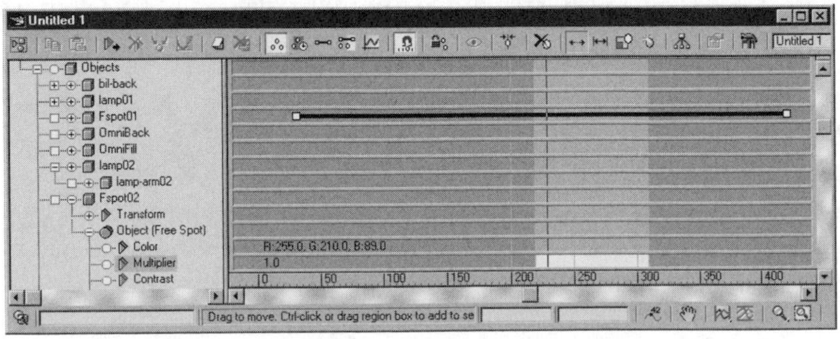

Figure 4.36
The Fspot02's Multiplier track is expanded.

Notice in the Track View that the current 90-frame section you assigned in the Time Configuration dialog is now a gray bar. That's pretty helpful.

5. Use the Zoom tool to zoom into the active time area in the Track View.

By scrubbing the time slider, you can hear the sound starting at frame 231. So you should start the flash at frame 230.

6. In the Track View, activate the Add Keys button and click to create a key at frame 230 in the Fspot02's Multiplier track. Right-click the key you just created to open the Fspot02\Multiplier dialog. Change the In: Tangent Type to Linear (as shown in Figure 4.37). Close the dialog.

Now you are assured that the Multiplier value will remain 1 before the key.

7. Click to add another key at frame 232 in the Multiplier track. Right-click it to open its dialog and change its Value to **2**. Close the dialog.

Now the intensity of the light will double over the course of two frames.

8. Click to add another key in the Multiplier track at frame 235, and right-click it to open its dialog. Change its Value to **0** (see Figure 4.38).

The Multiplier value of 0 will essentially "turn off" the light at frame 235.

9. Close the Track View.

The Fspot02 light now maintains a Multiplier value of 1 until frame 230, where it jumps up to a value of 2 by frame 232. The Multiplier value dips down to 0 by frame 235, and the light no longer casts any light.

Figure 4.37
The Fspot02\Multiplier dialog with a Linear In: Tangent Type.

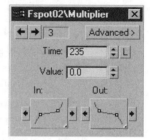

Figure 4.38
The Value is 0 at frame 235.

Exercise 4.8   Creating a Particle System

The light flashing and turning off is a good effect, but you decide to throw in some particles to give the appearance that the bulb burst and glass has shattered. Start by working with the particle system.

1. You don't need to see the lights anymore, so hide them (Shift+L).

2. Open the Create\Geometry panel and change the Standard Primitive type to Particle Systems. Click the Super Spray button, and then click and drag in the Top view to create a Super Spray emitter with an Icon Size of approximately 30 units (see Figure 4.39). Name it **ss-smash**.

Figure 4.39
The Super Spray emitter created in the Top view.

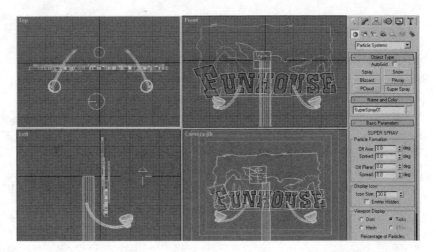

3. Open the Modify tab with the ss-smash particle system selected. Open the Particle Generation rollout, and in the Particle Timing group, change the Emit Start value to **229** and the Emit Stop value to **231**.

To see the particles being emitted, you need to change the Display Until value as well.

4. Change the Display Until value to **390** (see Figure 4.40); that is the last frame of the animation.

You have created a particle system and told it to emit particles between frames 229 and 231. You changed the Display Until value to 390 in order to view the particles until the end of the animation (if need be).

Figure 4.40
The Particle Generation rollout with the correct settings so far.

Exercise 4.9   Using the Align Tool to Direct the Particle Emission

Right now the particle system emitter is not in the right location. It needs to be inside the Lamp02 object. You can use the Align tool to place the emitter in the right place.

1. With the ss-smash particle system selected, click the Align button on the toolbar and then click the Lamp02 object. The **Align Selection (lamp02)** dialog opens. In the Align Position (World) group, select X Position, Y Position, and Z Position. In the Align Orientation (Local) group, select X Axis, Y Axis, and Z Axis (as shown in Figure 4.41). Click OK to close the dialog.

As you selected each axis in the dialog, the ss-smash particle system was interactively updated in the view. The ss-smash particle system is in the correct place now, but it faces the wrong direction. You need to rotate it 90 degrees.

2. Activate the Select and Rotate tool (Local X-axis) and rotate the ss-smash particle system X: **90** degrees.

The ss-smash particle system now points upward (see Figure 4.42).

If you play the animation, you will see a not-too-impressive particle effect. Between frames 229 and 231, you see a few particles shoot from the emitter in a straight line. That is some organized smashing glass! You'd better give those particles a little direction.

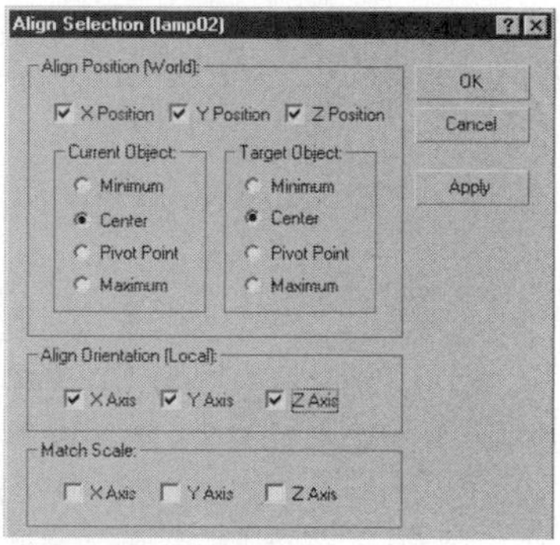

3. With the ss-smash particle system selected, open the Modify panel. Go to frame 240 and in the Viewport Display group of the Basic Parameters dialog, change the Percentage of Particles to **100**.

You can now see all the particles being generated in the view. You use a low value when you have an incredible amount of particles in your scene, and you only want to see an approximation of what the particles will do. In your scene, you can afford to see all the particles. It's time to break up that straight line of particles.

4. In the Particle Formation group of the Basic Parameters rollout, change the Off Axis Spread value to **90** degrees (as shown in Figure 4.43).

The particles are spread out now like a flat fan. It's time to add the third dimension.

Figure 4.41
The Align Selection (lamp02) dialog.

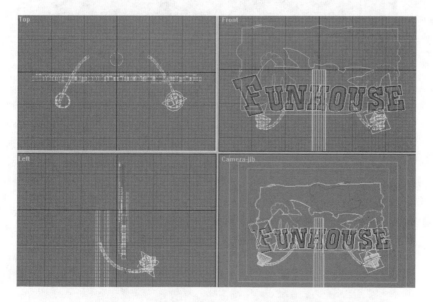

Figure 4.42
The correct orientation of the ss-smash particle system.

5. In the Particle Formation group of the Basic Parameters rollout, change the Off Plane Spread setting to **90**. If you drag the up and down arrows to change the value, you can see how the particles are spreading.

6. Play the animation again.

   It's starting to look better. But wouldn't it look even better if gravity was pulling the particles downward?

7. Open the Create/Space Warps panel and click the Gravity button. Click and drag in the Top view to create a Gravity Space Warp with an Icon Size of approximately 30 (see Figure 4.44). Leave the name **Gravity01**.

Figure 4.43
The particles with an Off Axis Spread value of 90 degrees.

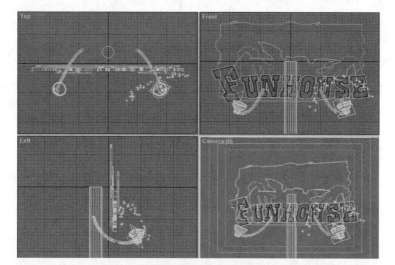

Figure 4.44
The Gravity Space Warp created in the Top view.

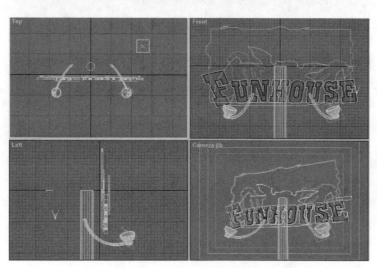

Now there is gravity in the scene, but nothing is bound to it. Bind the ss-smash particle system to the gravity space warp.

8. Activate the Bind to Space Warp tool, use it to select the ss-smash particle system, drag the mouse until the cursor is over the Gravity01 space warp, and release the mouse. The gravity space warp blinks to let you know it's bound.

9. Play the animation again. The particle system is really starting to take shape! The particles need a little more speed though.

10. Open the Modify panel and select the ss-smash particle system. In the Modify stack, select the Super Spray object. In the Particle Motion group of the Particle Generation rollout, change the Speed value to **20** and change the Variation value to **50%** (as shown in Figure 4.45).

Changing the Speed value from 10 to 20 doubled the speed at which the particles traveled. Applying a Variation value of 50% randomizes the speed the particles travel. This means that each particle could travel anywhere from a speed value of 10 to 30 (the Variation adds and subtracts the percent from the speed value).

Figure 4.45
The Speed and Variation Values in the Particle Generation rollout.

11. Play the animation again.

The speed of the particles looks great; however, they don't fall as quickly as they should. So increase the gravity.

12. Activate the Select Objects tool and select the Gravity01 space warp. Open the Modify panel and click the Play button to loop the animation. You can interactively change the Strength value of the gravity while the animation is looping. Enter a Strength value of **2** (see Figure 4.46).

Exercise 4.10   Creating Reflective Glass Particles

Now that you are happy with the motion of the particles, you need to adjust the appearance of the particles.

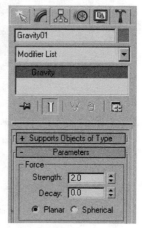

1. Go to frame 235 and click the Quick Render button to view the results.

The particles are so small you can't see them. Also, you need to apply a material to the particles. Do that now.

Figure 4.46
Change the Strength value to 2.

2. Select the ss-smash particle system and open the Material Editor. Select the third material preview slot and name it **ss-smash**. In the Shader Basic Parameters rollout, check 2-sided (because each particle is a single-sided triangle and you want to see both sides). In the Blinn Basic Parameters rollout, change the Opacity value to **0**. Click the Assign Material to Selection button.

Now make the material shiny like glass.

3. In the Specular Highlights group change the Specular Level value to **70** and the Glossiness value to **30** (as shown in Figure 4.47).

Now you have a clear glass-like material. To make the glass reflective, use Vince's great illustration as the reflection map.

4. Open the Maps rollout and click the Reflection Map button to open the Material/Map Browser. Choose Bitmap and click OK to close the browser. In the Select Bitmap Image File dialog, choose **\3ds4-ma\project1\maps\ finalclown.jpg** and click Open to close the dialog and load the image (see Figure 4.48). Name this map **ss-smash-rfl**.

Notice in the Coordinates rollout that the Mapping option is set to Spherical Environment. This means that the bitmap is mapped on an imaginary sphere surrounding the scene for the particles to reflect.

5. Click Go to Parent once to return to the root of the ss-smash material, and then change the Reflection Amount to **75**. The reflection isn't as bright now.

6. The material is finished, so close the Material Editor.

Now you're ready to work on the size of the particles.

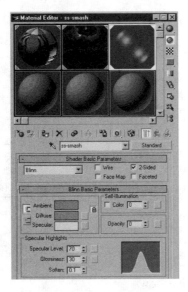

Figure 4.47
The Material Editor with the correct settings for the ss-smash material.

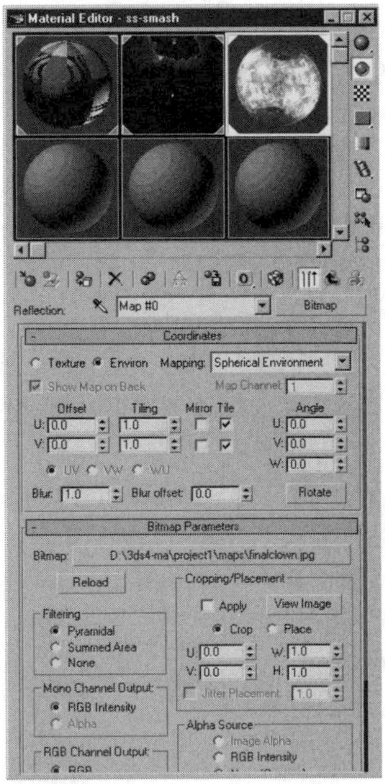

Figure 4.48
The Reflection map dialog.

7. Open the Modify panel and click the Super Spray object in the Modify stack. In the Particle Size group of the Particle Generation rollout, change the Size value to **2.5** and the Variation value of **50%**.

   The particles will be larger, and the Variation value ensures that the particles will be different sizes.

8. Also in the Particle Size group, change the Grow For and Fade For values to **0**.

   The Grow For and Fade For values instruct the particles to grow when created and shrink into dying. You don't want the glass particles to grow or shrink. You need to get a more accurate representation of the particles in the viewports.

9. In the Viewport Display group of the Basic Parameters rollout, click Mesh.

   Now you can see the triangular particles in the view (as shown in Figure 4.49).

   You can probably add a few more particles to the effect.

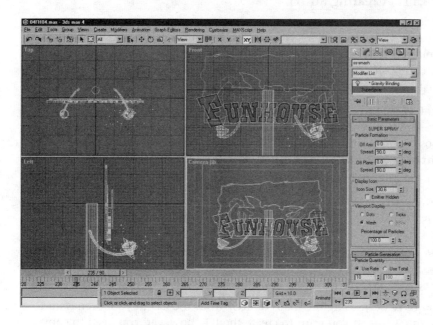

Figure 4.49
The Mesh Viewport Display is active.

10. In the Particle Generation rollout in the Modify panel, change the Particle Quantity to Use Total **300** (see Figure 4.50).

    Now there are plenty of particles in the scene—a total of 300 to be exact. It may look like there are too many, but when the effect is rendered, it will look good.

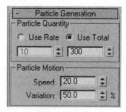

Figure 4.50
The Particle Quantity group with the correct settings.

11. Render frame 235 again. You will see the reflective glass particles in the rendering; they look great. If they were any smaller, it would be hard to see them when the animation is rendered because they travel so quickly. You are finished smashing the bulb, so save your scene.

12. Save your work as **04FH04.max**.

Adding Lightning

What's a scary night without lightning? I don't know either, but it's not as scary, that's for sure! The final touch you will add to your animation is some lightning. Gordon gave you the audio, so give it a listen and get on your way.

Exercise 4.11   Creating an IFL

You will add the lightning to your composite Environment map. However, at the current time, in your Maps folder you have four lightning TGA files with alpha. In essence, you need to create mini animations with them to insert into the Environment Map composite. To do so, you will create an Image File List (IFL). (An *IFL* is a text file that lists a group of bitmaps for 3ds max to load in sequence.)

1. With **04FH04.max** loaded, open the Track View, right-click the Sound track, and choose Properties to open the Sound Options dialog. Click the Choose Sound button and load **\3ds4-ma\project1\sounds\FH-Lightning&Thunder.wav**. Click OK twice to close both dialogs.

   You need to return the animation's length to 390.

2. Click the Time Configuration button to open the Time Configuration dialog. In the Animation group, change the Start Time to **0** and the End Time to **390**. Click OK to close the dialog.

3. In the Track View, offset the Sound track's bar to start at frame 30. Scrub the time slider through the animation and listen for the lightning strikes at frames 152 and 262. Close the Track View.

4. If you have been using the maps directly from the CD in your scenes up to now, that's fine. If you want to create the IFL, however, you need to copy the following five files to your local hard drive and use them from that drive to create the IFL:

   \3ds4-ma\project1\maps\light01.tga

   light02.tga

   light03.tga

   light04.tga

   lightblack.tga

The reason you need to copy these files to your local drive is that you will be creating a text file with an .IFL. It is easiest to create and save the .IFL file in the same folder as the images, and you wouldn't be able to write it to the CD. With that said, you're ready create the IFL.

5. Open the Material Editor and select the **env** map (it's in the second preview slot).

You need to add a new layer to the Composite map for the lightning IFL.

6. Click the Set Number button and change the Number of Maps to **4**. Click OK to close the dialog. Click the Map 4 button to open the Material\Map Browser. Choose Bitmap and click OK to close the browser.

7. Navigate the folder with the five tga files you copied. Select **light01.tga** and check Sequence (as shown in Figure 4.51).

Checking Sequence instructs the dialog to automatically generate an .IFL file in the folder using all the images in that numbered sequence.

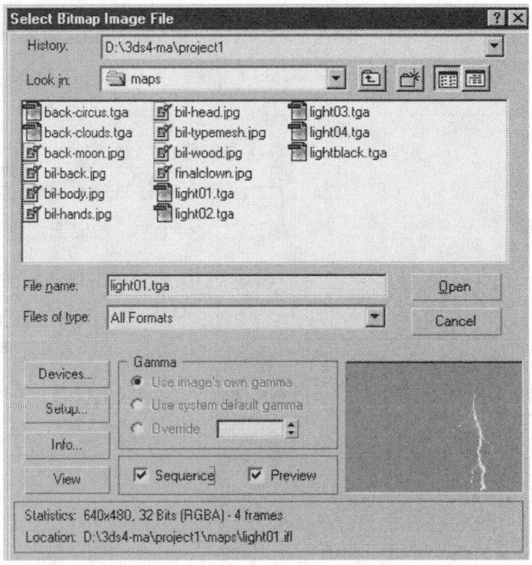

8. Click Open to open the Image File List Control dialog (shown in Figure 4.52). Click OK to accept the default settings and close the dialog. Name this map **env-lightning** (see Figure 4.53).

Here you can determine how the IFL should be created. The default settings are fine. You are going to manually edit the IFL yourself.

The lightning images need to be screen mapped. Otherwise, they will not appear correctly in the final rendering.

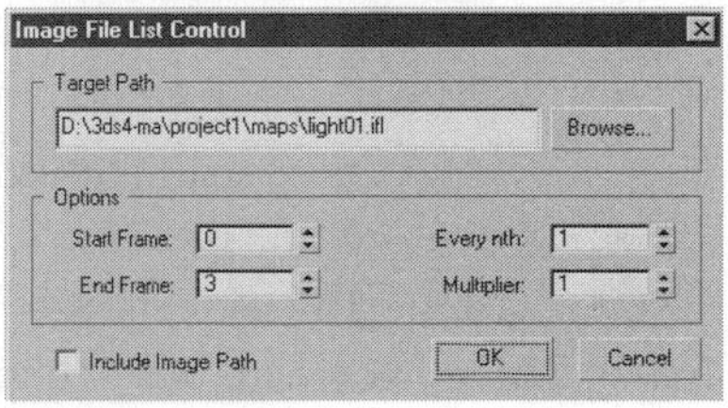

9. In the Coordinates rollout, change the mapping to Environ Mapping:Screen. Deselect Premultiplied Alpha in the Bitmap Parameters rollout.

The preview slot is an ugly shade of pink/purple. This is because the lightning tgas was created on this color background. Because the background is not black, the color shows up in the preview slot because you are using Premultiplied Alpha. If you deactivate that, everything should be fine.

Figure 4.51
In the Select Bitmap Image File dialog, choose light01.tga and check Sequence.

Figure 4.52
The Image File List Control dialog.

Ahh, there. That looks much better. If you scrub the time slider through the animation and watch the preview slot, you will notice that the four lighting images continue to loop throughout the entire animation. That's not good. You will now edit the IFL to cue the lightning to the sound.

To edit the IFL, you need to open a text editor program. I generally use the Notepad program (Start/Programs/ Accessories/Notepad).

10. Open Notepad. Choose File, Open and in the Open dialog, change Files of Type to All Files. Navigate to the folder to which you copied the four lightning images, choose **light01.ifl**, and click Open to load the text (see Figure 4.54).

Here you could see the sequence of images. When 3ds max 4 reads this IFL, it applies light01.tga to frame 0, light02.tga to frame 1, light03.tga to frame 2, and light04.tga to frame 3, and then it loops back to light01.tga at frame 4, and so on.

You don't want to have anything for the first 150 frames, so you need a blank image. That's what the fifth image you copied over (lightblack.tga) was for. It's a small targa file that is black with blank alpha. You can place this targa at the beginning of the IFL to create the first 150 non-lightning frames.

You could list lightblack.tga 150 times before the lightning images, but 3D Studio Max give you an easier way.

11. In Notepad, place the cursor before the "l" in "light01.tga" and press Enter to create a blank first line (as shown in Figure 4.55). In the first line, type **lightblack.tga 150** (see Figure 4.56).

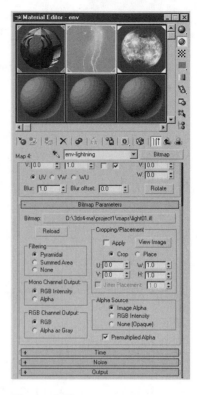

Figure 4.53
The env-lightning map.

Figure 4.54
Light01.ifl is loaded into Notepad.

Figure 4.55
The IFL with a blank
first line.

Figure 4.56
Add lightblack.tga 150 to
the IFL.

Lightblack.tga is now the first image in the IFL. By creating a space after the image and including the number 150, you tell 3ds max to hold that image for the first 150 frames. After that, it will move down the IFL to the next image. When it reaches the end of the IFL, it will loop back.

You want to see the lightning targa images in more than one frame each, and you want to have a few appear more than once. So edit the IFL to create a good lightning animation.

12. Edit the IFL to match the one shown in Figure 4.57.

    Now you have a ten-frame lightning flash animation. This will look great for the first flash at frame 150.

13. Save your IFL in Notepad and keep Notepad open.

14. In the Material Editor, click the Reload button in the Bitmap Parameters rollout.

    Scrub the time slider through frames 0–170, and you will see no lightning during frames 0–150. But throughout frames 150–159, you will see alternating streaks of lightning. After frame 160, there is no lightning because the IFL is looping. You need to finish the IFL now to create the second round of lightning at frame 270.

Figure 4.57
Edit your IFL to look
like this.

15. Edit your IFL to match Figure 4.58.

16. In Notepad, save your IFL and close Notepad.

   After the first lightning sequence, which ends at frame 160, you added a "lightblack.tga 100" entry. This adds a black image for a hundred frames, taking you to the start of the next lightning strike at frame 260. At the end of the IFL, you added a "lightblack.tga 1000" entry. That is just to hold the last frame well beyond the animation to prevent an accidental loop if you ever have to extend the Funhouse animation.

17. In the Material Editor, click Reload in the Bitmap Parameters rollout. Preview the environment by clicking the Make Preview button to open the Create Material Preview dialog (see Figure 4.59). Click OK to accept the default settings.

   When the preview finishes rendering, it will automatically open and play. You will see the lightning strike twice.

18. Close the Material Editor.

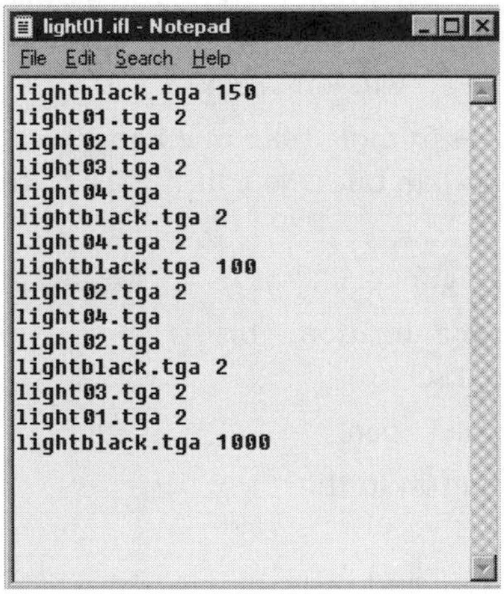

Figure 4.58
The finished IFL.

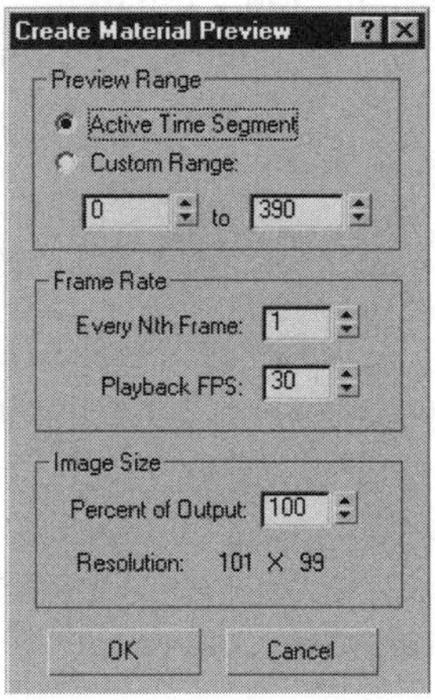

Figure 4.59
The Create Material
Preview dialog.

Rendering the Animation

The animation is finished. Rendering is the fun part…if, that is, you've done the work correctly.

Exercise 4.12   Rendering the Animation

You need to do just two things before you render the animation: Place the final audio in the Track View and add an Image Output Event to the Video Post Queue. So change the audio first.

1. Open the Track View. Right-click the Sound track's label and choose Properties. Click the Choose Sound button and choose **\3ds4-ma\ project1\sounds\FH-FullMix.wav**. Click OK twice to exit the dialogs.

2. Offset the Sound track's bar to start at frame 30 (as shown in Figure 4.60). Close the Track View.

Figure 4.60
In Track View, the FH-FullMix.wav is offset to frame 30.

Now set an output image event in the Video Post Queue, and then you can render this animation.

3. From the toolbar, choose Rendering/Video Post... to open the Video Post dialog.

4. Click the Add Image Output Event button to open its dialog (shown in Figure 4.61).

5. Click the Files button and choose an output destination, such as **\3ds4-ma\project1\images\ FH-Done.avi**. Click OK to close the Add Image Output Event dialog.

6. Save your work as **04FH05.max**.

7. When you are ready to render your animation, click the Execute Sequence button to open the Execute Video Post dialog. Make sure the Range is set to 0 to 390, choose an Output Size (such as 320×240), and click Render.

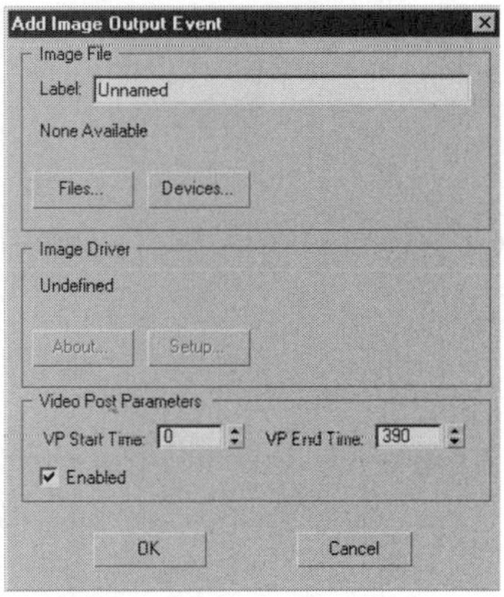

Figure 4.61
The Add Image Output Event dialog.

In Conclusion

Kick your feet up on your desk, turn on Jerry Springer, and relax for a while. When the animation is finished, call Mr. Boss, Vince, and Gordon over for a look. They will have to be duly impressed.

Part 2

2002 Vote Machine

The last presidential election brought to the forefront an issue that needed to be addressed: how the votes are recorded and counted. At MSNBC, we're already thinking about the next race, and so begins the scenario for the second project: "Congratulations on finishing your first project." Mr Boss says as he pulls you aside, "The Lynch family was thrilled with the funhouse animation. They didn't stop raving about it, and they can't wait to incorporate your animation into their new commercials. Great job!"

"For your next job, you will be working with Victor. He's working on a concept for an animation for a hip startup cable channel. The channel will be hitting the airwaves third quarter 2001, and the staff is preparing an identity for their United States 2002 elections. The station identity is very youthful and trendy. Keeping in that vein, Victor is putting together some interesting designs. You should stop by his workstation when you get a chance. Once again, great job on the 'Funhouse' project."

"Thanks Mr. Boss," you reply as he walks toward his next victim. Reflecting on what Mr. Boss said, you become excited at the notion of working with Victor. You've admired his work since your first day. Now you finally have the opportunity work on a project with him. You finish organizing your workplace and head over to talk to Victor.

Chapters 5 through 8 step you through the creation of the animation for a computerized voting machine.

Chapter 5

Building the Vote Machine

"Hello Victor, Mr. Boss sent me over to see what you are putting together for the 2002 elections. I have admired your work since I started here, and I am very excited to finally be working with you."

"Cool! Yeah dude, Bossman told me all about your work. He says you know your stuff. Here, let me take a second to show you what I'm up to."

Victor proceeds to open his version of Adobe Illustrator and loads a file (shown in Figure 5.1). "I heard the client wanted to be slightly lighthearted about the elections, especially after what happened last time around with Bush and Gore. So I invented this new computerized voting machine."

Figure 5.1
Victor's preliminary illustration of the 2002 vote machine.

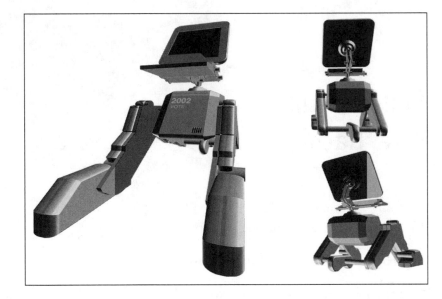

Victor then tells you that he is still working on the concept, but the vote machine isn't going to change. He explains that he built the machines in Illustrator using a 3D simulation plug-in. Because it was created in Illustrator, he can save his profiles so you can simply extrude and bevel them in 3ds max.

"Hey Victor, thanks for everything. I am looking forward to seeing your storyboards when they are finished." You take the disc with the Illustrator file and Victor's preliminary illustration back to your workstation.

In this chapter, you'll gain experience in the following areas:

- Importing Adobe Illustrator files
- Scaling with an XForm modifier
- Working in Shape sub-object level
- Welding vertices

Using an Adobe Illustrator File to Create the 2002 Vote Machine

As you walk back to your workstation with disc in hand, your mind whirls with the concept of the 2002 Vote machine. "It's kinda humorous," you think to yourself, "and very clever." The style is certainly modern; it looks like something straight from *The Jetsons*. As you sit down in your chair, you clear your mind and focus on the work at hand.

Settling into your chair, you put the disc Victor gave you into your machine. You think to yourself, "Well, I guess I'll import that Illustrator file now."

Exercise 5.1   Importing an Adobe Illustrator File

To start putting this project together, You can import Victor's Adobe Illustrator file as a single shape into the scene.

1. Choose File, Reset to reset 3ds max.

2. Select File, Import to open the Select File to Import dialog. Change the Files of Type entry to Adobe Illustrator (*.AI). Navigate to the \3ds4-ma\ project2\ai folder, choose **computer.ai**, and click Open to import the Illustrator file. The AI Import dialog opens (see Figure 5.2).

   Because you just reset 3ds max, it doesn't matter what you choose here; one option merges into the current scene (which is currently reset), and the other basically resets the scene and then imports the shapes.

3. Leave Merge Objects with Current Scene active and click OK to accept the default. The Shape Object dialog opens (see Figure 5.3).

   The Import Shapes As options are pretty straightforward. The shapes are imported either as one shape with multiple spline sub-objects or as individual shape objects with one spline each. You will leave the Illustrator file as a Single Object and decide later what items need to be individual shapes.

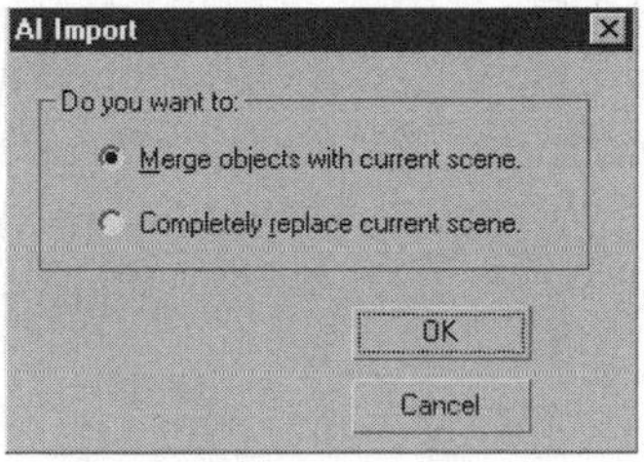

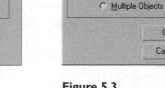

Figure 5.2
The import choices of the AI Import dialog.

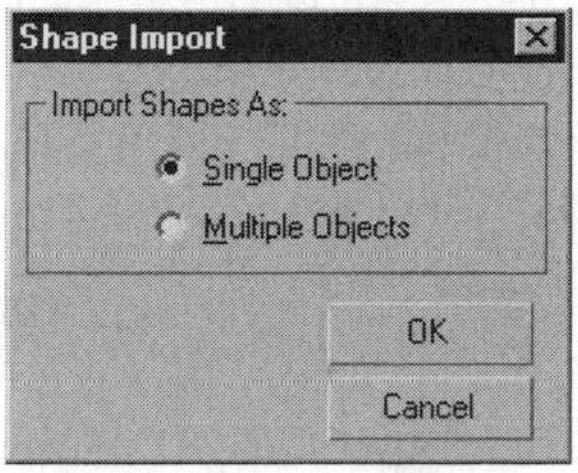

Figure 5.3
The Import Shapes As options of the Shape Import dialog.

4. In the Shape Import dialog, leave the default Single Object option active and click OK to import the shape (as shown in Figure 5.4). Rename the imported Illustrator shape **Vic01**.

Figure 5.4
Computer.ai is imported into 3ds max as one shape.

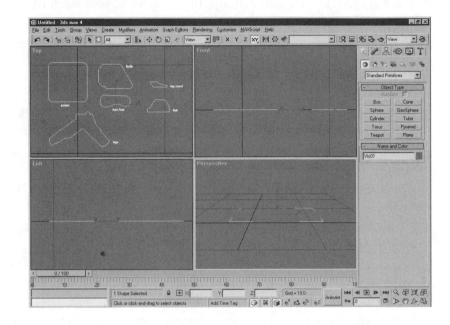

Correcting Problems That Occur in Imported Files

Often things aren't what they seem when you're importing Adobe Illustrator files. Sometimes the size of the object is wrong. Sometimes Bézier vertex handles are applied incorrectly. Another surprise often found in Illustrator imports are more vertices than are necessary to accomplish the shape. Some of these problems are the result of the Illustrator artist's working style; others are a direct result of the import process.

Scaling and Neatening the Imported Shape

It is important to examine the scale of the imported Illustrator file immediately after you import it. It has been my experience working in 3ds max that Illustrator files import amazingly small in the scene, even though they look fine in the viewports. To emphasize this point, you sometimes are going to conduct a little experiment.

Exercise 5.2   Exploring Two Methods for Correcting the Size of an Imported File

Measure the size of the imported Illustrator shape so you'll have a better understanding of what's going on here.

1. From the Create panel, choose Create, Helpers, Tape. While watching the Length value in the Create panel, drag the mouse in the Top view from the leftmost side of the imported splines to the rightmost side. Don't release the mouse button; just take note that the length of the tape is slightly over 15 units. Right-click to exit the tape creation.

   If you created a tape helper in your scene, you can select it and press the Delete key to delete it from the scene. The tape helper is very helpful when you need specific linear measurements. Often, you will only need to get a quick idea of the distance between two objects, for instance, so you could use the tape tool in the right-click non-permanent nature.

   So what did you learn? You learned that the shape is roughly 15 units across from left to right. What does that mean to you? It means that the shape isn't very large in the scene. The small size could have an adverse effect on your work down the road. Take a minute to examine why.

2. Make sure Vic01 is selected, open the Modify panel, and apply an Extrude modifier. In the Parameters rollout of the Extrude modifier, change the Amount to **1** (as shown in Figure 5.5).

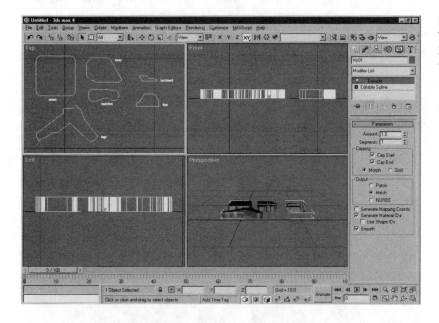

Figure 5.5
The Vic01 shape now has an extrusion of 1 unit applied.

The extrusion that resulted from an amount of 1 is far too large. When you're working on scenes, it's much easier to work in whole numbers than to keep enter decimal points. Therefore, you need to scale up the size of the shape; however, you have to be careful how you apply the scale.

You will apply the scale using two different techniques to understand the dangers of scaling the incorrect way.

3. In the Modify panel, delete the Extrude modifier from the Vic01 shape by clicking the Remove Modifier from the Stack button.

First, you will scale the Vic01 shape the correct way.

4. With Vic01 selected, apply an XForm modifier in the Modify panel. The XForm modifier allows you to apply transforms to objects before the rest of the stack affects them.

5. Activate the Select and Uniform Scale tool and activate Offset Mode Transform Type-In on the status bar. You should now be able to enter a value in only the X field of the Transform Type-In. With the XForm sub-object gizmo still active, enter X: **3000** percent in the Transform Type-In.

The XForm gizmo scales the shape to 3000 percent and the X: Value returns to 100 on the Transform Type-In (see Figure 5.6). There is no technical reason for choosing 3000 percent when scaling an Illustrator file. It's just a number that works with AI files. Now adjust the views to see the Vic01 shape again.

6. Click the Zoom Extents All button to view all of the Vic01 shape again (as shown in Figure 5.7).

It doesn't look much different than when you first imported it. However, to 3ds max, it looks much different: It's much larger. To see for sure, get the tape out again.

7. Choose Create, Helpers, Tape. Then, while watching the Length value in the Create panel, drag in the Top view from the leftmost side of the Vic01 shape to the rightmost side (see Figure 5.8). Right-click to cancel the tape helper.

The shape is about 460 units wide now, and you're ready to apply an Extrude modifier again to see how it looks.

Figure 5.6
The XForm modifier scales the Vic01 shape.

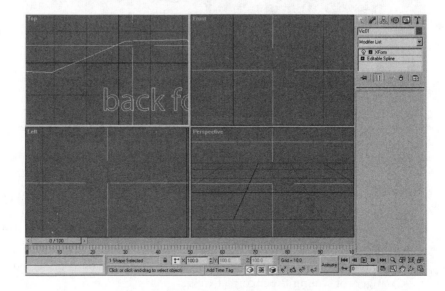

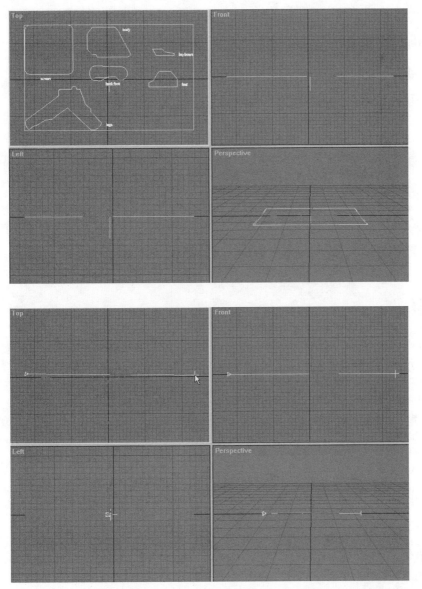

Figure 5.7
The scene with Zoom Extents All applied.

Figure 5.8
With the tape tool, measure the Vic01 shape in the Top view.

8. Make sure the Vic01 object is selected, and then open the Modify panel. Apply an Extrude modifier; the Amount should still be set to 1 (as shown in Figure 5.9).

The Extrude modifier applies an extrude with an amount of 1. Thanks to the scaling from the XForm gizmo, the Vic01 shape is much larger. This allows you to work with whole numbers when adjusting values in the Extrude and Bevel modifiers. Now see what would have happened if you had not applied the XForm before you scaled the shape 3000 percent.

Figure 5.9
The Extrude amount
of 1 is less obvious
now.

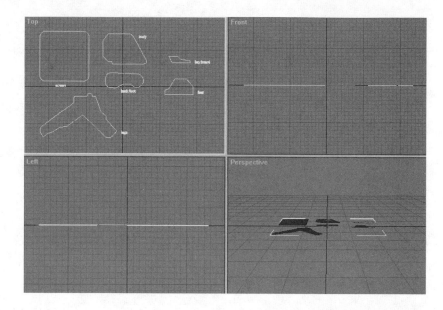

9. Activate the Select and Move tool (on the View XY-axis). In the Top view, Shift+drag the Vic01 object to the right. Place the new shape object slightly to the right of the original. Release the mouse button, and the Clone Options dialog opens (see Figure 5.10).

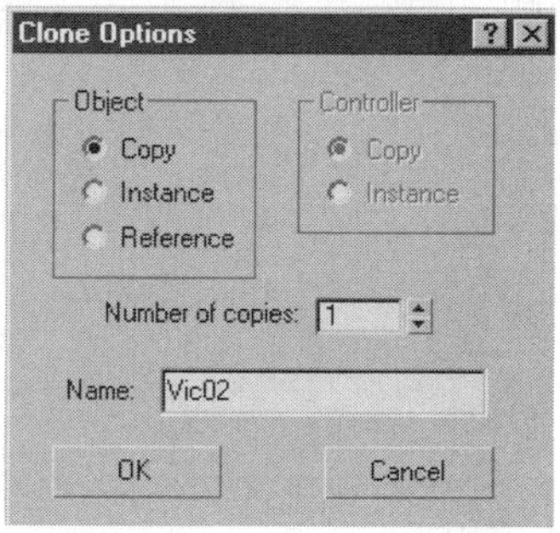

10. In the Clone Options dialog, leave the default settings and click OK to exit the dialog and clone the Vic01 shape. Click Zoom Extents All (see Figure 5.11).

    Now remove all the modifiers you just added from the Vic02 shape.

Figure 5.10
The Clone Options dialog.

11. Make sure the Vic02 shape is selected and open the Modify panel. Make sure the Extrude modifier is active and click the Remove modifier from the stack button to delete it. The XForm modifier should be selected now. Click the Remove modifier from the stack button to delete it (see Figure 5.12).

    When the modifiers have been removed from the Vic02 shape, it returns to its original tiny state. Now see what would have happened if you hadn't used the XForm modifier to scale the shape.

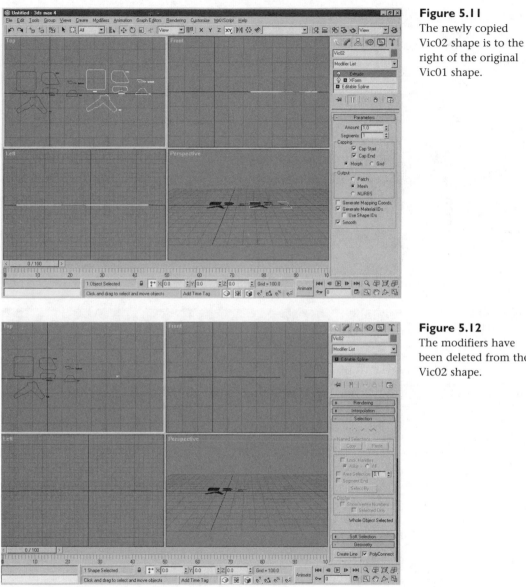

Figure 5.11
The newly copied Vic02 shape is to the right of the original Vic01 shape.

Figure 5.12
The modifiers have been deleted from the Vic02 shape.

12. With the Vic02 shape selected, activate the Select and Uniform Scale tool; Offset Mode Transform Type-In is still active. Enter X: **3000** to scale the Vic02 shape up 3000 percent (as shown in Figure 5.13).

Great, now you're back where you started.

13. With Vic02 selected, apply an Extrude modifier. Make sure that the Amount is 1 (as shown in Figure 5.14).

Figure 5.13
The Vic02 shape is
now 3000 percent
larger again.

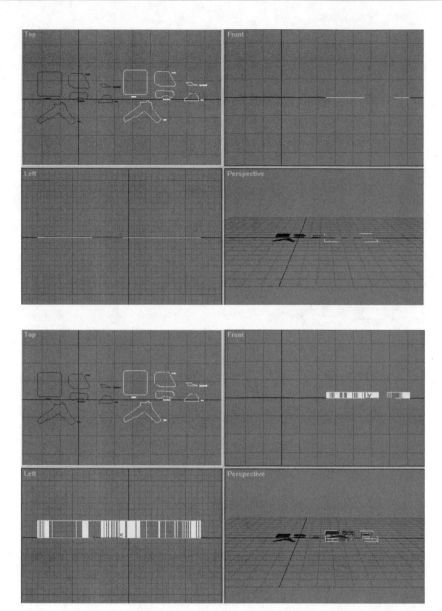

Figure 5.14
The Vic02 shape has
an Extrude of 1
applied.

Both shapes have an Extrude modifier with an amount of 1 applied to them.
The shape on the left was scaled up using an XForm modifier, applying the
extrude after the scale transform. The shape on the right was scaled up without an XForm modifier, so the extrude was applied before the scale transform.

Now that you know the importance of scaling using the XForm modifier,
you can clean up your scene a little.

14. With Vic02 selected, choose Edit, Delete to delete it from the scene. Click Zoom Extents All.

You no longer need the Extrude modifier on the Vic01 object, so go ahead and remove it.

15. Select Vic01 and in the Modify panel, click the Remove Modifier from the stack button to remove the Extrude modifier (see Figure 5.15).

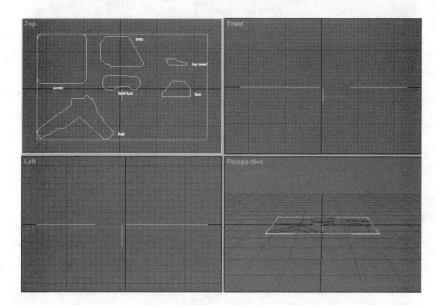

Figure 5.15
The Extrude modifier has been removed from the Vic01 shape.

Since you know you want to keep the scale that resulted from the XForm modifier, you will collapse the stack to Editable Shape.

16. In the Top view, right-click the Vic01 shape and choose Convert To, Convert to Editable Spline.

17. Save your work as **05VT01.max**.

Exercise 5.3   Using Shape Sub-Objects to Neaten Splines

Now that that Vic01 shape is the size in the scene that you desire, you can investigate the individual shapes to make sure everything is in order. Just sink your teeth into it.

1. Make sure **05VT01.max** is open and Vic01 is selected.

2. Click the Min/Max Toggle to maximize the Top view (as shown in Figure 5.16).

Now make a copy of the Vic01 shape to use as a backup in case of a mistake.

Figure 5.16
The Vic01 shape in
the maximized Top
view.

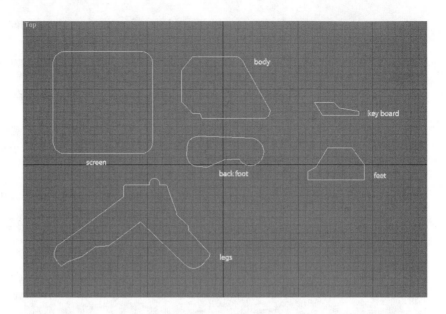

3. Select Edit, Clone to open the Clone Options dialog. Leave Copy selected, change the name to **Vic01-b** (as shown in Figure 5.17), and click OK to close the dialog and create the clone.

   The Vic01-b object is now selected, but you want to make sure it's a dark color when it's not selected.

4. Click the color swatch to the right of its name in the Modify panel to open the Object Color dialog (see Figure 5.18), and then choose a color. I usually choose dark purple, the fourth from the bottom left.

   As a default, you should deselect Assign Random Colors in the dialog. That way, no matter what shape or object you create, it will be created with the active color in the Object Color dialog.

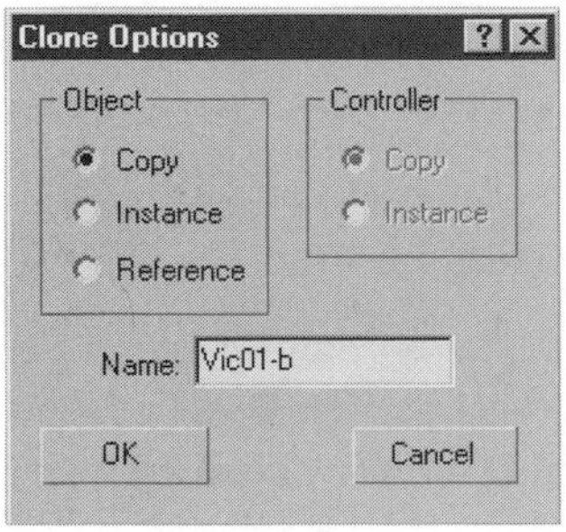

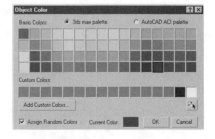

Figure 5.17
The Clone Options dialog for
the Vic01-b object.

Figure 5.18
The Object Color dialog for the
Vic01-b shape.

5. Deselect Assign Random Colors and click OK to close the dialog.

   Your backup shape is still selected; you need to select the original Vic01 shape.

6. Press H to open the Select Objects dialog, choose Vic01 (as shown in Figure 5.19), and click Select to close the dialog.

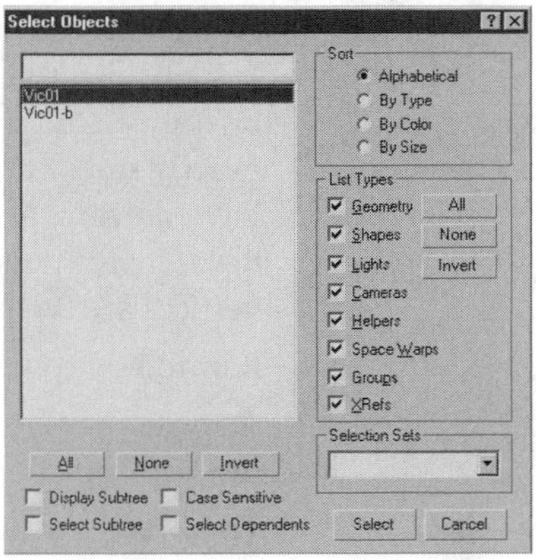

Improving the Screen

Because it is the most simple of the splines, you'll start your investigation with the screen spline. You will need to examine the shape and vertex count to make sure the shape will create a perfect object when you bevel it.

Figure 5.19
The Select Objects dialog with Vic01 selected.

Exercise 5.4   Removing Extra Verticies

Using sub-object mode, you will investigate the vertices of the screen shape and delete any extras you might find.

1. Right-click the Top view's label and deselect Show Grid. Use the Pan and Zoom tools to fill the Top view with the screen spline. Then activate Vertex sub-object mode (as shown in Figure 5.20).

   You can already see that your work is cut out for you. Only eight vertices are needed to create this rounded-cornered rectangle shape. To the eye, there are more than that. See how many are actually there.

2. Drag a rectangular selection around the screen spline to select all its vertices, paying attention to the number of vertices indicated in the Modify panel (shown in Figure 5.21).

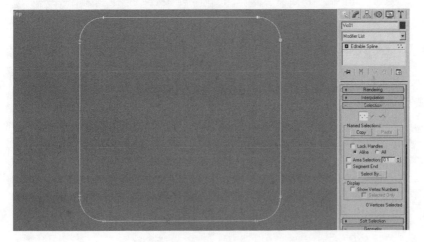

Figure 5.20
The screen shape is full in the Top view.

Notice the very bottom of the Selection rollout in the Modify panel. It informs you that there are 20 vertices selected on the shape. There should be only eight. Where did the rest of these vertices come from? You're not exactly sure, but you do know that they were all created in Illustrator and have nothing to do with the import process. Your best guess is that Victor used Boolean operations in Illustrator to join shapes and the miscellaneous vertices are the unfortunate byproduct.

Regardless, you need to delete the unwanted vertices.

3. Activate the Select Object tool. Drag a rectangular selection around the vertices on top of the left vertical segment (see Figure 5.22).

The Modify panel informs you that two vertices are selected. That makes it simple. You only need to delete one.

Figure 5.21
All the vertices of the screen spline are selected.

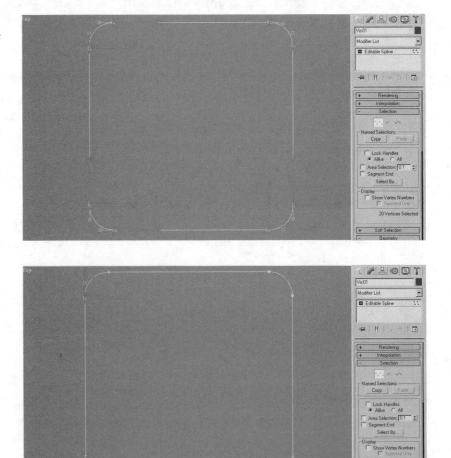

Figure 5.22
Two vertices are selected in the Top view.

4. Use the Select Object tool to select one of the two previously selected vertices. Press the Delete key to delete the selected vertex.

Now you need to get rid of the rest of the unwanted vertices.

5. Using the Select Object tool and selecting unwanted vertices, delete the unwanted vertices leaving only eight behind.

You might use Figure 5.23 to remind you where all the vertices are. Remember to leave eight vertices behind. Two or more vertices might be directly on top of one another. If that is the case, simply click one vertex at a time instead of dragging a selection around them. If you delete one too many, just click Undo.

Now you'll unify the vertices a little by changing their types.

6. Drag a rectangular selection around the eight remaining vertices to select them. Right-click one of the selected vertices and in the quad menu, change the vertex type to Smooth (as shown in Figure 5.24).

Now change them back to Bézier.

7. Right-click one of the selected vertices, and in the quad menu, change the vertex type to Bézier.

Now you can adjust the Bézier handles to create the original shape. You can use the backup shape you cloned as a template.

8. In the Selection rollout of the Modify panel, check Lock Handles. Now all the handles will adjust simultaneously.

9. Activate the Select and Move tool (View XY-axis). Adjust the lower Bézier handle of the vertex on top of the left vertical segment so that it is over the backup shape (see Figure 5.25).

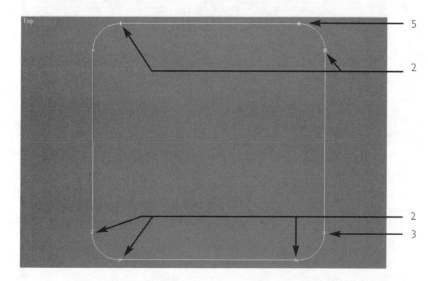

Figure 5.23
What looks at first glance like one vertex is actually a clump of 2, 3, or 5 vertices.

Figure 5.24
The eight remaining
vertices are now of
the Smooth type.

Figure 5.25
Every other Bézier
handle is correct.

Since Lock Handles was checked, all the handles moved concurrently. Doing this, you adjusted four vertices correctly and four vertices incorrectly. You need to deselect the vertices that are correct so you can adjust the ones that are misaligned.

10. Hold down the Alt key and click the vertices that are correctly aligned to deselect them. Use the Select and Move tool (View XY-axis) to adjust the remaining Bézier handles (as shown in Figure 5.26).

11. The screen shape is finished. Save your work as **05VT02.max**.

Figure 5.26
The correct position for the remaining Bézier handles.

Adjusting the Vertices in the Body

Now that the monitor spline is adjusted correctly, turn your attention to the body spline. All the splines of the vote machine are still in one shape, the Vic01 shape. You will separate them later when you are building the objects.

Exercise 5.5   Using the Weld Tool to Remove Unwanted Splines

Much like you did with the previous shape you edited, you will enter sub-object mode and investigate the vertices of the body shape. If you find any unnecessary vertices, you will be sure to delete them.

1. Make sure that **05VT02.max** is loaded and Vic01 is selected. Using the Pan and Zoom tools, adjust the Top view to observe the body spline. In the Modify panel, activate Vertex sub-object level (as shown in Figure 5.27).

2. Select all the vertices of the body shape, but do not select any of the vertices of the word "body" (see Figure 5.28).

Tip

You can use the Ctrl+click or the Ctrl+drag rectangular selection method to select. You can also Alt+click or Alt+drag to deselect vertices.

Notice in the Selection rollout of the Modify panel that 14 vertices are selected. If you were to go around and count how many vertices are needed to create the shape, you would count only 10. Some of the unnecessary vertices are obviously visible in the Top view. Other vertices are mysteriously stacked on top of one another, as you saw before when you were working on the monitor spline.

Figure 5.27
The body spline is visible in the Top view.

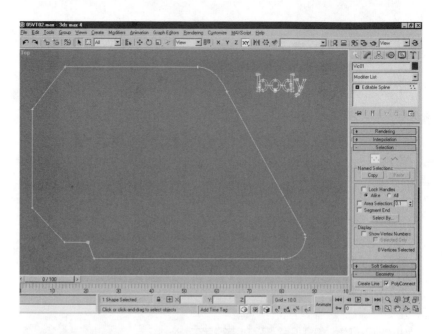

Figure 5.28
The 14 vertices of the body spline are selected.

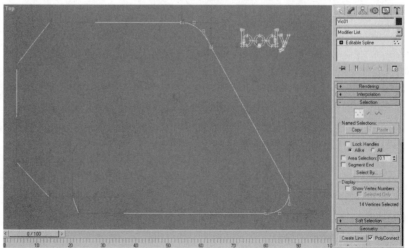

As you recall, when working on the monitor shape, you had to go around the shape and carefully check for the unnecessary vertices. There is an easier way to accomplish this—by using the Weld tool.

3. With all the vertices of the body spline selected, open the Geometry rollout in the Modify panel. Change the Weld value to **2** and click the Weld button (see Figure 5.29).

The Weld tool unites all the selected vertices within a 2-unit area of one another. All the vertices are then deselected. If you select all the vertices again, there will be only 10.

4. Re-select all the vertices of the body spline.

In the Selection rollout of the Modify panel, you can see that 10 vertices are selected (see Figure 5.30). Good. Well that was certainly easier than clicking around trying to find all the extra vertices.

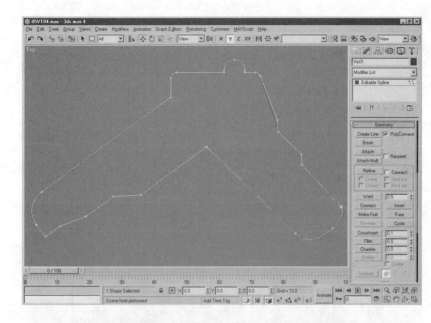

Figure 5.29
The selected vertices after a weld of 2 units is applied.

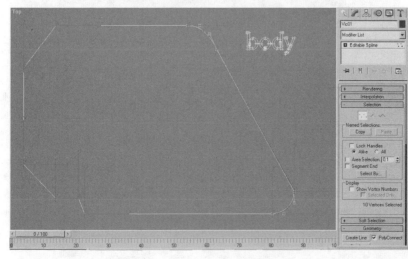

Figure 5.30
The 10 remaining vertices of the body shape are selected.

Even though the spline is acceptable for use, the perfectionism takes over—you cave in and start adjusting the remaining vertices. Notice that the vertices on the left side of the shape do not have tangent handles; this is because they are corner vertices. These vertices should remain this type.

The tangent handles of the four Bézier vertices are not as perfect as they could be. This is because one handle is directly on top of the vertex and the other is stretched out correctly. Make that adjustment now.

5. Alt+drag a rectangular selection around the six corner vertices to deselect them.

   Only the four Bézier vertices are selected now (as you can see in Figure 5.31).

   Now you'll temporarily change their vertex type to even out the length of the handles.

6. Right-click one of the selected vertices and choose Smooth from the quad menu.

   The vertices change from Bézier to Smooth (see Figure 5.32). Now you can change the vertices back to Bézier and adjust the tangent handles.

Figure 5.31
The four Bézier vertices are selected.

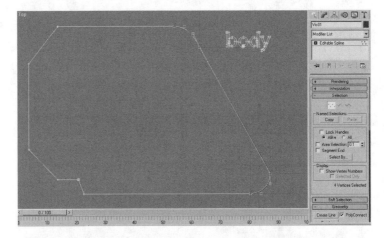

Figure 5.32
The selected vertices have been changed from Bézier to Smooth.

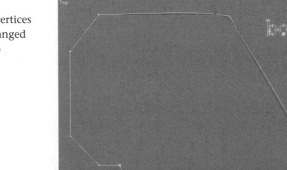

7. Right-click one of the selected vertices and choose Bézier from the quad menu. Activate the Select and Move tool (View XY-axis), turn off Lock Handles, and adjust the tangent handles to create the correct shape (shown in Figure 5.33).

The body shape is finished, and you adjusted it much more efficiently than you did the monitor shape—thanks to the Weld tool.

8. Save your work as **05VT03.max**.

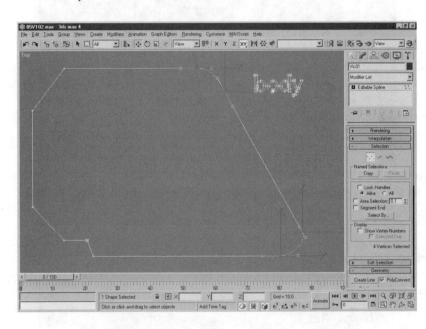

Figure 5.33
The Bézier tangent handles are in the correct configuration.

Working on the Back Foot

As you continue to examine the vote machine shapes, you turn your attention to the back foot shape.

Exercise 5.6   Removing Unwanted Vertices

Here you will examine the back foot shape to find unwanted vertices (as you did for the first two shapes). You will delete any unwanted vertices you find.

1. With **05VT03.max** loaded, make sure Vic01 is selected and Vertex sub-object is active in the Modify panel. Use the Pan and Zoom tools to observe the back foot spline (shown in Figure 5.34).

Just a quick glance at this spline, and you see that it contains far more vertices than are needed to generate the shape. Get rid of the unnecessary vertices.

2. Drag a rectangular selection around all the vertices of the back foot spline.

The Selection rollout informs us that 23 vertices are selected (see Figure 5.35).

See if you can use the Weld tool to remove some of the extraneous vertices.

3. In the Geometry rollout, make sure the Weld value is **2** and click the Weld button. Drag a rectangular selection around the back foot shape to select the remaining vertices (as shown in Figure 5.36).

Figure 5.34
The back foot spline in the Top view.

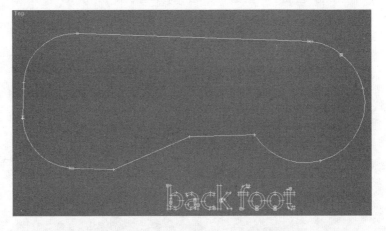

Figure 5.35
The 23 selected vertices of the back foot spline.

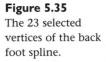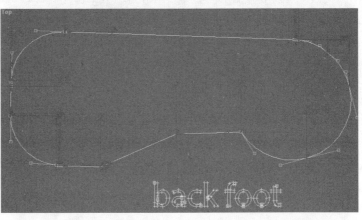

Figure 5.36
The remaining 11 vertices of the back foot spline.

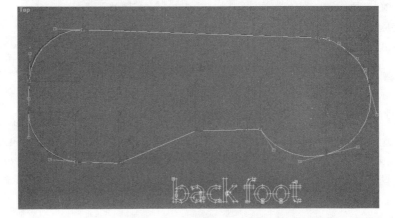

The Weld tool has removed 12 superfluous vertices from the back foot shape. You need to adjust the remaining vertices now. There is an unnecessary vertex in the upper-right of the back foot shape; delete that one first.

4. Select the vertex at 1 o'clock (shown in Figure 5.37) and press the Delete key to delete the vertex.

5. Activate the Select and Move tool (View XY-axis), select all the vertices of the back foot shape, change their vertex types to Smooth, and then change their types back to Bézier (see Figure 5.38).

   Having one XY-axis on each vertex of the spline can be annoying. But you can change how the axis is displayed.

6. On the toolbar, change Use Pivot Point Center to Use Selection Center (see Figure 5.39).

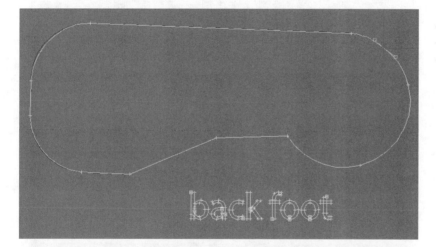

Figure 5.37
The unwanted vertex is selected; death is eminent.

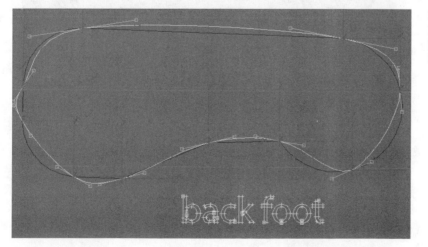

Figure 5.38
Every vertex of the back foot spline is Bézier type.

Only one red XY-axis appears in the Top view now. That's great.

Now that you can see what you are doing more clearly, you can continue to adjust the shape. Two vertices of the shape should actually be the Corner type, so go change them back.

7. Select the two hard corner vertices of the back foot spline (shown in Figure 5.40) and change their type to Corner.

The two vertices on the right curve are not arranged correctly for the curve they create. As a general rule, you should place vertices on a curve at 12, 3, 6, and 9 o'clock positions. So go ahead and fix that.

Figure 5.39
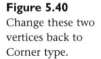
The Use Pivot Point Center flyout is now assigned to Use Selection Center.

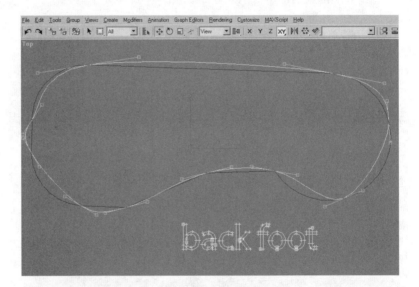

Figure 5.40
Change these two vertices back to Corner type.

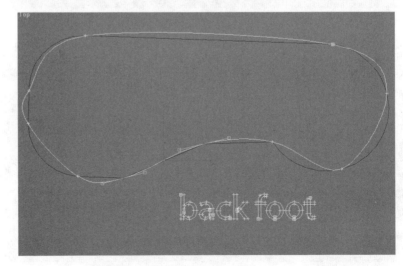

8. Using the Select and Move tool (View XY-axis), place the vertices on the right side curve appropriately (as shown in Figure 5.41).

The vertex to the left of the vertices you just changed needs attention as well (see Figure 5.42).

9. Select the vertex indicated in Figure 5.42 and change its type to Corner (see Figure 5.43).

The tangent handles of the vertex to the right of the vertex you just adjusted are causing the curve of the segment between them to overshoot the desired camber. To adjust this, you will adjust the tangent handle of the Bézier vertex to the right.

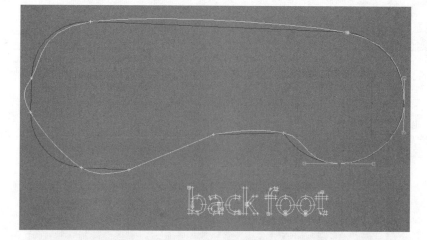

Figure 5.41
The two vertices are now arranged to optimize the curve.

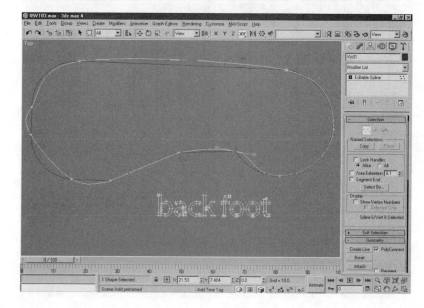

Figure 5.42
The type of this vertex needs to be changed.

10. Activate the Select and Move tool (View X-axis) and Shift+drag the tangent handle on the left to tighten the curve (see Figure 5.44).

When you Shift+dragged the tangent handle, you changed the type of the vertex from Bézier to Bézier corner. This allows the handles to be different lengths. You can now change the vertex back to Bézier, and the handles will remain the correct lengths. If you didn't change the vertex back to Bézier, there would be a seam in the smoothing when you beveled it later.

11. Right-click the vertex and choose Bézier from the quad menu.

12. Activate the Select and Move tool (View XY-axis), and using the techniques you learned previously, adjust the remaining vertices to appear like those in Figure in 5.45.

Note

Remember to change the types back to Bézier if you change the lengths of the handles.

13. Save your work as **05VT04.max**.

Figure 5.43
The vertex has been changed to Corner type.

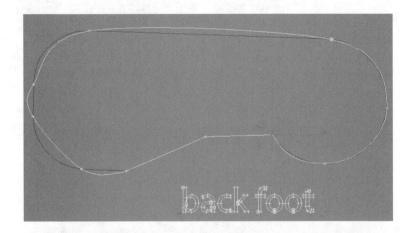

Figure 5.44
The tangent handles are correctly adjusted.

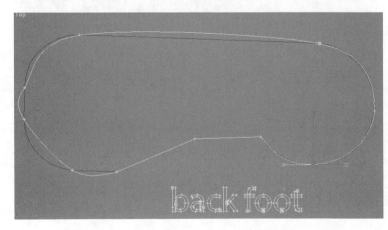

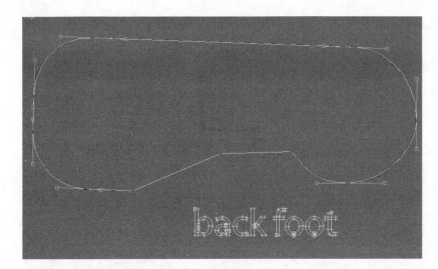

Figure 5.45
The correct placement
for all the vertices of
the back foot spline.

Fixing the Legs, Keyboard, and Remaining Feet

Three splines are left that you need to examine and edit: the legs, the keyboard, and the feet. The keyboard and the feet are going to be a breeze; the legs, on the other hand, will be the hardest of the shapes you've encountered so far. Because you're used to cleaning up this imported Illustrator file, and you know the Weld trick, this'll be a snap!

Exercise 5.7   Deleting Remaining Unwanted Vertices and Adjusting Shapes

You will now finish the imported shapes by checking for unwanted vertices and removing them. You will also adjust the shapes to return them to their original forms.

1. Make sure **05VT04.max** is open, Vic01 is selected, and Vertex sub-object is active. Using the Pan and Zoom tools, arrange the Top view to match Figure 5.46.

   Once again, a quick examination shows that many vertices need to be nixed. Let's start by welding the vertices. Because this spline contains more small details, you will need to lower the Weld value from 2 to .5 to keep the detail.

2. Drag a rectangular selection around the vertices of the leg spline. In the Geometry rollout of the Modify panel, enter a Weld value of **.5** and click the Weld button (see Figure 5.47).

   That removed most of the troublesome vertices but a few are left over. You can go in and manually delete them.

Figure 5.46
The Legs spline in the Top view.

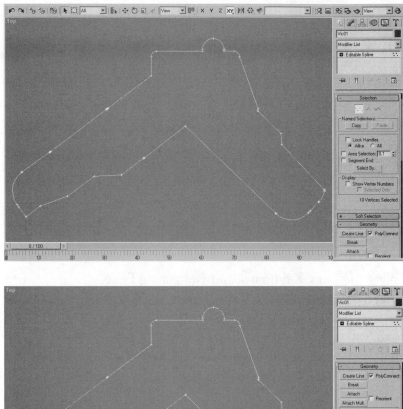

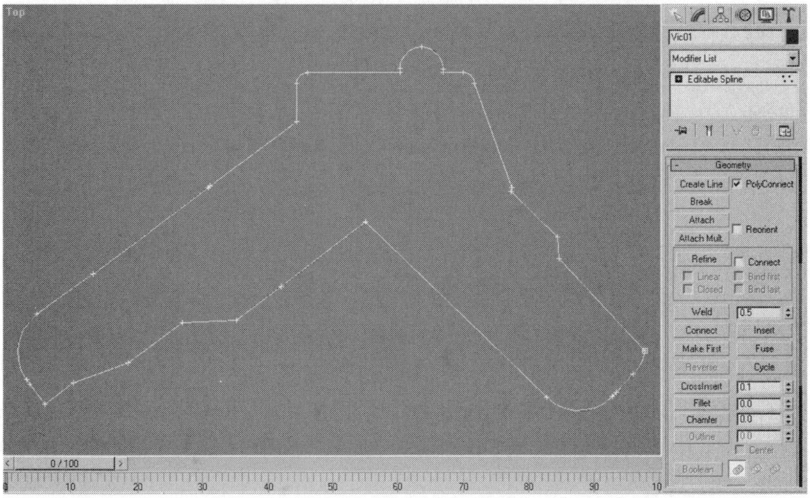

Figure 5.47
The vertices of the legs spline have been welded with a value of .5.

3. Select and delete the vertices indicated in Figure 5.48.

   There are no longer any unnecessary vertices on the legs spline. You know the drill: Change all the vertices to Smooth and then change them back to the appropriate types.

4. Drag a rectangular selection around all the vertices of the legs spline to select all the vertices. Right-click one of the selected vertices and choose Smooth from the quad menu. Then right-click one of the selected vertices again and change the type back to Bézier (as shown in Figure 5.49).

   Now change all the corner vertices into Corner type.

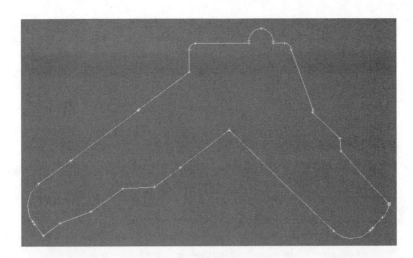

Figure 5.48
Select and delete
these vertices.

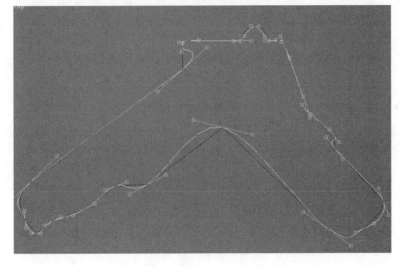

Figure 5.49
The vertices of the
legs shape are
changed to Bézier.

5. Select the vertices designated in Figure 5.50 and change their vertex types
   to Corner.

   Now that it's starting to take shape, it's time to turn your attention to the
   bump on the top of the spline.

6. Use the Zoom and Pan tools to view the knobby on the top of the legs
   spline. Using the Select and Move tool (View XY-axis), arrange the tangent
   handles to match those in Figure 5.51.

Note

Remember: To change the length of the handles, use Shift+drag. However, don't forget to
change the vertex type back to Bézier.

Figure 5.50
Select and change
these vertices to
Corner type.

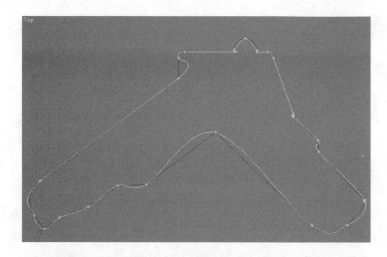

Figure 5.51
Arrange the tangent
handles of the
knobby to match
these vertices.

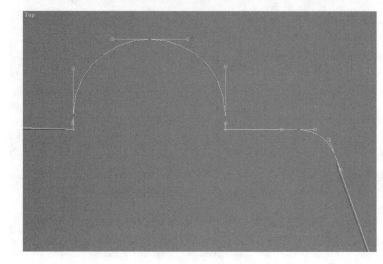

7. To finish adjusting the Bézier tangent handles, make sure the Select and
   Move tool is still active (View XY-axis) and adjust the vertices and tangent
   handles to match those shown in Figure 5.52. (You might have to move one
   or two of the vertices in the lower-right area to create the correct form.)

   One last thing: The line that steps down the upper-right side is not quite
   right. The vertices of the first step down are a little too close. Because you
   are going to bevel this shape, these two vertices might give you trouble in
   the future. Just move the top one a bit.

8. Activate the Select and Move tool (View XY-axis) and move the top vertex of
   the step upward and to the right to match what's shown in Figure 5.53.

   Having finished the leg shape, you're ready to move on to the last two
   shapes. They'll be easy.

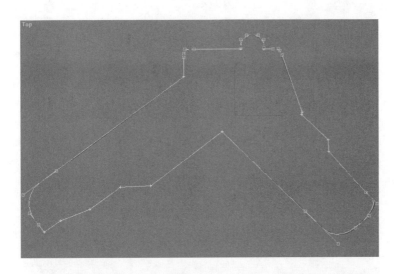

Figure 5.52
Adjust the Bézier tangent handles to match these.

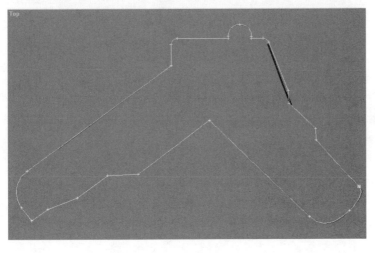

Figure 5.53
Use the Select and Move tool to move this vertex to this position.

9. Adjust the Top view to display the keyboard and feet shapes. Drag a rectangular selection around the vertices of both shapes to select all their vertices.

   The Selection rollout in the Modify panel says 13 vertices are selected. That's how many there should be. Great! You're done!

10. Save your work as **05VT05.max**.

In Conclusion

Whew! The imported Adobe Illustrator file is now in ship shape. Your grueling investigation of extra vertices has concluded. In the next chapter, you will use these shapes to create the vote machine objects.

Chapter 6

Assembling the 2002 Vote Machine

You lean back in your chair to relax your eyes for a moment and think about your progress. Now that you are through with the scrutinizing task of adjusting the imported Illustrator file, you realize the fruits of your labor are about to blossom.

You lean forward and acquaint your eyes with the monitor; as they focus on the interface, you prepare to erect the vote machine.

You realize that the vote machine will go together smoothly now that you have the necessary shapes to construct it. All you have to do is separate the splines into individual shapes and apply modifiers to produce the desired objects. It's time to work; you know what to do.

In this chapter, you gain experience in the following areas:

- Detaching splines from a shape
- Beveling and extruding modifiers
- Creating objects using Auto Grid
- Linking objects in a hierarchy
- Employing sub-object modeling techniques
- Smoothing groups and Auto Smooth
- Mirroring objects

Putting the Objects Together

Right now all you have are a bunch of great-looking splines in a shape. It's about time you start to turn them into something! Take a minute to review Victor's illustration of the vote machine (shown in Figure 6.1).

Figure 6.1
Victor's original illustration of the vote 2002 machine.

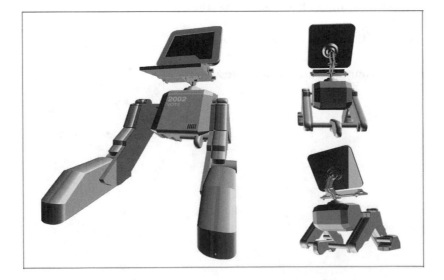

When Victor created the vote machine in Illustrator, he used a plug-in to create the appearance of extrusions and bevels in the shapes he provided for us. Even though you must spend a lot of time cleaning up the splines, Victor's hard work and creativity has made your job easier. All you need to do is re-create what Victor has made for you by extruding and beveling the shapes. If you examine the vote machine carefully, you will see, however, that Victor did not provide all the necessary shapes. You will have to create your own shapes for the monitor and keyboard armatures. In addition, you will also have to create a few cylinders.

The Body Object

Because the body object is the hub of the machine, you will model that object first. When the monitor's shape is detached from the Vic01 shape, you will add a bevel modifier to create the desired form for the object.

Exercise 6.1   Detaching a Spline from a Shape

Before you get started with your work on the body object, clean up the workspace a little. First, make some sense out of your visual space.

 1. Open **05VT05.max**. If you have not exited Vertex sub-object mode, return to the root of the Vic01 shape now. Select Zoom Extents All to view the entire shape (see Figure 6.2).

    Now get rid of the old backup copy you created in the beginning of the project.

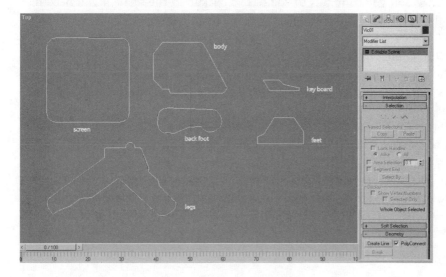

Figure 6.2
The Vic01 shape is full in the Top view again.

2. Open the Select Objects dialog by clicking the Select By Name button or by pressing the H key. Select Vic01-b (see Figure 6.3) and click Select to exit the dialog and select the backup shape.

3. Choose Edit > Delete or press the Delete key to delete the old shape.

4. Select the Vic01 shape and in the Modify panel, activate Spline sub-object level. Select the body spline and use the Select and Move tool (View XY-axis) to Shift+drag the spline to copy it (see Figure 6.3).

Figure 6.3
The body shape was copied by Shift+dragging it with the Select and Move tool.

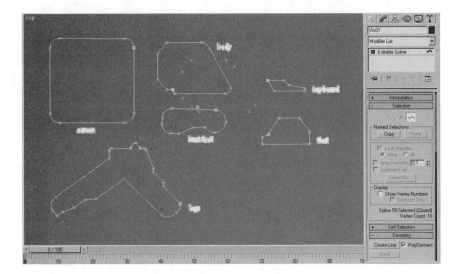

The reason you copy it is so you have a backup in the scene if you need it. Now you can detach the copied body shape from the Vic01 shape and create the object.

5. With Spline sub-object still active and the copied body spline selected, click the Detach button in the Geometry rollout of the Modify Panel. In the Detach dialog, enter the name **body01.** Click OK to detach the shape. Exit Spline sub-object mode.

The shape is now detached from the Vic01 shape and is ready to be turned into an object. Stand it up in the scene before you start.

6. Minimize the Top view either by pressing the W key or by clicking the Min/Max toggle button. Select the body01 shape, activate the Select and Rotate tool (View Z-axis), and change the Use Center Flyout to Use Selection Center. Press the Spacebar to activate the Selection Lock Toggle (see Figure 6.4).

7. In the Front view, drag the mouse downward and rotate the body01 shape
Z: **90** degrees (as shown in Figure 6.5).

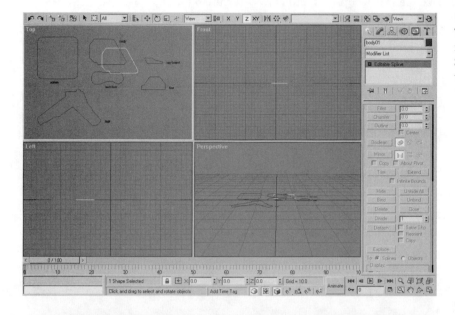

Figure 6.4
The body01 shape
is selected, and the
Select and Rotate
tool is active.

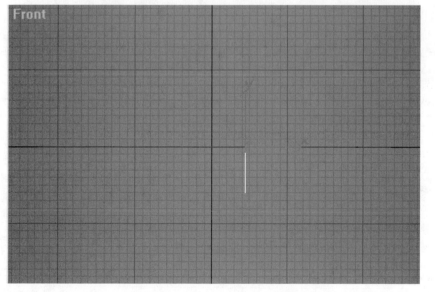

Figure 6.5
The body01 shape
has been rotated Z:
90 degrees in the
Front view.

8. To complete the standing up process, drag the mouse upward in the Left view to rotate the body01 object Z: **–90**.

The shape is now upright and correct (Figure 6.6).

Figure 6.6
The body01 shape is correctly oriented in the scene.

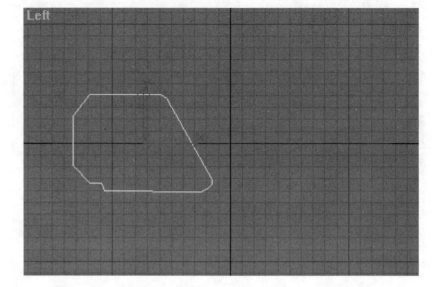

Finally, the fun part! You get to bevel this. Take a look at Victor's illustration one last time before you start.

9. Choose File > View Image File. In the View File dialog, choose \3ds4-ma\ project2\images\computer1.jpg and click Open to view the image.

Examine the body section of the machine. You will notice that a rather large bevel is placed on the sides. You can easily duplicate this. You might want to minimize this illustration but keep it open because you will be referring to it frequently.

10. With the body01 object still selected, open the Modify panel. Apply a Bevel modifier. Enter these settings in the Bevel Values rollout:

Level 1:   Height: **15** Outline: **5**

Level 2:   Height: **80** Outline: **0**

Level 3:   Height: **15** Outline: **–5**

Click Zoom Extents All Selected.

The object looks about right. However, if you look at the lower-right corner of the body01 object in the Left view, you can see that the corner could be a little tighter. You can adjust the outline of the bevel to make the adjustment.

11. In the Bevel Values rollout, drag the Start Outline value arrows downward until the value is –5.

The profile of the shape is reduced by five units, making the corner tighter (as shown in Figure 6.7).

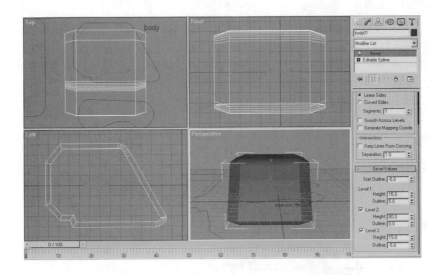

Figure 6.7
The finished body01 object.

The body01 object is finished. Now adjust its pivot point and place it correctly in the scene before you move on.

12. Open the Hierarchy panel and activate the Affect Pivot Only button. Click the Center to Object button to move the object's local pivot point to the center of its space. Deactivate the Affect Pivot Only button.

    Now position it to the center of the world.

13. Activate the Select and Move tool. In the Transform Type-In, change the position to XYZ: **0, 0, 0**. Click Zoom Extents All (see Figure 6.8).

14. Save your work as **06VT01.max**.

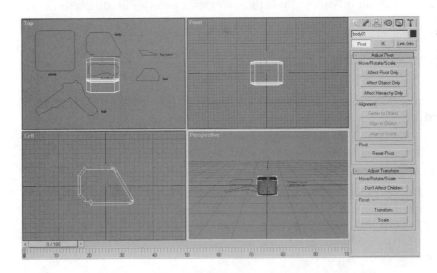

Figure 6.8
The body01 object is positioned in the center of the world.

The Legs

The next objects you will construct are the leg objects on either side of the body object. You will simply build one complete leg and then mirror it to the other side of the body object. If you view Victor's illustration of the machine closely, you will see that two leg objects actually create each leg (see Figure 6.9).

Figure 6.9
Combined, these two objects create one leg.

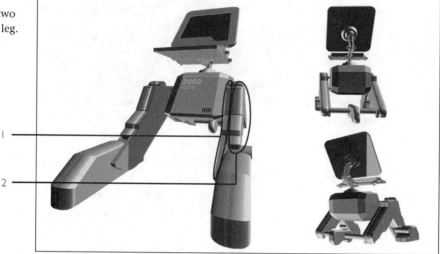

The first leg object is the long leg shape you already have from the Illustrator import. The other shape is a shorter modification of the long leg shape you already have. Focus your attention on the longer leg, and then you can modify it to create the second, shorter leg.

Exercise 6.2   Centering a Shape's Pivot

Detach the long leg object shape from the Vic01 shape and get started.

1. Make sure **06VT01.max** is open. Select the Vic01 shape (you may have to deactivate the Selection Lock Toggle). Open the Modify panel and activate Spline sub-object level. Activate the Select and Move tool (View XY-axis) and Shift+drag the leg shape in the Top view to copy it.

   Next you will detach the long leg shape from the Vic01 shape.

2. With the copied leg shape still selected, click the Detach button in the Geometry rollout of the Modify panel. In the Detach dialog, name the object **leglongR01,** and then click the OK button to detach the shape. Click the yellow Editable Spline bar in the Modify panel to return to the root of the Vic01 shape.

You need to make the leglongR01 shape stand up in the world, much like you did with the body01 shape.

3. Select the leglongR01 shape and activate the Select and Rotate tool (View Z-axis—Use Selection Center). Activate the Selection Lock toggle and in the Top view, drag upward to rotate the leglong01 shape Z: **–90** degrees (as shown in Figure 6.10).

The leg is now pointing forward, but it's still not standing up.

4. In the Front view, drag downward to rotate the leglongR01 shape Z: **90** degrees. Activate the Perspective view and use the Arc Rotate, Pan, and Zoom tools to get a better look at the scene (see Figure 6.11).

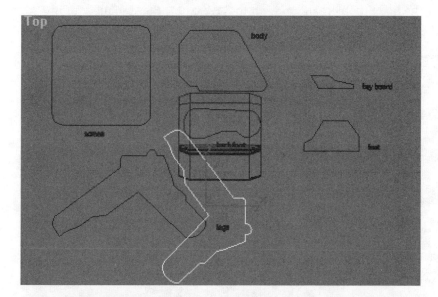

Figure 6.10
The leglongR01 shape is rotated –90 degrees in the Top view.

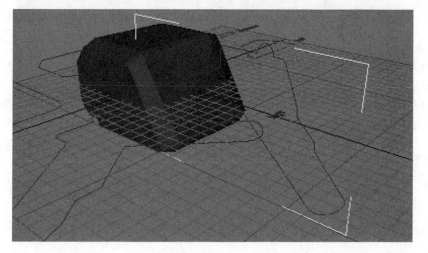

Figure 6.11
The Perspective view is Arc Rotated for a better view.

Before you proceed any further with creating the long leg object, center leglongR01's pivot to itself.

5. Open the Hierarchy panel and activate Affect Pivot Only. Click the Center to Object button.

   The pivot is now centered to the shape. Deactivate the Affect Pivot Only button. Now let's place the leg shape on the world's ground plane.

6. Activate the Select and Move tool and move the leglongR01 shape to XYZ: **–60, 0, 56** Absolute World. Click Zoom Extents All Selected to zoom in on the leglong01 shape.

   Now you need to lift the body01 shape into position.

7. Select the body01 object and move it to XYZ: **0, 17, 88** Absolute World (as shown in Figure 6.12).

Figure 6.12
The body01 object is in the correct position in conjunction with the leglong01 shape.

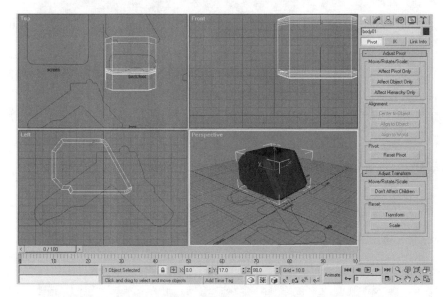

The vote machine is beginning to take form. To continue your work with the long leg object, it's time to turn this shape into an object.

8. Select leglongR01 shape. In the Modify panel, apply a Bevel modifier. In order to see the object more clearly in the Perspective view, right-click the Perspective view label and check Edged Faces (see Figure 6.13).

   Well, the leglongR01 shape is certainly beveled now! Because of the "sticky" settings, the bevels applied to the leglongR01 object are identical to those of the body01 object. That's okay, you can change the settings easily.

9. In the Bevel Values rollout of the Modify panel, change the settings to:

Start Outline: **0**

Level 1: Height: **1** Outline: **1**

Level 2: Height: **4** Outline: **0**

Level 3: Height: **1** Outline: **–1**

The leglongR01 object looks much better now (see Figure 6.14).

10. Save your work as **06VT02.max**.

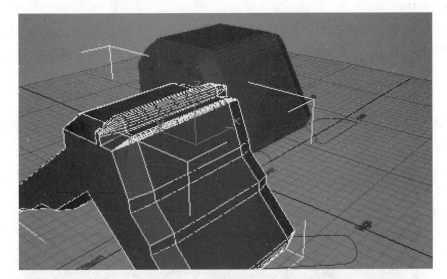

Figure 6.13
The beveled leglongR01 object in the Perspective view.

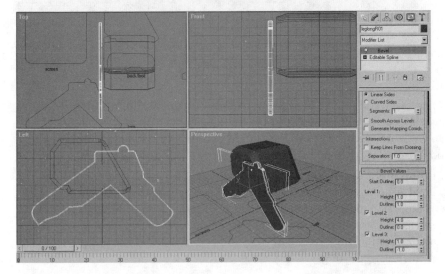

Figure 6.14
The leglongR01 shape has the correct bevel settings now.

Exercise 6.3   Working with the Parameters of the Bevel Modifier

As mentioned earlier, the short leg object is a slight modification on the long leg object. Therefore, creating it should be pretty easy. To create the short leg object, you will copy the long leg object, make modifications to its shape, and change the parameters of the Bevel modifier.

1. With **06VT02.max** still loaded make sure the leglongR01 object is selected. Choose Edit > Clone and in the Clone Options dialog, leave Copy selected and change the name to **legshortR01**. Click OK to close the dialog and create the copy.

   Now move the legshortR01 object into position.

2. Activate the Select and Move tool and move the legshortR01 object to XYZ: **–66, 0, 56** (as shown in Figure 6.15).

Figure 6.15
The legshortR01 object is next to the leglongR01 object.

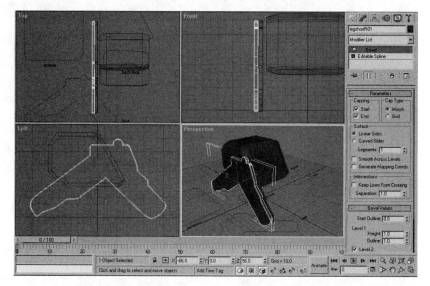

Now you need to make modifications to the shape to shorten the leg. Take another look at Victor's illustration \3ds4-ma\project2\images\computer1.jpg. On the vote machine in the lower-right corner, you can see a bump by the foot. You're going to add that now.

It is important to remember, however, this isn't an exact science. Victor created his illustration in Illustrator using a 3D simulation plug-in. The lens angles are different on all three of the illustrations in computer1.jpg. Basically, Victor's illustration is more of a visual reference, or instructions on how to assemble the piece. You will not be able to build it exactly the way it appears, but you will get it very close.

3. With legshortR01 selected, open the Modify panel and activate the Editable Spline event in the stack. Select Vertex sub-object mode, maximize the Left view, and use the Pan and Zoom tools to observe the front base of the leg.

Now to add the bump, you will add more vertices to the shape.

4. In the Geometry rollout, activate the Refine button and click to create the two vertices indicated in Figure 6.16. Right-click to exit Refine mode.

The Refine tool allows you to add vertices to the shape without affecting the appearance of the shape. The two vertices you add will act as anchors, holding the form of the shape as you move the vertices below them. However, there are three vertices below the two new vertices we added, and you need only two. So delete the extraneous one.

5. Select the vertex indicated in Figure 6.17 and press the Delete key to delete the vertex.

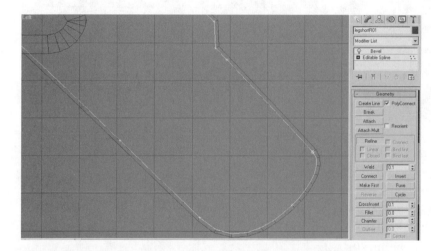

Figure 6.16
Activate Refine and click to add these two vertices.

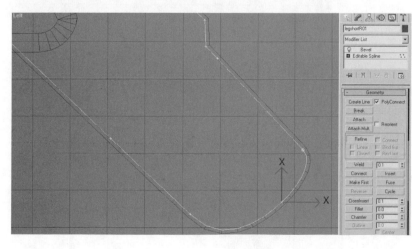

Figure 6.17
Select and delete this vertex.

Now to add the bump.

6. Activate the Select and Move tool (View XY-axis) and adjust the vertices and tangent handles to create the shape illustrated in Figure 6.18.

Figure 6.18
Adjust the vertices to match these.

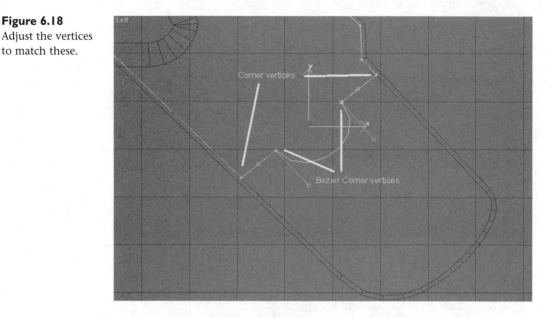

You have added the bump to the short leg shape. Pretty easy, wasn't it? All that's left to do now is to modify the bevel.

7. Minimize the Left view using the Min/Max toggle. In the Modify panel, return to the root of the legshortR01 shape and click the Bevel modifier in the stack to activate it. Change the Bevel Values to the following:

Start Outline: **0**

Level 1: Height: **4** Outline: **2**

Level 2: Height: **5** Outline: **0**

Level 3: Height: **4** Outline: **−2**

As you can see in Figure 6.19, the object is starting to take form.

The object looks pretty good. However, in Victor's illustration, the bevel is smoothly rounded, not linearly stepped. You can take care of that.

8. With the legshortR01 object selected, open the Parameters rollout in the Modify panel. In the Surface group, activate Curved Sides, change Segments to **2**, and check Smooth Across Levels (see Figure 6.20).

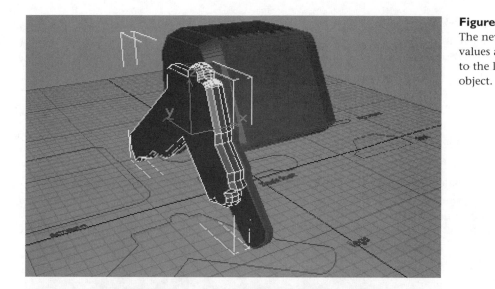

Figure 6.19
The new bevel values are applied to the legshortR01 object.

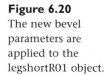

Figure 6.20
The new bevel parameters are applied to the legshortR01 object.

The Curved Sides parameter instructs the bevel to be rounded instead of linear. However, without more than one Segment, the curved effect is not apparent on the model because there are not enough faces. Smooth Across Levels applies the same smoothing group to all the levels of the bevel, so the smoothing does not step when the object is rendered.

The legshortR01 object is finished for now.

9. Save your work as **06VT03.max**.

Exercise 6.4   Creating a Cylinder Primitive Using Auto Grid

As you look at Victor's illustration of the vote machine, you decide the most exaggerated piece is, hands down, the feet. The large image on the left of Victor's illustration depicts the feet in a fashion like that of the Sphinx. The reality of the matter, as you can see in the lower-right illustration, is that the foot is much more square and compact. The foot object could almost be confused for a sandal a Spice Girl would wear. With that in mind, start working to create the foot object for the vote machine.

1. With **06VT03.max** loaded, select the Vic01 shape. Activate Spline sub-object level and, using the Select and Move tool (View XY-axis) in the Top view, Shift+drag the foot shape to copy it (see Figure 6.21). In the Geometry rollout, click the Detach button and name the new shape **footR01**.

Figure 6.21
Using the Select and Move tool, copy the foot shape.

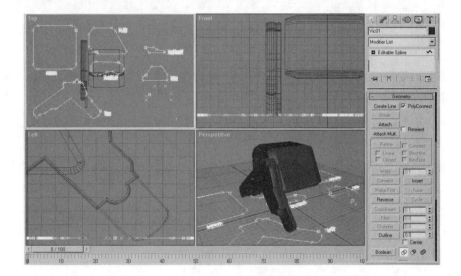

You need to make the shape stand up in the scene and move it into position.

2. Return to the root of the Vic01 object and select the footR01 shape. Activate the Select and Rotate tool (View Z-axis—Use Selection Center) and activate the Selection Lock toggle. Click Zoom Extents All. In the Top view, drag upward to rotate the footR01 shape Z: **–90**. In the Front view, drag downward to rotate the footR01 shape Z: **90**.

The foot is now upright in the scene. Center its pivot to itself and move the foot into position in the scene.

3. Open the Hierarchy panel and activate the Affect Pivot Only button. Click the Center to Object button to center the pivot to the object. Deactivate the Affect Pivot Only button. Activate the Select and Move tool and move the footR01 shape to XYZ: **–66, –103, 21** (as shown in Figure 6.22).

The foot is in the right place now, but when you look at how the foot relates to the leg, it seems a little too tall. Jump into Vertex sub-object mode and make a few modifications.

4. Maximize the Left view and activate the Select and Move tool (View Y-axis). With footR01 selected, open the Modify panel and select the Vertex sub-object mode. Deactivate the Selection Lock Toggle and drag a rectangular selection around all the vertices except the two touching the floor. Place the mouse over one of the selected vertices and drag downward to move the vertices down approximately 3 units (see Figure 6.23).

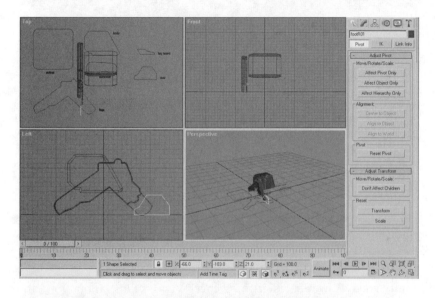

Figure 6.22
The foot is in the correct location in the scene.

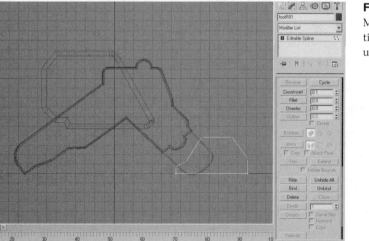

Figure 6.23
Move these two vertices approximately –3 units on the Y-axis.

5. Drag a rectangular selection around the top two vertices and drag them down approximately **–5** units (see Figure 6.24).

Figure 6.24
The vertices of the foot are in the correct position now.

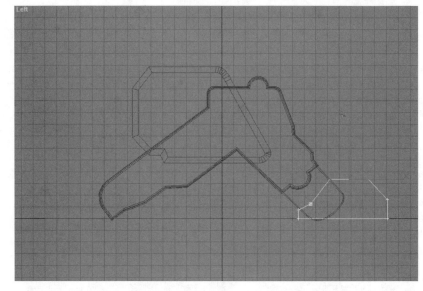

The foot looks much better now. You can bevel it and call it a day.

6. Return to the root of the footR01 object and minimize the Left view. Select the legshortR01 object to load those "sticky" bevel settings, and then re-select the footR01 shape. Apply a Bevel modifier in the Modify panel. Adjust the Perspective view for a better look.

Looks pretty good. However, when you recheck Victor's illustration, you can see that the foot should be wider.

7. In the Bevel Values rollout of the Modify panel, change the Bevel Values to the following:

Start Outline: **0**

Level 1: Height: **7** Outline: **2**

Level 2: Height: **8** Outline: **0**

Level 3: Height: **7** Outline: **–2**

The foot is perfect now (see Figure 6.25).

The foot is finished now, but before you save your work, add the ankle cylinder. You can easily see the ankle cylinder on the lower-right of Victor's illustration. Adding it will be a snap; you'll use the cylinder primitive and Auto Grid.

8. Maximize the Perspective view and adjust it to have a clear view of the ankle area of the leg.

9. Open the Create panel and in the Object Type rollout, click the Cylinder button and check Auto Grid. Click in the back center of the ankle and drag to create the radius of the cylinder. Then release the mouse and push the mouse to give the cylinder height (see Figure 6.26).

Auto Grid lets you automatically create objects on the surface of other objects by generating and activating a temporary construction plane based on the normal of the face you click. This serves as a more efficient way of stacking objects as you create them, rather than building objects and then aligning them. That's why the cylinder was created directly on the surface of the ankle, pretty cool! Let's change some of the parameters of the Cylinder and save our work.

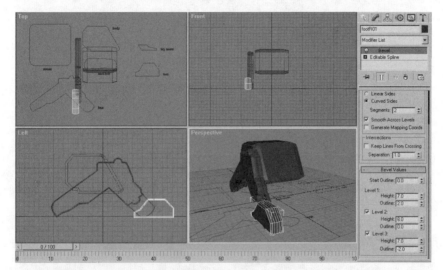

Figure 6.25
The bevel of the footR01 shape is finished.

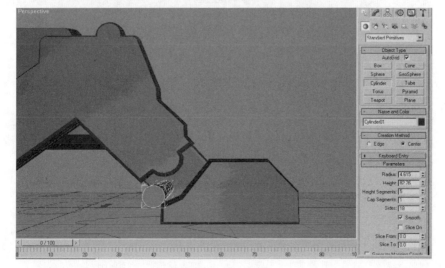

Figure 6.26
The cylinder has been created on the ankle.

10. Name the cylinder **legankleR01** and in the Parameters rollout, change the Radius to **5**, Height to **30**, and Height Segments to **1**. Feel free to adjust the Perspective view to examine the leg objects (see Figure 6.27).

11. If you want to move the legankleR01 object to better center it on the leg, use the Select and Move tool (Local XY-axis) to position the leg as in Figure 6.28.

    You are all finished with the first leg. Congratulations!

12. Save your work as **06VT04.max**.

Figure 6.27
The finished ankle object on the leg.

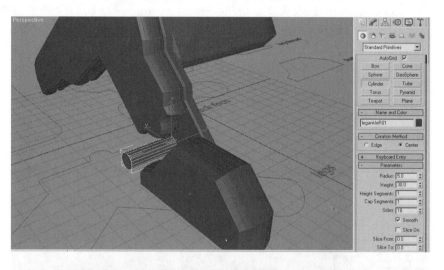

Figure 6.28
The correct location for the legankleR01 object.

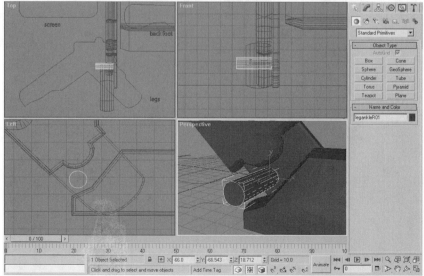

Exercise 6.5   Creating a Hierarchy to Hold an Object Together

Now that you have created the first leg, the second leg will be a breeze. All you have to do is create a hierarchy to hold the leg together, mirror the objects, and then move them into position.

1. With 06VT04.max still open, press H to open the Select Objects dialog. Select footR01, legankleR01, and legshortR01, and then click Select to select the objects and close the dialog.

   These objects will be the children in the hierarchy you are creating. You will parent them to the leglongR01 object.

2. Activate the Select and Link tool and press the H key to open the Select Parent dialog. Select leglongR01 and click Link to link the objects and close the dialog.

   The leg objects are all linked to the leglongR01 object. Now you can mirror the objects. But first, you need to select all the leg objects.

3. Activate the Select Object tool and press the H key to open the Select Objects dialog. In the Select Objects dialog, check Display Subtree to show the hierarchy (see Figure 6.29).

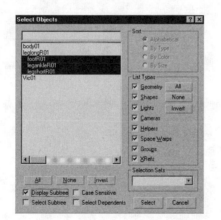

Figure 6.29
The Select Objects dialog displaying the hierarchy subtree.

Here you can see that the three leg objects are in fact linked to the leglongR01 object. Good. Now select all four objects and mirror them.

4. In the Select Objects dialog, select all four leg objects: leglongR01, footR01, legankleR01, and legshortR01. Click Select to close the dialog. Make sure the Reference Coordinate System is Local, and on the toolbar, click the Mirror Selected Objects button to open the Mirror: Local Coordinates dialog. In the Mirror Axis: group, choose Z, and in the Clone Selection group, choose Instance (as shown in Figure 6.30). Click OK to close the dialog.

You probably noticed that when you changed values in the Mirror: Local Coordinates dialog the objects changed interactively. That makes it much easier to achieve the desired results quickly because you don't have to know exactly which axis you want to mirror. The left leg is now created, but it isn't in the correct location.

5. Select only the leglongR02 object and activate the Select and Move tool. In the Transform Type-In dialog, move the leglongR02 shape to XYZ: **60, 0, 56** (as shown in Figure 6.31).

Figure 6.30
The Mirror: Local Coordinates dialog with the correct mirror settings.

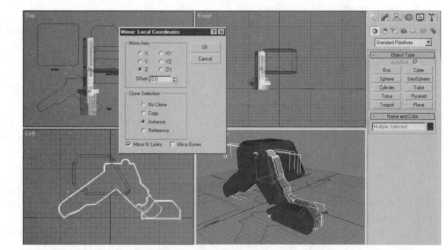

Figure 6.31
The left leg in the correct position.

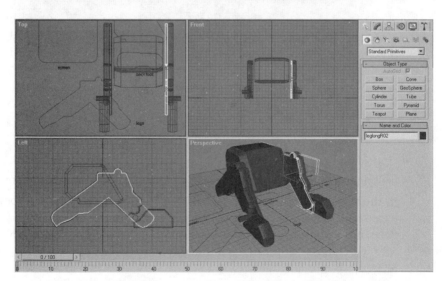

With the left leg in the correct position, you might think you were finished with it. However, you named all the right leg objects with an "R" in their names. Now all the left leg objects are named with an "R" as well. You should change that now, before you forget.

6. Select the four left leg objects and rename them accordingly:

   leglongR02 > **leglongL01**

   legshortR02 > **legshortL01**

   legankleR02 > **legankleL01**

   footR02 > **footL01**

   The left leg is finished. Wasn't that a cinch?

7. Save your work as **06VT05.max**.

Exercise 6.6   Beveling a Shape and Centering Its Pivot

To finish the bottom half of the vote machine you still need to add the back foot and the support beams. You already have the back foot shape created and ready to be beveled, so this is going to go quickly.

1. Make sure **06VT05.max** is loaded. Select the Vic01 shape and activate Spline sub-object level. Click Zoom Extents All.

2. Select the back foot spline and, using the Select and Move tool (View XY-axis), in the Top view, Shift+drag the back foot spline to copy it (see Figure 6.32).

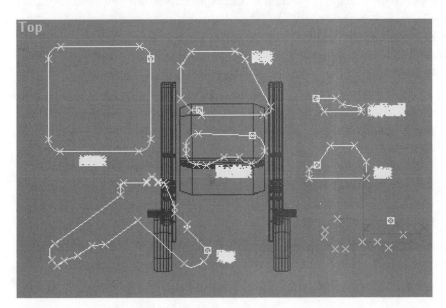

Figure 6.32
The back foot spline is copied in the Top view.

3. In the Geometry rollout, click the Detach button and name the shape **backfoot01**. Return to the root of the Vic01 shape and select the backfoot01 shape.

Now you need to orient backfoot01 to face the correct direction.

4. Activate the Select and Rotate tool (View Z-axis—Use Selection Center) and activate the Selection Lock Toggle. Drag upward in the Top view to rotate the backfoot01 shape –90 degrees.

Figure 6.33
The backfoot01 shape in the correct orientation.

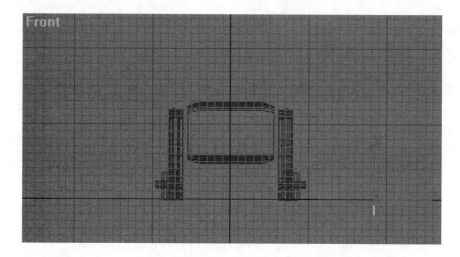

The backfoot01 shape is facing the correct direction, but you need to stand it up.

5. Drag downward in the Front view to rotate the backfoot01 shape Z: **90** degrees (as shown in Figure 6.33).

Now bevel the back foot shape before you put it into position.

6. Open the Modify panel and with backfoot01 selected, apply a Bevel modifier. Click Zoom Extents All Selected and change the Bevel modifier's values to the following:

Start Outline: **0**

Level 1: Height: **2** Outline: **2**

Level 2: Height: **10** Outline: **0**

Level 3: Height: **2** Outline: **–2**

In the Surface group of the Parameters rollout, choose Linear Sides, change Segments to **1**, and uncheck Smooth Across Levels (see Figure 6.34).

The backfoot01 object is finished. Now put it into position on the vote machine.

7. Open the Hierarchy panel and activate Affect Pivot Only. With the back-foot01 object selected, click Center to Object; deactivate the Affect Pivot Only button. Click Zoom Extents All and adjust the Perspective view to observe the back of the vote machine (see Figure 6.35).

Now put that backfoot01 object in its place!

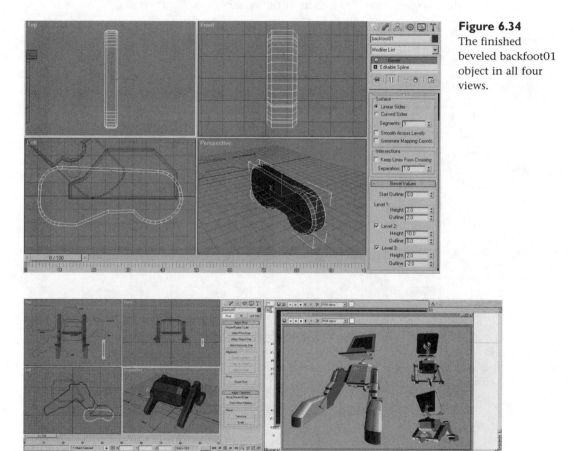

Figure 6.34
The finished beveled backfoot01 object in all four views.

Figure 6.35
The Perspective view has been arranged so you can view the back of the vote machine.

8. Activate the Select and Move tool and move the backfoot01 object to XYZ: **0, 85, 21** (as shown in Figure 6.36).

Next you will put in the support beam. Use the Auto Grid tool again to create a cylinder.

9. Open the Create panel and click the Cylinder button; Auto Grid should still be selected. Maximize the Perspective view and drag on the inside of the leglongL01 object to draw the radius of the cylinder. Move the mouse to the right to designate the height of the cylinder (see Figure 6.37).

Figure 6.36
The backfoot01 object in its correct location.

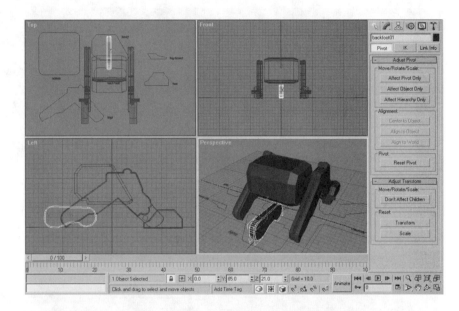

Figure 6.37
Use Auto Grid to create a cylinder in the Perspective view

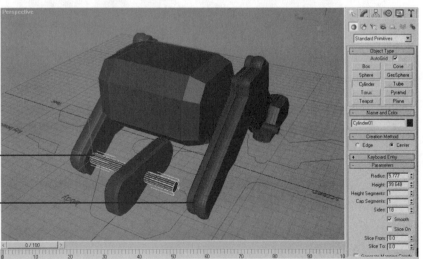

Drag here to create the radius.

Move the mouse to the right to designate the height.

10. In the Parameters rollout of the cylinder you just created, change the Radius to **4** and the Height to **120**. Name this object **backbeam01** (see Figure 6.38).

11. Just to make sure it's in the right place, minimize the Perspective view and activate the Select and Move tool. Move the backbeam01 object to XYZ: **60, 82, 22** Absolute World (see Figure 6.39).

12. Save your work as **06VT06.max**.

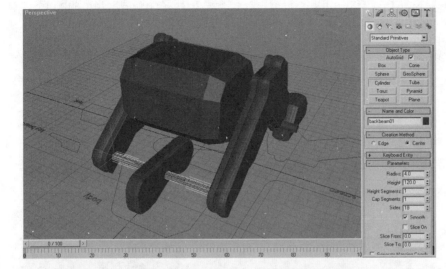

Figure 6.38
The backbeam01 object with the correct settings.

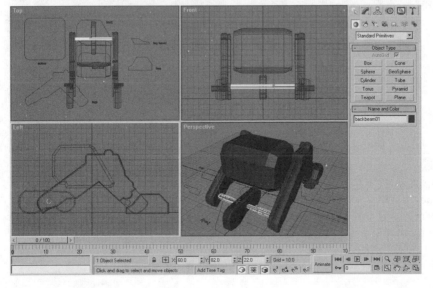

Figure 6.39
The finished backbeam01 object in the correct position.

The Keyboard

Now it's time for the simplest of the objects in the project: the keyboard. To create the keyboard, you will apply a simple extrude to the shape.

Exercise 6.7   Extruding a Shape

To create the keyboard, you need to detach the keyboard shape, move it into position, and extrude it. It doesn't get much easier than that!

1. Make sure **06VT06.max** is open and select Vic01. Activate Spline sub-object mode and select the keyboard shape. Using the Select and Move tool in the Top view, Shift+drag the keyboard shape to copy it. Click the Detach button and name the new shape **keyboard01**. Return to the root of Vic01 and select the keyboard01 shape (see Figure 6.40).

Figure 6.40
The keyboard shape has been copied, detached, and selected.

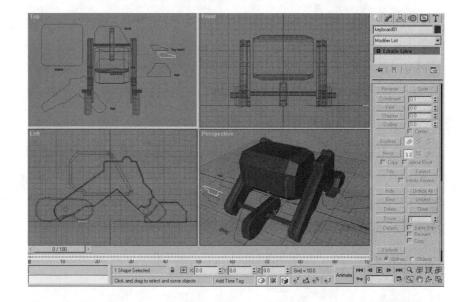

2. To rotate the keyboard shape so it is in the correct orientation, activate the Select and Rotate tool (View Z-axis—Use Selection Center) and with the keyboard01 shape selected, activate the Selection Lock Toggle. Drag the mouse upward in the Top view to rotate the keyboard01 shape Z: **–90** degrees. In the Front view, drag the mouse down to rotate the keyboard01 shape Z: **90** degrees (as shown in Figure 6.41).

   Next you need to adjust the pivot point and move the keyboard shape into place.

3. With the keyboard01 shape selected, open the Hierarchy panel and activate the Affect Pivot Only button. Click the Center to Object button and deactivate the Affect Pivot Only button. Activate the Select and Move tool and move the keyboard01 shape to XYZ: **60, –35, 145** Absolute World. Adjust the Perspective view to view the front of the vote machine (see Figure 6.42).

Now for the hard part: extruding the shape. Oh, did I say hard? I meant the *easy* part.

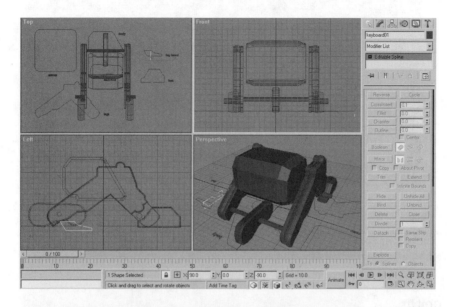

Figure 6.41
The keyboard01 shape is in the correct orientation to the world.

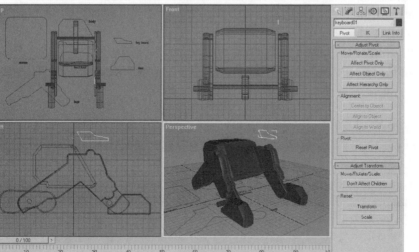

Figure 6.42
The keyboard01 shape is in the correct position and orientation.

4. With the keyboard01 shape selected, open the Modify panel. Apply an Extrude modifier and change the Amount to **115** (see Figure 6.43). Deactivate the Selection Lock Toggle.

Figure 6.43
The finished keyboard01 object is in place in the scene.

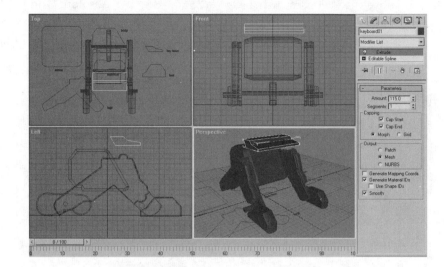

The keyboard is finished. You will attach it to the machine after you complete the monitor object.

5. Save your work as **06VT07.max**.

The Monitor

You have finished all but one of the shapes Victor provided you with in his Illustrator file. The one that remains is the monitor object. If you take another look at the illustration he provided (in \3ds4-ma\project2\computer1.jpg), you will see that even though it's a simple object, it has its complexities. The complicated aspect of the monitor object is the recessed screen.

Exercise 6.8   Using an Object-Level Boolean

To build the object, first you will bevel the shape that Victor provided, and then you will use an object-level Boolean operation to add the recessed screen.

1. Make sure **06VT07.max** is loaded. Select the Vic01 shape (for the last time, Hooray!) and enter Spline sub-object mode. Select the screen shape, create a copy of it, and detach it with the name **monitor01**. Return to the root of the Vic01 shape and select the monitor01 shape (see Figure 6.44).

As you did for all the other shapes so far, you need to rotate the monitor01 shape into the correct orientation in the scene. When the object is facing the correct way, you will move it into a more realistic position.

2. Activate the Select and Rotate tool (View Z-axis—Use Selection Center), and with the monitor01 shape selected, activate the Selection Lock Toggle. Drag upward in the Top view to rotate the shape Z: **–90** degrees. In the Left view, drag upward to rotate the shape Z: **–90** degrees.

You need to adjust the pivot point and position the monitor shape on the machine.

3. With the monitor01 shape selected, open the Hierarchy panel and activate the Affect Pivot Only button. Click the Center to Object button and deactivate the Affect Pivot Only button. Activate the Select and Move tool and move the monitor01 shape to XYZ: **0, 13, 230** Absolute World (as shown in Figure 6.45).

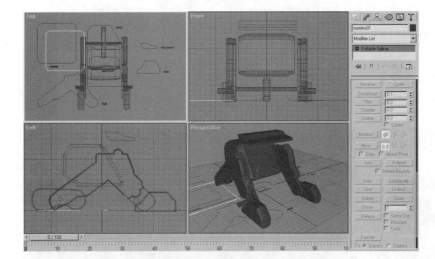

Figure 6.44
The monitor01 shape is detached from the Vic01 shape.

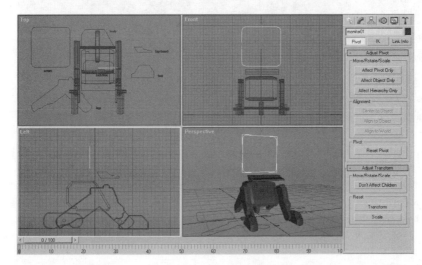

Figure 6.45
The monitor01 shape is in the correct position.

Looking at the monitor in the Front and Perspective views, you see that the monitor shape looks a little too square. It would also look better if it was not quite so high. Jump into sub-object mode and make a quick modification.

4. With monitor01 selected, open the Modify panel and enter Vertex sub-object mode. In the Front view, drag a rectangular selection around the top four vertices of the monitor spline. Activate the Select and Move tool (View Y-axis) and move the four vertices down approximately Y: **–15** units. Exit sub-object mode.

Let's bevel this bad boy.

5. With monitor01 still selected, apply a Bevel modifier and change the Bevel Values to the following:

Start Outline: **0**

Level 1: Height: **2** Outline: **2**

Level 2: Height: **5** Outline: **0**

Level 3: Height: **(3)** Outline: **–2**

The monitor01 object takes shape (Figure 6.46).

Figure 6.46
The monitor01 shape is now a beveled object.

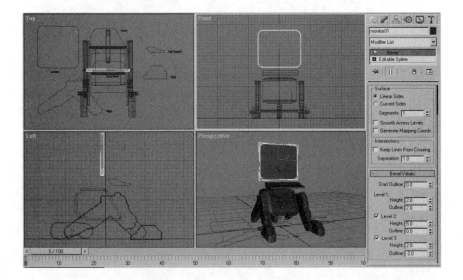

The monitor01 object finally has dimension. However, there is no screen on it. Earlier, I had mentioned that we would be using object level Boolean operations to create the screen. In order to successfully complete this process, we need to create a second object to "subtract" from the monitor01 object. Let's crank a subtraction object out.

6. Maximize the Perspective view and with the monitor01 object selected click
   Zoom Extents Selected. Open the Create > Shapes panel and click the Rectangle
   button (Auto Grid should still be active). Drag from the upper-left of the
   monitor01 object to the lower-right, creating a rectangle shape (Figure 6.47).

7. To make sure the rectangle is centered from side to side, activate the Select
   and Move tool, and in the Transform Type-in, move the Rectangle to
   XYZ: **0, 4, 224**. In the Parameters rollout of the Modify panel, change the
   Length to **90** and Width to **110**.

   If you take a peek at Victor's original illustration again, you will see a tab in
   the lower-left corner of the screen. The easiest way for you to add it will be to
   do a little spline level Boolean operations. (Hey, it never hurts to practice!)

8. Right-click the Rectangle01 shape and from the quad menu, choose Convert
   To > Convert to Editable Spline. Activate Spline sub-object level. Activate the
   Select and Move tool (Local XY-axis) and Shift+drag to create a copy of the
   rectangle spline to the lower-left corner of the original (see Figure 6.48).

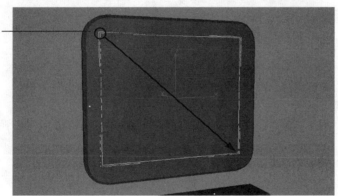

Start drag here.

Figure 6.47
A rectangle shape
has been created on
the surface of the
monitor01 object
using Auto Grid.

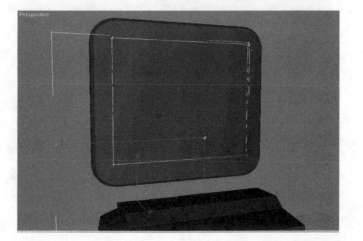

Figure 6.48
Create a copy of the
original rectangle
spline and move it to
the lower left.

9. In spline sub-object mode, select the
   original rectangle spline. Activate the
   Boolean button and activate the subtraction button as well (see Figure 6.49).
   Click the copied spline and the subtraction result is displayed (as shown in
   Figure 6.50).

   Not bad, but you need to give a little
   angle to the tab.

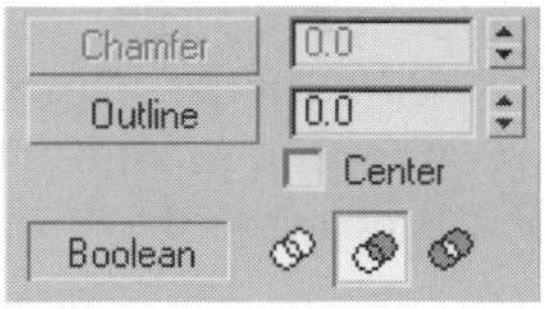

Figure 6.49
Use the Boolean subtraction button
to subtract one spline from the other.

10. Activate the Select and Move tool (Local X-axis) and activate Vertex sub-
    object level. Select the two vertices creating the vertical line in the center of
    the rectangle shape and change their type to Corner. Move these vertices to
    a more aesthetic position (see Figure 6.51).

Figure 6.50
The result of the
Boolean subtraction
of the rectangle
shape.

Figure 6.51
The tab of the screen
shape is angled now.

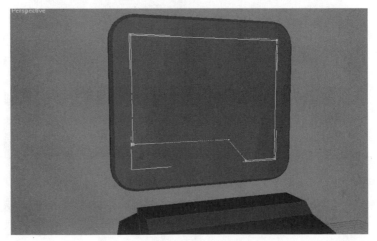

That looks much better. However, in the example, the horizontal line of the tab is a little bit too high. So you are going to fix that.

11. Activate the Select and Move tool (Local Y-axis) and select the two vertices that form the tab's horizontal line to move them down (see Figure 6.52). Return to the root of the Rectangle01 shape.

Now that you have an appealing screen shape, extrude it and then use it to subtract a screen area from the monitor.

12. With the Rectangle01 shape selected, apply an Extrude modifier with an Amount of **5**. Minimize the Perspective view and click Zoom Extents All Selected. Using the Select and Move tool (Local Z-axis), move the Rectangle shape approximately A: **−4** units (as shown in Figure 6.53).

Figure 6.52
The tab is less obtrusive now.

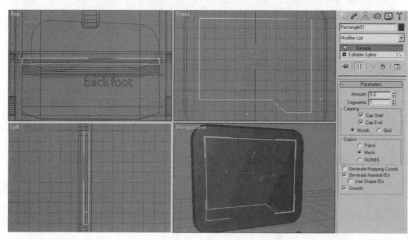

Figure 6.53
The Rectangle01 shape is in the correct position for the Boolean operation.

With the Rectangle01 shape in the correct position, you can create your first object-level Boolean operation. Put on your rubber gloves.

13. Select the monitor01 shape and choose Create > Geometry > Compound Objects. Click the Boolean button and in the Pick Boolean rollout, click the Pick Operand B button. Click the Rectangle01 object.

The Rectangle01 object is subtracted from the monitor01 shape (see Figure 6.54).

Figure 6.54
The Boolean subtraction was successful!

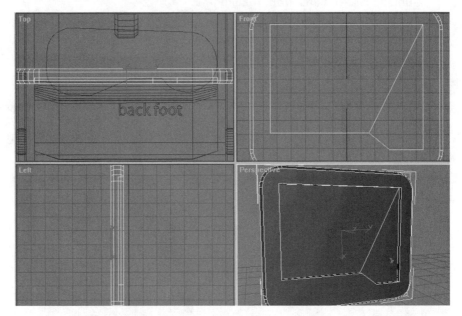

Excellent! It worked like a charm. Looks to me as though the monitor01 object is finished. Before you save your work, hide the Vic01 shape because you won't need it anymore.

14. Click Zoom Extents All to view all the objects in the scene. Select the Vic01 shape and right-click it. In the quad menu, choose Hide Selection to hide the shape. Don't worry, you can always unhide it from the Display panel.

15. Click Zoom Extents All again and save your work as **06VT08.max**.

The Armature

The only pieces needed to build the vote machine that Victor didn't provide in the Illustrator file are the sections that build the armature. That's okay though, because those pieces are relatively simple to build. Looking at Victor's illustration of the vote machine, \3ds4-ma\project2\images\computer1.jpg, you will see the armature links holding the monitor and keyboard to the base object.

It's a little complicated to see their detail from the small image, and kind of M.C. Escher-esque because it's hard to see what link is in front of what. That's okay, once again, because this image is just a visual reference on how the machine is supposed to appear, not instructions on how it is built. You can use creative license to build the armature correctly.

Exercise 6.9   Modifying a Cylinder Object in Sub-Object Mode

The most important part of the armature is the mount to which the armature is connected. The mount's form is relatively simple and could easily be created by lathing a cross-section. However, you can create it more easily by modifying a cylinder object in sub-object mode.

1. With **06VT08.max** loaded, maximize the Perspective view. Using the Pan, Zoom, and Arc Rotate tools, adjust the view to observe the top of the body01 object as viewed from behind (see Figure 6.55).

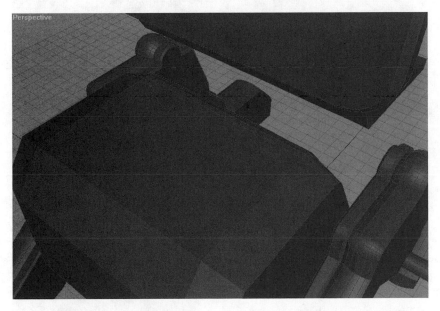

Figure 6.55
The Perspective view shows the top of the body01 object.

Now you will use Auto Grid again to create a cylinder primitive on the top surface of the body01 object. However, for clarity in the figures, I have lightened the color in which the armature will be created in order to contrast it from the rest of the vote machine objects.

2. Open the Create > Geometry > Standard Primitives panel. Click the Cylinder button and make sure Auto Grid is checked. Drag from the center of the top surface of the body01 object outward to create the radius of the cylinder.

Then move the mouse upward to create the height, and click the left button to complete the cylinder. Name the object **mountB01** and in the Parameter rollout, enter the following values:

Radius: **20**

Height: **3**

Height Segments: **1**

Cap Segments: **1**

Sides: **32**

The mount begins to take shape, as you can see in Figure 6.56.

Figure 6.56
The mountB01 object is created on the top surface of the body01 object using Auto Grid.

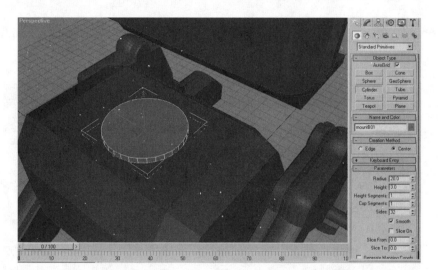

Now make sure the mountB01 object is centered on the body01 object. Because the body01 object is centered on the world's X plane, all you have to do is move the cylinder to X: 0 Absolute world.

3. With the mountB01 object selected, activate the Select and Move tool. In the Transform Type-In, enter X: **0**. You could also adjust the Y: value to center the cylinder object front to back on the body01 object. Change the Y: value to Y: **34** (see Figure 6.57).

Now you can perform the sub-object modifications to finish the mountB01 object.

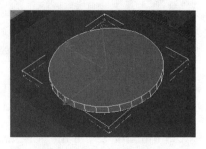

Figure 6.57
The mountB01 object is centered on the body01 object.

4. Right-click the selected mountB01 object and choose Convert To > Convert to Editable Poly. Activate Polygon sub-object level and select the top polygon (see Figure 6.58).

You will first change the extruded cylinder into a beveled profile.

5. In the Edit Geometry rollout, enter an Outline value of **–3**. The top face is scaled smaller, and the Outline value returns to zero (see Figure 6.59).

Now you need to create a flat section on the top surface of the cylinder before you bevel it again. To accomplish that, you will use the Extrusion tool to create the necessary faces to create the plateau. Then you will apply an Outline to reduce its size.

6. In the Edit Geometry rollout of the Modify panel, drag the Extrusion spinner upward to change its value. Then—without releasing the mouse—return the value back to zero and release the mouse button. This creates extra extrusion faces; you just don't see them yet.

7. To create the plateau, enter an Outline value of **–3** (as shown in Figure 6.60).

Now you need to give it one more beveled extrusion.

8. Enter an Extrusion of **3** and follow it up with an Outline of **–3** (see Figure 6.61).

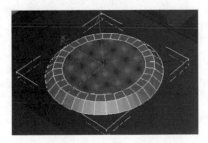

Figure 6.58
The top polygon of the cylinder shape is selected. (Shade Selected Faces is activated for figure clarity.)

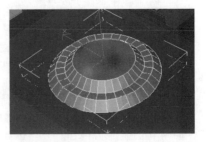

Figure 6.59
The cylinder has a more beveled profile now.

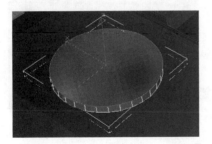

Figure 6.60
The Outline value of –3 creates the plateau on the surface of the cylinder.

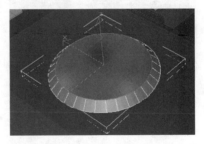

Figure 6.61
A second beveled extrusion is created on the cylinder.

Now you need to add the post that everything will mount to. You will use the Extrude to 0 technique to create another flat surface.

9. Without releasing the mouse button, drag the Extrusion spinner to change the value and return it to zero. Then release the mouse button. Enter an Outline of **–7** to make it look like Figure 6.62.

Now add the post.

10. Enter an Extrusion value of **15** (see Figure 6.63).

The post may not be the correct length, but you can always go back and change it later. Otherwise, the mountB01 object looks pretty good. However, if you were to render a frame, you could see that smoothing groups are missing on the object.

Because the smoothing groups aren't correctly configured, areas of the mountB01 object appear faceted. You can easily take care of that in the Surface Properties rollout by using Auto Smooth.

Figure 6.62
The second plateau is created on the top surface.

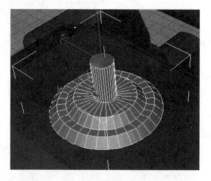

Figure 6.63
The post is created on the mountB01 object.

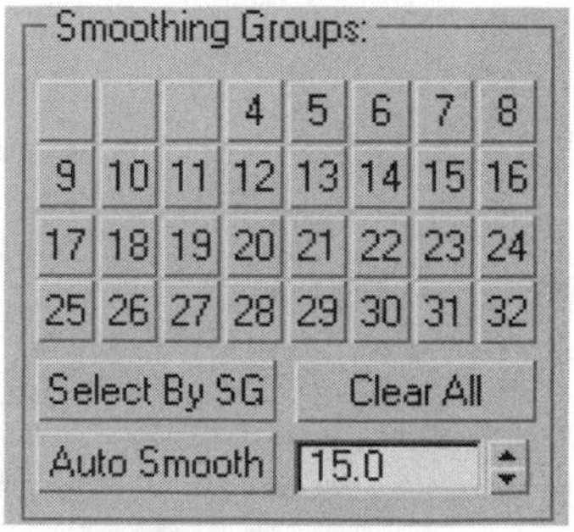

11. Activate Element sub-object mode and select the mountB01 element. In the Surface Properties rollout, change the Auto Smooth value to **15** and click the Auto Smooth button (as shown in Figure 6.64).

If you render the mountB01 object again, you will see that the smoothing groups were corrected.

Auto Smooth sets the smoothing groups based on the angles between polygons. Any two adjacent polygons will be put in the

Figure 6.64
The Auto Smooth button in the Surface Properties dialog.

same smoothing group if the angle between their normals is less than the threshold angle, which is set by the spinner to the right of the Auto Smooth button.

The mountB01 object is finished. Before you save your work, however, you should instance the mountB01 object and position it on the monitor01 object.

12. Return to the root of the mountB01 object. Choose Edit > Clone to open the Clone Options dialog. In the Object group, choose Instance and change the name to **mountM01**. Click OK to create the instance.

13. Adjust the Perspective view to see the back of the monitor. Click the Align button on the toolbar, and then click the monitor01 object to open the Align Selection dialog. In the Align Position (World) group, check Y Position and Z Position. In both the Current Object and Target Object sections, check Pivot Point. In the Align Orientation (Local) group, check Z Axis (as shown in Figure 6.65). Click OK to close the dialog.

The mount is in the correct place, but it's backward (see Figure 6.66). You can fix this easily by mirroring the mountM01 object.

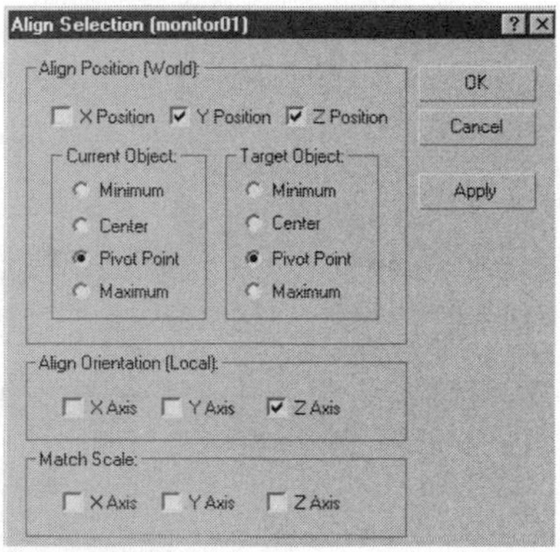

Figure 6.65
The Align Selection dialog with the correct settings.

Figure 6.66
The mountM01 object is in the correct location, but it faces the wrong way.

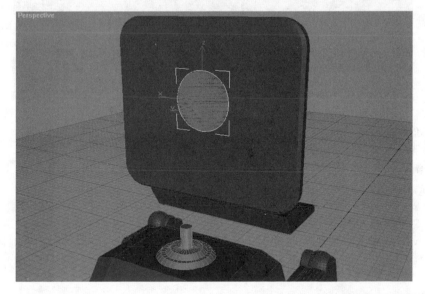

14. With the mountM01 object selected, click the Mirror Selected Objects button. The Mirror: World Coordinates dialog opens. In the Mirror Axis group, check Y and make sure No Clone is active in the Clone Selection dialog (see Figure 6.67). Click OK to close the dialog.

As you can see in Figure 6.68, that's much better.

15. Save your work as **06VT09.max**.

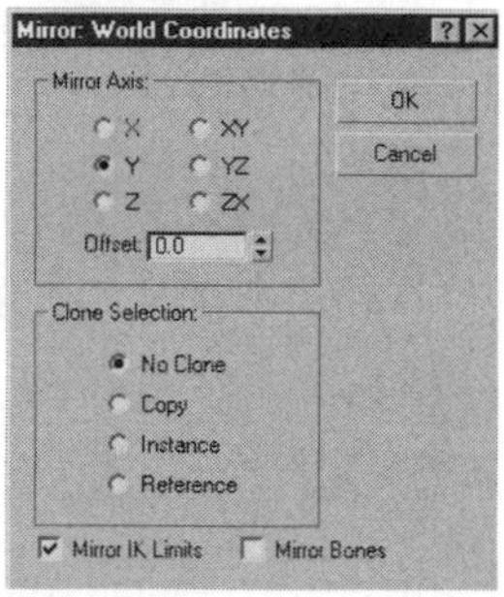

Figure 6.67
The Mirror: World Coordinates dialog with the correct settings.

Figure 6.68
The mountM01 object is in the correct position and orientation.

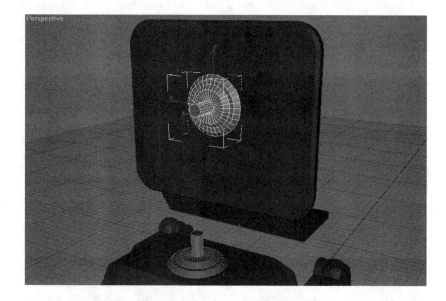

Attaching the Keyboard to the Body

The next step toward completing the vote machine is connecting the keyboard object to the body. The detail in Victor's illustration isn't the best, but it gives you an idea of how to create the attachment.

Exercise 6.10   Using Copying Instead of Instancing

First you will create a bracket to sandwich on either side of the post of the mountB01 object. Then you will attach a rod to the bracket, and then attach a bracket on each side of the keyboard to attach the keyboard to the rod.

1. With **06VT09.max** loaded, minimize the Perspective view and maximize the Left view. Right-click the Left view label and deselect Show Grid. Then adjust the Left view to match Figure 6.69.

Now you will create the first bracket shape for the keyboard mount.

2. Select Create > Shapes, and in the dialog that appears, click the Circle button. Deactivate Auto Grid and drag to create a circle shape with a Radius of 12 units. Name that object **bracketKA01**. Activate the Select and Move tool and move the bracketKA01 shape to XYZ: **0, 34, 148** Absolute World (see Figure 6.70).

3. Right-click the selected bracketKA01 shape and choose Convert To > Convert to Editable Spline. Activate Spline sub-object level and select the circle spline. Activate the Select and Move tool (View X-axis) and Shift+drag the circle shape, copying it to XYZ: **0, 11, 148** Absolute World.

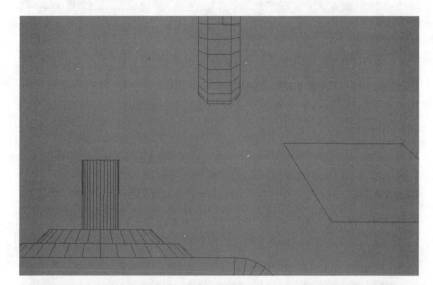

Figure 6.69
Adjust the Left view to observe this viewpoint.

Figure 6.70
The first circle shape that's needed to make the keyboard bracket.

Now do a Boolean operation to unite the two shapes.

4. In the Geometry rollout, activate the Boolean Union buttons and click the unselected circle shape to unite the two circles (see Figure 6.71).

5. Activate Vertex sub-object mode, select the top vertex that was created by the Boolean union, and delete it. Then select the lower vertex created by the Boolean and change its vertex type to Smooth. Activate the Select and Move tool (View Y-axis) and move the Smooth vertex down approximately Y: **–3** units (see Figure 6.72).

Figure 6.71
The Boolean united circle shapes.

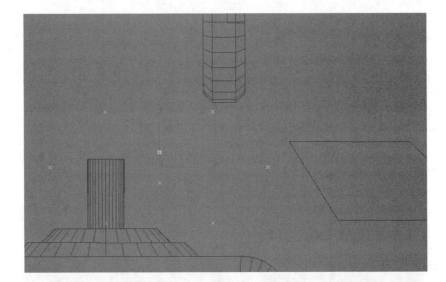

Figure 6.72
The finished bracketKA01 shape.

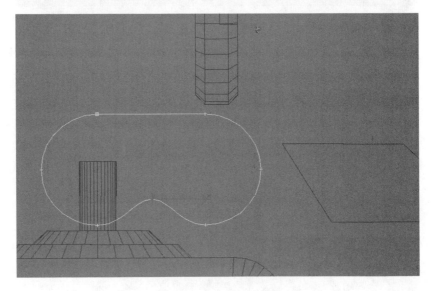

The bracketKA01 shape is finished. You can apply a Bevel modifier to turn it into an object.

6. Minimize the Left view and return to the root of the bracketKA01 shape. Click Zoom Extents All Selected. With bracketKA01 selected, apply a Bevel modifier with the following Bevel values:

Start Outline: **0**

Level 1: Height: **.5** Outline: **.5**

Level 2: Height: **.5** Outline: **0**

Level 3: Height: **.5** Outline: **–.5**

Move the bracketKA01 object to XYZ: **–4, 34, 148** (as shown in Figure 6.73).

Next, you need to copy the bracket object so it hugs both sides of the post.

7. Select Edit > Clone to open the Clone Options dialog. Choose Copy, and then click OK to close the dialog and create the clone. Move the new object to XYZ: **5.5, 34, 148**.

The reason you are copying the bracket instead of instancing it is that you want to join the two objects so they are attached. For you to attach two objects to one another, they must be unique. Therefore, you need to copy instead of instance.

Because both of these brackets will act as one piece, you can attach them so they will be the same object.

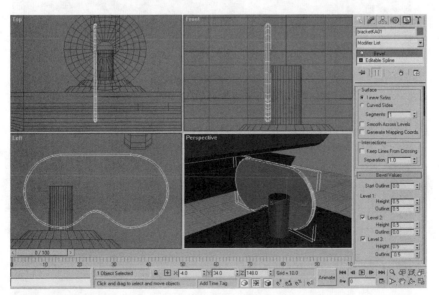

Figure 6.73
The beveled bracket hugs one side of the post.

8. Select the bracketKA01 object, right-click it, and choose Convert To > Convert to Editable Poly. In the Edit Geometry rollout, click the Attach button and click the copied bracket object. The two objects are combined into one object (see Figure 6.74). Deactivate the Attach button.

9. Save your work as **06VT10.max**.

Exercise 6.11   Joining Shapes with Sub-Object Boolean Operations

You can now create the brackets that will hold the keyboard to the post.

1. With **06VT10.max** loaded, maximize the Left view and adjust the view to observe the post bracket and the keyboard (see Figure 6.75).

Figure 6.74
The two bracket objects are now attached.

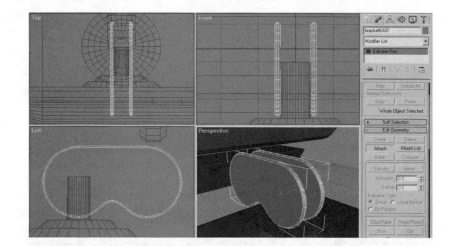

Figure 6.75
Adjust the Left view to this viewpoint.

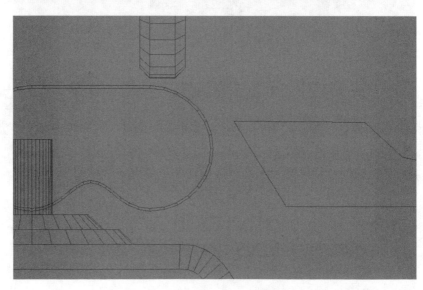

2. Select Create > Shapes and create a circle with a radius of 10. Move it to
   XYZ: **0, 11, 148** and name the shape **bracketKB01** (see Figure 6.76).

3. Convert the circle to an editable spline. Activate Spline sub-object mode and
   the Select and Move tool (View X-axis). Shift+drag the circle spline to copy
   it to XYZ: **0, –17, 148**.

4. Activate Vertex sub-object mode and move the two closest vertices to match
   Figure 6.77.

Figure 6.76
Create a circle with
a radius of 10 at
XYZ: 0, 11, 148.

Figure 6.77
Move the two vertices
to match this.

5. Use Spline sub-object level Boolean Union to join the two splines.

6. Activate Vertex sub-object level and select the two vertices that were created by the Boolean operation. Change their vertex types to Smooth.

7. To round out the form of the bracket, leave the two Smooth vertices selected and activate the Select and Non-Uniform Scale tool (View Y-axis—Use Selection Center). Activate the Selection Lock Toggle and drag upward to scale the vertices apart Y: **150** percent (as shown in Figure 6.78). Return to the root of the shape.

Figure 6.78
The two new vertices have been scaled Y: 150 percent apart.

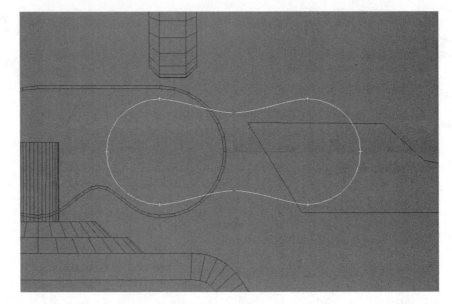

The bracketKB01 shape is finished. You can apply a Bevel modifier to turn it into an object.

8. In the Modify panel, apply a Bevel modifier. The settings should be "sticky" from the last bracket:

    Start Outline: **0**

    Level 1: Height: **.5** Outline: **.5**

    Level 2: Height: **.5** Outline: **0**

    Level 3: Height: **.5** Outline: **–.5**

9. Minimize the Left view, click Zoom Extents All, and adjust the Front and Perspective view to see the keyboard (see Figure 6.79).

    It seems as though you made the keyboard a little too short on one side. If you look at the Front view, you see the keyboard is touching the grid line on the right side, but it is too short on the left side. You can fix this quickly.

10. Select the keyboard01 object. In the Modify panel, change the Amount to **120**. The keyboard is equal on both sides now.

11. Select the bracketKB01 object and move it to XYZ: **–60, 11, 148**. Copy the bracketKB01 object and move the copy to XYZ: **61.5, 11, 148**, as shown in Figure 6.80.

    Now you can attach the two objects to make them one object.

12. Select the bracketKB01 object and convert it into an Editable Polygon. In the Modify panel, click the Attach button, and then click the bracketKB02 object to attach it (see Figure 6.81). Deselect the Attach button.

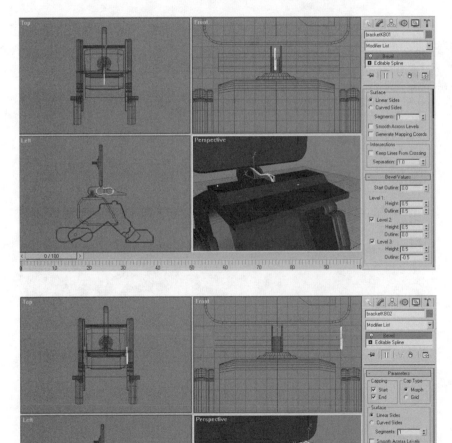

Figure 6.79
Adjust the Front and Perspective view to observe the keyboard.

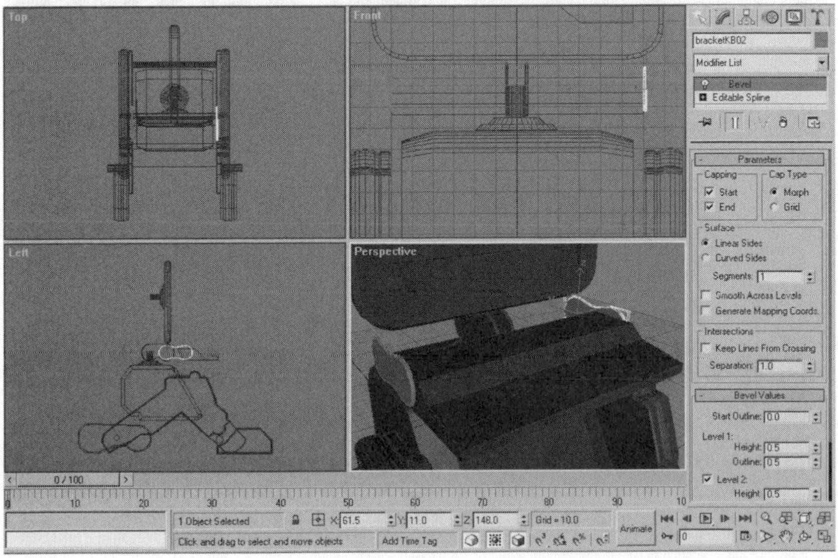

Figure 6.80
The copied bracket is in the correct position.

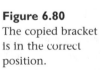

Before you save your work, position the keyboard so it's more centered to the bracket, and then adjust its pivot point.

13. Maximize the Left view and click Zoom Extents Selected. Select the Keyboard and move it to XYZ: **60, –35, 148**.

14. To adjust the pivot point, open the Hierarchy panel and activate the Affect Pivot Only button. Move the pivot to XYZ: **60, –17, 148** (see Figure 6.82). Then deselect the Affect Pivot Only button.

    The keyboard will now pivot on the center of the bracketKB01 sprocket.

15. Save your work as **06VT11.max**.

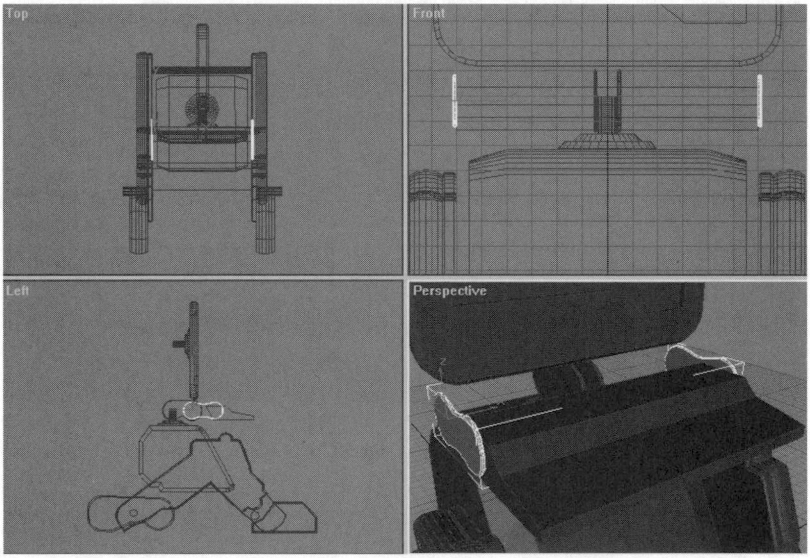

Figure 6.81
The two KB brackets are attached.

Figure 6.82
The keyboard and the keyboard's pivot are in the correct positions.

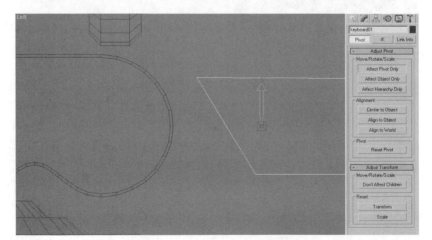

Exercise 6.12   More Practice Using Cylinder Primitives

The brackets for the keyboard are finished. All that's left to finish on the keyboard armature are the rods. You will use cylinder primitives to create the rods.

1. With **06VT11.max** open, minimize the Left view. Open the Create > Geometry panel and click the Cylinder button. In the Left view create a cylinder with a Radius of **4**, a Height of **140**, and Sides of **18**. Name the object **rodKA01** (see Figure 6.83).

2. Move the rodKA01 object to XYZ: **70, 11, 148** (as shown in Figure 6.84).

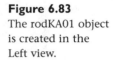

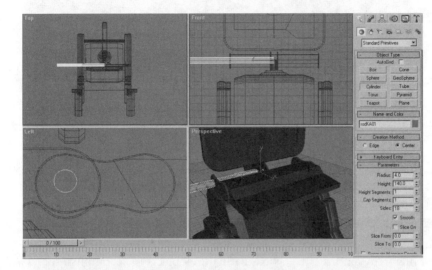

Figure 6.83
The rodKA01 object is created in the Left view.

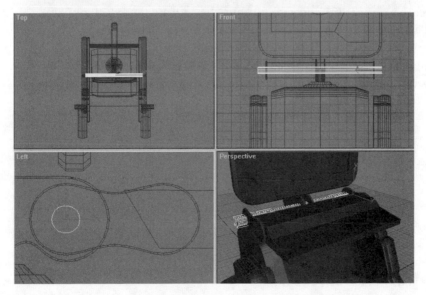

Figure 6.84
The rodKA01 object in the correct position.

Now that you have created one rod, you can simply instance it and move it to the keyboard.

3. Create an instance of the rodKA01 object by choosing Edit > Clone, choosing Instance, and naming the new object **rodKB01**. Move the rodKB01 object to XYZ: **70, –17, 148** (see Figure 6.85).

Figure 6.85
The instanced rodKB01 object is moved into the correct position.

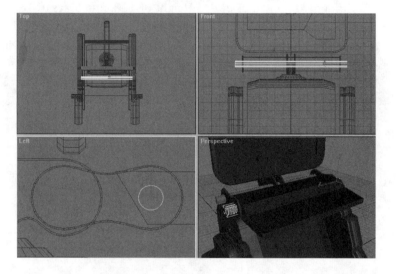

You have finished the armature, but it is not functional yet. This means that when you rotate one object, the others don't follow. You need to create a linked hierarchy among the keyboard armature objects to accomplish that.

4. Select the keyboard01 and rodKB01 objects. Activate the Select and Link tool and press the H key to open the Select Parent dialog. Select bracketKB01 and click Link.

5. Activate the Select Object tool and select the bracketKB01 and rodKA01 objects. Activate the Select and Link tool and link the two objects to the BracketKA01 object.

6. Activate the Select Object tool and select the bracketKA01 object. Activate the Select and Link tool and link the bracketKA01 object to the mountB01 object.

7. Using the Select and Link tool, select the mountB01 object and drag to link it to the body01 object. Activate the Select Object tool and press the H key to open the Select Objects dialog. Check Display Subtree and compare your hierarchy to that in Figure 6.86. When you finish, close the Select Objects dialog.

The keyboard armature hierarchy is finished. Good work! Now whenever one of the pieces of armature is rotated, the children will follow.

8. Save your work as **06VT12.max**.

Figure 6.86
The finished keyboard armature hierarchy.

Attaching the Monitor to the Body

You have successfully attached the keyboard to the mount on the body. Now you need to apply the same techniques to attach the monitor. You need to create two more pair of brackets to hold the monitor to the base mount. The bracket, in this case, will be identical, so production should go smoothly.

Exercise 6.13   Creating Shapes in Sub-Object Mode

Start by creating the bracket pair connected to the mount on the base object.

1. Make sure **06VT12.max** is loaded. Maximize the Left view and adjust it to see both mount objects (as shown in Figure 6.87).

   You will now create a circle shape and start to build the bracket object.

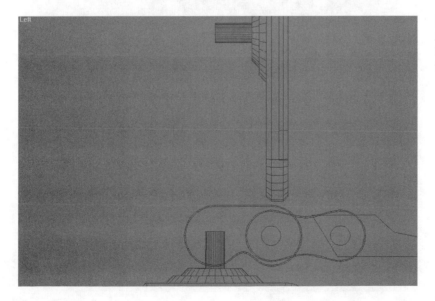

Figure 6.87
Adjust the maximized Left view to match this viewpoint.

2. Create a circle shape with a Radius of **12** and name it **bracketMA01** (see Figure 6.88). Move it to XYZ: **0, 34, 148**.

3. Convert the bracketMA01 shape into an editable spline, enter Spline sub-object mode, and select the circle spline. Activate the Select and Move tool (View Y-axis) and Shift+drag upward to create a copy of the circle. Move it to XYZ: **0, 34, 195**.

   Now, as you did with the keyboard bracket, you will move the two vertices to cross the two splines. You will then use a Boolean Union to join the two splines into one.

4. Activate Vertex sub-object level. Using the Select and Move tool (View Y-axis), move the two vertices (approximately 15 units each) so that they cross as shown in Figure 6.89.

Figure 6.88
Create a circle shape with a Radius of 12.

Figure 6.89
Cross the two vertices as illustrated here.

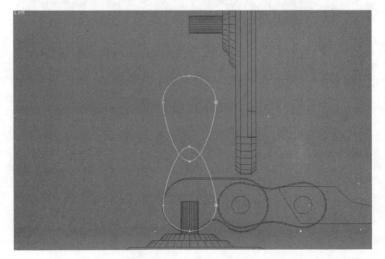

5. Activate Spline sub-object level, and then use Boolean Union to join the two circle splines.

6. To smooth out the profile of the bracket, activate Vertex sub-object level, select the two new vertices, and change their types to Smooth (see Figure 6.90).

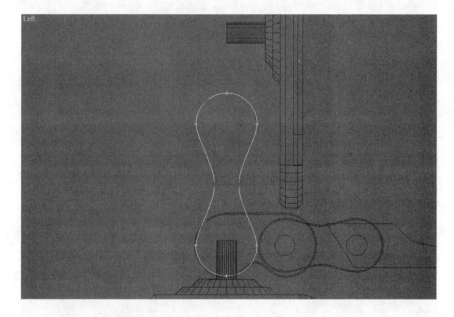

Figure 6.90
The two vertices that resulted from the Boolean Union are now smooth.

When the bracket shape is finished, you need to turn it into an object by applying a Bevel modifier.

7. Return to the root of the object and apply a Bevel modifier with the following "sticky" settings:

Start Outline: **0**

Level 1: Height: **.5** Outline: **.5**

Level 2: Height: **.5** Outline: **0**

Level 3: Height: **.5** Outline: **–.5**

Minimize the Left view and adjust the views to see the bracketMA01 object clearly (as shown in Figure 6.91).

The bracket needs to be moved to the outside of the keyboard bracket.

8. Move the bracketMA01 object to XYZ: **–5.5, 34, 148**.

It is now on the outside of the keyboard bracket (see Figure 6.92).

You need to create the second bracket to complete the pair.

Figure 6.91
The four views
are adjusted for
optimal viewing of
the bracketMA01
object.

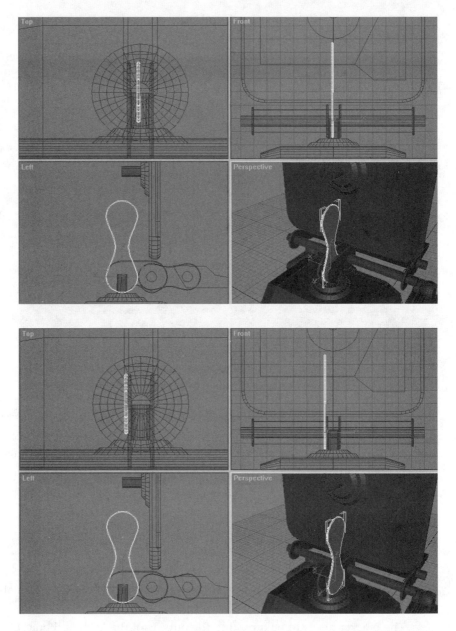

Figure 6.92
The bracketMA01
object is in the
correct position.

9. Copy bracketMA01 and accept the default name that's used, **bracketMA02**.
   Move it to XYZ: **7, 34, 148** so it hugs the keyboard bracket precisely
   (see Figure 6.93).

Because the second bracket pair will use the same object, all you have to do is copy one of the first brackets.

10. Select bracketMA01 and create a copy of it named **bracketMB01**. Move it to XYZ: **–4, 34, 195** (as shown in Figure 6.94).

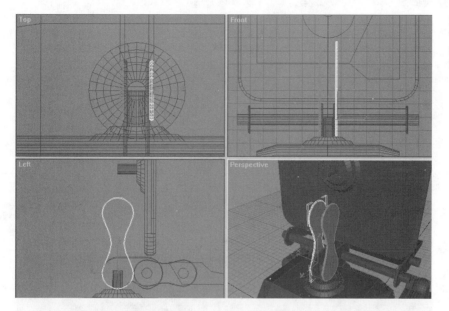

Figure 6.93
The pair of brackets hug the keyboard brackets precisely.

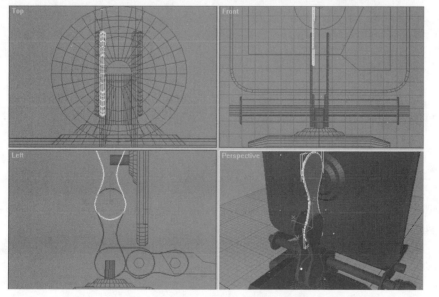

Figure 6.94
The bracketMB01 object in the correct position.

The bracketMB01 object should hug the inside surface of the bracketMA01 object. Now you need to copy the bracketMB01 object and position it to snugly hug the bracketMA02 object.

11. Copy the bracketMB01 object and keep the default name that's used, **bracketMB02**. Move it to XYZ: **5.5, 34, 195** (see Figure 6.95).

Figure 6.95
The two bracketMB objects are in the correct positions.

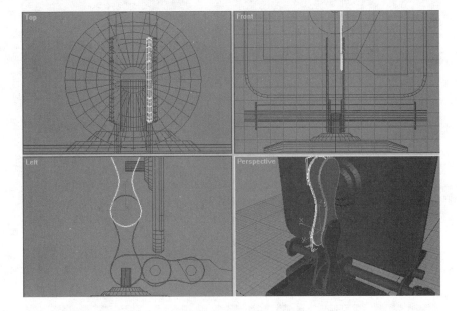

Exercise 6.14   Using Cylinder Objects as Rods

Now you will add the rods that will attach the brackets to one another and attach the brackets to the mounts.

1. Adjust the Perspective and Left views until you can see all of both monitor bracket pairs.

   Now you will create the first rod.

2. In the Left view, create a Cylinder primitive with a Radius of **4** and a Length of **26** and name the cylinder **rodMA01**. Move the rodMA01 object to XYZ: **13, 34, 148** (see Figure 6.96).

   The rodMA01 object is in its correct location on the armature. You now need to instance it twice to pin all the joints together.

3. Instance the rodMA01 object and name it **rodMB01**. Move it to XYZ: **13, 34, 195** (see Figure 6.97).

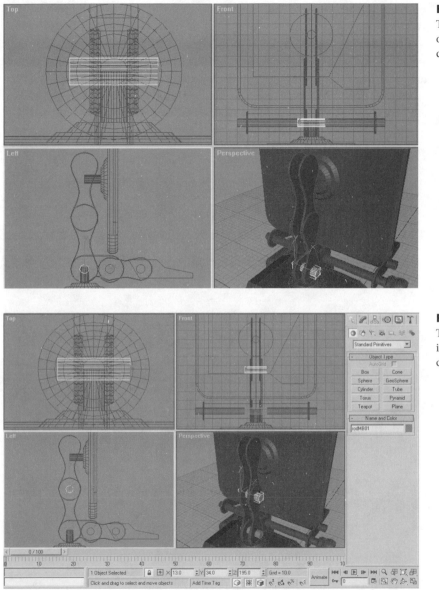

Figure 6.96
The rodMA01 object in its correct location.

Figure 6.97
The rodMB01 instance in its correct position.

4. To create the final rod, instance the rodMB01 object and name it **rodMC01**. Move it to XYZ: **13, 34, 242** (see Figure 6.98).

   You are so close to finishing the vote machine that you can almost taste it! All you need to do is create the hierarchy linking and adjust the armature to actually hold the monitor object.

Before you do that, however, adjust the height of the post on the mountB01 object. Remember, you weren't so sure if it was the correct height. Well, it would be better to make it a little shorter.

5. Maximize the Left view, select the mountB01 object, and click Zoom Extents Selected. Enter Vertex sub-object mode and drag a rectangular selection around the top vertices. Activate the Select and Move tool (View Y-axis) and lower the vertices approximately Y: **–2** (see Figure 6.99). Then return to the root of the mountB01 object and minimize the Left view.

6. Save your work as **06VT13.max**.

Figure 6.98
The final rod, rodMC01, is in the correct position.

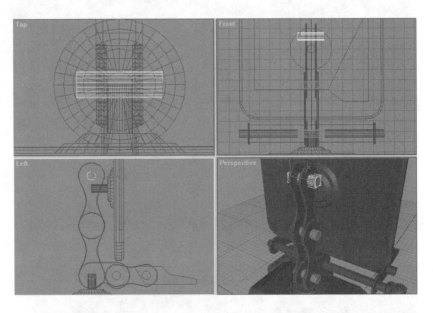

Figure 6.99
The top vertices have been lowered approximately –2 units.

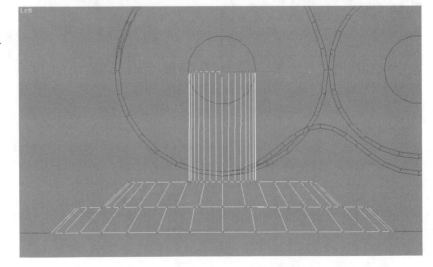

Creating the Monitor Armature Hierarchy

You have finished creating all the objects for the vote machine. However, for the vote machine to be functional, you must create the link hierarchy for the monitor armature. You will first link all the brackets and rods together with the base. Then you will orient the armature to meet the monitor object correctly, and then you will add the monitor object to the hierarchy.

Exercise 6.15   Using the Attach List Dialog

Before you can create the hierarchy, you need to attach the bracket pairs.

1. Make sure **06VT13.max** is open and maximize the Perspective view.

   Because the rod objects will be moving in unison with the brackets, you can just attach them to the bracket pairs as you create them.

2. Select bracketMA01 and convert it to an Editable Poly. Click the Attach List to open the Attach List dialog. Select bracketMA02 and rodMA01 (see Figure 6.100). Click the Attach button to attach the objects (see Figure 6.101).

   Now you will attach the top bracket assembly.

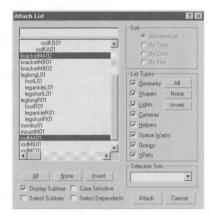

Figure 6.100
The two bracketMA objects and the bottom rodMA01 object are attached as one object.

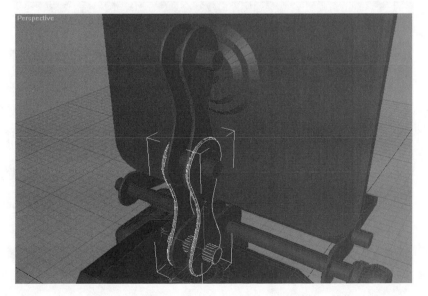

Figure 6.101
The elements of the bottom monitor bracket assembly are attached.

3. Select the bracketMB01 object and convert it into an Editable Poly. Open the Attach List dialog and select the bracketMB02, rodMB01, and rodMC01 objects (see Figure 6.102). Click Attach to attach the objects (see Figure 6.103).

With the two monitor bracket assemblies attached, you're ready to create the hierarchy.

4. Activate the Select and Link tool and select the bracketMA01 object. Drag from the bracketMA01 object to the mountB01 object and release the mouse button.

The mountB01 object flashes momentarily to indicate the successful completion of the link.

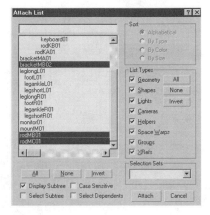

Figure 6.102
The Attach List dialog with the objects selected.

5. Select the bracketMB01 object and, using the Select and Link tool, drag from the bracketMB01 object to the bracketMA01 object. Release the mouse button, and the bracketMA01 object flashes.

The hierarchy is almost complete. In order to attach the armature to the monitor, you need to adjust the orientation of the armature to better meet the monitor's mount object.

Figure 6.103
The elements of the top monitor bracket assembly are attached.

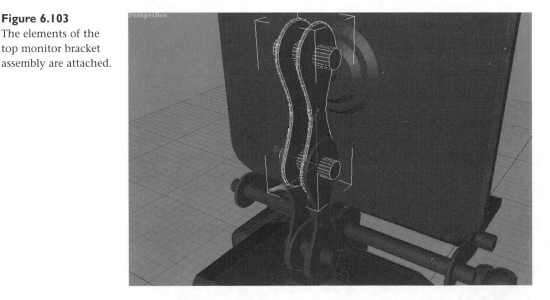

6. Minimize the Perspective view and maximize the Left view. Adjust the Left view to observe the monitor armature (as shown in Figure 6.104).

7. Activate the Select and Rotate tool (View Z-axis) and rotate the bracketMA01 object Z: **30** degrees.

8. Select the bracketMB01 object and rotate it Z: **–60** degrees (see Figure 6.105).

Figure 6.104
Adjust the Left view to this viewpoint.

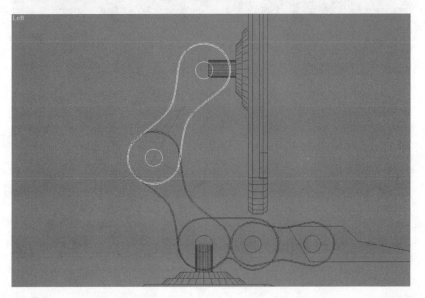

Figure 6.105
The bracketMB01 object is rotated to the correct orientation.

The rod of the bracket is almost perfectly touching the post of the mount. Now you will link the mount object to the monitor and then move the mount into position.

9. Activate the Select and Link tool. Select the monitor01 object, drag from the monitor01 object to the mountM01 object, and release the mouse.

   The mountM01 object flashes, indicating the link is complete.

10. Activate the Select and Move tool (View XY-axis) and move the mountM01 object to divide the rod of the top bracket precisely in half.

    All that's left to do is to link the mount to the armature.

11. Activate the Select and Link tool and select the mountM01 object. Drag from the mountM01 object to the bracketMB01 object to link them.

    The bracketMB01 object flashes, indicating a successful link.

12. To test the link hierarchy, activate the Select and Rotate tool (View Z-axis— Use Pivot Point Center). Select the bracketMA01 object, press and hold down the left mouse button, and drag up and down. Then right-click to exit the rotation.

Figure 6.106
All these objects should rotate along with the bracketMA01 object.

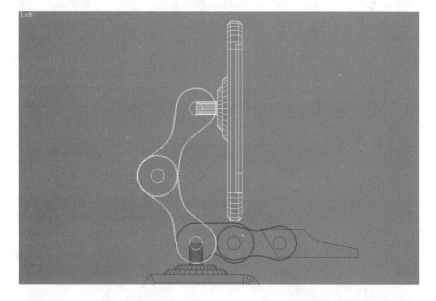

All of the monitor armature should rotate accordingly (see Figure 6.106). If you accidentally released the mouse and rotated the object permanently from its original orientation, click Undo.

Now check the remaining pivots for the monitor armature.

13. With Select and Rotate (View Z-axis) active, select bracketMB01 and test its rotation. It should rotate about the lower rod (see Figure 6.107). Make sure you return the bracketMB01 object to its original orientation.

14. Select the mountM01 object and rotate it.

    Oops! Something isn't right here. The mountM01 object is rotating from where it meets the monitor, not the post. You'll need to adjust its pivot point.

15. Open the Hierarchy panel and activate the Affect Pivot Only button. Activate the Select and Move tool (View X-axis) and move the pivot point to be centered with the top rod of the bracketMB01 object (see Figure 6.108). Deactivate the Affect Pivot Only button.

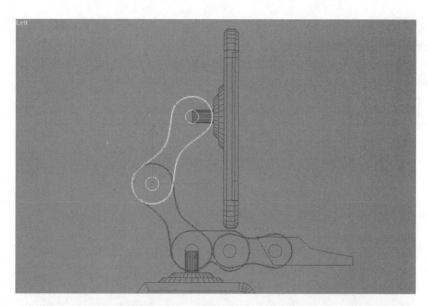

Figure 6.107
The bracketMB01 object should rotate about this axis.

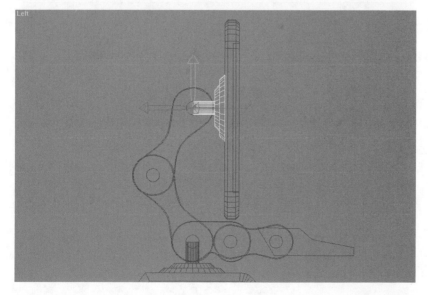

Figure 6.108
The correct placement of the mountM01 object's pivot point.

If you rotate the mountM01 object (View Z-axis) again, it will rotate correctly on the rod.

You're finished building the vote machine. Did you ever think you'd make it this far?

16. Save your work as **06VT14.max**.

In Conclusion

You have successfully completed the vote machine. Both Victor and Mr. Boss are going to be quite proud of you and excited to hear the good news and view the fruits of your labor. In the next chapter, you'll have a good time adding materials and lights and creating the environment. It's going to feel like a vacation compared to all the work it took to get you this far! Good work!

Chapter 7

Adding Materials to the Vote Machine and Creating the Environment

Shortly after finishing the vote machine, you give Victor a call and say, "Hey Victor, do you have a second to come over here and check this out?" He responds with, "Sure thing," and heads your way.

When you finish spinning the vote machine around in the Perspective view, presenting all the machine's angles, Victor nods with approval.

"Great job, Dude," Victor affirms. "I just finished up the storyboard. I put it on this disk for you. It's at \3ds4-ma\project2\images\vote-board.jpg." You open it up to see the images shown in Figure 7.1.

"Looks great Vic," you reply. "So I guess there are straight cuts that go from view to view?"

"Yeah, real clean straight cuts. Gordon is putting together some audio for the animation, but he isn't finished yet, so you could sync the cuts to the score."

Figure 7.1
Victor's finished storyboard.

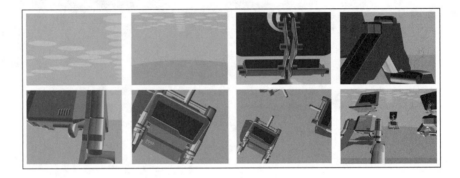

"Oh, by the way Victor, is anything supposed to be shown on those monitors?" you ask.

Victor nods his head and replies, "Among the texture maps I'm giving you, three are for the screen. The first one is a red texture that mimics the circle star theme on the ceiling; use that as the background. The other two textures are text. One reads '2002,' and the other reads 'VOTE.' They both have alpha, so you can composite them right over the background. Maybe you can animate the type sliding in from the sides?"

"Thanks Victor," you respond, "I'll do that, it sounds cool."

As Victor heads back to his workstation, you think to yourself "Boy that guy is sure busy." Speaking of busy, you'd better get to work.

This chapter teaches you about the following:

- Adding reflection maps
- Using the Isolate tool
- Creating composite maps
- Instancing materials

- Adding shadows
- Copying colors from bitmap images

Adding Materials to the Vote Machine

Victor's illustrations roughly depict how the vote machine should appear. From the looks of things, it will be made up of three materials: the gray metallic material, the khaki colored body faceplate material, and the monitor screen material. The gray metallic material is the base material that appears on every object, so create that one first. Then you'll turn to the faceplate because it is a simple application of a texture map. Finally, you'll create the animated material for the monitor screen.

Creating the Metal Material for the Body of the Vote Machine

Examining Victor's illustration, you can see that the gray material is a matte finished metal. It's not the run-of-the-mill polished chrome that most people are used to seeing. The material is a little more refined and subdued, and it has only a hint of reflection. Try to capture that quality on your material.

Exercise 7.1   Using the Phong Shader to Create a Matte Finish

Because the gray metal on Victor's illustration has a matte finish, you shouldn't use the Metal shader. Instead you will use the Phong shader. The metal shader's specular highlights are calculated far too severely to duplicate the type of material you are trying to create. The Phong shader, on the other hand, works well for creating more plastic-appearing materials, which is right on target with the effect you are trying to achieve.

1. Open **06VT14.max** and minimize the Left view. Open the Material Editor and name the top left material **metal**.

2. In the Shader Basic Parameters rollout, change the Blinn shader to Phong.

3. In the Specular Highlights group of the Phong Basic Parameters rollout, change the Specular Level to **28** and the Glossiness to **21** to add a little shininess to the material (see Figure 7.2).

   The settings you entered for the Specular Highlight have created a subtle highlight on the sample sphere. It's just what you were looking for. All the material needs now is a little reflection.

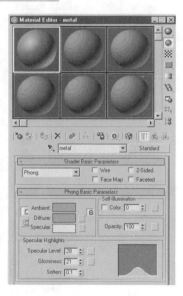

Figure 7.2
The specular highlight is appropriate for the material you are creating.

4. Open the Maps rollout and click the Reflection button to open the Material/Map Browser. Choose Bitmap (see Figure 7.3) and click OK to open the Select Bitmap Image File dialog. Choose **\3ds4-ma\project2\maps\ metal-ref.jpg** and click Open to close the dialog and load the image.

The metal-ref.jpg is applied to the metal material at 100 percent. That's far too bright, but you can adjust that as soon as you finish adjusting the reflection map's parameters.

If you click the View Image button in the Bitmap Parameters rollout, you can view the reflection map you applied to the material. Figure 7.4 shows a black and white image of a mountain range. The mountain range is from a photo I took while hiking in Colorado, and the sky is from one of the standard maps that ship with 3ds max. I composited them in Photoshop and darkened the top and bottom of the image to disguise the pinched seam that occurs at the top and bottom of a spherically mapped reflection map.

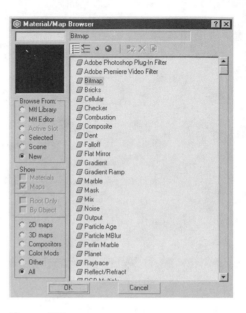

Figure 7.3
The Material/Map Browser with Bitmap selected.

Figure 7.4
The metal-ref.jpg image you've applied as a reflection map.

Although the image is slightly blurry, it still needs to be blurred a little more so the reflection isn't as obvious on the material. Close the Specify Cropping/ Placement dialog if you opened it to view the image.

5. In the Coordinates rollout, change the Blur Offset to **.01**. You will see the reflection soften on the preview sphere. Name this map **metal-rfl** (as shown in Figure 7.5).

The reflection map looks great on the material, but it is far too bright. You need to lessen the intensity.

6. Click the Go To Parent button to return to the root of the metal material. In the Maps rollout, change the Reflection setting to **35** (see Figure 7.6).

   The metal material looks very good, but it might also be just a tad too bright. Darken it a little.

7. In the Phong Basic Parameters rollout, click the Diffuse color swatch to open the Color Selector: Diffuse Color dialog. Change the Color to RGB: **130, 130, 130** (as shown in Figure 7.7). Click Close to close the dialog.

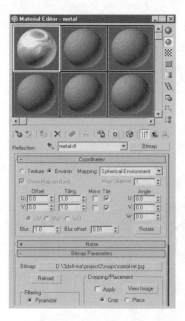

Figure 7.5
The finished metal-rfl reflection map.

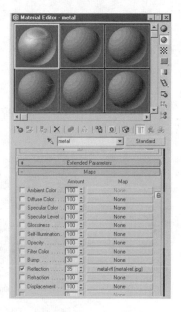

Figure 7.6
Change the Reflection setting to 35.

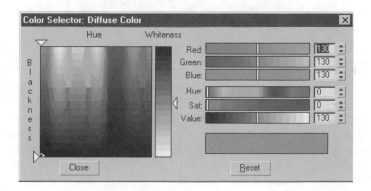

Figure 7.7
Enter RGB: 130, 130, 130 in the Color Selector: Diffuse Color dialog.

Now the material is perfect. Apply it to all the objects in the scene and render a test frame.

8. Choose Edit > Select All to select all the objects in the scene. In the Material Editor, click the Assign Material to Selection button and close the Material Editor. The metal material is now applied to all the objects in the scene.

9. Adjust the Perspective view to view the front of the vote machine at an angle. With the Perspective view active, click the Quick Render button to render an image.

    It looks great to me. When you light it later, it will be outstanding!

10. Save your work as **07VT01.max**.

Creating the Material for the Faceplate of the Vote Machine

The body of the vote machine is mostly the metal material with the exception of the faceplate. The khaki-colored faceplate has the words "2002 Vote" printed on the upper-left corner, and air vents are mapped in the lower-right corner (see Figure 7.8). This is one of the textures Victor was kind enough to provide you with.

Figure 7.8
The file \3ds4-ma\ project2\maps\ bodyface.jpg contains the body's faceplate texture.

Exercise 7.2   Preparing an Object for a Material Map

In essence, it's as if you have a decal or sticker that you can just stick on the front of the body01 object. To accomplish that, you will create a multi/sub-object material much like you did on the Funhouse project. This time, however, you will convert the body01 object into an Editable Poly, change all its polygons to Material ID 1, and then select the faceplate and change its Material ID to 2. While the faceplate polygon is selected in sub-object mode, you will also apply a UVW Map modifier to provide mapping coordinates.

1. With **07VT02.max** open, click Zoom Extents All and select the body01 object (see Figure 7.9).

   Now you want to isolate the body01 object to work on it. Instead of hiding all the unselected objects, you can simply use the Isolate tool so you will be able to do the necessary work on the body01 object.

2. Ctrl+right-click the body01 object and choose Isolate tool. The other objects disappear. Click Zoom Extents All again to zoom in on the body01 object (as shown in Figure 7.10).

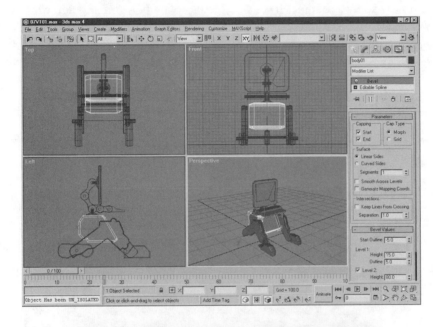

Figure 7.9
Click Zoom Extents All to view all the objects in all the views.

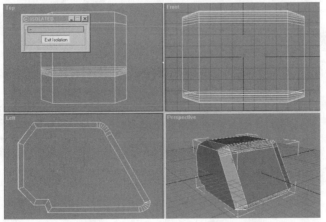

Figure 7.10
The body01 object is isolated.

When you finish working on the body01 object, you can click the Exit Isolation button and the other objects will reappear. Gotta love that Isolate tool! Now you have to convert the body01 object into an Editable Poly so you can change its Material IDs.

3. Right-click the body01 object and choose Convert To > Convert to Editable Poly. Activate Element sub-object level and click the body01 object to select it. In the Surface Properties dialog, change the Material ID to 1 (as shown in Figure 7.11).

You can now apply a Material ID of 2 to the faceplate polygon and add the UVW Map gizmo.

4. Activate Polygon sub-object level. Click the faceplate polygon to select it and change its Material ID to **2** (see Figure 7.12).

Figure 7.11
Assign Material ID 1 for all the faces of the body01 object.

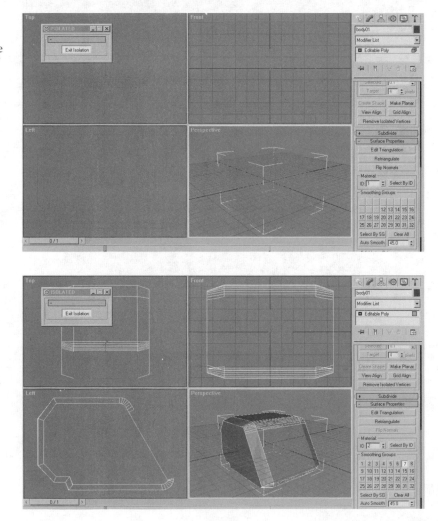

Figure 7.12
Change the face-plate's Material ID to 2.

Now that the faceplate polygon has a unique Material ID, you can apply a UVW Map modifier to that face, providing the correct mapping coordinates for the faceplate texture.

5. Leave Polygon sub-object level active and the faceplate polygon selected. Apply a UVW Map modifier.

The faceplate polygon now has UVW mapping coordinates, but they are not applied correctly. Notice that the mapping gizmo is facing you in the Left view (see Figure 7.13). This indicates that the coordinates are facing sideways. They need to be facing forward.

6. To change the alignment of the mapping gizmo, click X in the Alignment group (see Figure 7.14).

The gizmo is facing forward now. However, it is also too narrow now so it isn't sized completely to the face. Another thing that would be nice is if you could get the gizmo to lie flat on the faceplate polygon. You can easily make the correct adjustments.

7. To lay the UVW Map Gizmo down on the surface of the faceplate polygon, activate the Normal Align button in the Alignment group. Briefly drag the pointer over the surface of the faceplate polygon.

The gizmo aligns itself to the polygon (as shown in Figure 7.15), but it is sideways. The top of the gizmo, indicated by the line rising from the middle, is facing to the left (from your view). You need to stand it back up.

8. Activate sub-object Gizmo and the Select and Rotate tool (Local Z-axis). Rotate the gizmo Z: **–90** degrees so the gizmo points upward (as shown in Figure 7.16).

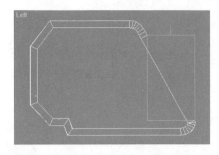

Figure 7.13
The faceplate polygon has a UVW Map modifier applied.

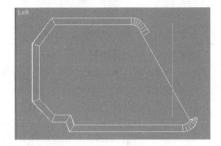

Figure 7.14
The mapping gizmo with an X alignment.

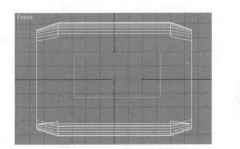

Figure 7.15
Normal Align aligns the gizmo to the polygon.

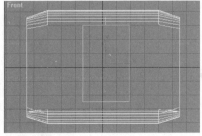

Figure 7.16
The gizmo is now in the correct orientation.

Although the gizmo is now correctly orientated on the body01 object, it is not sized to fit the faceplate polygon correctly. You better fix that.

9. In the Alignment group, click the Fit button.

The gizmo is sized correctly to the polygon (see Figure 7.17). You might notice that the Normal Align tool didn't rotate the gizmo perfectly on the face of the object; the gizmo isn't laying flat on the surface. In this case, it is good enough as it is. However, if you wanted to be a perfectionist, you could rotate the gizmo on its Local X-axis to make the adjustment.

10. Exit Gizmo sub-object and save your work as **07VT02.max**.

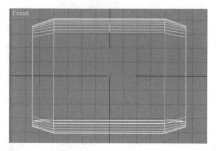

Figure 7.17
The UVW Map gizmo is correctly applied to the faceplate polygon.

Exercise 7.3   Creating a Multi/Sub-Object Material

Now you have the body01 object ready to receive its brand-spanking new material, so you have to create one for it. You will be creating a multi/sub-object material for the body01 object. Because the metal part of the body should have the same metal material you already created, you can just instance the original metal material into the sub-material 1 slot. In the second sub-material slot, you will create the faceplate panel material. Don't delay!

1. With **07VT02.max** open, open the Material Editor and select the second preview slot. Click the Standard button to open the Material/Map Browser. Choose Multi/Sub-Object (see Figure 7.18) and click OK to close the browser. In the resulting Replace Material dialog, choose Discard Old Material?, and then click OK to close the dialog.

   By default, the Multi/Sub-Object material has 10 sub-objects; you need only two.

2. Click the Set Number button and change the Number of Materials to **2**.

3. Click the sub-material 1 button to open its parameters. Click the Standard button to open the Material/Map Browser. In the Browse From group, choose Scene and select the metal material (as shown in Figure 7.19). Click OK to load the material as a sub-material. In the Instance or Copy? dialog, choose Instance and click OK to instance the material as the sub-material.

Figure 7.18
The Material/Map Browser with Multi/Sub-Object selected.

The metal material appears in the sub-material 1 slot now. Because it is an instance, if you were to make changes to the metal material in either the original location or as this sub-material, both would be changed. However, because you made the metal material so perfect, I doubt you'll need to change it.

Turn your attention to putting the faceplate texture on the body object now.

4. In the Material Editor, click the Go To Parent button to return to the root of the multi/sub-object material. Name this material **body** and click the sub-material 2 button to open its parameters. Name this sub-material **faceplate**.

5. To add the faceplate texture, click the gray square to the right of the Diffuse color swatch in the Blinn Basic Parameters rollout (see Figure 7.20) to open the Material/Map Browser.

6. In the Material/Map Browser, check New in the Browse From group. Choose Bitmap (refer to Figure 7.20) and click OK to close the dialog.

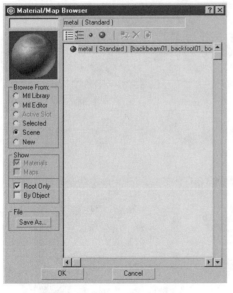

Figure 7.19
Select the metal material in the Material/Map Browser.

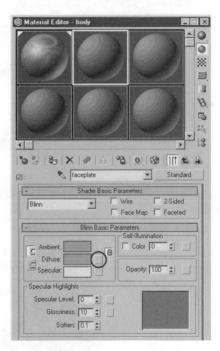

Figure 7.20
Click the blank square to open the Material/Map Browser.

7. In the resulting Select Bitmap Image File dialog, choose **\3ds4-ma\project2\maps\bodyface.jpg** and click Open to load the bitmap. Name this map **faceplate-dif** and click the Assign Material to Selection button (assuming the body01 object is still selected). Click the Show Map in Viewport button.

The map appears in the shaded Perspective view (as shown in Figure 7.21). It seems that you're finished with the materials of the body01 object. Render a test frame to make sure.

8. With the Perspective view active, click Render Last to render a frame (Figure 7.22).

Figure 7.21
The faceplate-dif map is visible on the body01 object in the shaded Perspective view.

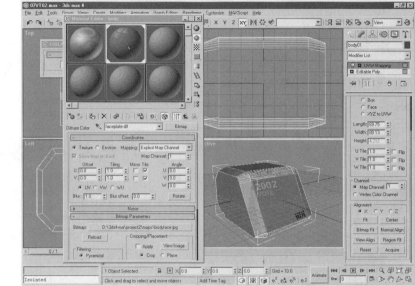

Figure 7.22
The finished body01 object.

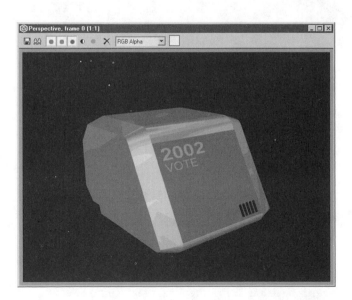

Looks great. Now clean up a bit and save your file.

9. Close the Material Editor and click the Exit Isolation button. Click Zoom Extents All to view all the objects in all the views (as shown in Figure 7.23).

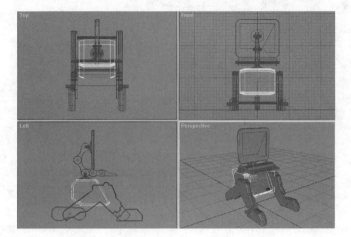

Figure 7.23
All the vote machine objects reappear when you click Exit Isolation.

10. Save your work as **07VT03.max.** You can render the Perspective view again if you want to sneak a peek at the whole vote machine again.

Creating the Material for the Monitor Screen

You are almost finished completing the vote machine. All you need to do is create a material for the monitor01 object. Thinking back to your conversation with Victor, you recall that three textures need to be composited in the screen. That should be pretty simple. You can just copy the faceplate material and change it to spec.

Exercise 7.4   Applying the Mapping Coordinates to the Screen

In this exercise, you use drag and drop to create the new material. Then you change the diffuse map of sub-material 2 to the monitor background map and make the necessary edits to the monitor01 object before you're ready to apply the map.

1. With **07VT03.max** open, select the monitor01 object, click Zoom Extents All Selected, and open the Material Editor. Drag the faceplate material preview sphere to the third material preview slot and release the mouse button. Name the material **monitor** and click the Assign Material to Selection button (see Figure 7.24).

Before you edit the monitor01 object, change the diffuse map of sub-material 2 to the monitor background map. Then you'll make the necessary edits to the monitor01 object so that it will correctly accept the material.

Figure 7.24
The monitor material
has been applied to
the monitor01 object.

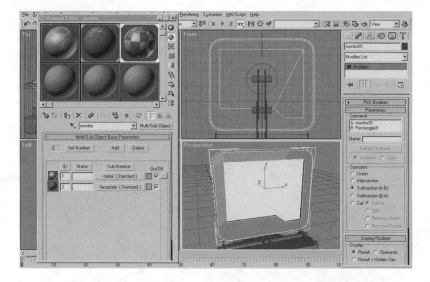

2. Click the sub-material 2 button to
   open its parameters. Rename the sub-
   material from faceplate to **screen**.
   Click the Diffuse map button and in
   the Bitmap Parameters rollout, click
   the Bitmap button. In the Select
   Bitmap Image File dialog, choose
   **\3ds4-ma\project2\maps\
   redstar.jpg**. In the Select Bitmap
   Image File dialog, click the View button to view the file (see Figure 7.25).

   Notice that redstar.jpg is square.
   Actually it's 500 pixels by 500 pixels.
   You need to keep that in mind when
   applying the UVW Map modifier.

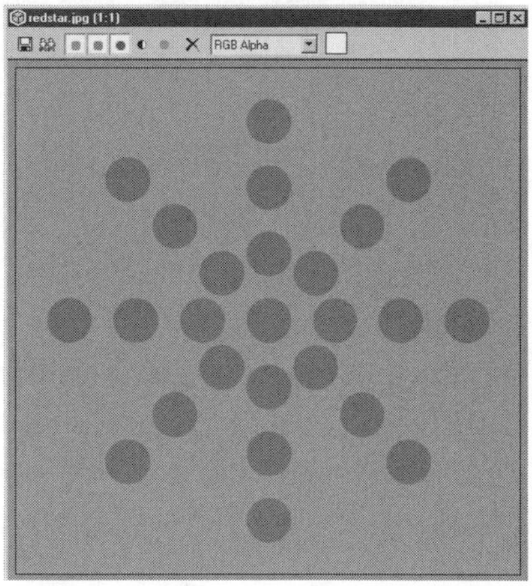

3. Close redstar.jpg and click Open to
   load the map into the Material Editor.

Figure 7.25
View redstar.jpg by clicking the View
button.

   Now you can start to make modifica-
   tions to the monitor01 object. You will need to change the Material IDs
   correctly, much as you did with the body01 object.

4. Close the Material Editor and convert the monitor01 object to an Editable
   Poly. Activate Element sub-object level and click the monitor01 object to
   select it (see Figure 7.26).

5. In the Surface Properties rollout, change the Material ID to 1. Activate Polygon sub-object mode and select the screen. (You might have to Ctrl+click the two faces to select them both.) Change the Material ID to **2** (as shown in Figure 7.27).

Now that the Material IDs are correct, you can add a UVW Map modifier to the selected screen faces.

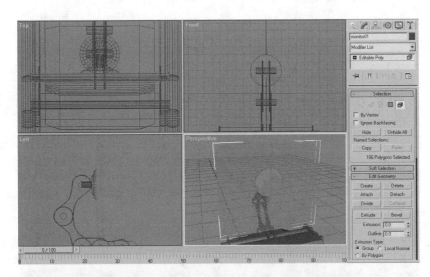

Figure 7.26
The monitor01 object is selected in Element sub-object mode.

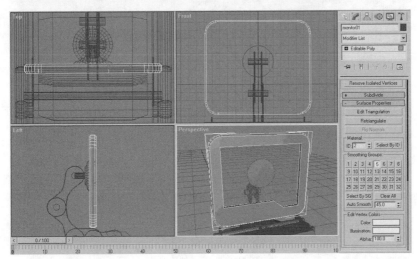

Figure 7.27
The screen is selected, and its Material ID is changed to 2.

6. Leave Polygon sub-object mode active and leave the screen polygons selected. Apply a UVW Map modifier (see Figure 7.28).

The UVW Map is flat on the surface of the screen, which is good. The bad thing is that it's pointing to the right (from your view). Since the screen is planar to the Front view, you can easily fix that with the View Align button.

7. Activate the Front view and click the View Align button.

The UVW Map gizmo orients itself upright (as shown in Figure 7.29), but it does not fit the size of the screen. Remember, however, that the maps Victor gave you were square. So instead of clicking the Fit button, you can manually enter the Gizmo's size.

Figure 7.28
The UVW Map modifier has been applied to the screen polygons.

Figure 7.29
The UVW Map gizmo is upright, thanks to View Align.

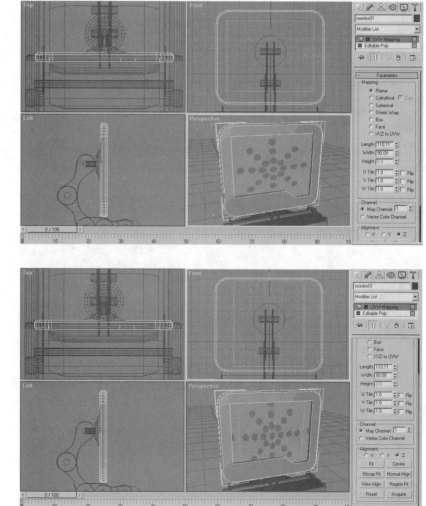

8. In the Mapping group, change the Length and Width to **110** (see Figure 7.30).

   The UVW Map Gizmo is square now, but it needs to be raised a bit so that the star shape will be centered between the top of the tab and the top of the screen.

9. Activate the Select and Move tool (View Y-axis) and activate Gizmo sub-object level. In the Front view, move the gizmo upward approximately 6 units to better center the star shape. Deactivate Gizmo sub-object level and return to the top-level (see Figure 7.31).

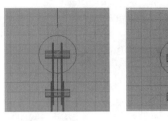

Figure 7.30
The UVW Map Gizmo is now square.

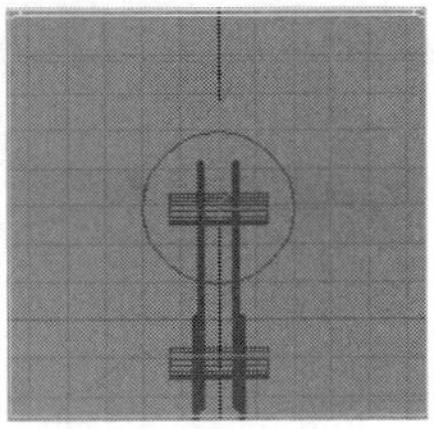

Figure 7.31
The star shape is more centered on the screen now.

Exercise 7.5   Creating a Composite Map

The monitor01 object now has the correct Material IDs and UVW mapping coordinates, and you have created and applied the material for the monitor01 object. All that's left for you to do is to create the composite map using the remaining two textures Victor provided you with.

Victor mentioned that the text images included alpha. What this means is that the image has the normal 24-bit color information plus an extra 8 bits of opacity information. Figure 7.32 shows the 24-bit color information of 2002.tga. Figure 7.33 shows the 8-bit opacity information. The 8-bit opacity information allows you to easily composite the images over one another. Give it a go.

Figure 7.32
The 24-bit color information of 2002.tga.

Figure 7.33
The 8-bit opacity information of 2002.tga.

1. Open the Material Editor. With the faceplate-dif map selected, change the Sample Type from sphere to cube (see Figure 7.34).

2. Click the Bitmap button to open the Material/Map Browser. Choose Composite (as shown in Figure 7.35) and click OK to close the browser. In the Replace Map dialog, choose Keep Old Map a Sub-Map? and click OK to close the dialog.

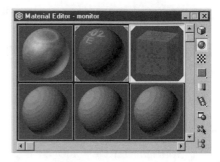

Figure 7.34
Change to the cube sample type.

3. Change the name of the map to **screen**.

   Click the Set Number button, change the Number of Maps to **3**, and click OK to exit the dialog. Three maps are in the composite now (see Figure 7.36).

   The map in the Map 1 slot is the red star map. You better name it so you don't get confused later.

4. Click the Map 1 button and change the name of the map to **screen-star**. Click Go To Parent to return to the root of the composite map.

   Now you can add the other two text images to the composite. Start with the 2002 type.

5. Click the Map 2 button to open the Material/Map Browser. Choose Bitmap and click OK to close the browser. In the Select Bitmap Image File dialog, choose **\3ds4-ma\project2\maps\2002.tga**. Click Open to load the image.

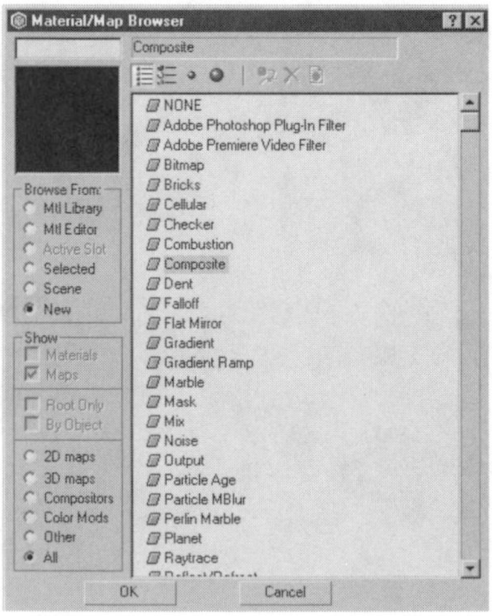

Figure 7.35
The Material/Map Browser with Composite selected.

Figure 7.36
The Composite map has three maps.

The 2002 type is automatically composited over the star shape; however, it made the star shape brighter because Premultiplied Alpha is checked in the Bitmap Parameters.

6. Uncheck Premultiplied Alpha and name this map **screen-2002** (as shown in Figure 7.37).

Premultiplied Alpha determines how alpha is treated in the bitmap. When it's turned on (the default), premultiplied alpha is expected in the file. When it's turned off, the alpha is treated as non-premultiplied, and any RGB values are ignored.

Because Image Alpha is selected in the Alpha Source group, the 2002 type is composited using its stored alpha. Pretty neat!

Now add the VOTE type and call this material done.

7. Click Go To Parent to return to the root of the composite map. Click the Map 3 button and in the Material/Map Browser, choose Bitmap and click OK. In the Select Bitmap Image File dialog, choose **\3ds4-ma\project2\maps\vote.tga** and click Open to load the map. Name the map **screen-vote** and deselect Premultiplied Alpha (see Figure 7.38).

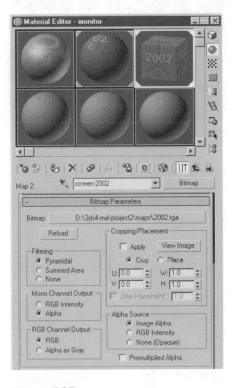

Figure 7.37
With Premultiplied Alpha deselected, the color returns to normal.

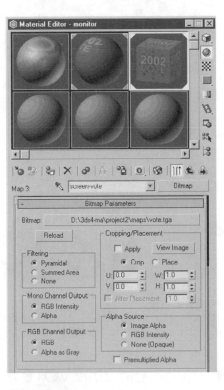

Figure 7.38
The finished screen-vote map.

The composite map is finished for now. Later when you are animating the scene, you will animate these maps to add more interest to the animation.

Because a computer screen is backlit, you should backlight your screen map as well. Adding self-illumination will certainly do the trick.

8. Click Go To Parent twice to return to the root of the screen material. In the Blinn Basic Parameters rollout, change the Self-Illumination to **100** (as in Figure 7.39).

Now render a test frame.

9. Render the Perspective view by clicking the Render Last button. Figure 7.40 shows the rendered image.

It looks great! Save your work and take a much-deserved break.

10. Save your work as **07VT04.max**.

Figure 7.40
The rendered monitor01 object with the new screen sub-material applied.

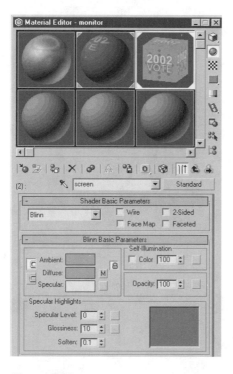

Figure 7.39
The screen's self-illumination is changed to 100, which creates a backlight effect.

Creating the 2002 VOTE Environment

You examine Victor's storyboard and decide the environment looks pretty simple. It consists of a solid powder blue sky and a slightly darker solid blue ground with shadows casting. The ceiling of the environment has the familiar star shape that's created out of circles. It looks pretty straightforward.

Before you start constructing the environment, however, you should instance the vote machine twice so the scene will have three vote machines in a circular fashion, like Victor's storyboard does.

Finishing the Hierarchy

Earlier, when you built the vote machine, you created a partial hierarchy to group crucial objects together. Before you instance the vote machine, you should finish the object's hierarchy so it transfers to all the instances as well.

Exercise 7.6   Linking the Vote Machine Together in One Hierarchy

You need to link the backbeam01, backfoot01, leglongL01, and leglongB01 objects to the body01 object to complete the hierarchy. Then all the vote machine objects will be parented to the body01 object.

1. Make sure **07Vt04.max** is open. Click Zoom Extents All, right-click the Top view label, and check Show Grid. Use Zoom All to zoom out all the views a bit (as shown in Figure 7.41).

2. Open the Select Object dialog, check Display Subtree, and select the backbeam01, backfoot01, leglongL01, and leglongB01 objects (as in Figure 7.42) and click Select to select the objects.

   Now link these objects to the body01 object.

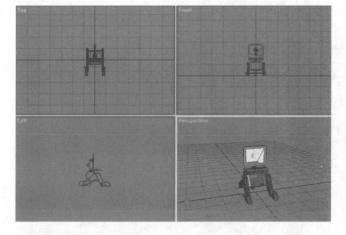

Figure 7.41
The four views have been zoomed out using the Zoom All tool.

Figure 7.42
Select these objects in the Select Object dialog.

3. Activate the Select and Link tool, and then press the H key to open the Select Parent dialog. Choose body01 and click Link to close the dialog. Activate the Select Object tool and open the Select Objects dialog again (see Figure 7.43).

The hierarchy is sound now, and everything is connected to the body01 object.

4. Click Cancel to exit the Select Objects dialog.

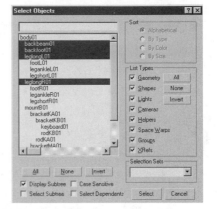

Figure 7.43

The correct hierarchy for the vote machine objects.

Instancing the Vote Machine

You will use the center of the world grid (where the thick black lines cross) as the center of your scene. You need to offset the vote machine in order to create three vote machines surrounding the center.

Exercise 7.7   Instancing with Shift+Rotate

You will move the vote machine into a forward position and then Shift+Rotate it on the World Z-axis to instance the remaining two vote machines.

1. Activate the Select and Move tool, select the body01 object, and move it to XYZ: **0, –225, 88** (see Figure 7.44).

Now that the vote machine is offset from the center of the world, you can use the world's center to instance the other two voting machines.

Figure 7.44

The body01 object is moved to XYZ: 0, –225, 88.

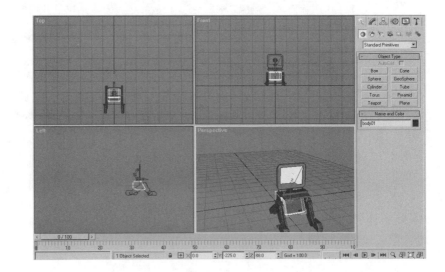

2. Drag a rectangular selection around all the objects to select them. Activate the Select and Rotate tool (World Z-axis—Use Transform Coordinate Center). Shift+drag the selected objects to rotate them 120 degrees, and then release the mouse button. In the Clone Options dialog, check Instance, set Number of Copies to **2** (as shown in Figure 7.45), and click OK to accept the default name. Click Zoom Extents All to see the screen shown in Figure 7.46.

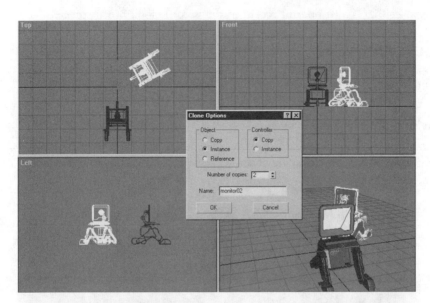

Figure 7.45
The Clone Options with the correct settings.

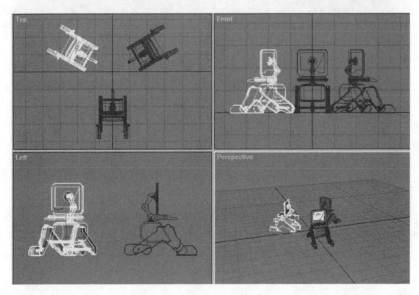

Figure 7.46
The two instanced vote machines are in the correct position and orientation.

Thank goodness for Use Transform Coordinate Center. It allowed you to pivot the rotation of the vote machine on the center of the world. Pretty neat!

3. Save your work as **07VT05.max**.

Creating the Circle Star Ceiling

The circle star ceiling is a wonderful accent to the graphic look of this piece.

Exercise 7.8   Using the Clone to Element Option

You can easily add this accent to your world by creating a circle shape, converting it into a mesh, and instancing it, much as you instanced the vote machines. This should go very smoothly.

1. Make sure **07VT05.max** is open.

2. Activate the 3D Snap toggle. Select Create > Shapes and click the Circle button. Click at the center of world space and create a circle shape with a radius of 73. Name the circle shape **ceiling** (see Figure 7.47).

Figure 7.47
Create a circle shape
at XYZ: 0, 0, 0.

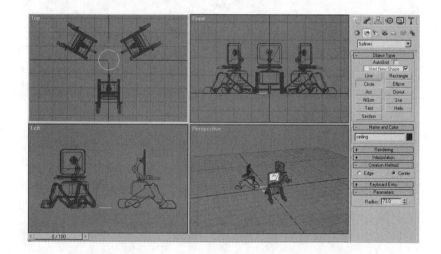

With the first circle shape in the scene, you can use that to build the rest of the ceiling. The first thing you need to do is convert it into an Editable Poly. When it is a polygon, you can copy it to create the rest of the pattern.

3. Right-click the ceiling shape and convert it into an Editable Poly. Then maximize the Top view and zoom out to match Figure 7.48.

Now enter Polygon sub-object level and create the rest of the ceiling pattern.

4. Enter Polygon sub-object level and activate the Select and Move tool (View Y-axis). Select the circle polygon and activate the Selection Lock Toggle. With 3D Snap still active, place the cursor at the center of the circle poly, and the crosshair will turn blue. Shift+drag to create a copy of the circle polygon at XYZ: **0, –200, 0**. In the Clone Part of Mesh dialog, choose Clone to Element (as shown in Figure 7.49) and click OK to create the clone.

   You've just created the first cloned circle poly for the ceiling. You need to create four more the same way.

5. Using the Shift+move technique to copy the circle polygon, make four more copies at (XZ: **0,0**) Y: **–400**, Y: **–600**, Y: **–800**, and Y: **–1000** (see Figure 7.50). Deactivate 3D Snap and Selection Lock Toggle.

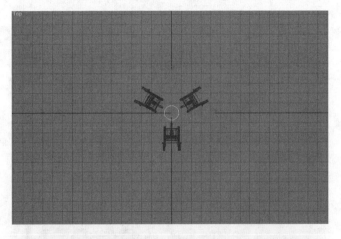

Figure 7.48
Zoom out the Top view to match this viewpoint.

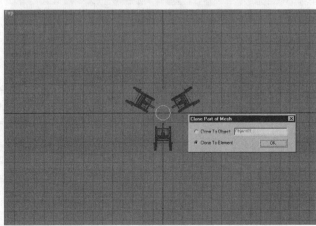
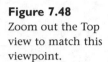

Figure 7.49
The Clone Part of Mesh dialog with Clone to Element selected; notice the position of the cloned circle poly.

Great! You now have six circle polygons. Next, select the outer five circle polygons and clone them by rotating them about the World Transform coordinate system.

6. Drag a rectangular selection around the last five circle polygons you created. Activate Selection Lock Toggle and activate the Select and Rotate tool (World Z-axis—Use Transform Coordinate Center). Figure 7.51 shows the result.

Notice that the axis is in the center of the world. You will create the remaining seven rows of circle polygons now.

7. Activate the Angle Snap toggle. Shift+drag downward to rotate the five circle polygons 45 degrees and release the mouse button. In the Clone Part of Mesh dialog, leave Clone To Element active and click OK to create the clones (see Figure 7.52).

Figure 7.50
The positions for the six circle polygons.

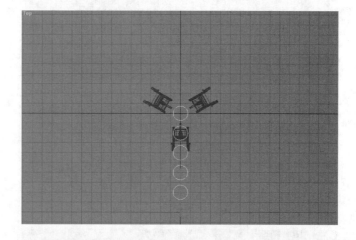

Figure 7.51
The outer five circle polygons are selected, and Selection Lock Toggle is activated.

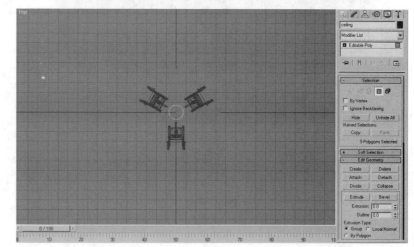

8. Using the Shift+Rotate technique, create six more rows of circle polygons 45 degrees apart (as shown in Figure 7.53). Deactivate Polygon sub-object mode.

   When you finish the ceiling object, you're ready to move it into position.

9. Minimize the Top view and click Zoom Extents All. Activate the Select and Move tool and move the ceiling object to XYZ: **0, 0, 500**, the correct position (as shown in Figure 7.54).

The circle polygons you created to make the ceiling pattern are only one sided, which means only one side of the circle polygon will render. Currently, that side is facing toward the sky; you want it to point toward the ground. To fix this, you simply rotate the ceiling 180 degrees.

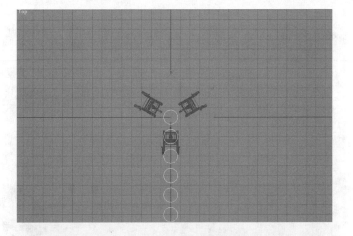

Figure 7.52
The cloned circle polygons form a row at a 45 degree angle to the original row.

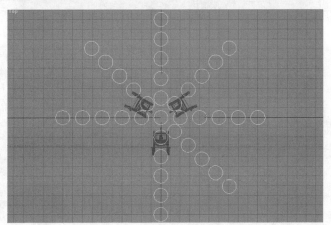

Figure 7.53
The finished ceiling object.

10. Activate the Select and Rotate tool (View Z-axis) and in the Front view, rotate the ceiling object 180 degrees. Adjust the Perspective view to view the scene from a low angle. You will see the shaded circle polygons from below (see Figure 7.55).

   After creating the ceiling object, you can add the material to it. Looking at Victor's storyboard, the material is going to be a simple self-illuminated material.

11. Open the Material Editor and select the first preview slot in the second row. Name this material **ceiling** and assign it to the ceiling objects.

   To get the perfect color for the ceiling, you can just borrow it from Victor's storyboard.

Figure 7.54
The ceiling is now in the correct position

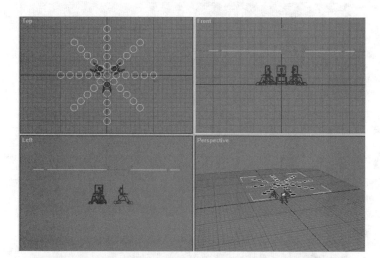

Figure 7.55
The ceiling has been rotated 180 degrees.

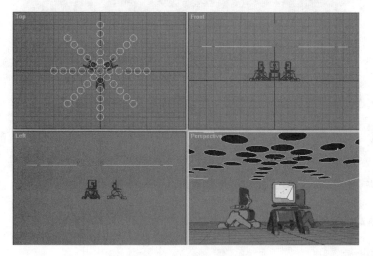

12. Use File > View Image File to open Victor's storyboard image (**\3ds4-ma\ project2\vote-board.jpg**). Right-click on one of the bright circles, and the color is copied to the color swatch above (see Figure 7.56).

13. Copy the color swatch from the vote-board.jpg image to the Diffuse color swatch in the Material Editor. In the Copy or Swap Colors dialog, choose Copy. The light blue color copies into the Diffuse slot (it should be roughly RGB: 100, 204, 243). In the Blinn Basic Parameters rollout, change the Self-Illumination setting to **100**. Then render the Perspective view; it should look like Figure 7.57.

    It's fantastic! Looks to me as though the ceiling is finished. Be sure to save your hard work.

14. Save your work as **07VT06.max** and close the Material Editor.

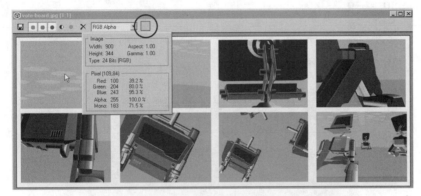

Figure 7.56
You can get the exact color by right-clicking on the image.

Figure 7.57
The rendered Perspective view, with the new self-illuminated light blue ceiling.

Adding Lights and Creating the Floor

The scene is almost finished. All you need to do is add a few lights and a floor to catch the shadows and change the environment background color. Start by adding two lights, and then add the floor.

Exercise 7.9   Creating Omni Lights

To illuminate the scene, you decide to add two lights. One light will act as the primary light or the key light. The second light will be the fill light, brightening the areas that the key light leaves in shadow. Add the key light first.

1. With **07VT06.max** open, select Create > Lights, activate the Omni button, and click in the Top view to create an Omni light. Name the light **OmniKey**. Then activate the Select and Move tool and move the light to XYZ : **–650, –850, 350** (as shown in Figure 7.58).

Figure 7.58
Create the OmniKey light and move it to XYZ: –650, –850, 350.

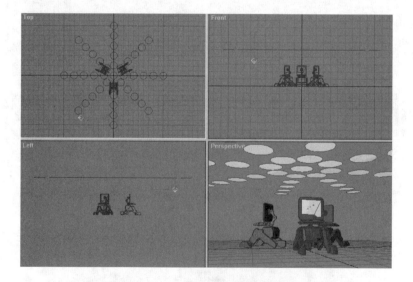

You might want to make a few adjustments to the OmniKey light.

2. With the OmniKey light selected, open the Modify panel. In the General Parameters rollout, change the light's color to RGB: **180, 180, 180** and check Cast Shadows (see Figure 7.59).

You need to examine the shadow casting settings to make sure they are correct.

Figure 7.59
The General Parameters rollout for the OmniKey light, with the correct parameters applied.

3. Open the Shadow Parameters rollout and change the Shadow Map to Ray Traced Shadows (as shown in Figure 7.60).

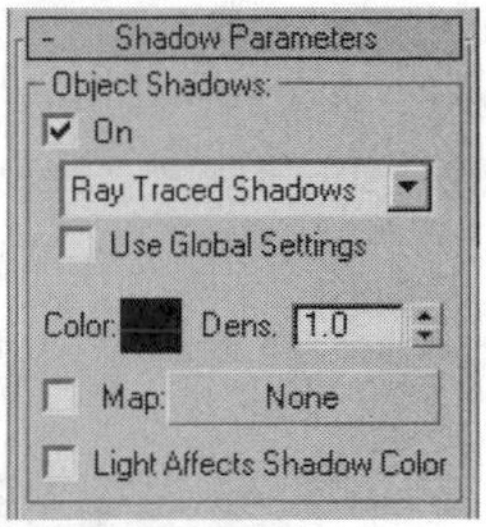

Ray Traced shadows, generated by tracing the path of rays sampled from a light source, are more accurate than Shadow Mapped shadows. They always produce a hard edge. A Shadow Map is a bitmap that the renderer generates during a pre-rendering pass of the scene. It is projected from the direction of the spotlight. This method provides a softer edge and can require less calculation time than Ray Traced shadows do, but the Shadow Map is less accurate. In this scene, you want hard graphic edges, so you need to use Ray Traced shadows.

Go ahead and add the fill light while you are at it.

Figure 7.60
In the Shadow Parameters dialog, select Ray Traced Shadows.

4. Create an Omni light in the Top view, name it **OmniFill**, and move it to XYZ: **–450, –175, 800** (see Figure 7.61).

Figure 7.61
The OmniFill light in the correct position.

The fill light is in place in the scene. However, you also want it to cast shadows, so you'll have to activate them.

5. With the OmniFill light selected, open the Modify panel. In the Shadow Parameters rollout, select On and make sure Ray Traced Shadows is selected (as shown in Figure 7.62).

Figure 7.62
Checking On is the same as checking Cast Shadows in the General Parameters rollout.

The lights are in pretty good positions. You might want to adjust their positions when you animate the scene, but you have a good base to start with.

6. Adjust the Perspective view and render a frame (see Figure 7.63).

7. Save your work as **07VT07.max**.

Figure 7.63
The rendered
Perspective view with
Ray Traced shadows.

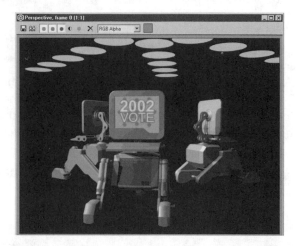

Exercise 7.10   Using Ray Traced Shadows

Add the floor, which will catch some of those hard-edged Ray Traced shadows.

I. With **07VT07.max** open, select Create > Shapes and click the Circle button. In the Top view, create a circle with a Radius of **1000** at XYZ: **0, 0, 0** (you can use the 3D Snap toggle to accurately create it). Name it **floor** (see Figure 7.64).

Figure 7.64
The circle shape will
be the floor object.

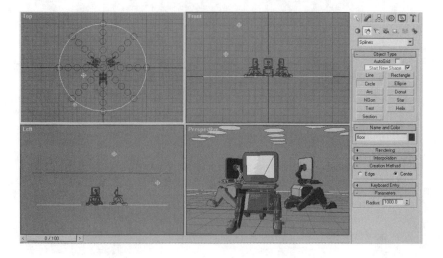

The circle shape is exactly that, a shape. You need to convert it into an object before it can receive shadows.

2. With the floor shape selected, right-click it and convert it into an Editable Poly. If you render the Perspective view, you will see shadows cast on the floor (see Figure 7.65).

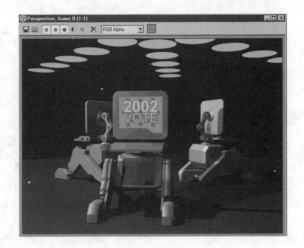

Figure 7.65
The floor shape has been converted into an Editable Poly.

The floor is certainly serving purpose in the scene, receiving shadows and giving something for the vote machines to rest on. Now you need to give the floor the correct material.

3. With the floor object selected, open the Material Editor. Select the second material preview slot in the second row and name it **floor**. Apply the floor material to the floor object. To attain the color of the floor, open Victor's storyboard from \3ds4-ma\project2\images\vote-board.jpg. Right-click the floor color and drag the color swatch from the image to the Diffuse slot in the Material Editor (the color should be roughly RGB: 0, 148, 196).

To achieve a more graphic, solid color on the floor (which will brighten up the harsh shadows), you can add a little self-illumination to the floor material as well.

4. Change the Self-Illumination value to **50**. Close the Material Editor, but keep Victor's storyboard open.

There is one thing left to do: change the background color from black to blue. You can steal that color from Victor's storyboard image.

5. Choose Rendering > Environment to open the Environment dialog. Right-click on the blue background color of Victor's storyboard, and then copy the color swatch to the Background Color swatch in the Environment dialog (the color should be roughly RGB: 0, 178, 236). Close the storyboard image and the Environment dialog.

6. Render the Perspective view (see Figure 7.66).

7. Save your work as **07VT08.max**.

Figure 7.66
The rendered
Perspective view
shows the scene to
this point.

In Conclusion

The scene is now completely built. As you animate it, you might need to make a few tweaks here and there to the lights and such, but the scene is certainly constructed. It has been a long road to get to this point, but in the next chapter, you will breath some life into the scene by adding animation and audio!

Chapter 8

Animating and Rendering the 2002 Vote Machine

You've built the vote machine and the environment in which it lives. You've rendered a frame or two and you are happy with the results. To animate the scene, you need to corner Gordon and ask him if he is finished creating the score for the animation.

In this chapter, you'll learn about the following:

- Adding music
- Using the Array tool to create multiple copies
- Animating to a storyboard
- Rendering multiple cameras with Field of View

Adding the Musical Score

You find Gordon and politely ask if he's finished creating the music. He turns to look at you and smiles. He plays a funky futuristic track while doing his best Mr. Roboto dance routine. "Wow, that's pretty cool Gordon! How appropriate," you exclaim.

"Thanks," Gordon responds. "It's on the disk for you to use. Anything else you need?"

"Nah, but thanks Gordon," you say with a wave as you walk away replaying his robot dance in your mind.

Exercise 8.1   Adding the Music to the Scene

Now that you have the music for the animation in your possession, you can add it to the scene and start to plan your attack.

1. With **07VT08.max** open, open the Track View. In the Track View, select and right-click the Sound track title and choose Properties to open the Sound Options dialog. Click Choose Sound and choose **\3ds4-ma\project2\ sounds\VoteMachine3D.wav** (see Figure 8.1). Click OK to close the Sound Options dialog. Close the Track View for now as well.

   The audio is twelve seconds long. So you'll want to adjust your scene length to match.

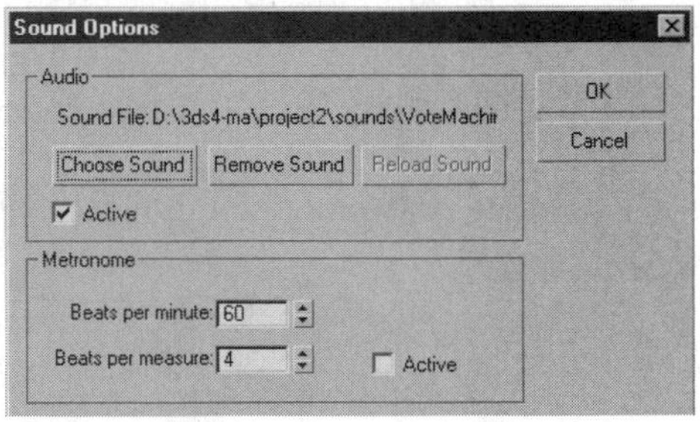

Figure 8.1

The Sound Options dialog with the VoteMachine3D.wav loaded.

2. Click the Time Configuration button to open its dialog. In the Animation group, change the End Time to **360** (as shown in Figure 8.2) and click OK to close the dialog.

   The scene is now twelve seconds long as well. You don't need pad or pre-roll because this animation is going to air as a 12-second spot. It will be created to precisely fit the designated time. Now that the audio is in the scene, you can hear it for the first time loaded into 3ds max.

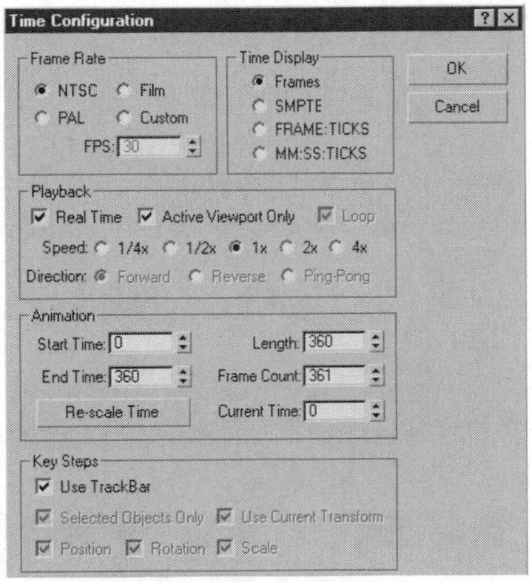

Figure 8.2
Enter the new End Time in the Time Configuration dialog.

3. Click the Play Animation button. You hear the music play as the time slider moves through the timeline.

4. Save your work as **08VT01.max**

Animating the Scene

The time has come for you to animate this scene. There are a few things you need to consider, however, before you start. First, you need to plan the animation. Then you will add depth of field to the cameras using the Depth of Field Multi-Pass Effect. This is the cleanest, most accurate way to create focus in 3ds max.

You will also use multiple cameras to animate this scene. To render the animation, you might think you could create a queue in Video Post and render all the cameras out in one pass. That is a good idea, but the sad reality is that Multi-Pass Effects do not render in Video Post. This is unfortunate, but it is better that you find it out now rather than later.

So instead of animating all the cameras and rendering them all at the end, you will animate one camera and then render it. Then you will animate the next camera and render it. And you will follow this suit until the animation is finished. When you finish rendering all the frames, you will build a Video Post queue to assemble the five shots with the audio.

Planning the Animation to the Storyboard and Music

Take a look at Victor's storyboard one more time (see Figure 8.3). The scene can be broken down into five separate shots:

- Shot 1: The first two panels of the storyboard, showing the empty scene

- Shot 2: The third panel of the storyboard, showing the camera moving behind the monitor

- Shot 3: The fourth and fifth shot of the storyboard, showing the camera moving around the vote machine's leg to the front of the faceplate

- Shot 4: The sixth and seventh panels of the storyboard, showing the camera pulling back from a one-shot to a three-shot

- Shot 5: The eighth panel of the storyboard, showing the vote machines from a low angle

Figure 8.3
Victor's storyboard for the 2002 Vote animation.

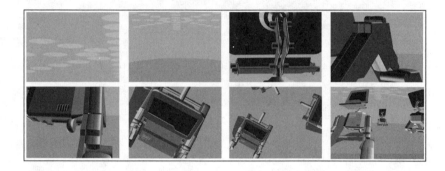

For all intents and purposes, you will stick to that 5-shot game plan. However, you need to figure out where and how you will make the transitions between these shots in the animation. First they need to be timed to the music.

The first shot should occur in the time before the first base drum sounds. If you play the animation or drag the time slider, you will hear the base drum hit around frame 46. So you will transition to the second shot one frame before the base drum hit. This means the first shot will use frames 0 through 44.

The second shot should be paced equal to the first shot in order to keep the rhythm of the animation moving. The music is in 4/4 time, making four beats per measure. The second shot starts on the one-count, so the third shot should as well. Listening carefully to the music, you hear the base drum of the second one-count strike on frame 103. So you should end shot two by frame 101. This means the second shot will use frames 45 through 101.

The third shot should be one measure long as well, making it last four beats. If you examine the music carefully, you hear the base drum of the one-count hit again at around frame 160. So you should end the third shot at frame 158. This means the third shot will use frames 102 through 158.

The fourth shot should be longer than the other shots because it will show the screen of the vote machine. This is where you can play up the 2002 Vote textures you added to the screen. Two measures, or eight beats, will provide plenty of time for this shot. Listening to the music, you hear the base drum hit at frame 270. So you should end this shot by frame 268. This means the fourth shot will use frames 159 through 268.

By default the fifth shot will use frames 269 through 360.

To recap, and for easy reference, here are the timings for the five shots of the animation:

> Shot1: Frames 0–44
>
> Shot2: Frames 45–101
>
> Shot3: Frames 102–158
>
> Shot4: Frames 159–268
>
> Shot5: Frames 269–360

It's always a good idea to go through and break the animation down before you start to keyframe. That way you won't have to think about what you are animating while you animate, and there will be no unexpected surprises.

Animating Shot One

Shot one is the establishing shot of the animation. The storyboard shows the environment without the machines. Because you are rendering the animation shot by shot, you could simply hide the vote machines and render the scene without them—which is exactly what you're going to do.

Exercise 8.2   Hiding Unwanted Elements and Creating Camera Jibs

In this exercise, you will hide the vote machines and add the first camera to the scene.

1. With **08VT01.max** open, open the Display panel and in the Hide rollout, click Hide by Name to open the Hide Objects dialog. Make sure Display Subtree and Select Subtree are checked. Select body01, body02, and body03, and the children will automatically be selected as well because Select Subtree is activated. The only four things that should not be selected are ceiling, floor, OmniFill, and OmniKey (see Figure 8.4). Click Hide to hide the vote machines.

Now you can create a camera in the scene. While working on the Funhouse project, you used dummy helpers to create a jib for the camera. You will implement the same technique in this animation.

2. Activate the 3D Snap toggle, open the Create > Camera panel, and click the Free button. Click in the Front view at XYZ: 0, 0, 0 to create a camera. In the Parameters rollout, click the 35mm Stock Lenses button (see Figure 8.5).

Figure 8.4
The Hide Objects dialog with the vote machines selected.

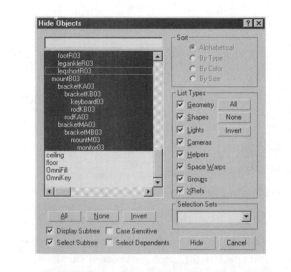

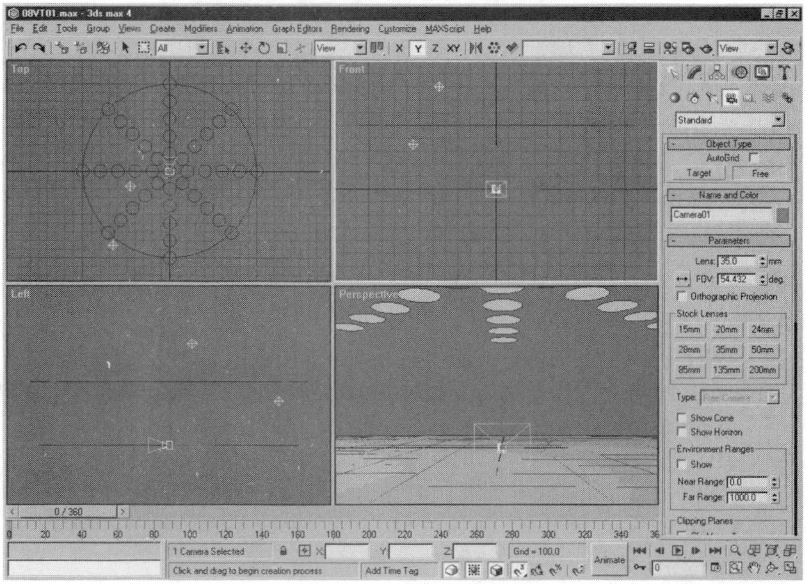

Figure 8.5
Click in the Front view to create a camera with a 35mm lens.

3. Activate the Select and Move tool and move the camera to XYZ: **0, −300, 0**.

   Now you will create the Dummy helpers to create the jib arm.

4. Open the Create > Helpers panel and click the Dummy button. Create two dummy helpers in the Top view, one larger than the other, at XYZ: **0, 0, 0** (as shown in Figure 8.6). Deactivate the 3D Snap toggle; you no longer need it.

5. Activate the Select Objects tool and select the smaller dummy helper; name it **DummyTilt01**. Select the larger dummy helper and name it **DummyPan01** (see Figure 8.7).

   Now link the dummy helpers and the camera to create your jib.

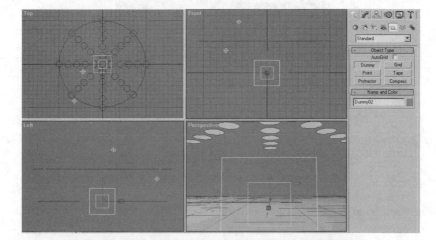

Figure 8.6
Two dummy helpers have been created for the jib.

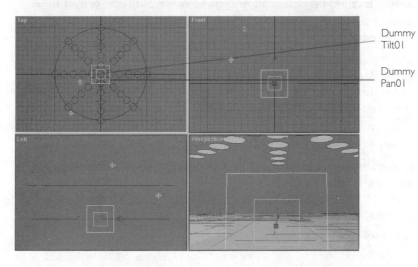

Dummy
Tilt01

Dummy
Pan01

Figure 8.7
Name the dummy helpers appropriately.

6. Zoom in the Top view to observe the camera jib elements more closely. Activate the Select and Link tool.

Select Camera01 and drag to the DummyTilt01 helper (the smaller one) to link them together. Select the DummyTilt01 object and drag to the DummyPan01 object to link them. Activate the Select Objects tool and open the Select Objects dialog to check your hierarchy. Select all three jib elements (as shown in Figure 8.8). Click Select to select them and exit the dialog.

Figure 8.8
The dummy helpers and Camera01 are linked correctly.

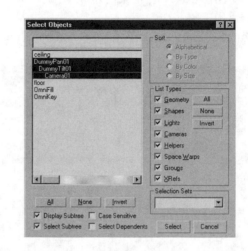

Having completed the camera jib assembly, copy it four times so you will have one for each of the shots. To create the copies, you will not use the Edit > Clone method because it allows you to make only one copy a time. Instead you will use the Array tool, which allows you to make as many copies you desire.

7. With the three jib elements selected, click the Array button in the toolbar to open the Array dialog. In the Array Dimensions group, leave 1D active and change the Count to **5**. The Count number includes the original, so you need five total (see Figure 8.9). Click OK to exit the Array dialog and create the copies.

You only need one camera jib at a time, so just hide the ones you don't need.

8. Activate the Display panel in the Hide rollout and click Hide by Name to open its dialog. With Display Subtree and Select Subtree active, select DummyPan02, DummyPan03, DummyPan04, and DummyPan05 (see Figure 8.10). Click Hide to close the dialog and hide the extra jibs.

9. Save your work as **08VT02.max**.

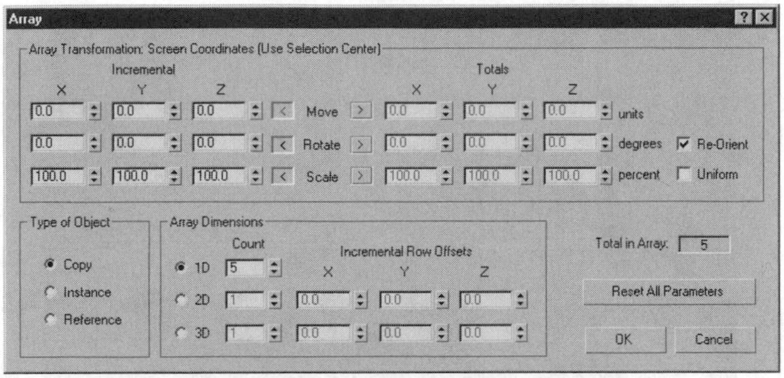

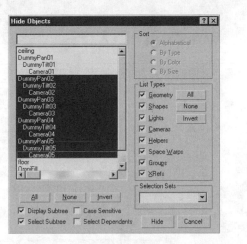

Figure 8.9
The Array dialog with the proper settings.

Figure 8.10
The Hide Objects dialog with the extra jibs selected.

Exercise 8.3   Animating a Scene

Now that you have a camera jib to work with, you can finally add motion to the scene. Move the camera to its start position.

1. With **08VT02.max** open, activate the Perspective view and press the C key to change it to a camera view. In the Select Camera dialog, choose Camera01 (see Figure 8.11) and click OK to close the dialog.

2. Activate the Select and Move tool and move the DummyPan01 helper to XYZ: **–150, –500, 300** (as shown in Figure 8.12).

3. Activate the Select and Rotate tool (Local Z-axis) and rotate the DummyPan01 helper Z: **25** degrees (see Figure 8.13).

   Now tilt the camera so you can look up at the ceiling.

4. Activate the Select and Rotate tool (Local X-axis) and rotate DummyTilt01 X: **30** degrees (as shown in Figure 8.14).

Figure 8.11
The Select Camera dialog with Camera01 selected.

Figure 8.12
The DummyPan01 object is in its start position.

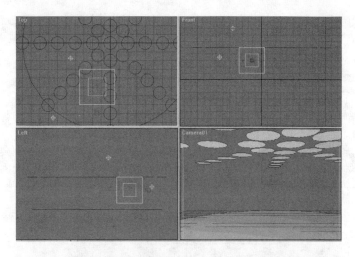

Figure 8.13
The DummyPan01 object is rotated Z: 25 degrees on its local axis.

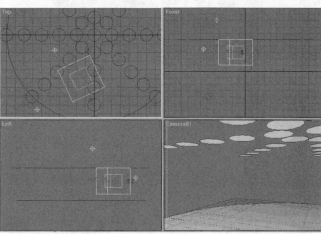

Figure 8.14
The camera is in its start position.

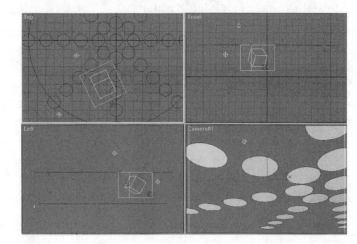

The camera is in the correct position for the start of the animation. You can now move to frame 44 and set the camera's end orientation.

5. Advance to frame 44 and activate the Animate button. Activate the Select and Move tool and move the DummyPan01 helper to XYZ: **0, –500, 250** (see Figure 8.15).

6. Activate the Select and Rotate tool (Local Z-axis) and rotate DummyPan01 Z: **–25** to move the camera into its end orientation (see Figure 8.16).

7. Activate the Select and Rotate tool (Local X-axis) and rotate the DummyTilt01 helper X: **–30** to return it to XYZ: **0, 0, 0** so you can move the camera into its end orientation (see Figure 8.17).

You are finished animating the camera for the first scene. Deactivate the Animate button and play the animation, and then you'll be ready to set up the depth of field.

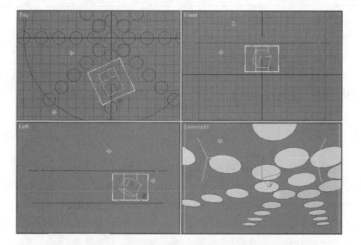

Figure 8.15
The DummyPan01 helper is centered on the world's X-axis.

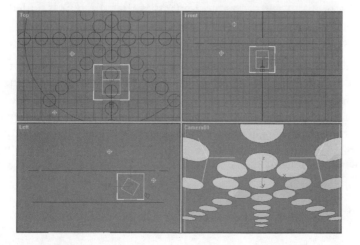

Figure 8.16
The DummyPan01 helper is rotated to XYZ: 0, 0, 0.

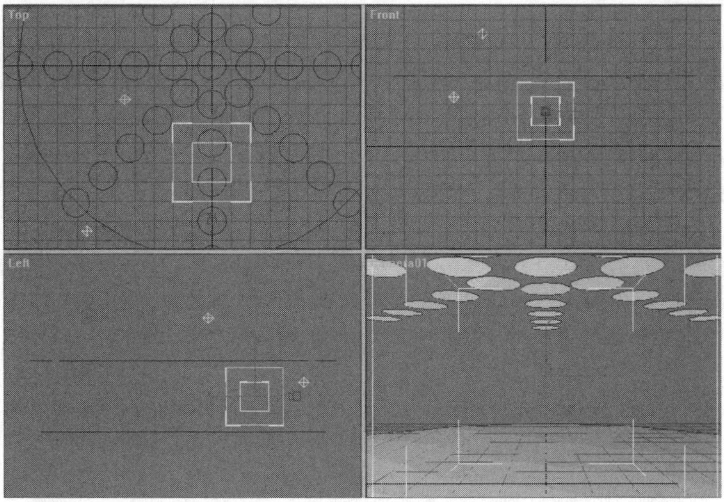

Figure 8.17
The camera is in the
correct final position.

8. Deactivate the Animate button. Activate the Camera01 view and click the Play Animation button to view the camera move.

   At frame 0, the camera is looking upward at the ceiling. As time moves forward toward frame 44, the camera tilts down, pans to the right, and centers to the world grid.

9. Save your work as **08VT03.max**.

Exercise 8.4   Adding Depth of Field and Rendering Shot One

Victor's storyboard images have a hint of depth of field, or in simpler terms "focus," applied. You will add this effect to your animation as well. There are several ways to apply the depth of field effect to a rendering inside 3ds max. For example, there is a Depth of Field post effect in Render Effects and a Focus effect in Video Post. The problem with these post effects is that the blur is added after the effect is rendered, and when multiple objects overlap, the blur effect is not rendered cleanly.

A more effective way to render depth of field is to use the multi-pass effect, which is new to 3ds max R4. It creates the depth of field effect by rendering the frame several times, offsetting the camera slightly each pass. When all the iterations are combined into one frame, the image appears to be blurred. The multi-pass depth of field effect allows you to use the camera's target as the center of the offset, meaning the least amount of offset occurs where the target is located, keeping that area in focus. As objects get further and further away from the target, the blurring effect becomes more and more obvious.

The only drawback to using this technique is that it escalates rendering times considerably. As mentioned above, to create the focus effect, you must render the frames a particular number of times, as defined by the user. The more iterations, the better the effect.

In this exercise, you will experiment with the depth of field effect as you apply it in the scene.

1. With **08VT03.max** open, select Camera01 and open the Modify Panel. Advance to frame 10. In the bottom of the Parameters rollout, check Enable the Depth of Field Multi-Pass Effect. With the Camera01 view active, click the Preview button (see Figure 8.18).

   The multi-pass renders a preview in the Camera01 view. However, everything seems out of focus. See if you can adjust that by changing the Target Distance.

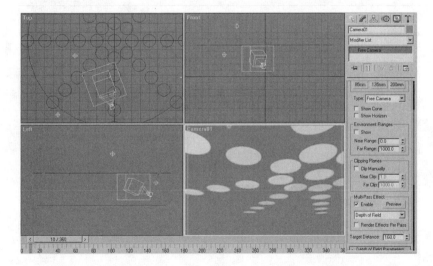

Figure 8.18
The multi-pass effect renders in the Camera01 view.

2. At the very bottom of the Parameters rollout, change the Target Distance to **300**. Click Preview again, and you'll see that the focus is better (as shown in Figure 8.19).

   That's much more acceptable. However, I would like to see a little more blur in the distance. To adjust that, you change the Sample Radius value. The Sample Radius is the radius by which the scene is shifted to generate blurriness. Increasing the value increases the overall blurriness of the effect. So increase the value and see what happens.

3. In the Depth of Field Parameters rollout, change the Sample Radius to **3** and click Preview again (see Figure 8.20).

Figure 8.19
The Target Distance of 300 creates a better effect.

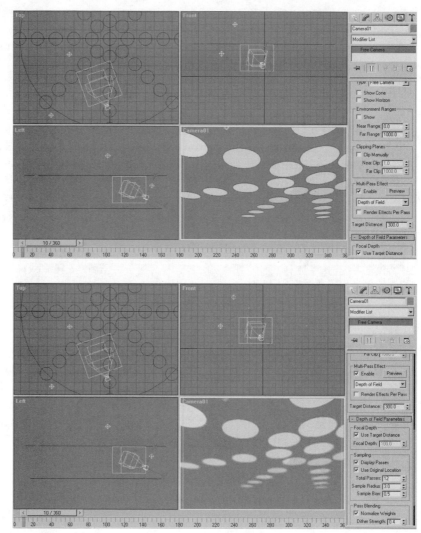

Figure 8.20
The field of view effect is more dramatic.

The field of view effect is perfect now. But you can check it for sure by rendering a frame.

4. Click the Render Scene button to open the Render Scene dialog. In the Time Output group, leave Single active, and in the Output Size group, click the 320×240 button (as shown in Figure 8.21). Click Render to render a frame (see Figure 8.22).

Right now the renderer is rendering 12 passes to create the focus effect. You could probably get away with half that many passes and still have an acceptable effect. Give it a try.

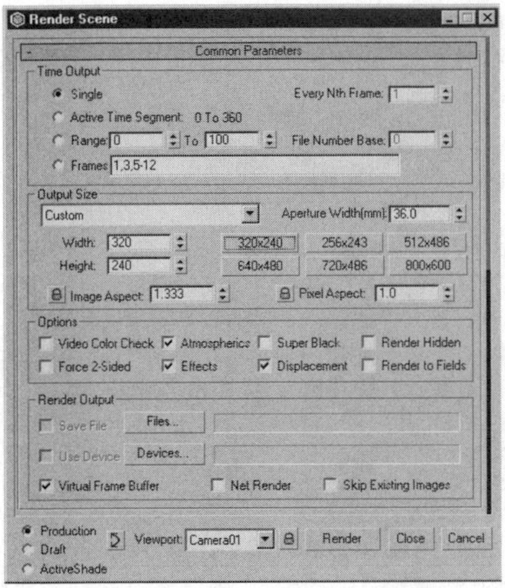

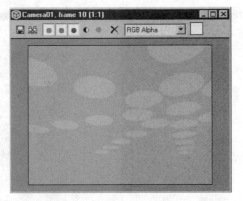

Figure 8.22
The rendered field of view effect.

Figure 8.21
The Render Scene dialog with correct settings.

5. In the Depth of Field Parameters rollout, change the Total Passes to **6** (as shown in Figure 8.23). Then render frame 10 again from the Camera01 view.

   The rendered effect looks the same. Leave the Total Passes set to 6. You can now render the first shot. You will render frames 0 through 44 as individual frames into their own folders. You will render all the frames from all the cameras into this folder. In my case, it's going to be \3ds4-ma\project2\images\jpg\vote.jpg. You can render to any folder you desire as long as you remember where it is. If you are concerned about quality, you can render the images as Targa (TGA) files; although they take up more space that way, they are uncompressed images.

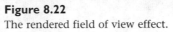

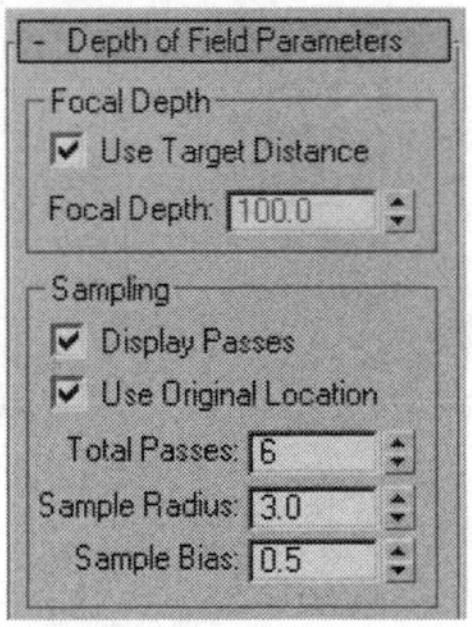

Figure 8.23
The Depth of Field Parameters rollout with Total Passes changed to 6.

6. In the Time Output group of the Render Scene dialog, activate Range and change the values to **0** and **44**. In the Render Output group, click the Files button and choose an output folder, file type, and name.

7. When you are finished (see Figure 8.24), save your work as **08VT04a.max** and click the Render button.

   You are saving your work with the letter "a" after it so you can easily recall that it is the first shot. After a few minutes, the 45 frames should be finished rendering. You are ready to start the next shot! One down, four to go.

Figure 8.24
The Render Scene
dialog, ready to
render.

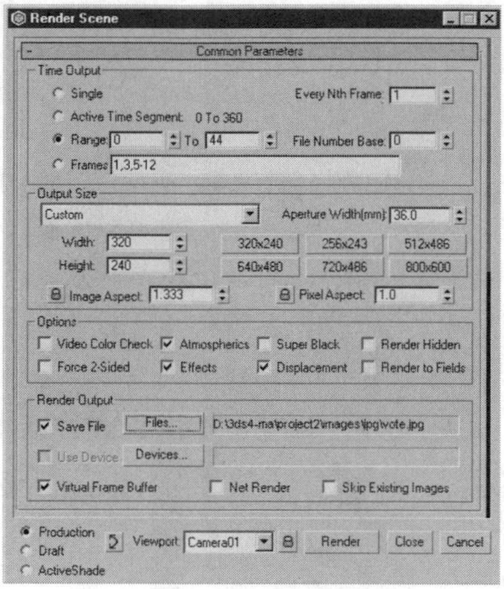

Animating Shot Two

The second shot, as indicated on the storyboard, takes place behind the monitor and focuses on its armature. To add interest to the shot, you will animate the rotation of the armature and the monitor to create the sense that the machine is assembling. You will also animate the camera to have a slow orbit around the vote machine to add interest and movement. First, prep the scene.

Exercise 8.5   Unhiding Objects and Positioning the Camera Jib

You know what you have to do; now it's just a matter of doing it. Before you can start animating the scene, you need to do a little housework in the scene. You need to hide the first camera jib and unhide the second camera jib. Also, you can't forget to unhide the three vote machines as well!

1. With **08VT04a.max** open, close the Render Scene dialog. Open the Display panel and click Hide by Name to open the Hide Objects dialog. Select DummyPan01, DummyTilt01, and Camera01. Then click Hide to hide them.

2. To unhide the second camera, click the Unhide by Name button to open its dialog. Make sure that both Display Subtree and Select Subtree are checked. Select body01, body02, body03, and DummyPan02 (as shown in Figure 8.25) and click Unhide to unhide the objects.

3. With the Camera01 view active, press the C key to open the Select Camera dialog. Choose Camera02 and click OK to close the dialog and change the view to Camera02 (as shown in Figure 8.26).

    Now move the camera into its start position.

Figure 8.25
You need to unhide the three vote machines and the second camera jib.

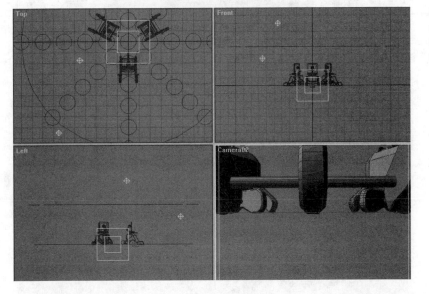

Figure 8.26
Change from Camera01 view to Camera02 view.

4. Activate the Select and Move tool and move the DummyPan02 helper to XYZ: **0, –185, 190** (see Figure 8.27).

   DummyPan02 is in the right place. However, it is facing the wrong direction. Adjust that now.

5. Activate the Select and Rotate tool (Local Z-axis) and rotate the DummyPan02 helper Z: **–100** (as shown in Figure 8.28).

   The camera is at the right viewpoint now, but it is too far away from its subject. You'll need to push it closer.

Figure 8.27
The DummyPan02 helper is in the correct position.

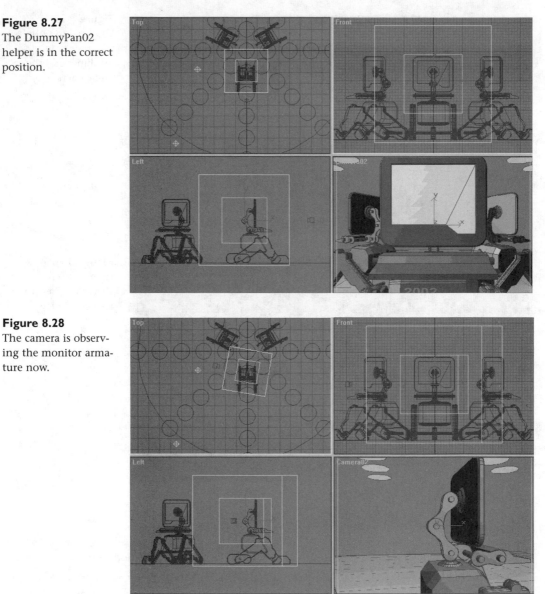

Figure 8.28
The camera is observing the monitor armature now.

6. Activate the Camera02 view, right-click the Camera02 view label, and choose Show Safe Frame. The view is now cropped to match the rendering output. Activate the Dolly Camera tool. Dolly the camera toward the armature until the armature nearly fills the view (as shown in Figure 8.29).

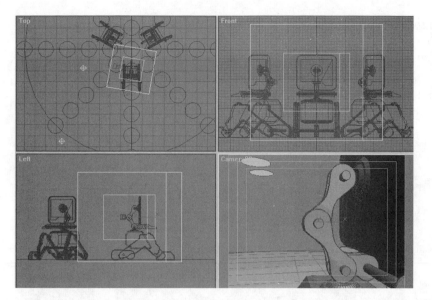

Figure 8.29
The camera gives a close-up view of the armature now.

Exercise 8.6   Animating an Armature

You'll set the armature's start orientation first, and then you will activate the Animate button and animate it.

 1. Adjust the Left view for a close-up of the monitor's armature. Activate the Select and Rotate tool (View Z-axis), and in the Left view, rotate the bracketMA01, bracketMB01, and mountM01 objects (in that order) to match Figure 8.30.

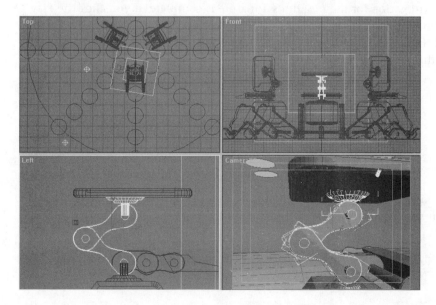

Figure 8.30
Rotate these objects into these positions.

The second shot will encompass frames 45 through 101. So you will advance to frame 101, activate the Animate button, and set the end orientation for the monitor armature.

2. Advance to frame 101 and activate the Animate button. Using the Select and Rotate tool (View Z-axis) in the Left view, match the armature orientation to that shown in Figure 8.31. Then deactivate the Animate button.

Figure 8.31
The final orientation for the monitor armature at frame 101.

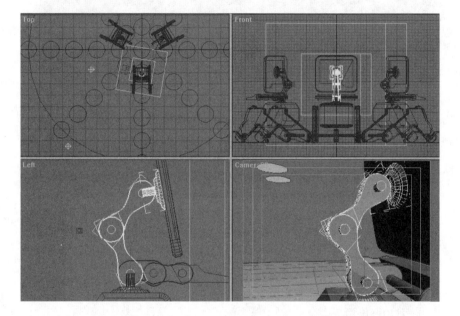

The animation for the monitor's armature is complete. If you click the Play Animation button, you will see the armature unfold between frames 0 and 101. However, it is supposed to unfold between frames 45 and 101. You can fix this very easily in the track bar.

3. Select all three of the armature objects (bracketMA01, bracketMB01, and mountM01). In the track bar, drag the red key square from 0 to 45 (see Figure 8.32).

Note

The Status Panel tells you what frame the key is located at as you drag it.

If you were to play the animation now, you would see that the armature animates between frames 45 and 101. Pretty cool!

4. Save your work as **08VT05.max**.

Figure 8.32
You can move the key from frame 0 to frame 45 on the Track Bar; the Status Panel keeps you informed about its location.

Exercise 8.7   Animating the Camera for Shot Two

The second shot is almost finished. All that's left to do is to animate the camera and configure its depth of field settings. Now that you know better what the armature is going to do, you will be able to animate the camera much more accurately.

The shaded view might be hindering the real-time playback of the animation, so turn off Smooth+Highlights in the Camera02 view.

1. With **08VT05.max** open, right-click the Camera02 label and check Wireframe.

   Now compose a better start position for the camera.

2. Move to frame 0 and activate the Select and Move tool. Move the DummyPan02 helper to XYZ: **0, –200, 190**.

   As you can see in Figure 8.33, the composition is a little more centered and balanced now. Rotate the camera up to look downward on the armature.

3. Activate the Select and Rotate tool (Local X-axis) and rotate the DummyTilt02 helper X: **–8** to look slightly downward at the armature (as shown in Figure 8.34).

   You now have a fantastic start orientation for the camera, so advance to frame 101 and set the end orientation.

4. Advance to frame 101 and activate the Animate button. Activate the Select and Rotate tool (Local Z-axis) and rotate the DummyPan02 helper Z: **–65** (see Figure 8.35).

Figure 8.33
The composition is balanced after you reposition the camera jib.

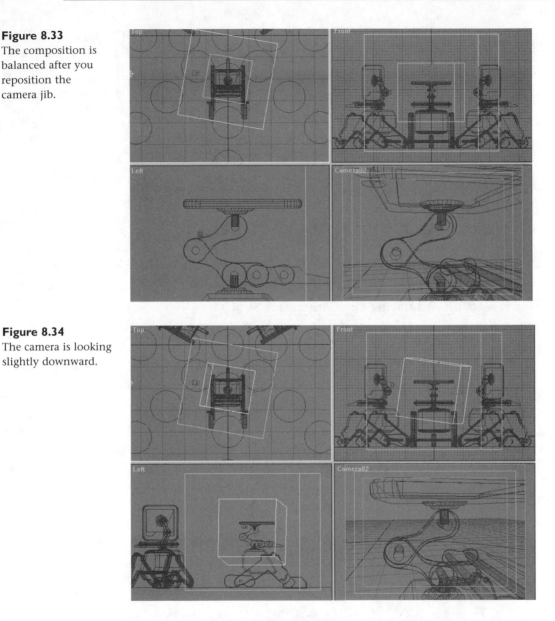

Figure 8.34
The camera is looking slightly downward.

To add a little more interest to the move, animate the DummyTilt01 helper to slowly drop the camera downward during the move.

5. Activate the Select and Rotate tool (Local X-axis) and rotate the DummyTilt02 helper X: **16** (see Figure 8.36). Deactivate the Animate button since you are no longer animating.

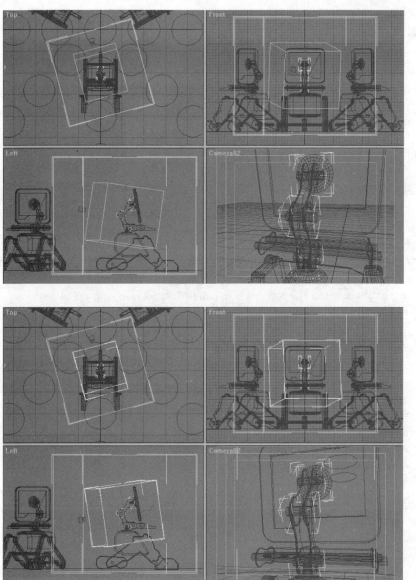

Figure 8.35
The camera is now more behind the monitor.

Figure 8.36
The camera is tilted lower.

Although the move is finished, it is animated between frames 0 and 101; remember, it needs to be animating between frames 45 and 101. You can move these keys the same way you adjusted the keys of the armature.

6. Select the DummyTilt02 and DummyPan02 helpers and on the Track Bar, drag the key from frame 0 to frame 45. (If you are currently at frame 0, you will see a only blue bar, but the key is there and you can drag it.)

7. Play the animation again. You will see that the camera jib only animates between frames 45 and 101. Good work!

Before you get excited and click that Render button, you need to add the depth of field effect to the camera.

8. Advance to frame 70 (a good in-between frame) and select Camera02. Open the Modify panel and in the Parameters rollout, check Enable in the Multi-Pass Effect group. Click Render Last to render a frame (see Figure 8.37).

There is a whole lot of rendering and not much depth of field happening, isn't there? That is because the Target Distance is currently 160, and that's too far away to make a noticeable difference in the scene.

Something else stands out to me. The monitor01 object is casting a very dark shadow on the top of the armature. I am not sure I like that effect so much. Instead of repositioning the light or turning off shadows, you can simply instruct the monitor01 object to not cast shadows. You can then change it back when you are rendering the other views.

9. Select and right-click the monitor01 object and choose Properties to open the Object Properties dialog. In the Rendering Control group, deselect Cast Shadows (as shown in Figure 8.38) and click OK to close the dialog.

Now when you render the camera again, the monitor will not cast shadows.

Getting back to the depth of field, move the camera's target closer to try to create a more appealing depth of field effect.

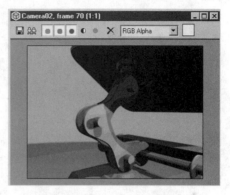

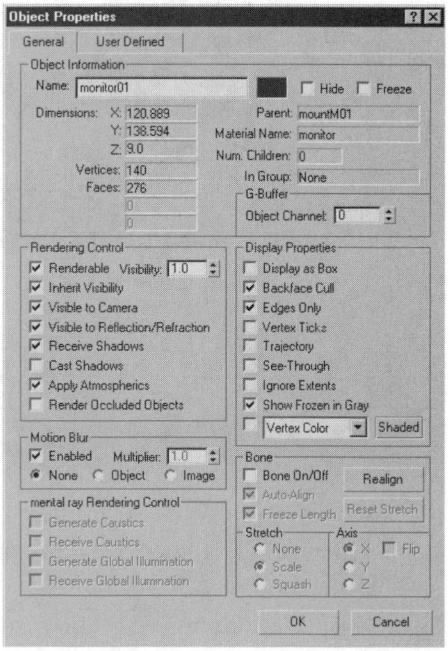

Figure 8.37
Frame 70 is rendered with the default Depth of Field applied.

Figure 8.38
The Object Properties dialog with Cast Shadows deselected.

10. Select Camera02 and at the very bottom of the Parameters rollout, change
the Target Distance to **120**. Render frame 70 again.

The closer target distance improves the depth of field by bringing its offset
point closer to the camera. You might notice a little blurring/focus effect on
the top of the monitor and the keyboard.

The depth of field effect looks pretty good, but it takes a considerably long
time to render because of the 12 passes it requires to render the effect. Once
again, you can decrease the Total Passes to 6, and then you shouldn't be able
to tell the difference. Also, you want the blur to be more pronounced, so
boost the Sample Radius as well.

11. In the Depth of Field Parameters rollout, change the Total Passes to **6** and
the Sample Radius to **6**. Render frame 70 once more.

The depth of field effect is perfect now, and it renders in half the time,
thanks to the lower value in the Total Passes option.

Before you click the Render button, take a second to think ahead. In the
third shot, you will animate the keyboard to raise from a lowered position to
the position it is currently in. If you render the scene as-is right now, a savvy
viewer will notice that the keyboard is higher in this, the second shot, and
has dropped magically in the third shot. To ensure the true continuity of the
piece, you should drop the keyboard now before you render it.

12. Activate the Select and Rotate tool (View Z-axis) and adjust the Left view to
observe the keyboard. In the Left view, rotate the bracketKA01, bracketKB01,
and keyboard01 objects to match Figure 8.39.

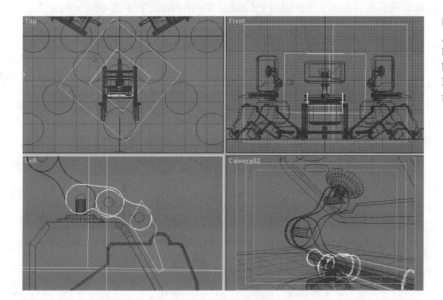

Figure 8.39
Adjust the
bracketKA01,
bracketKB01, and
keyboard01 objects to
match the Left view.

That is much better, and just think: It's a step you don't have to do in the next section! Yeah! You are now ready to render the second shot.

13. Open the Render Scene dialog. In the Time Output group, make sure Range is still active and change the range to **45** To **101**. At the bottom of the dialog, make sure the Viewport is Camera02 (see Figure 8.40).

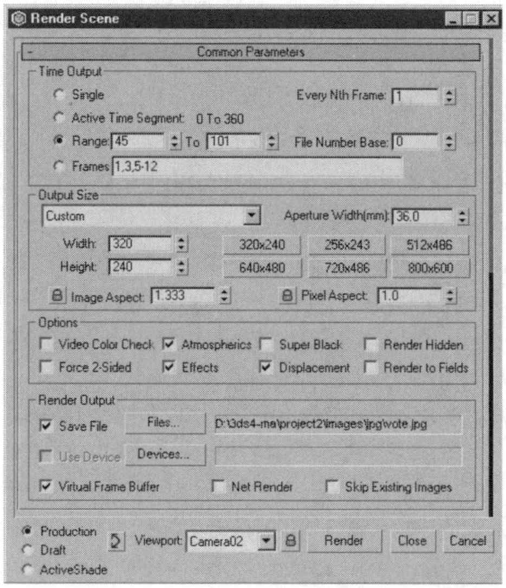

Figure 8.40
The Render Scene dialog with the correct settings.

If you have worked continuously with your file from the first shot, you shouldn't have to enter a different filename for the Save File. If you are ready to take a nice break, you could render the range now, or you could always come back and render it later.

14. Save your work as **08VT06b.max**. Click Render if you want to take a break, I sure do.

You were told to save the file with a "b" at the end to remind you that this is the finished shot two file. Just for your information, I am working on a dual 500MHz Pentium III. Rendering this shot two took approximately 1 hour. If your machine can't turn out the frames as quickly as you desire, you can always turn off the Multi-Pass effect or lower the Total Passes value. However, lowering the Total Passes value below 6 will not create a very good effect in most cases, so you may want to just go without. You might also improve rendering time by turning off the Ray Traced shadows on the OmniFill light; the final rendered result is more than acceptable. You could leave the OmniFill light shadows off for the whole animation if you feel it improves your rendering time.

Animating Shot Three

Shots one and two are out of the way, so now you can turn your attention to shot three. In this shot, you will look at the side of the vote machine's leg as you come around front to see the "2002 VOTE" text that's revealed by the rising keyboard. Because you are getting so good at banging out the shots, this one is going to fly by in no time flat. That is, until you click the Render button.

Exercise 8.8   Preparing the Camera

You need to hide the camera jib of the second shot and unhide the camera jib for the third shot. Do that now.

1. Make sure **08VT06b.max** is open.

2. Open the Display panel and click the Hide by Name button. Select DummyPan02, DummyTilt02, and Camera02 (as shown in Figure 8.41), and then click Hide to hide them.

   Now you have to unhide the camera03 jib.

3. In the Display panel, click the Unhide by Name button. In the Unhide Objects dialog, select DummyPan03, DummyTilt03, and Camera03. Click Unhide to unhide them.

4. With the Camera02 view active, press the C key, and in the Choose Camera dialog, choose Camera03.

   Now move the camera into its starting position.

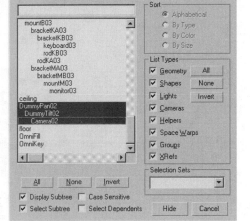

Figure 8.41
Hide these objects.

5. Activate the Select and Move tool and move DummyPan03 to XYZ: **–40, –240, 110**. Activate the Select and Rotate tool (Local Z-axis) and rotate the DummyPan03 helper Z: **–75** (see Figure 8.42).

   The camera is too far away from the vote machine; you want to see a close-up. Make that adjustment now.

6. Activate the Camera03 view and use the Dolly Camera tool to dolly the camera in for a closer look (as shown in Figure 8.43).

   The camera tilting in the second shot worked so well, you might as well put it in this shot too.

Figure 8.42
Move and rotate the
DummyPan03 helper
into this position.

Figure 8.43
Dolly the camera in
for a close-up.

7. Activate the Select and Rotate tool (Local X-axis) and rotate the
DummyTilt03 helper X: **–10** (see Figure 8.44).

The camera is now ready to be animated.

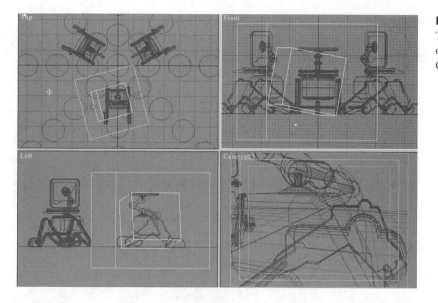

Figure 8.44
The start orientation for Camera03.

Exercise 8.9   Animating the Camera and Vote Machine for Shot Three

The camera's start orientation is on the money. You need to set the camera's end orientation next. The third shot consists of frames 102 through 158. So you will need to set the end orientation to frame 158.

1. Activate the Animate button and advance to frame 158.

2. Activate the Select and Rotate tool (Local Z-axis) and rotate the DummyPan03 helper Z: **60** degrees (as shown in Figure 8.45).

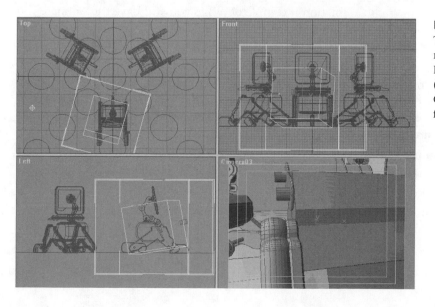

Figure 8.45
The correct Z rotation for the DummyPan03 helper (shading is active in Camera03 for clarity of figure).

Now animate the tilt.

3. Activate the Select and Rotate tool (Local X-axis) and rotate the DummyTilt03 helper X: **20** degrees (see Figure 8.46).

The camera animation is correct now. However, the start key is at frame 0, and you need to move it to frame 102.

Figure 8.46
Camera03 in its end orientation.

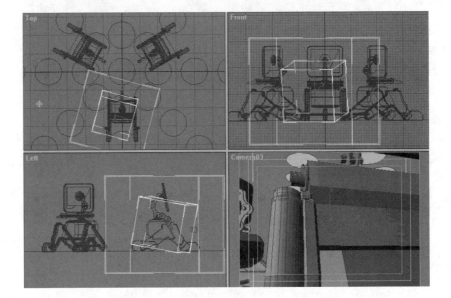

4. Select the DummyTilt03 and DummyPan03 helpers and drag the red key on the Track Bar to frame 102.

The camera jib animation is complete. While you still have the Animate button active, you might as well animate the keyboard rising into position. Because it's already in its start orientation, this is going to go fast.

5. Advance to frame 158 and adjust the Left view to observe the keyboard and its armature. Using the Select and Rotate tool (View Z-axis) in the Left view, rotate the keyboard into the upright orientation by rotating the bracketKA01, bracketKB01, and keyboard01 objects (see Figure 8.47). Deactivate the Animate button.

You need to move the keyboard armature's keys from frame 0 to frame 102.

6. Select the bracketKA01, bracketKB01, and monitor01 objects, and on the track bar, drag their keys from frame 0 to frame 102.

Because you are modifying the vote machine, you should activate shadow casting on the monitor01 object again.

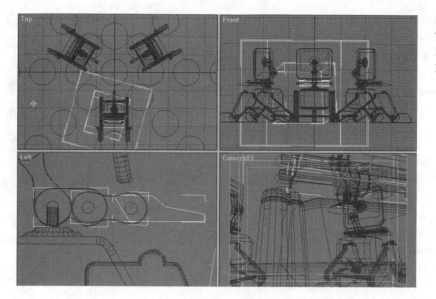

Figure 8.47
The keyboard is
in the correct
position.

7. Select and right-click the monitor01 object to open its Object Properties dialog. Check Cast Shadows and click OK to close the dialog.

You are becoming quite proficient at adding depth of field to your animations. It should be a cinch to add the depth of field to camera03.

8. Select Camera03 and open the Modify panel. Check Enable to enable the Depth of Field Multi-Pass effect.

Because the Target Distance of 120 worked so well in the second shot, try it again here.

9. In the Parameters rollout, change the Target Distance to **120**. In the Depth of Field Parameters rollout, change the change the Total Passes to **6** and the Sample Radius to **2**. Then advance to frame 135 and click the Render Last button.

The depth of field looks pretty good, but the focal plane is a little too far away. You should bring it closer to the camera so the leg objects aren't so out of focus.

10. Change the Target Distance to **110** and render frame 135 again (see Figure 8.48).

It isn't as bad now as it was. The most important thing about the shot is that you can read the "2002 VOTE" type as the camera spins around. Move to frame 158, render it, and see how it fairs.

Figure 8.48
Frame 135 rendered with a Target Distance of 110.

11. Advance to frame 158 and render it through the Camera03 view (as shown in Figure 8.49).

Darling, it looks marvelous! It seems as though shot three is finished. Go ahead and render it.

12. Open the Render Scene dialog. In the Time Output group, make sure Range is still active and change the range to **102** To **158**. On the bottom of the dialog, make sure the Viewport is Camera03.

13. Save your work as **08VT07c.max**, and if you are ready for a break, click Render. Otherwise, you can continue and then load this file later and render at your leisure.

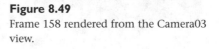

Figure 8.49
Frame 158 rendered from the Camera03 view.

Animating Shot Four

The fourth shot in this animation will be the first shot in which you actually see the monitor of the vote machine, as well as the other two vote machines in their entirety. It is the first shot where the viewer will gain an understanding of what he or she has been looking at over the course of the animation. That's why it's twice as long as the other shots.

Also, the red 2002 VOTE animation will be playing in the monitor as well, emphasizing the purpose of the animation. The first step toward completing the fourth shot would be to animate the 2002 VOTE graphic in the monitors.

Exercise 8.10   Animating Layers of a Composite Material

When you created the materials for the vote machine, you created a composite material with three layers to play in the screen of the monitor object. The three layers consisted of the red star background, the 2002 type, and the VOTE type. You will animate all three of these layers, creating an interesting graphic element in the monitor and the 3D animation plays through.

Because the red star background is the bottommost layer, animate it first. You will put a simple Z-axis (or in the UVW coordinate world a W-axis) rotation animation on it. This will result in a slow clockwise rotation of the red star in the monitor.

1. With **08VT07C.max** open, open the Material Editor and select the monitor material. Click the sub-material 2 button (screen) to open its parameters. Click the Diffuse map button to open the Composite map. Click the Map 1 button to open the screen-star map's parameters (see Figure 8.50).

I mentioned that you would be putting a slow clockwise rotation on the star map. To accomplish this, you will animate the W Angle in the Coordinates rollout.

2. Advance to frame 360 and activate the Animate button. In the Coordinates rollout, change the W Angle value to **360** (as shown in Figure 8.51). Deactivate the Animate button.

The screen-star map now rotates 1 degree every frame. You can click the Make Preview button to create an animated material preview if you desire. You will see the screen-star map rotating clockwise behind the 2002 VOTE type.

The movements of the VOTE type and the 2002 type will counter one another. The Vote type will enter the screen from the left, and the 2002 type will enter the screen from the right. You don't want to see any of the type when you first see the screen on frame 159; you want to see the type make its appearance shortly after that. You should be able to easily create that effect by turning off Tile and animating the map's U Offset.

3. With screen-star being the current map, click the Go Forward to Sibling button to change to the screen-2002 map. In the Coordinates rollout, change the U Offset to **.5** (as shown in Figure 8.52).

By changing the U Offset of the screen-2002 map, you pushed it to the right. However, because Tile is checked, a new tiled 2002 is pushing in from the right. If you uncheck U Tile, the 2002 on the left will disappear.

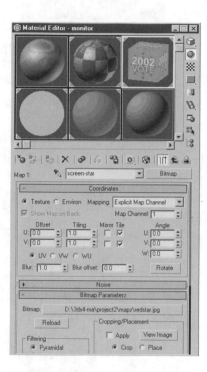

Figure 8.50
The screen-star map's parameters.

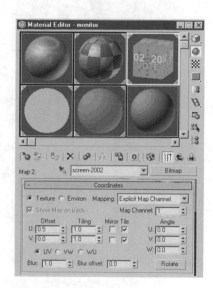

Figure 8.52
The screen-2002 map is offset by .5.

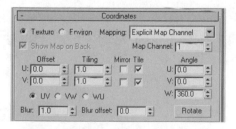

Figure 8.51
The Coordinates rollout with the W Angle changed to 360 at frame 360.

4. In the Coordinates rollout, deselect U Tile (as shown in Figure 8.53).

   With U Tile off, you see only one 2002 pushed off the right of the screen. At the beginning of the fourth shot, you want the 2002 type to be completely pushed out of the right side so you will be able to animate in from the right.

5. In the Coordinates rollout, change the U Offset to **1**. The 2002 type disappears altogether.

6. Now, to animate the texture, advance to frame 360 and activate the Animate button. Change the U Offset to **–1** and deactivate the Animate button (see Figure 8.54).

   The U Offset is currently set to animate from 1 to –1 over the course of frames 0 to 360. Because Shot 4 starts at frame 159, you want to advance the U Offset key at frame 0 to frame 160. This ensures that you can't see the 2002 type until well into the fourth shot.

7. Select the monitor01 object.

   On the track bar, you will see a red key square. This is because the track bar's default filters include all keys associated with that object, including materials. This works out to your advantage because you don't have to open the Track View and expand all the tracks—what a pain!

   However, there are two keys at frame 0: the screen-star's W Angle rotation and the screen-2002 U Offset key. You only want to advance the U Offset key.

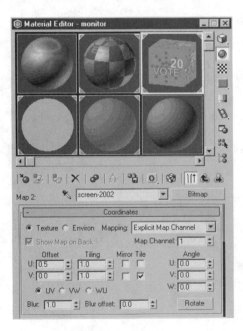

Figure 8.53
Deselect U Tile.

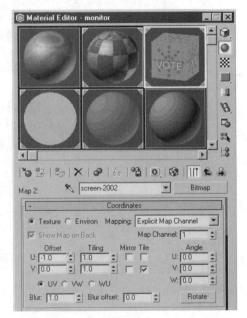

Figure 8.54
The U Offset is animated to –1 at frame 360.

8. Right-click the red key square at frame 0 on the track bar. From the resulting menu, choose **monitor01: U Offset** to open its key settings. Change the Time value to **160** (Figure 8.55) and close the dialog.

The key is no longer at frame 0; it is at frame 160. The screen-2002 map is correctly animated now.

The VOTE type will be animated much like the 2002 type was, the only difference being that it will be animated to enter from the left and move out to the right. Because you've already done this once, you can animate this one in seconds.

9. With the screen-2002 map as the current map, click the Go Forward to Sibling button to view the screen-vote map's Coordinates rollout.

10. Change the screen-vote's U Offset to **–1** and uncheck U Tile. The VOTE type disappears (well, it moves off the screen to the left).

11. Make sure you are still on frame 360 and activate the Animate button. Change the U Offset to **1** and deactivate the Animate button. Close the Material Editor.

12. Right-click the key at frame 0 on the track bar and choose Monitor01: U Offset. Change the time to **160** (as shown in Figure 8.56) and close the dialog.

You are finished animating the screen material.

13. Save your work as **08VT08.max**.

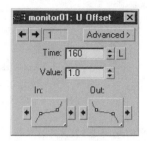

Figure 8.55
The monitor01: U Offset dialog with the correct settings.

Figure 8.56
The Monitor01: U Offset dialog for the screen-vote map.

Exercise 8.11   Animating the Camera for Shot Four

By now you know the drill: You have to hide the camera03 jib and unhide the camera04 jib. When you see camera04 in the viewport, you can start to orient it the way you want to see it at the beginning of the shot at frame 159. You will then advance to frame 268 and animate the camera into its final orientation. You will then drag the keys on the track bar from frame 0 to frame 159. It's cut and dry, right?

1. Open the Display panel and click the Hide by Name button. Hide DummyPan03, DummyTilt03, and Camera03. In the Display panel, click the Unhide by Name button and unhide DummyPan04, DummyTilt04, and Camera04. Activate the Camera03 view and press the C key. In the Select Camera dialog, choose Camera04.

Now you are ready to place camera04 into its start orientation. Here you will diverge from the storyboard a little; instead of starting with a high angle close-up, you'll start with a low angle close-up. As the camera animation progresses, it will change to a high angle wide shot.

2. Advance to frame 160 so you can see the monitor01 object in its upright orientation. Activate the Select and Move tool and move DummyPan04 to XYZ: **0, –250, 220** (see Figure 8.57).

3. Activate the Select and Rotate tool (Local Z-axis) and rotate the DummyPan04 helper Z: **20** degrees. Activate the Camera04 view and use the Dolly Camera to dolly the camera toward the screen until it matches Figure 8.58.

Figure 8.57
The DummyPan04 helper in the correct start position.

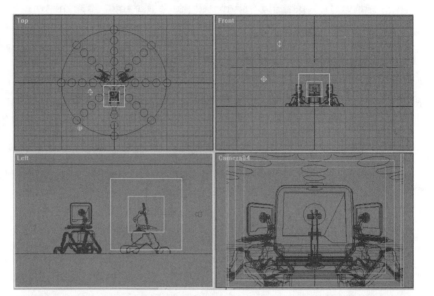

Figure 8.58
Dolly the camera to view a close-up of the screen.

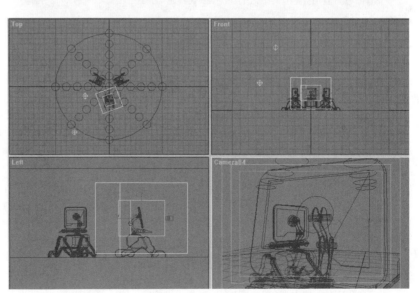

Now you want to set up that low angle shot.

4. Activate the Select and Rotate tool (Local X-axis) and rotate the DummyTilt04 helper X: **20** (as shown in Figure 8.59).

You now have your start orientation for camera04. Activate that Animate button and set the end orientation.

5. Advance to frame 268 and activate the Animate button. Activate the Select and Rotate tool (Local Z-axis) and rotate the DummyPan04 helper Z: **–25** (see Figure 8.60).

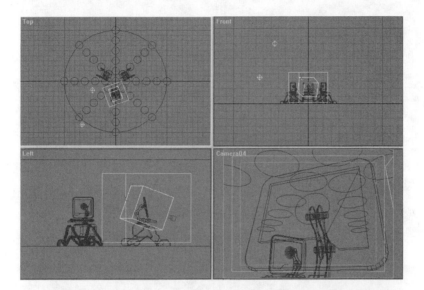

Figure 8.59
Adjust the DummyTilt04 helper to match this figure.

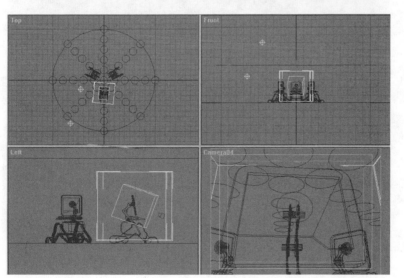

Figure 8.60
The DummyPan04 helper has been rotated to XYZ: 0, 0, –5.

6. Activate the Select and Rotate tool (Local X-axis) and rotate the DummyTilt04 helper X: **–60** (see Figure 8.61).

Now pull the camera back to create a wide shot.

7. Activate the Camera04 view and activate the Dolly Camera tool. Then pull the camera back to match Figure 8.62.

Figure 8.61
The DummyTilt04 helper has been rotated to attain a high angle shot.

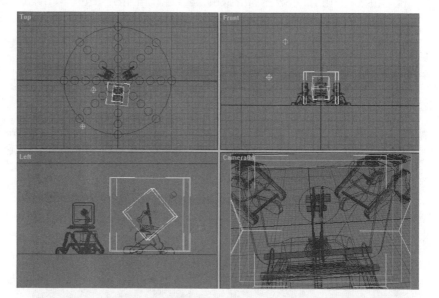

Figure 8.62
Pull back Dolly Camera04 to match this viewpoint.

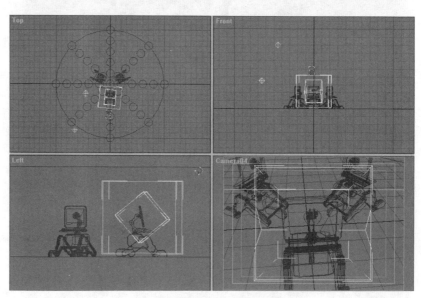

8. Activate the Select and Move tool and move the DummyPan04 helper to XYZ: **0, –170, 220** (as shown in Figure 8.63). Deactivate the Animate button.

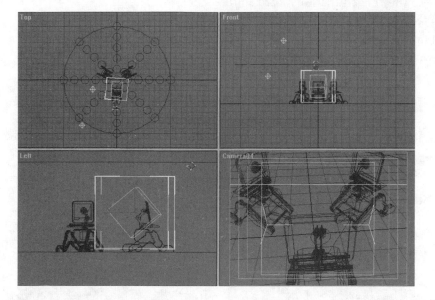

Figure 8.63
The final orientation for Camera04.

To finish the camera move, you need to move the start key from frame 0 to frame 159.

9. Select DummyPan04, DummyTilt04, and Camera04 and drag the keys from frame 0 on the track bar to frame 159.

   The animation is complete. Now quickly add some depth of field, and this shot will be ready for rendering.

10. Advance to frame 215, a good in-between frame, and select Camera04. Open the Modify panel and check Enable in the Multi-Pass Effect group. Leave Target Distance set to 160 for now and in the Depth of Field Parameters dialog, change the Total Passes to **6** and Sample Radius to **2**. Render frame 215 through the Camera04 view.

    The resulting image is a little out of focus. The target is too close to the camera; move it a little further away.

11. Change the Target Distance to **250** and render frame 215 again (see Figure 8.64).

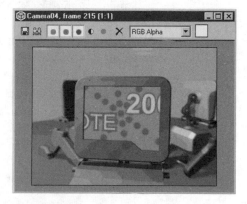

Figure 8.64
Frame 215 rendered with a target distance of 250.

The depth of field looks much better now. Before you go ahead and render this shot, though, tilt the monitors of the back two vote machines back a little so they match the storyboard a little better.

12. Activate the Select and Rotate tool (Local X-axis) and select the mountM02 and mountM03 objects. Rotate the selected objects back X: **–10** degrees (as shown in Figure 8.65).

Figure 8.65
The mountM02 and mountM03 objects are rotated back X:–10 degrees.

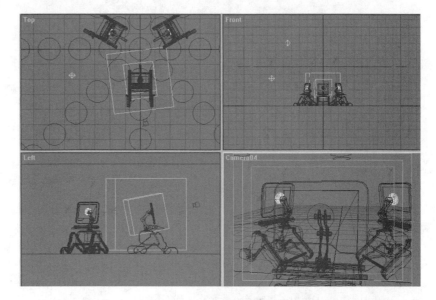

13. Open the Render Scene dialog. In the Time Output group, make sure Range is active and change the range to **159** To **268** (as shown in Figure 8.66). At the bottom of the dialog, make sure the Viewport is Camera04.

14. Save your scene as **08VT09d.max**. If you are ready for an extended break, you can click Render now. However, if you prefer, you can wait until later to load this file and render the frames.

Shot four is complete.

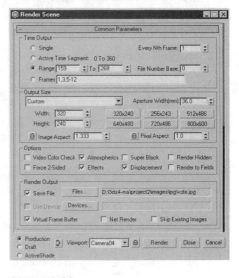

Figure 8.66
The Render Scene dialog with the correct settings.

Animating Shot Five

You are most certainly over the hump; the rest of this project is easy coasting. The final shot of the animation will consist of a very simple low-angle camera shot in which the camera orbits from left to right, remaining at the same height.

Exercise 8.12   Animating the Camera for Shot Five

I'm sure you are all very anxious to finish this animation so you can sit back in your chairs and let your eyes soak in the sweet candy you've created.

1. With **08VT09d.max** open, open the Display panel and click the Hide by Name button. Select and hide DummyPan04, DummyTilt04, and Camera04. Click Unhide by Name and unhide DummyPan05, DummyTilt05, and Camera05. Activate the Camera04 view and press the C key to open the Select Camera dialog. Choose Camera05 and click OK.

   Now you need to move the camera into its start position.

2. Activate the Select and Move tool and move the DummyPan05 helper to XYZ: **0, 0, 170**. Activate the Select and Rotate tool (Local X-axis) and rotate the DummyTilt05 helper X: **11** degrees (as shown in Figure 8.67).

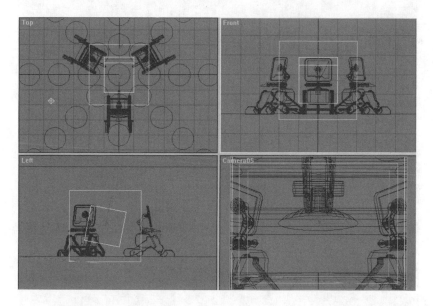

Figure 8.67
The DummyTilt05 helper is rotated X: **10** degrees.

Now dolly the camera back to view the vote machine in its entirety.

3. Activate the Camera05 view and activate the Dolly Camera tool. Advance to frame 215 and dolly back the camera until the top and bottom of the vote machine are touching the orange safe frame (see Figure 8.68).

Now rotate the DummyPan05 helper to place the camera in its start orientation.

4. Activate the Select and Rotate tool (Local Z-axis) and rotate the DummyPan05 helper Z: **–15** degrees (see Figure 8.69).

What a gorgeous low angle shot of the vote machines! To animate this shot, all you are going to do is rotate the DummyPan05 helper to the right. That's all—short, sweet, and simple.

Figure 8.68
Dolly the camera back into a comfy position.

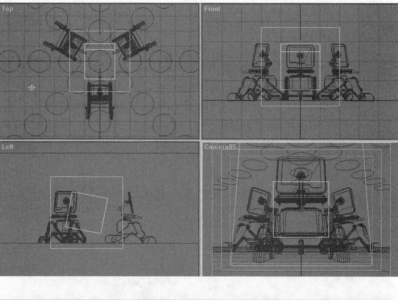

Figure 8.69
The camera's start orientation.

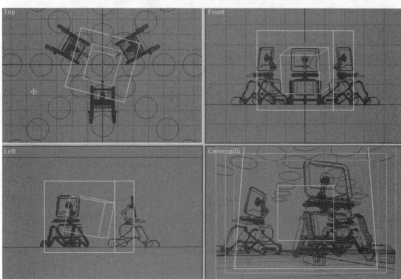

5. Advance to frame 360 and activate the Animate button. With the Select and Rotate tool (Local Z-axis) active, rotate the DummyPan05 helper Z: **30** degrees (as shown in Figure 8.70). Deactivate the Animate button.

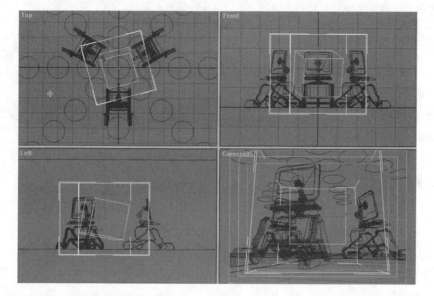

Figure 8.70
The end position for Camera05.

Because DummyPan05 is the only object that is animated, you don't have to select the other camera jib objects to move their keys to the start frame (frame 269).

6. With DummyPan05 selected, move the key from frame 0 to frame 269 on the track bar.

7. Save your work as **08VT10.max**.

You need to add depth of field to shot five before you can render it. First set up the depth of field as you have in the other shots of the animation.

8. With **08VT10.max** open, select Camera05 and open the Modify panel. In the Parameters rollout, check Enable in the Multi-Pass Effect group, and in the Depth of Field Parameters rollout, change Total Passes to **6** and Sample Radius to **2**. Render frame 290, which should look like Figure 8.71.

The image is blurry because the Target Distance is too close to the camera. You need to change that.

Figure 8.71
Frame 290 is rendered with depth of field applied.

9. Change the Target Distance to **500** and render frame 290 again (see Figure 8.72).

That looks pretty good. Everything is almost in focus, and for once it should be. This gives the viewer a chance to soak it all in.

Exercise 8.13   Creating a Rack Focus

Because shot five is the last shot in the animation, you will end the animation with an abrupt defocus that times out with the last sound in the music. The defocus, or "rack focus," will act as the final punctuation of the animation, more or less saying, "This is the end."

Figure 8.72
Frame 290 rendered again with a target distance of 500.

You are going to animate this rack focus between frames 305 and 325. This means the camera is suddenly going to go out of focus. This defocus is timed to the music. You're ready to add that now.

1. Advance to frame 325 and activate the Animate button. With Camera05 selected, change the Target Distance to **100** and the Sample Radius to **5**. Render frame 325 (as shown in Figure 8.73). Then deactivate the Animate tool.

The rack focus looks more like someone's drunken, drugged-up flashback than a softly blurred rack focus. This is because of the Total Passes setting and the way the renderer creates the depth of field effect. You could improve the blur by adding more passes to the effect, and you can even animate the Total Passes value. However, the render times would go through the roof.

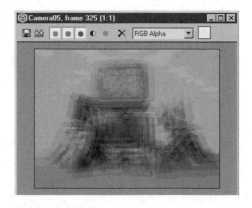

Figure 8.73
Frame 325 rendered with a Sample Radius of 5 and a Target Distance of 100.

The rack focus effect you created may not be a perfect rack focus, but it is a neat effect nonetheless. So you will keep it this way. But you still need to move the keys from frame 0 to frame 305.

2. With Camera05 selected, drag the keys from frame 0 to frame 305 on the track bar.

You're now ready to render the scene.

3. Open the Render Scene dialog in the Time Output group, make sure Range is active, and change the range to **269** To **360** (as shown in Figure 8.74). At the bottom of the dialog, make sure the Viewport is Camera05.

4. Save your work as **08VT11e.max**, and if you are ready for a break, click the Render button. Keep in mind that you must have all five shots rendered to go any further with the tutorial.

In the next section, you will take all the rendered image files, join them with the music, and render them as a QuickTime or AVI so you can watch the finished product. You've done great this far; you deserve the break. Render time is often the best part of the job.

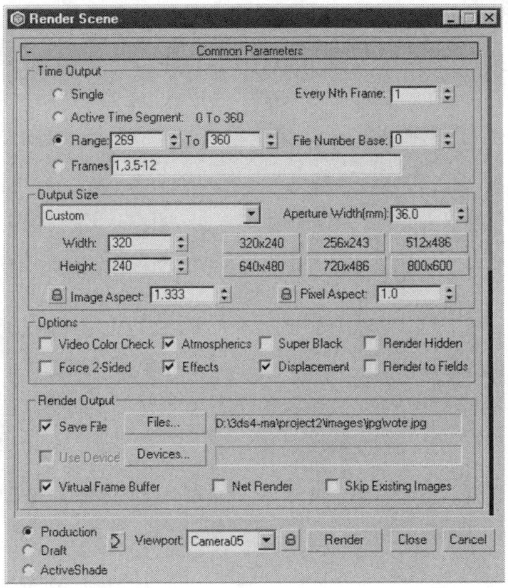

Figure 8.74
The Render Scene settings for shot 5.

Putting the Rendered Images to the Music

Because you had to render all the shots separately, you couldn't render an AVI or QuickTime movie from the beginning. However, now that you have all the images rendered, you can go into Video Post, put a quick queue together, and render the piece with music.

In order for the music score to be included with the AVI, you must put a scene event into the queue. This is because you have included the music in the scene; adding the scene event will add the music. However, you don't want to have to re-render anything unnecessarily, so you can simply hide everything in the scene and render one of the orthographic views (Left, Front, or Top). You don't want to render the Camera view because it has the multi-pass effect active, and it would render each frame six times.

Exercise 8.14   Creating a Video Post Queue

If you're like me, you can't wait to see the piece rendered with the music. Go ahead and set up that queue so you can get the show on the road.

1. With **08VT11e.max** open, open the Display tab and click Hide by Name to open its dialog. Under the list of objects, click All to select everything in the scene (see Figure 8.75), and then click Hide to hide them.

   Now you can build the Video Post queue.

2. Choose Rendering > Video Post to open the Video Post dialog (shown in Figure 8.76).

   Now you can add the music to the queue by adding a scene event.

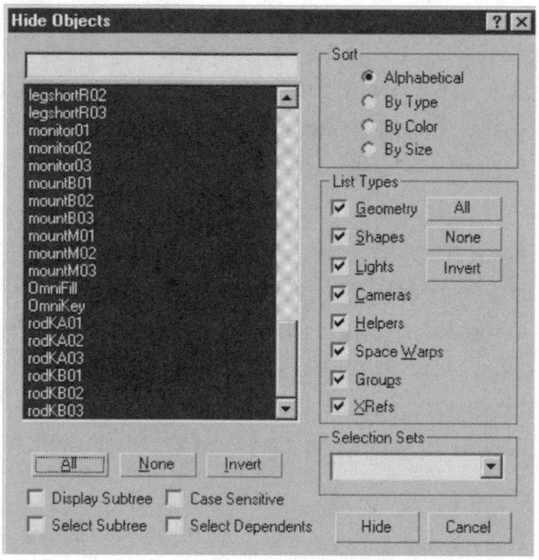

Figure 8.75

Click All under the list of objects to select everything in the scene.

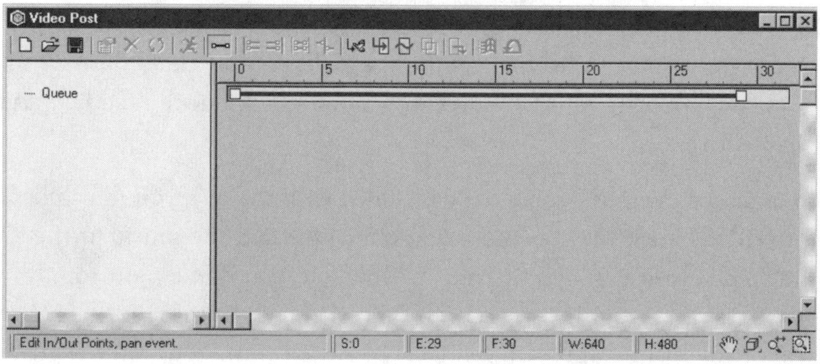

Figure 8.76

The Video Post dialog.

3. Click the Add Scene Event button to open the Add Scene Event dialog. In the View group, choose Front (as shown in Figure 8.77) and click OK to add the event. The Front event is added to the queue (as shown in Figure 8.78).

   Now you can add the rendered images.

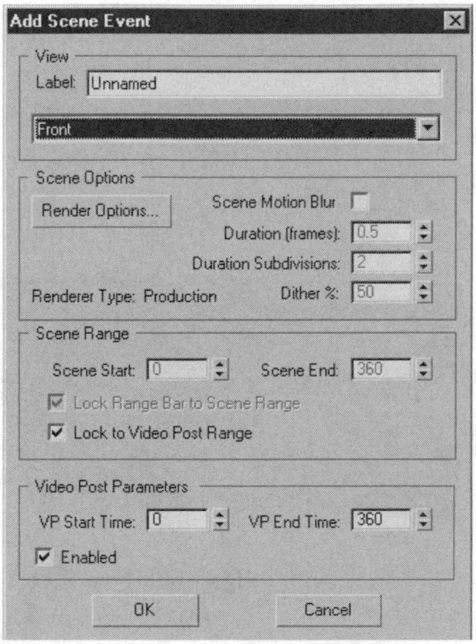

Figure 8.77
The Add Scene Event dialog with Front chosen.

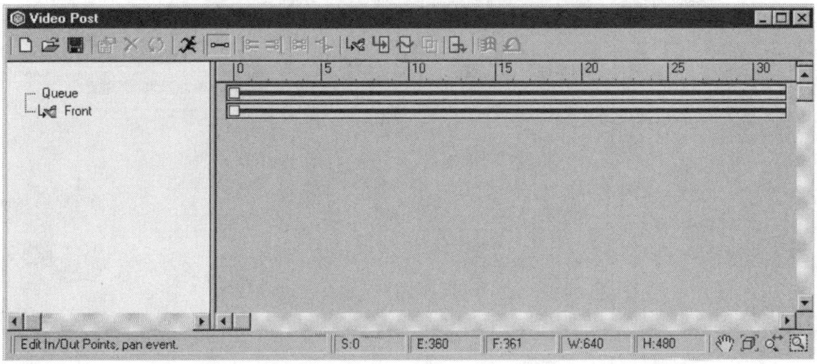

Figure 8.78
The Video Post queue with the Front scene event added.

4. Make sure the Front event is not selected and click the Add Image Input Event button to open the Add Image Input Event dialog. In the Image Input group, click the Files button to open the Select Image File for Video Post Input dialog. Open the folder to which you rendered the frames, and then select the first image in the folder. In the bottom of the dialog, check Sequence (see Figure 8.79). Choosing Sequence will load all the individual frames into an animated sequence. Click Open to open the Image File List Control dialog, which opens because you have checked Sequence (see Figure 8.80). Click OK to accept its default settings. Click OK to add the image input event (see Figure 8.81).

All you need to do now is add an Image Output Event, and then you can render the queue.

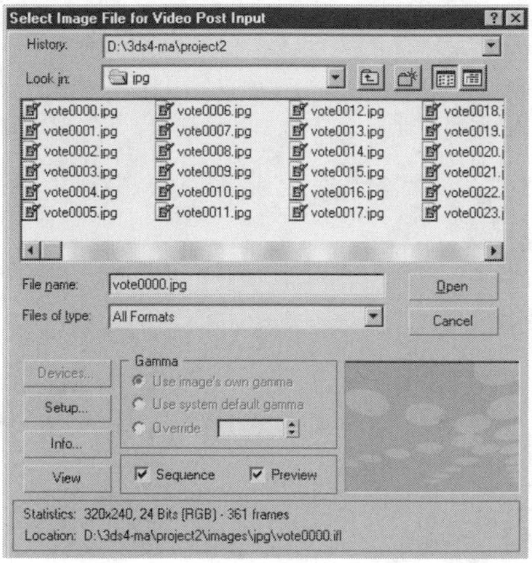

Figure 8.79

The Select Image File for Video Input dialog.

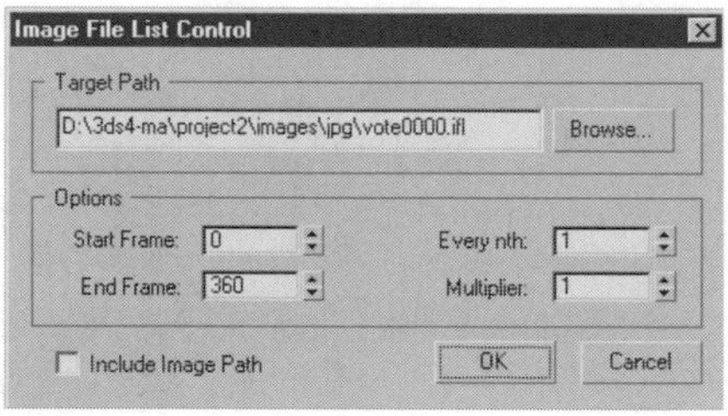

Figure 8.80

The Image File List Control dialog.

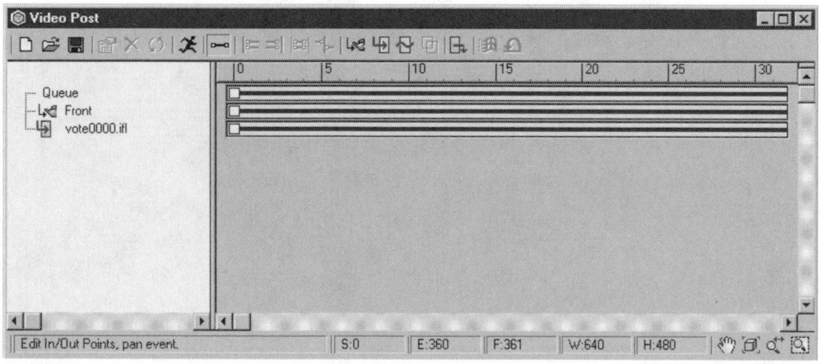

Figure 8.81

The Video Post queue with the vote0000.ifl image input event added.

5. Make sure nothing is selected in the queue, and then click the Add Image Output Event button to open the Add Image Output Event dialog. Click the Files button to open the Select Image File for Video Post Output dialog. Enter a folder and a filename, and in the Save As Type area, choose either AVI File or MOV Quick Time File (see Figure 8.82). My personal preference is MOV Quick Time File, but if you have a reason to choose AVI, feel free to do so. Click Setup, and in the Compressor group of the Compression Setting dialog, choose Animation and Millions of Colors and specify High in the Quality group (as shown in Figure 8.83); once again, this is my personal preference. Click OK to exit the Compression Settings dialog and click Save to exit the Select Image File for Video Post Output dialog. Click OK to exit the Add Image Output Event dialog.

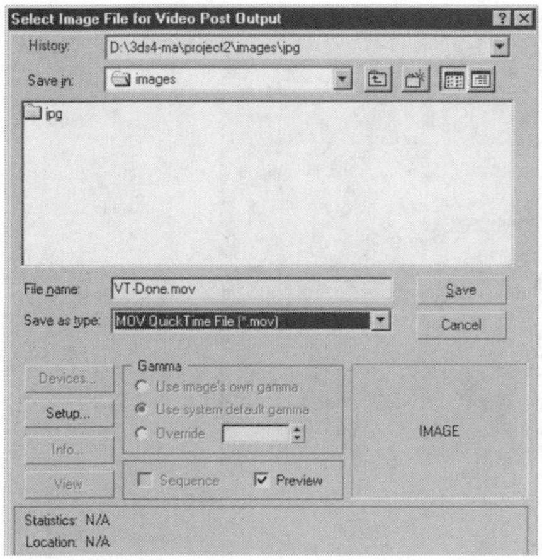

Figure 8.82
The Select Image File for Video Post
Output dialog.

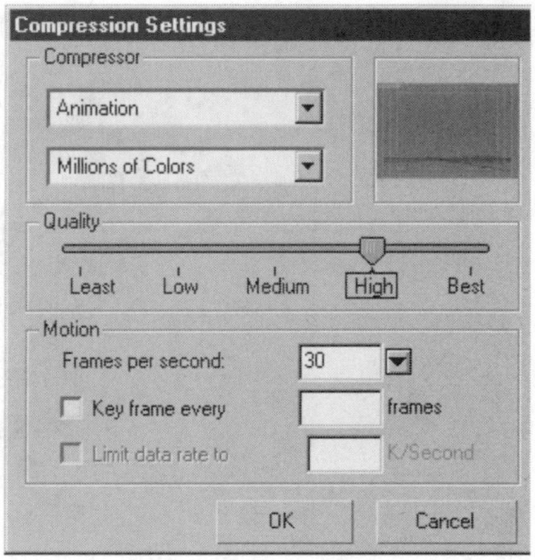

Figure 8.83
The Compression Settings dialog set
to my preference.

The Image Output event is shown in the queue (see Figure 8.84).

You're ready to render.

6. Click the Execute Sequence button to open the Execute Video Post dialog.
   Leave Range 0 To 360 active and change the Output Size to 320×240 (see
   Figure 8.85). Click Close to close the Execute Video Post dialog.

7. Save your work as **08VT12.max**. Click the Execute Sequence button to
   open its dialog, and then click Render to render the queue.

8. When the render is finished, choose File > View Image File from the main
   toolbar, locate the file, and sit back and enjoy the show!

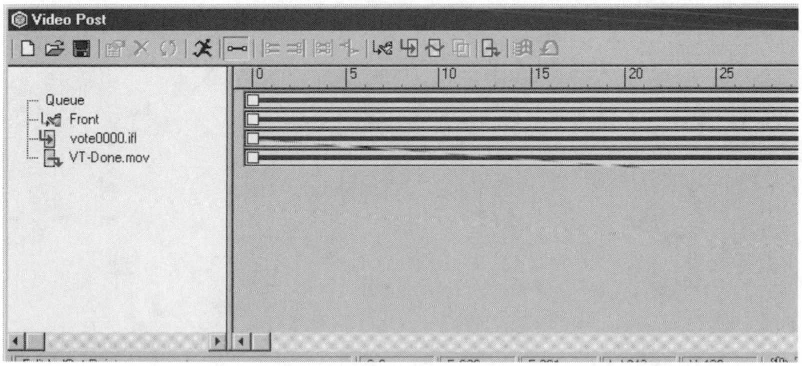

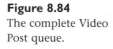

Figure 8.84
The complete Video
Post queue.

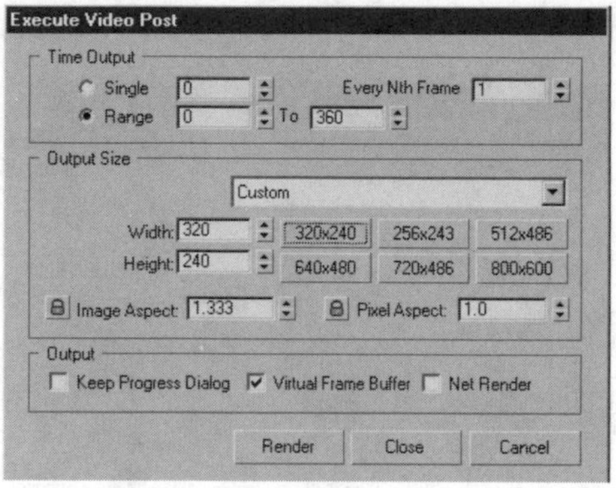

Figure 8.85

The Execute Video Post dialog with correct settings.

In Conclusion

The project is officially finished, and everyone is thrilled with your work! It took a great deal of time, skill, patience, and concentration to pull off this animation, and you accomplished it with flying colors. Keep up the great work!

Part 3

TV 3 News Open

The third project for this book gives you a crack at traditional media animation for a TV station. Here's the scenario... You've been given a few days to kick back, relax, and recover from the back-to-back projects you've just knocked out over the last few days. You are basking in a tranquil moment as you gaze at the progress of your system backup. You feel good about yourself for doing such good work and backing it up in case you need it again someday.

Mr. Boss stops by and engages you in a conversation. "The Vote 2002 animation turned out great! The client was thrilled." You modestly reply with, "Thanks, I'm just doing my job." "Anyway, I stopped by to let you know you are on a new project—the news open for TV 3. John Hudson has put together some storyboards for you. You should pay him a visit." "I'll get right on it, Bossman. Thanks!"

Chapters 9 through 11 step you through creating the TV 3 project.

Chapter 9

Creating the Globe Environment

You head over to John's workstation and look at the storyboards (see Figure 9.1). John then begins to explain that he would like to see a real world, with wireframe latitude/longitude lines and solid metal continents.

"This is just the concept for the animation," John adds. "It's up to you to really stylize it."

You nod and then inquire about his intent for the logo's manifestation: "Do you see the camera traveling through those blue Venetian blinds as a transition to the logo?" John confirms your hunch, informing you that the project is basically two animations: the globe environment and the logo. The transition element will be the blue Venetian blinds that remain behind the logo.

Figure 9.1

John's storyboard for the TV 3 News opening.

You turn to John and add, "Thanks John, I'll do the best I can to bring this to life," and you turn to head back to work.

By examining the storyboards and talking with John, you've learned you will need to make two scenes in order to create the animation. To see a JPG image of the storyboard, just open **\3ds4-ma\project3\images\news-board.jpg**. The first scene will be the globe environment, illustrated by the first three storyboard panels, and that is what you will create in this chapter. You'll animate the scene in the next chapter.

In this chapter, you're going to learn the following:

- Deciding whether to use Wire materials or Circle shapes
- Creating renderable splines
- Creating an Include list to illuminate particular isolated objects
- Effectively using Opacity Maps
- Working with Raytrace reflection maps and materials
- Using a Specular Level map

Creating the Objects

In this chapter you will be building and adding lights to the globe scene. When you examine the storyboard, you see that the objects are all basic primitive objects, mostly a sphere and tube primitives. Using these primitive shapes, however, it is up to you to develop their materials and bring them to life.

Setting Up the Wireframe-Like Object

Talking with John, you learned that the globe needs to appear as though there are solid metal continents on a wireframe frame. You will build this framework first so you can place the metal continents over it.

At first you think, "I can just create another sphere and assign a Wire material to it." Then you remember the pitfalls of Wire materials (see Figure 9.2). To create this Wire material, all you had to do was check Wire in the material's Shader Basic Parameters rollout (shown in Figure 9.3). Checking that box instructs the renderer to render the object in a wireframe representation. The thickness of this wireframe representation is adjusted in the Wire group of the Extended Parameters rollout. Using Pixels instructs the renderer to render all the lines the same thickness, regardless of their distance from the camera. Using Units instructs the renderer to render the lines in varying thickness, as determined by their distance from the camera.

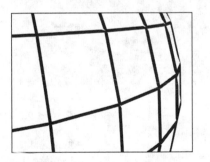

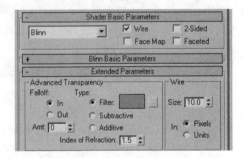

Figure 9.2
A sphere rendered with a Wire material.

Figure 9.3
You can check Wire in the Shader Basic Parameters rollout to create a wireframe material.

The pitfalls of using Wire to generate a wireframe effect in your renders is obvious in Figure 9.2. When the renderer creates the polygons on the wireframe to be rendered, it often leaves gaps and undesired triangular artifacts. A Wire material works if you are in a pinch; however, you will need to create the wireframe globe frame a different way.

Exercise 9.1   Using Circle Shapes to Create the Illusion of a Wireframe Object

To create the frame, you will build longitudinal and latitudinal lines using renderable circle shapes.

1. Choose File > Reset 3DS Max and activate the 3D Snap toggle. Open the Create > Shapes panel, click the Circle button, and in the Front view, create a Circle Shape at XYZ: **0, 0, 0** with a Radius of **60** (as shown in Figure 9.4). Leave the name **Circle01**.

Note

In my scene I have colored the shape blue by clicking the color swatch next to its name. This helps me to visually organize my scene because I know I will be adding a blue material to it later.

Figure 9.4
Create a circle shape in the Front view at XYZ: 0, 0, 0.

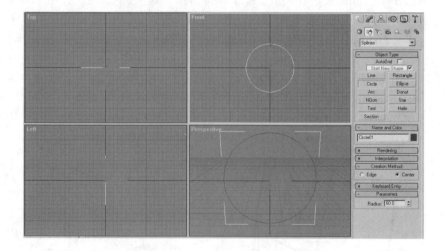

This circle is the first of the globe's longitude lines. Right now, if you rendered any of the views, nothing would render. 3ds max, however, allows you to make shapes renderable with precise control. Make those adjustments now.

2. With Circle01 still selected, open the Modify panel and expand the Rendering rollout. Check Renderable (as shown in Figure 9.5) and Render the Perspective view (shown in Figure 9.6).

Figure 9.5
Check Renderable to make the shape render.

That was easy—making the Circle01 shape render that is—however the shape is stepping far too much. By saying, "stepping," I mean there aren't enough polygons to create the illusion of roundness. You need to add more steps to the shape. The Sides value in the Rendering rollout does not add more sides to the circle; instead it adds more sides to the cross-section that is lofted along the shape, in turn creating the rendered object. Currently, the Sides value is 12, and that is more than enough sides for what you will be doing with the shape; your concern is with adding more steps to the shape.

3. Open the Interpolation rollout, change the Steps value to **20** (as shown in Figure 9.7), and render the Perspective view once more (see Figure 9.8).

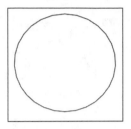

Figure 9.6
The rendered Circle01 shape (the background is changed to white for figure clarity).

Figure 9.7
The Steps value in the Interpolation is increased to 20, making a smoother circle shape.

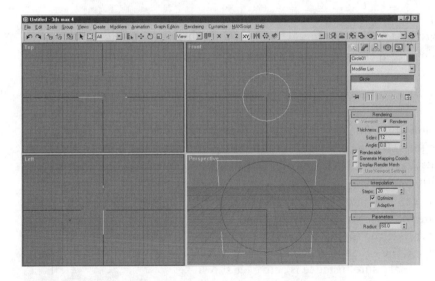

The circle is much smoother now. Now that you have one perfect longitude line, you can instance the circle around itself to create the others.

4. Activate the Select and Rotate tool (View Z-axis). Deactivate the 3D Snap toggle and activate the Angle Snap toggle. In the Top view, Shift+drag the circle to rotate it Z: **–30** degrees. In the Clone Options dialog, choose Instance and change the Number of Copies to **5** (as shown in Figure 9.9). Click OK to create the instances. Then render the Perspective view (see Figure 9.10).

You chose to create 5 instances because you rotated the circle 30

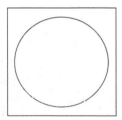

Figure 9.8
The rendered circle shape with a Steps value of 20 (the background is changed to white for figure clarity).

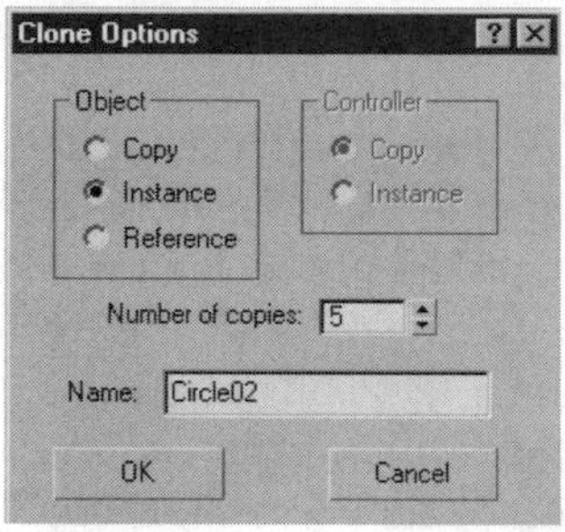

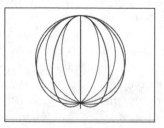

Figure 9.9
The Clone Options dialog with
the correct settings to create
the remaining longitude lines.

Figure 9.10
The rendered longitude lines
from the Perspective view.

degrees. 180 degrees is half a full rotation, and 180 (degrees) divided by 30 (degrees) is 6 (circles). Subtracting the initial circle, you need 5 instances.

The rendered circles are too thick for my taste. You need to thin them.

5. In the Rendering rollout of the Modify Panel, with any Circle shape selected, change the Thickness value to **.5** and render the Perspective view again.

The longitude lines are perfect now. Now you can start to lay out the latitude lines. For the equator, you can simply instance a circle that we already created. For the others, you will have to copy a circle shape, move it into position, and size it accordingly.

6. Select Circle04 and activate the Select and Rotate tool (View Z-axis). In the Front view, Shift+rotate the Circle04 shape Z: **–90** degrees to create the equator. In the Clone Options dialog, make sure Instance is active (as shown in Figure 9.11) and click OK to create the instance (see Figure 9.12).

You have created the equator, now you need to create its fellow latitude lines.

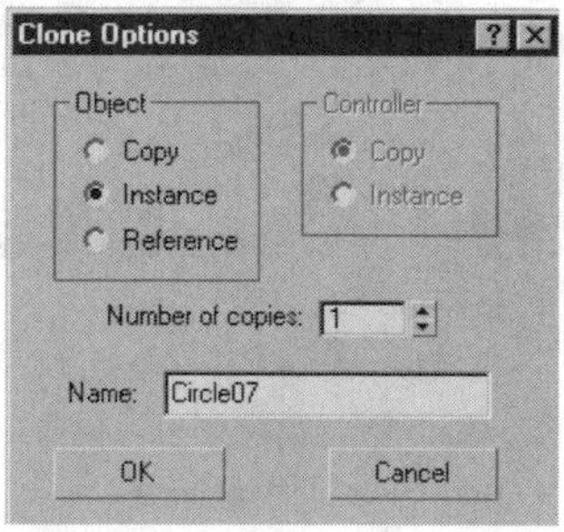

7. Deactivate the Angle Snap toggle and activate the 3D Snap toggle. Activate the Select and Move tool (View Y-axis), and in the Front view, Shift+drag the Circle07 (equator) shape upward Y: **30**. In the Clone Options dialog, choose Copy in the Object area and click OK to create the copy.

Figure 9.11
The Clone Options dialog with
the correct Instance settings.

The circle shape is too large and doesn't fit on the longitude framework snugly. You can easily fix this by adjusting the circle shape's Radius.

8. Use the Pan and Zoom tools to view the upper-right quadrant of the frame. Right-click the Front view label and uncheck Show Grid. With the Circle08 shape selected, open the Modify panel and lower the Radius value until the circle touches the latitude lines (as shown in Figure 9.13). In my scene, I came up with a Radius of 51.95.

You left a large gap between the equator and your newly created latitude line. This is because the gold rings surrounding the earth will fill in that gap. Any extra latitude lines in that area would simply clutter up the globe's design. Having just a few latitude lines will be enough to hold it together visually, yet that will not detract from the more important aspects in the scene. To finish the northern hemisphere, you will create one more latitude line.

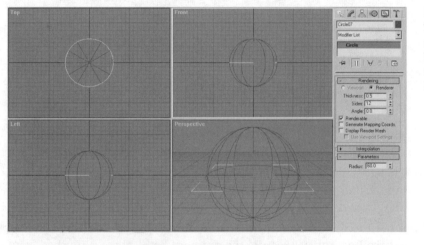

Figure 9.12
The horizontal equator has been added to the vertical longitude lines.

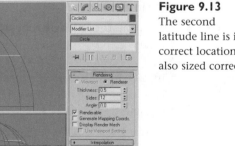

Figure 9.13
The second latitude line is in its correct location and is also sized correctly.

9. With the Select and Move tool (View Y-axis) active, Shift+move the Circle08 shape up Y: **20** in the Left view. In the Clone Options dialog, make sure Copy is active and click OK to create the copy (see Figure 9.14).

Now, just as you did for the previous latitude line, you need to size the Radius to fit snugly on the longitude lines.

Figure 9.14
The new latitude line is in position.

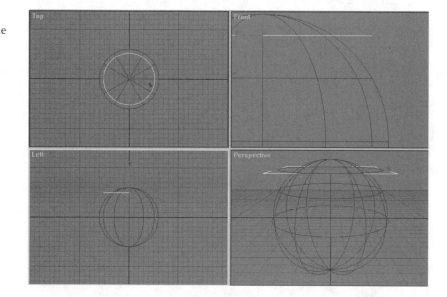

10. With Circle09 selected, open the Parameters rollout of the Modify panel. Adjust the Radius value until the circle shape fits snugly against the longitude lines. In my scene, I came up with a Radius of 33.1.

All you need to do to finish the wireframe latitude/longitude frame is create the southern hemisphere. Because the northern hemisphere is finished, you can simply instance it.

11. Deactivate the 3D Snap toggle and activate the Angle Snap toggle. Activate the Select and Rotate tool (World Y-axis—Use Transform Coordinate Center). Select the two latitude lines of the northern hemisphere (Circle08 and Circle09) and Shift+rotate the two circle shapes Y: **180** degrees. In the Clone Options dialog, choose Instance and click OK to create the instances (see Figure 9.15).

The framework of the globe is complete.

12. Save your work as **09TV01.max**.

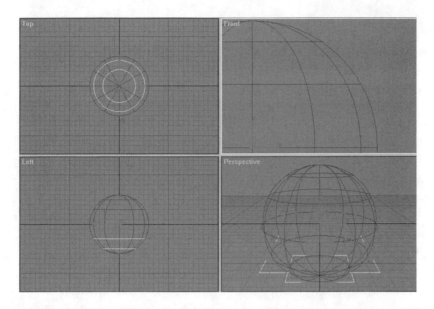

Figure 9.15
The finished wire-frame frame for the globe.

Exercise 9.2   Using a Phong Shader to Create a Blue Metallic Material

Next you'll apply the material to the wireframe globe so you don't have to worry about that later.

1. Make sure **09TV01.max** is open, select all 11 of the Circle shapes, and open the Material Editor. Make sure the first material preview slot is active and name the material **wireframe**.

   Because the storyboard does not depict the desired globe, you must use your own artistic sense and creative judgment. You know that the globe must be blue metal; so put a shiny blue material on the wireframe globe.

2. Click the Ambient color swatch and enter RGB: **105, 105, 250** into the Color Selection: Ambient Color dialog (shown in Figure 9.16). Click Close to close the color selector.

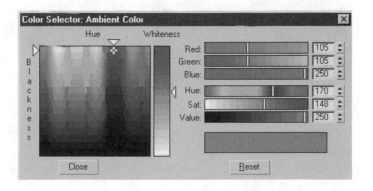

Figure 9.16
The correct shade of blue is selected in the Color Selector.

Now you need to make the material shinier. To create the metallic effect, you will use a Phong shader. The Phong shader is ideal for creating plastic materials. However, you can also use it to create a metallic material. The metal shader, although also good for creating metallic materials, is not as versatile as the phong shader because it does not allow the user to change the specular color.

3. In the Shader Basic Parameters rollout, change the shader from Blinn to Phong. In the Phong Basic Parameters rollout, change the Specular Level to **88** and Glossiness to **17** (as shown in Figure 9.17).

4. With all 11 circle shapes selected, click the Assign Material to Selection button. Then render the Perspective view (see Figure 9.18).

    That looks good, however you need to add a little Self-Illumination to it to brighten the color in the darker areas.

5. In the Phong Basic Parameters rollout, change the Self-Illumination value to **50** (see Figure 9.19). Render the Perspective view again.

    In the rendered Perspective view, you will notice the Self-Illumination brightening up some of the dark areas of the wireframe objects. The material is perfect now.

6. Save your work as **09TV02.max** and close the Material Editor.

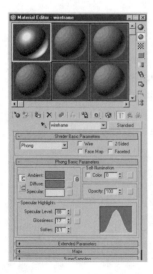

Figure 9.17
The wireframe material with the correct settings so far.

Figure 9.18
The rendered wireframe material in the Perspective view.

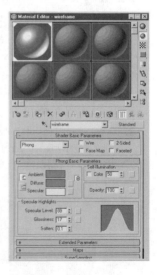

Figure 9.19
The finished wireframe material in the Material Editor.

Adding the Globe and Its Rings

Now that you've created the internal wireframe structure of the globe, you can place the continents on top of it. You will not be placing the continents directly on the surface; instead you will opacity map the continents above the wireframe structure on a sphere, thereby creating depth and interest. Then you will create the rings that wrap around the globe.

Exercise 9.3   Working with the Sphere and Tube Shapes and the Mirror Tool

In one step, you can create the globe. Then it's on to using Tube, the Use Transform Coordinate Center option, the World Coordinate system, and the Mirror tool to set up the rings the way you want them. It's a lot easier than it sounds.

I. Make sure **09TV03.max** is open, deactivate the Angle Snap toggle if it is still active, and activate the 3D Snap toggle. Open the Create > Geometry panel, click the Sphere button, and in the Top view, create a sphere at XYZ: **0, 0, 0** with a Radius of **70**. Change its name to **Globe**. Make the roundness of the globe smoother by changing the Segments value to **64** (see Figure 9.20).

The globe object is finished; you will create the continents by using maps in the material. But before you apply the material to the globe, you should add the rings.

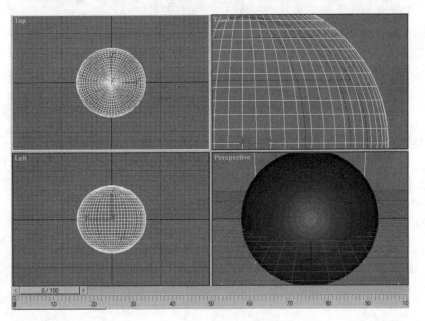

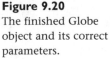

Figure 9.20
The finished Globe object and its correct parameters.

2. In the Create > Geometry panel, click the Tube button and in the Top view, create a tube with these settings:

   Radius 1: **85**

   Radius 2: **70**

   Height: **1**

   Height Segments: **1**

   Sides: **64**

   Name this object **Ring01** (as shown in Figure 9.21). Deactivate the 3D Snap toggle.

   The ring object is the correct size, but it is not in the correct location. It needs to be offset from the equator, and then you will instance another ring to be equally offset on the other side of the equator. The result will be two rings symmetrical to the equator.

Figure 9.21
The Ring01 object with the correct parameters.

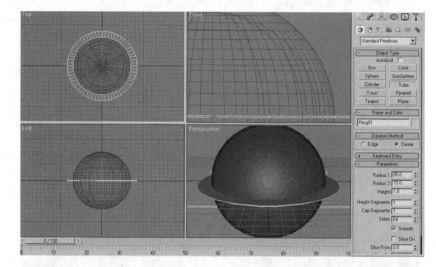

3. Activate the Select and Move tool and move the Ring01 object to XYZ: **0, 0, –12.** With Ring01 selected, activate the Select and Move tool (World XY-axis—Use Transform Coordinate Center), as shown in Figure 9.22.

   When Use Transform Coordinate Center is active on the World Coordinate system, the transform axis moves to the center of the world (XYZ: 0, 0, 0). The Mirror tool will use the axis as it is currently being used. Therefore, if you use the Local Coordinate system, the object would mirror, but it would mirror on its local axis and therefore would not be positioned the way you want it. If you use the World Coordinate system, however, the axis is in the center of the globe (XYZ: 0, 0, 0), and the object will mirror symmetrical to the world.

4. Click the Mirror Selected Objects button on the toolbar to open the Mirror: World Coordinates dialog. In the Mirror Axis group, change the axis to **Z** and in the Clone Selection dialog, choose Instance (as shown in Figure 9.23). Click OK to create the instance (see Figure 9.24).

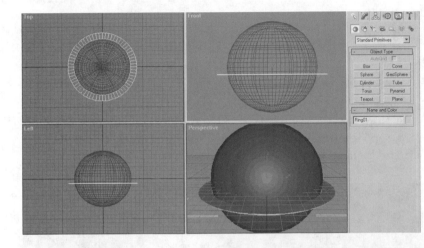

Figure 9.22
Ring01 is selected with the Select and Move tool set to Use Transform Coordinate Center.

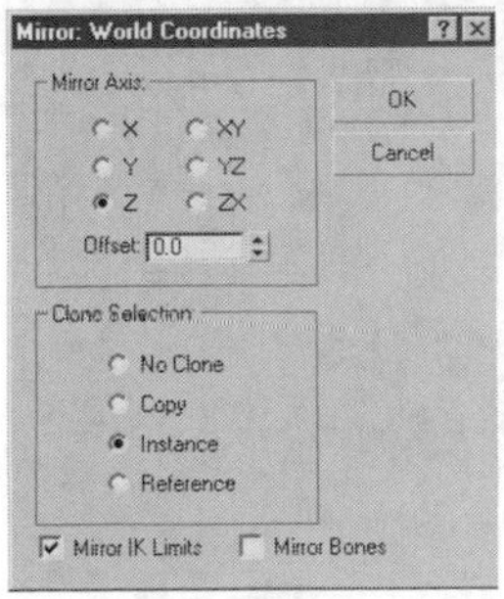

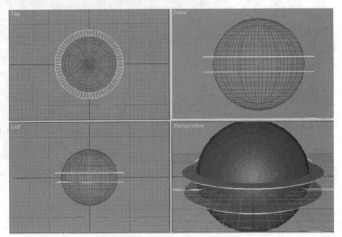

Figure 9.23
The Mirror: World Coordinates dialog with the correct settings.

Figure 9.24
By mirroring the Ring01 object on the World Coordinate Center, you have created the Ring02 object.

There is one final ring that orbits the globe. It is larger than the symmetrical rings you just created, so you can't simply instance one that is already in the scene. You will simply create a new, larger tube and place it in the correct location.

5. Activate the 3D Snap toggle and in the Create > Geometry panel, click the Tube button. In the Front view create a Tube with these settings:

XYZ: **0, 0, 0**

Radius 1: **170**

Radius 2: **110**

Height: **10**

Name this object **RingLarge** (see Figure 9.25).

The RingLarge object is centered to the world when viewed through the Front view. However, it is not centered to the world when you peer down on it from the Top view. You will need to center the RingLarge's local pivot to its height and then center the object to the world.

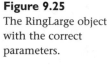

Figure 9.25
The RingLarge object with the correct parameters.

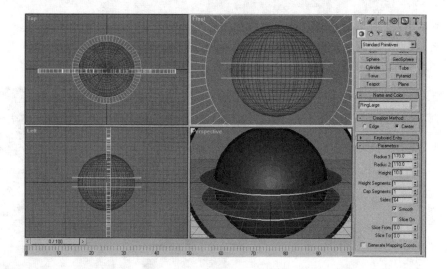

6. With RingLarge selected, open the Hierarchy panel. Activate the Affect Object Only button and click the Center to Pivot button so that the RingLarge object is centered to pivot and to the world (as shown in Figure 9.26). Deactivate the Affect Object Only button.

All three ring objects are now properly created and oriented in the scene.

7. Save your work as **09TV03.max**.

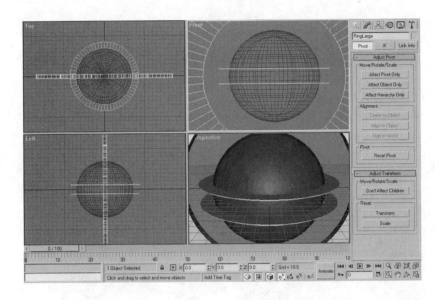

Figure 9.26
The Ring Large object is centered to the world.

Shedding Light on the Scene

As a general rule of thumb, I place the main light of my scene to the front-right of the objects. This light is "key light" in our scene. Another rule of thumb I have is to always start with a luminance of 180 units emitting from any light. That way you are creating your materials for optimal viewing for that amount of light. However, if more light is needed, you can increase the value up to 255. If the 255 value still isn't enough light, you can increase the Multiplier value of the light. However, I change the multiplier only in extreme cases in which I need additional light or negative light (which removes light from the scene).

You should also add a backlight to "pop" the objects off the background. You may need to add "special" lights to illuminate certain areas of particular objects. To do so, you can create lights with Include lists. The Include list allows the light to illuminate designated objects.

Exercise 9.4   Using Lighting to Aid in the Creation of Materials and to Create a Dramatic Effect

The globe object and the rings are now ready to have materials applied to them. Before you go ahead and start placing materials on the objects, add a few lights to the scene. This will allow you to more accurately view our materials.

1. With **09TV03.max** open, open the Create > Lights panel. Click the Omni button and click in the Top view to create an Omni light. Activate the Select and Move tool and move the Omni to XYZ: **235, –140, 15**. You will need to use the Zoom All tool to see the Omni light (see Figure 9.27).

Adjust the light so its value is only 180 units.

2. In the Modify panel, with the Omni01 light selected, change its color to RGB: **180, 180, 180**. Also, rename the light **Omni-Key** (as shown in Figure 9.28).

   The key light is finished in the scene. You should also add a back light to the scene to illuminate the upper-right area of the globe object. This back light will help to "pop" the globe off the background.

3. In the Create > Lights panel, click the Omni button and create an Omni light in the top view. Move it to XYZ: **630, 350, 380** and name it **Omni-Back**. You will need to use the Zoom All tool to see it (see Figure 9.29).

Figure 9.27
Create the Omni light and move it to XYZ: 235, –140, 15.

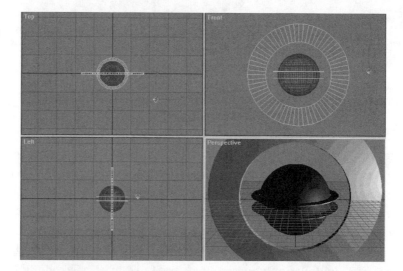

Figure 9.28
The Omni-Key light with correct settings.

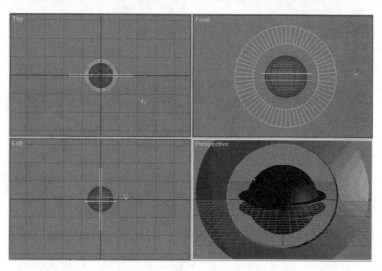

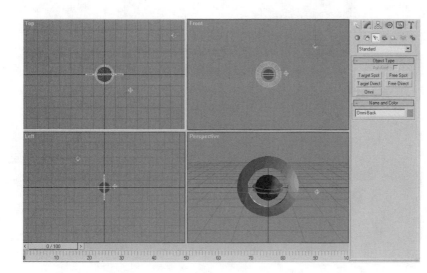

Figure 9.29
The Omni-Back light
is named and in
position.

Because the back light should be more subtle, you need to
lower its intensity to be less than the key light's, which currently is 180. Also, to create a dramatic effect you will also add
a little color to the back light.

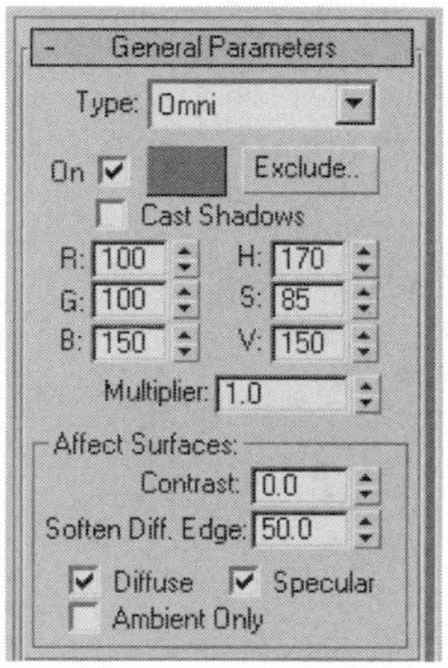

4. With Omni-Back selected, open the Modify panel. Change its
color to RGB: **100, 100, 150** (as shown in Figure 9.30).

The back light now has a bluish hue that will add a little
drama to the scene.

Looking at John's storyboard, you can see that the sides of
the rings that face one another are brightly lit, especially in
the second panel of the storyboard. You will add a light in-
between the rings orbiting the globe object.

5. Create an Omni light in the Top view and move it to XYZ: **78,
0, 0**. Name the light **Omni-SpecialRing01**. Open the Modify
panel and change its color to RGB: **180, 180, 180**. You might
need to adjust your view to see the Omni light clearly (as
shown in Figure 9.31).

This light should not cast light on any objects except for the Ring01 and
Ring02 objects. Luckily, you can create an Include list, which enables you to
accomplish that very task.

6. In the Modify panel, with Omni-SpecialRing01 light selected, click the
Exclude button in the General Parameters rollout. In the Exclude/Include
dialog, choose Include, select Ring01 and Ring02, and click the arrow pointing to the right (see Figure 9.32). Click OK to create the Include list.

Figure 9.30
The Omni-Back light has
the correct parameters.

Figure 9.31
The Omni-
SpecialRing01 light
is in the correct
position with the
correct parameters.

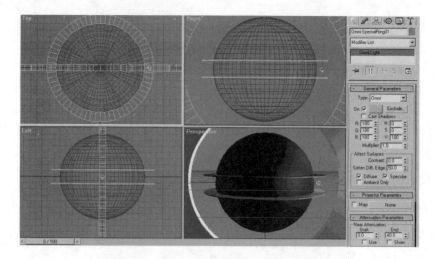

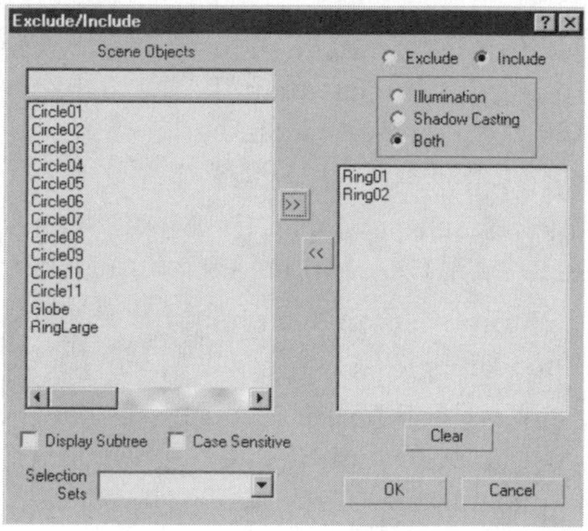

Figure 9.32
The Include list
includes the Ring01
and Ring02 objects.

Since you created the Include list, the Omni-SpecialRing01 light will illuminate only the Ring01 and Ring02 objects. Save your work before adding the
materials.

7. Save your work as **09TV04.max**.

Applying a Material to the Globe Object

You now have the groundwork for the scene laid out correctly, lights and all. That
said, you could begin to apply the materials to the objects. You will start by creating the material for the globe object.

Exercise 9.5   Using an Opacity Map to Create the Illusion of Oceans

Earlier when you spoke with John, he told you that he envisioned the globe having metallic blue continents floating off the wireframe latitude/longitude lines. You will create that effect by using an opacity map to make the oceans of the globe invisible, allowing the wireframe to show through. Go ahead and get started.

1. With **09TV04.max** open, select the Globe object and open the Material Editor. Activate the second material preview slot of the top row and name it **Globe**. Click the Assign Material to Selection button to apply the material to the Globe object.

   Now make the material appear to have a polished blue metallic appearance.

2. In the Shader Basic Parameters rollout, change the shader from Blinn to Metal. Click the Ambient color swatch and change its color to RGB: **80, 80, 240**. Because the Ambient and Diffuse colors are locked (the buttons next to their titles appear to be pressed in), both colors change simultaneously. Change the Specular Level to **100** and Glossiness to **60**.

   A reasonably good metal material, a dark blue polished metallic, appears (see Figure 9.33).

   The globe material is still solid. You need to add the Opacity map in order for the oceans to disappear. Add the Opacity map now.

3. In the Metal Basic Parameters rollout, click the Opacity button (it's to the right of the spinner) to open the Material/Map Browser. In the Material/Map Browser, choose Bitmap and click OK to open the Select Bitmap Image File dialog. Choose **\3ds4-ma\project3\maps\globe.jpg** and click the View button to see the screen shown in Figure 9.34.

   The "(1:2)" that appears after "globe.jpg" in the title bar indicates that you are currently viewing the image at one-half its actual size, which means the bitmap has a pretty large resolution. One of the most valued images a media animator could possess is a good texture of the earth to map on spheres. Let's face it, everybody and their brother wants a spinning globe in their logo somewhere, especially when it comes to news. The resolution needs to be large in case you need to view a particular location of the globe and still want the edges of the continents to appear crisp. This globe image may not be 100 percent geologically correct, but it is a fantastic representation.

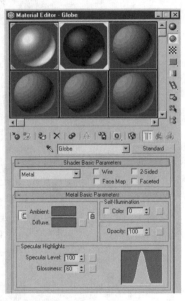

Figure 9.33
The Globe material has a dark blue polished metallic appearance.

Figure 9.34
The Globe.jpg
dialog opens after you
click View in the
Select Bitmap Image
File dialog.

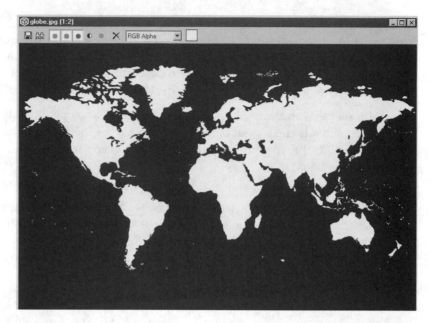

4. Close the globe.jpg (1:2) image and click
Open to load globe.jpg as the Opacity map.
Change the name to **Globe-opc** (as shown
in Figure 9.35).

Notice in the material preview slot that the
oceans have sort of been removed from the
material. The reality is that only the diffuse
and ambient colors of the globe are transparent. The black pixels of the image result with
a transparent ambient and diffuse channels,
and the white pixels of the image result with
opaque ambient and diffuse channels. For
any gray pixels would apply partial opacity,
the brighter the pixel, the more opaque it is.

The specular highlight remains. There are
two ways to mask the specular highlight: by
applying a map to the Specular Level, or by
applying a map to the Glossiness level.
Both are effective, but they yield slightly
different results. Putting the opacity map
on the Specular Level channel gets rid of
the specular color; putting it on the
Glossiness channel changes the sharpness
of the specular highlights.

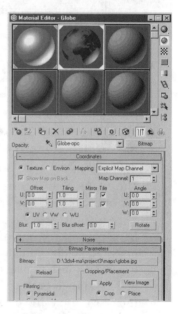

Figure 9.35
The Globe-opc opacity map
is loaded.

In this exercise, you will choose to map the glossiness because that creates a sparkling artifact on the shoreline where the oceans meet the land. This effect will become evident when you apply the map.

5. Click Return to Root to return to the root of the Globe material. In the Metal Basic Parameters dialog, drag the Opacity map button to the Glossiness map button and release the mouse. In the Copy (Instance) Map dialog, choose Copy and click OK to copy the map (see Figure 9.36).

   Hmm, very interesting. It seems as though the exact reverse of what you wanted to happen happened. The specular highlight is showing up on the oceans instead of the continents. If you invert the output of the globe.jpg in the Glossiness map channel, it will create the desired effect.

6. Click the Glossiness map button to open its parameters. Change its name to **Globe-gls** and open the Output rollout. Check Invert. The effect is faint, but correct. Click Go to Parent to return to the root of the Globe material.

   The Glossiness map is now doing its job, it's just not doing it very well. You can tweak the material's settings to improve the effect.

7. In the Specular Highlights group of the Metal Basic Parameters dialog, change the Glossiness value to **100**. Open the Maps rollout and change the Glossiness map amount to **50**. The effect improves, but you can strengthen it by dramatically increasing the Specular Level value. In the Specular Highlights group of the Metal Basic Parameters dialog, change the Specular Level value to **300** (see Figure 9.37).

   By making a few adjustments to the Glossiness and Specular Level values, you have created the perfect blue metallic globe material. Render a frame to see the results. Before you do though, change the background color.

8. Choose Rendering > Environment to open the Environment dialog. Click the Background Color swatch and change its color to RGB: **150, 150, 150**. Close the Environment dialog. Adjust the Perspective

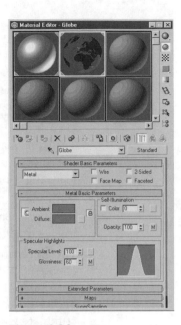

Figure 9.36
The Globe material with the Opacity map copied to the Glossiness map button.

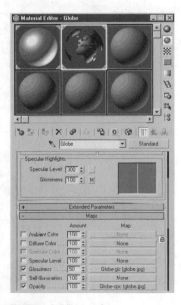

Figure 9.37
The Globe material with correct Glossiness and Specular Level settings.

view until the globe fits comfortably in the view, and then render the Perspective view (see Figure 9.38).

Note

Be sure to use the Zoom tool and not the FOV tool to adjust the view. Using the Zoom tool to adjust the view allows you to correctly view environment later in the chapter.

The globe material looks great on the globe. However, you are currently seeing the continents on only one side of the globe. Make the material two sided to place the continents on both the outside and the inside of the globe.

9. With the Globe material selected in the Material Editor, check 2-Sided in the Shader Basic Parameters rollout. Render the Perspective view again (see Figure 9.39).

The globe now has continents on both the outside and inside. When you checked 2-Sided in the material's parameters, the material was applied to both sides of the polygons creating the globe. Because the same material is on both the inside and outside, it might become difficult at times to discriminate what is the front and what is the back. To take care of this issue, you will apply an entirely different and much darker material to the inside of the globe. You will do so by changing the Globe material into a double-sided material.

Figure 9.38
The globe rendered through the Perspective view.

Figure 9.39
The globe material is now two sided.

10. In the Shader Basic Parameters dialog, uncheck 2-Sided to return the globe material to its original setting. Click the Standard button to open the Material Map Browser. Choose Double Sided and click OK to create the new material. In the Replace Material dialog, leave Keep Old Material As Sub-Material? selected and click OK.

Now the original Globe material is in the Facing Material sub-material slot. The default gray material is in the Back Material sub-material slot. If you were to render the Perspective view again, you would see that the front of the globe looks fine. However, the inside is now a solid gray material (as shown in Figure 9.40).

You now need to add a globe material to the Back Material sub-material slot as well in order to put the continents on the inside again. The continents on the inside will be solid black. To create the back material, you will simply copy the facing material and adjust its settings.

11. In the Material Editor, drag the Facing Material button over the Back Material button and release the mouse. In the Instance (Copy) Material dialog, choose Copy and click OK to copy the material.

The facing globe material is now copied into the back material slot. You can now open the material and adjust its parameters.

Figure 9.40
The new double sided material rendered in the Perspective view.

12. Click the Back Material button to open its parameters, and then change its name to **Globe-Back**. Because the material is going to be black, you no longer need any Specular Highlights. In the Metal Basic Parameters roll-out, drag the Specular Level button (to the right of its spinner) over the Glossiness map button. The map is removed from the Glossiness channel. Change both the Specular Level and Glossiness values to **0** (as shown in Figure 9.41).

    The specular highlight has been removed from the Globe-Back sub-material. To finish this sub-material, you need to change its color to black.

13. Click the Ambient swatch and change its color to RGB: **0, 0, 0**. Render the Perspective view again (see Figure 9.42).

    The globe material, as a whole, looks great. Add a raytraced reflection map to the facing sub-material to add a little Hollywood to it.

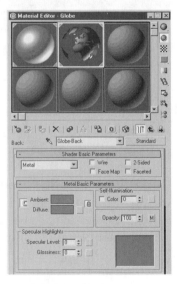

Figure 9.41
The Globe-Back back sub-material.

Figure 9.42
The Rendered double-sided globe material.

14. In the Material Editor, click the Go Forward to Sibling button to access the facing sub-material settings. Expand the Maps rollout and click the Reflection button to open the Material/Map Browser. Choose Raytrace and click OK to load the map.

You have just crossed the line from "relatively quick renders" to the world of "unbelievably long renders." Raytraced reflections are the most realistic reflections you can create in 3ds max. It uses complex algorithms to trace rays of light as they bounce through the scene until they reach the camera. All of this calculation takes a great deal of time.

By default, no antialiasing is applied in the raytrace calculations. Therefore, the reflection may seem pixilated and not smooth. If you are working on a machine with a fast processor, you can turn Antialiasing on by clicking the Options button in the Raytracer Parameters rollout; in the Global column check Antialiasing (see Figure 9.43). This will result in a cleaner effect.

However, in this scene, you will leave Antialiasing deactivated. You will only be applying a subtle reflection, so you might be able to get away with not using antialiasing.

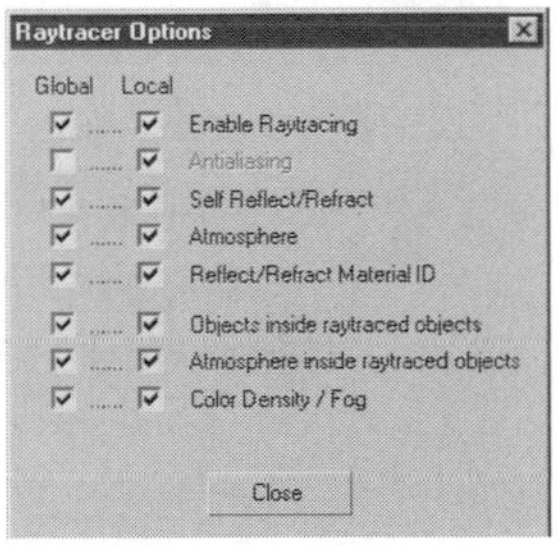

Figure 9.43
By default, Global Antialiasing is deactivated; for better quality, you can check Global Antialiasing.

15. Name this map **Globe-rfl** and click the Go to Parent button to return to the root of the Globe facing sub-material. In the Maps rollout, change the Reflection Amount to **50** and render the Perspective view again (see Figure 9.44).

You can now see the rings reflected on the globe. Pretty cool, isn't it? Since you didn't mask the reflection, the reflection is applied to the entire globe, not just the continents. For this particular scene, this will work well. Right now your background color is a bright gray. But when the scene is finished, the background will be almost black, so the reflection on the globe will not be as bright.

16. Save your work as **09TV05.max**.

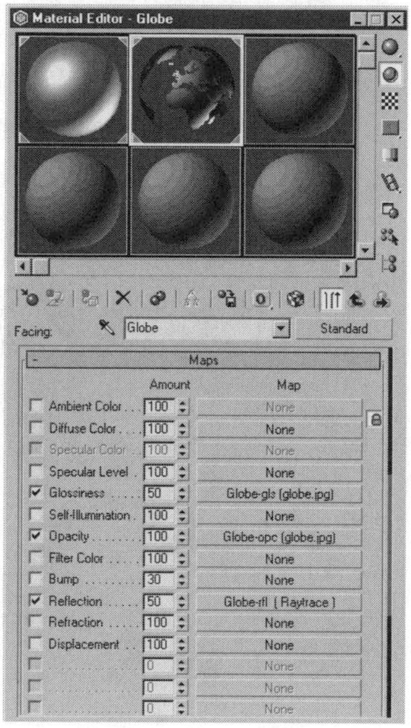

Applying a Material to the Ring Objects

You just finished the globe material, complete with a raytrace reflection map. You also want the ring objects to have raytraced reflections. Instead of using the raytrace reflection map, however, you will use the raytrace material to create the reflective gold material for the ring objects.

Figure 9.44
The Globe-rfl amount has been changed to 50 to reduce the overall appearance of the reflection.

3ds max has both a raytrace map and a raytrace material. Each has its own strengths and weaknesses. The major difference is that the Raytrace map has more extensive attenuation controls than the Raytrace material does. If you are having problems creating a certain effect using the Raytrace map, you might want to try to create it using the Raytrace material. Often you can achieve much different results experimenting with both.

Exercise 9.6   Creating a Reflective Gold Material

You will be adding a reflective Raytrace material to the ring objects. The reflective effect should be very similar to what you accomplished with the Globe material.

1. Make sure **09TV05.max** is open, and select all three ring objects (Ring01, Ring02, and RingLarge). In the Material Editor, select the third material preview slot in the top row and name it **GoldRing**. Click the Standard button

and in the Material/Map Browser, choose Raytrace and click OK to load the material.

The material type has been changed from Standard to Raytrace. You can now adjust its parameters to create a gold reflective material.

2. In the Raytrace Basic Parameters rollout, change the Ambient color to RGB: **240, 100, 60** and change the Diffuse color to RGB: **255, 150, 40**. Deselect Reflect and enter a value of **15**. Click the Assign Material to Selection button and render the Perspective view (see Figure 9.45).

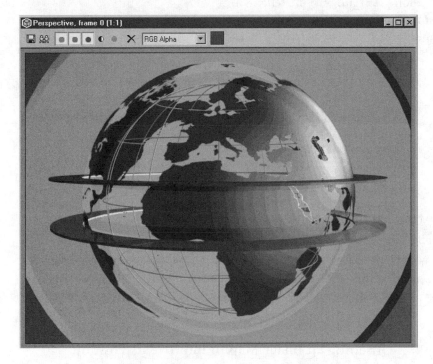

Figure 9.45
The GoldRing material is rendered on the ring objects.

The gold ring material is starting to take shape. The reason you deselected Reflect was to access its numeric value. If you were to leave Reflect checked, and then you changed the color in the swatch, the reflection would appear but would be tinted to that color. In this scene, however, you want the colors to reflect as realistically as possible. Therefore, you will use the value spinner.

The material would look better with a more pronounced gold-colored specular highlight. Make the necessary adjustments now.

3. In the Specular Highlight group, change the Specular Color to RGB: **255, 195, 80**. Change the Specular Level value to **143** and the Glossiness to **27** (as shown in Figure 9.46).

If you were to render the Perspective view again, you would notice that the specular highlights on the rings are larger and more gold colored. Creating this material is a testament to how quickly you can create complex and attractive materials in 3ds max.

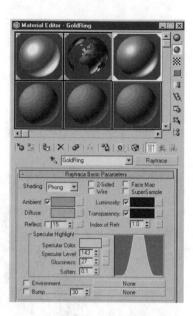

Figure 9.46
The parameters of the finished GoldRing material.

Note

You can significantly speed up renderings by reducing the (Rendering) Sides of the circles. Reducing the number of sides from 12 to 4 can almost cut the rendering time in half.

Adding the Environment

You are really starting to fine-tune the materials and the rendered appearance of the scene, so get rid of that drab gray background and add the environment map. Looking at John's storyboard, you can see that the environment background appears to be blue Venetian blinds. To accomplish that effect, you will load a blue-striped image into the environment map channel.

Exercise 9.7   Offsetting an Image Map to Improve Its Position

Adding the Environment map will be a breeze. You will load a JPG image and map it on Spherical Environment Mapping. After you have accomplished that, you will use the offset values to position the image so it renders in the correct location.

1. Choose Rendering > Environment to open the Environment dialog. In the Background group, click the Environment Map button to open the Material/Map Browser, choose Bitmap, and click OK to open the Select Bitmap Image File dialog. Choose **\3ds4-ma\project3\maps\streakblue.jpg** and click View to view a sample of the image.

The image is a square image that is mostly black. In the center of the image is a hi-tech circle shape that is created by dark blue horizontal lines of varying thickness. This image was created in Photoshop by basically creating a blurred circle image, applying a pixelate > color halftone filter to it, and applying some horizontal motion blur and contrast (see Figure 9.47).

Figure 9.47
The three basic steps to creating the streak-blue.jpg image: blurred circle, color halftone, motion blur.

2. Close the preview image and in the Select Bitmap Image File dialog, click Open to open the streakblue.jpg (as shown in Figure 9.48).

By default, the environment map is mapped using screen mapping, meaning the image is resized to fit perfectly in the view, no matter where the camera is pointed. You want the environment to interact with the camera, so you will need to change its mapping type to spherical.

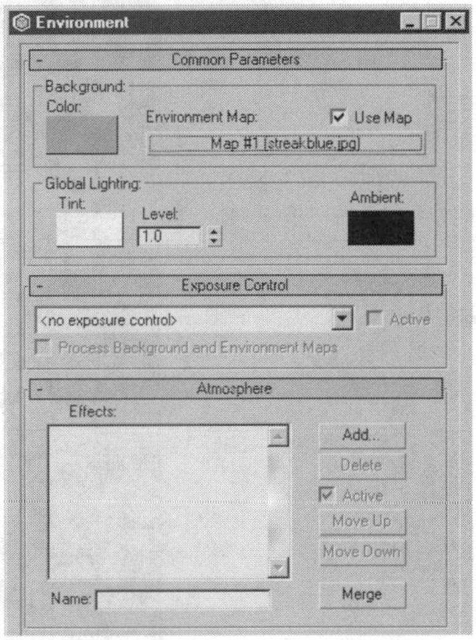

3. Drag the Environment Map button from the Environment dialog to the first material preview slot of the second row in the Material Editor. In the Instance (Copy) Map dialog, choose Instance and click OK to instance the map into the Material Editor. Close the Environment dialog. Name this map **Env** and in the Coordinates rollout, change the Mapping from Screen to Spherical Environment. The streakblue.jpg is now mapped on an imaginary sphere surrounding the scene. Render the Perspective view (see Figure 9.49).

Figure 9.48
The streakblue.jpg is loaded into the environment map slot.

Hmm, the blue streaks don't seem to be behind the globe. That's because they are in front of the globe. In fact, you can see them reflected on the continents. You need to offset the map in order to position the blue streaks behind the globe.

4. In the Coordinates rollout of the Env map, change the U Offset to **.5**. The blue streaks disappear from the preview slot. Render the Perspective view again (see Figure 9.50).

That looks much better. The scene is really starting to shape up. Save your work and continue adding the remaining objects.

5. Save your work as **09TV06.max** and close the Material Editor.

Figure 9.49
The new
streakblue.jpg spheri-
cal environment
mapped as the envi-
ronment background.

Figure 9.50
The rendered perspec-
tive view with the
blue streaks offset
correctly.

Adding the Type Elements

You need to create only two more objects to finish this scene: the large type that
orbits the globe and the small type that is on the lower ring object (you can see it
on the first and second panels of the storyboard).

Exercise 9.8   Using an Opacity Map to Create Type

You will add the large GlobalNews type to the scene first. To do so, you will opacity map the text on a cylinder, in much the same way as you opacity mapped the
continents on the globe.

   1. With **09TV06.max** open, open the Create > Shapes panel. Activate the 3D
      Snap toggle, click the Circle button, and in the Top view, create a circle at
      XYZ: 0, 0, 0 with a radius of **75**. Name the circle **GlobalNews** (as shown in
      Figure 9.51).

You now have a circle shape that you will extrude to create the cylinder to map the type on. The reason you are creating the cylinder by creating a circle and extruding it (as opposed to creating a cylinder primitive object) is that when you extrude it, you can turn off Start and End capping so the cylinder will have no top or bottom. You don't need the top or bottom; you only need the curved side to map the type on.

2. With GlobalNews selected, open the Modify panel and apply an Extrude modifier. Enter an Amount of **8** and deselect Cap Start and Cap End (as shown in Figure 9.52).

   With The GlobalNews object finished, move it into position and apply its material.

3. Activate the Select and Move tool and move the GlobalNews object down to XYZ: **0, 0, –4** (see Figure 9.53).

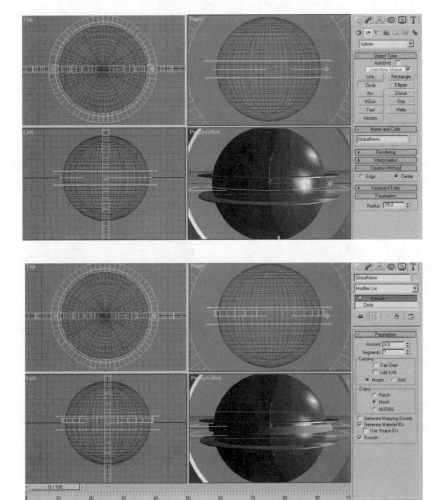

Figure 9.51
Create the GlobalNews circle shape at XYZ: 0, 0, 0.

Figure 9.52
The extruded GlobalNews shape.

Figure 9.53
The GlobalNews
object is moved into
position.

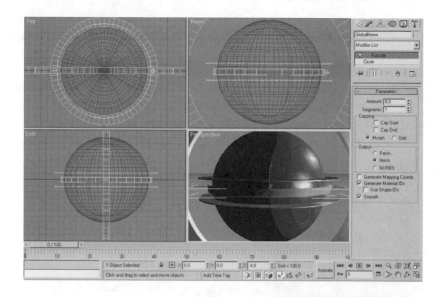

The material for the GlobalNews object is
going to be simple. It will consist of a 100
percent self-illuminated white material
with no specular highlight. The type will
be "cut out" with an opacity map.

4. Open the Material Editor and select the
second material preview slot in the second
row. Name this material **GlobalNews** and
assign it to the GlobalNews object. Change
the Diffuse color to RGB: **255, 255, 255**
and change the Self-Illumination value to
100 (see Figure 9.54).

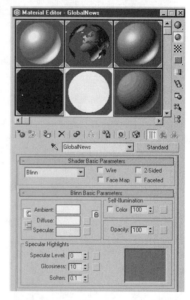

Figure 9.54
The GlobalNews material to
this point.

As of now, you have a 100 percent self-
illuminating white material with no
specular highlight. Now you need to apply
the opacity map to finish this material.

5. In the Blinn Basic Parameters rollout, click
the Opacity button (to the right of the
spinner) to open the Material/Map
Browser. Choose Bitmap and click OK to
close the browser. In the Select Bitmap
Image File dialog, choose **\3ds4-ma\
project3\maps\GlobalNewsBlur.jpg** and click Open to load the image
as an opacity map. Name this map **GlobalNews-opc** and render the
Perspective view (see Figure 9.55)

Dang, that looks good. It is a bit stretched though. Let's change its U Tiling amount to thin the letters a tad.

6. In the Coordinates rollout of the GlobalNews-opc map, change the U Tiling to **1.5** (as shown in Figure 9.56), and then render the Perspective view again (see Figure 9.57).

Figure 9.55
The GlobalNews material is applied to the GlobalNews object.

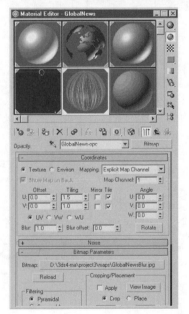

Figure 9.56
The GlobalNews-opc map thus far.

Figure 9.57
The rendered
Perspective view.

The strand of type now appears 1 and a half times around the GlobalNews object. You don't want to see the extra half on the ring, so you will deselect Tile to ensure it only appears once on the ring.

7. To view the map in the shaded Perspective view, click the Show Map in Viewport button. To get rid of the extra tiled map, deselect U Tile in the Coordinates rollout. The extra type caused by the tile disappears in the shaded view (see Figure 9.58).

Figure 9.58
The
GlobalNewsBlur.jpg
type appears only
once on the
GlobalNews object.

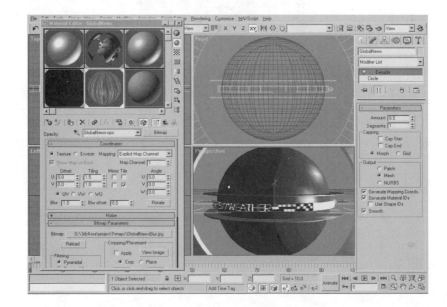

If you render the Perspective view again, you will see that the map no longer tiles (see Figure 9.59).

The Global News object and material are finished. Save your work.

8. Save your work as **09TV07.max** and close the Material Editor.

Figure 9.59
The GlobalNews-opc map no longer tiles.

Exercise 9.9   Opacity Mapping Text from Glossy Material

You must tend to one last embellishment before you can say you are finished creating all the objects in your scene. That object is the type on the edge of the bottom ring. To create that effect, you will approach it very similarly to the way you created the GlobalNews type object. You will extrude a circle shape and add the texture.

1. Make sure **09TV07.max** is open and make sure the 3D Snap toggle is active. Open the Create > Shapes panel and click the Circle button. In the Top view, create a circle shape with a Radius of **86** at XYZ: 0, 0, 0. Name the shape **RingType**. Because the rings have 64 faces around their perimeter, you should have 64 faces around the perimeter of your circle shape as well. Because 4 vertices create the circle shape, each segment should have 16 steps in order to create 64 segments (16 × 4 = 64). Expand the Interpolation rollout and change the Steps value to **16** (as shown in Figure 9.60).

The radius of the circle is 86—one unit larger than the rings. You want to place the RingType object so that it will be rendered over the side of the ring objects.

Extrude the circle and move it into position.

2. With RingType selected, open the Modify panel and apply an Extrude Modifier with an Amount of 1. Make sure Cap Start and Cap End are not checked. Activate the Select and Move tool and move the RingType object to XYZ: 0, 0, –12 (see Figure 9.61).

Because the object is so small in the view, you should adjust the Perspective view to observe a more realistic image.

3. Use the Zoom and Pan tools to adjust the Perspective view to roughly match Figure 9.62. What is important is to see the RingType object more closely.

Instead of using an opacity map to map out the opacity of the material, you will make the material completely transparent. You will map the shininess of the material to create the text.

4. Open the Material Editor and select the third material preview slot of the second row. Name the material **RingType** and apply it to the RingType object. In the Blinn Basic Parameters rollout, change the Opacity value to **0**. The RingType object disappears in the shaded Perspective view.

Now you will map the Specular level of the material to make the type appear.

Figure 9.60
The correct parameters for the RingType circle shape.

Figure 9.61
The RingType object is extruded and positioned correctly.

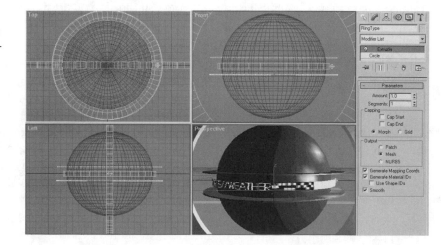

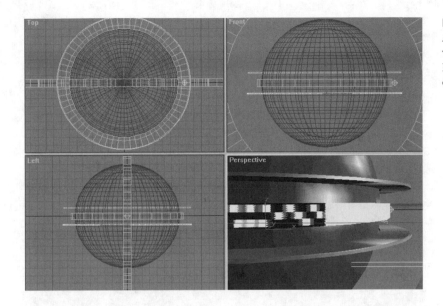

Figure 9.62
Adjust the Perspective view to observe the RingType object more closely.

5. In the Specular Highlights group of the Blinn Basic Parameters rollout, click the Specular Level map button (to the right of the spinner) to open the Material/Map Browser. Choose Bitmap and click OK to open the Select Bitmap Image File dialog. Choose **\3ds4-ma\project3\maps\ type-ring.jpg** and click View to view the image (see Figure 9.63). This is the type you will be mapping around the RingType object. Notice the amount of blank space before the word "Business," and note how close "Entertainment" is to the edge of the bitmap. This map was created to tile seamlessly. Therefore, you can increase Tile value (in whole numbers), and the map will seamlessly create an endless wrap of text around the object. Close the type-ring.jpg preview window and click Open to load the map into the Specular map slot. Name this map **RingType-spc,** click Show Map in Viewport, and render the Perspective view (see Figure 9.64).

   The effect looks good. However, you need to tile the RingType-spc map along its U-axis in order to make the type more legible.

6. In the Coordinates rollout of the RingType-spc map, change the U Tiling to **5** (as shown in Figure 9.65), and then render the Perspective view again (see Figure 9.66).

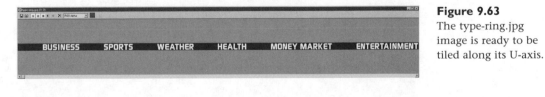

Figure 9.63
The type-ring.jpg image is ready to be tiled along its U-axis.

Figure 9.64
Stretched type
appears around the
lower ring object.

Figure 9.65
The correct Tiling
coordinates for the
RingType-spc map.

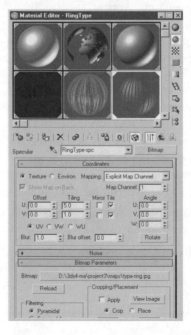

Figure 9.66
The type looks much
better now that it's
tiled five times.

The material looks great. The text looks like a hologram floating in front of the ring objects. Neat! Let's save our work and get ready to animate this scene.

7. Save your work as **09TV08.max**.

In Conclusion

You are finished creating the objects and applying the appropriate materials, and you have added lights in the scene to illuminate the objects in a dramatic and artistic manner. By examining test images you've rendered through the Perspective view, you know that your scene matches the mood of John's storyboard.

In the next chapter, you will key the animation, add any necessary special effects, and render the first scene.

Chapter 10

Animating the Globe Environment

In the previous chapter, you built and

added materials to all the objects you will

need to create the first half of the TV 3

news animation. In this chapter, you will

add the music, animate the scene, and render it. This rendering will be used as the screen mapped environment background for the second half of the animation.

In this chapter, you gain experience in the following areas:

- Animating to Audio
- Grouping objects
- Applying the Video Post Lens Flare filter
- Adding Inferno to a Lens Flare effect

Adding Sound to the Scene

Gordon provided you with a piece of audio to sync your animation to. Because you have already had the experience of adding sound in the previous projects, it'll be easy this time. Add it to the scene, and then listen to what you have.

Exercise 10.1   Adding the Soundtrack

While you are adding the soundtrack to the scene, you need to be aware that you will need pre-roll and pad for this animation. Keeping this in mind, you should examine the audio to see if you need to offset the time the music starts to add pre-roll.

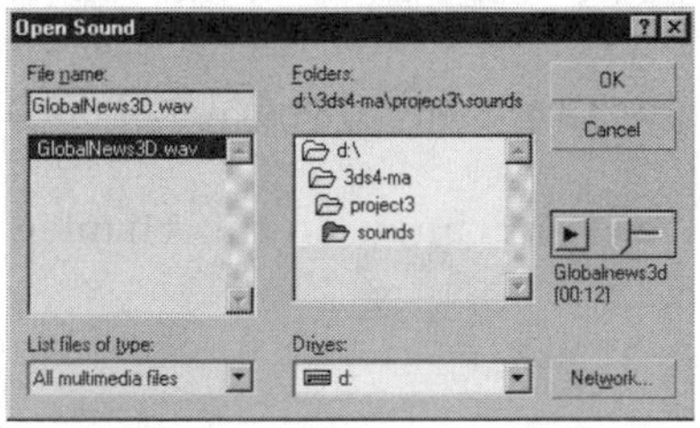

1. With **09TV08.max** open, open the Track View. Select the Sound track title, right-click it, and choose Properties from the resulting list to open the Sound Options dialog. Click the Choose Sound button and choose **\3ds4-ma\project3\sounds\ GlobalNews3D.wav**. Notice that this .wav file is 12 seconds long (see Figure 10.1). Click the Play button to preview the audio. That certainly sounds like news music to me! Click OK to open the sound, and then click OK again to close the Sound Options dialog.

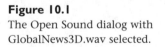

Figure 10.1
The Open Sound dialog with GlobalNews3D.wav selected.

The music does not have pre-roll included, so you need to add pre-roll to this animation. To do so, you will offset the sound's starting point by 30 frames.

2. In the Track View, expand the Sound track. Use the Zoom tool to view time in 10 frame intervals. Using the Move Keys tool, move the track forward 30 frames (as shown in Figure 10.2). Close the Track View.

Note

You should not hear anything during the first 30 frames. However, because the music loops, you can hear the faint ending of the music during the first 30 frames before the music starts to play. 3ds max allows you to work with audio for choreographic purposes, not to add a music track in the final product. Usually when you finish an animation, you will take it into a composite software such as Combustion or After Effects and color correct, add extra effects, and add the final audio track.

The music doesn't start until after frame 30, which gives you plenty of pre-roll. However, your scene is still 100 frames long. If the music is 12 seconds (360 frames) and you add 1 second (30 frames) of pre-roll, the animation will be 13 seconds or 390 frames long. However, this scene is only half the animation. Therefore, you need to figure out where the transition will occur so you know how long to make this scene.

3. Click the Time Configuration button to open the Time Configuration dialog. In the Animation group, change the Length to **390** (see Figure 10.3). Click OK to exit the dialog. Then play the animation to hear the music again.

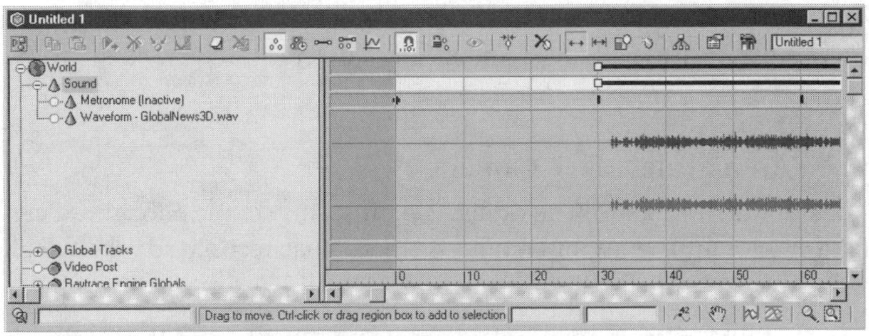

Figure 10.2
The sound track is off-set forward 30 frames in the Track View.

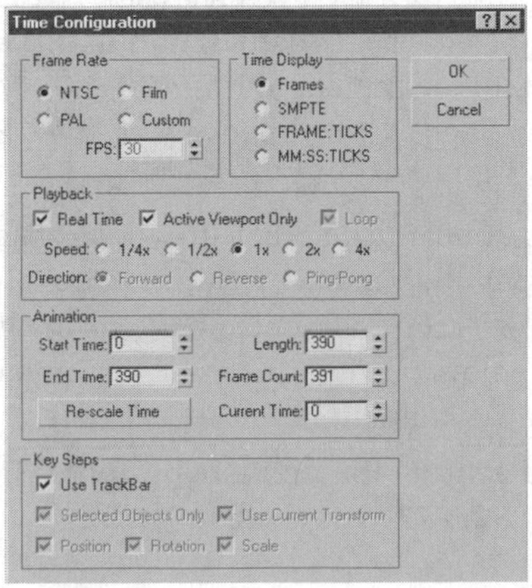

Figure 10.3
The animation is now 390 frames long.

The music is in 4/4 time, meaning there are four beats to a measure. Examining the storyboard and listening to the music, it seems logical that the globe animation will encompass the first two measures, or eight beats. By the ninth beat (the first beat of the third measure), you will see the Venetian blinds (from the second scene's animation) moving in over the globe animation. The globe animation should be completely gone by the first beat of the fourth measure (around frame 180), but you should add an extra second, just in case you need it. That means the length of the animation should be 210 frames long, and that will be more than you'll need to complete the animation.

4. Click the Time Configuration button again and change the Length to 210. Click OK to close the dialog. Save your work as **10TV01.max**.

Animating the Camera

The animation of this scene is relatively simple. The most complicated aspect of this scene is the camera move. This is because the camera will start close to the objects and move to examine them, and then it will quickly accelerate to pull away from the globe. You need to create the camera and its animation before you do anything else in the scene.

Exercise 10.2   Animating a Free Camera

Take a good look at the storyboard. The camera's path seems simple enough, so create the animation without the use of Dummy helpers (that technique we have all grown to love).

1. Make sure **10TV01.max** is open. Select Create > Cameras, and then click the Free button. Click in the Front view to create a Free camera. In the Stock Lenses group, click 35mm to use a standard 35mm lens. Move the camera to XYZ: **55, –68, –8** and rotate the camera to XYZ: **90, 30, 0**. Activate the Perspective view and press the C key to change it to the Camera01 view (shown in Figure 10.4).

   The camera's view is very similar to the first storyboard panel. Basically all you need to do now is dolly the camera backward to get a wider view of the globe. You should, however, keep the camera close to the globe for a few beats so the viewers can enjoy the close-up and can familiarize themselves with what is going on in the animation.

2. Advance to frame 60 and activate the Animate button. With Camera01 still selected, move it to XYZ: **52, –77, 1** (see Figure 10.5).

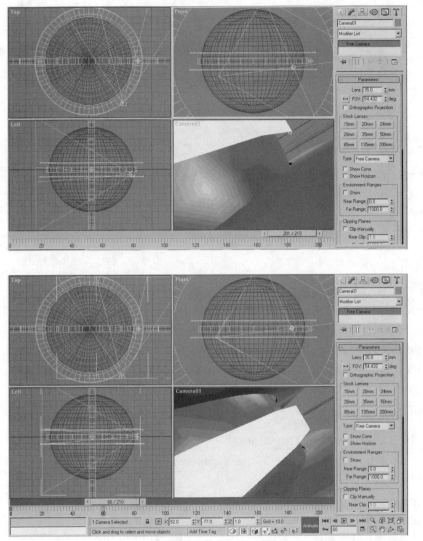

Figure 10.4
Camera01 is in the correct position and orientation

Figure 10.5
Camera01 is moved to XYZ: 52, –77, 1 at frame 60.

To complete the animation, you need to dolly it back further and rotate a slight counterclockwise turn to the camera.

3. Advance to frame 210, and with the Animate button still active, move Camera01 to XYZ: **38, –270, 5**. Rotate Camera01 to XYZ: **90, 15, 0** (as shown in Figure 10.6). Then deactivate the Animate button.

The animation for the camera is complete. Feel free to play the animation and view the results. The camera should linger on a close-up of the globe and then slowly dolly backward to a wider shot.

Figure 10.6
Camera01 is in the correct position and orientation at frame 210.

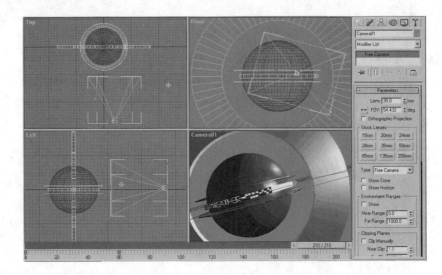

Bringing the Scene to Life

Now that you know what the camera move is, you can animate the globe exactly the way you want it to rotate. You should keep in mind that the earth rotates counterclockwise (if you were looking down on the North Pole). You don't want to play god and change the ways of nature, so you better rotate the continents in that direction. The wireframe, on the other hand, will rotate in the opposite direction, adding visual interest to the scene.

Exercise 10.3   Animating the Objects

Before you can animate the rotation of the continents, you need to see them in the shaded Camera01 view.

1. Open the Material Editor and select the Globe material. Navigate to the Facing Material: Globe material and open its Opacity map's parameters. Click Show Map in Viewport. Close the Material Editor. The continents are visible in the shaded Camera01 view now (as shown in Figure 10.7).

   Because you are in the United States, you want to focus on North America. If you want to view any other continent during your animation, feel free to do so.

2. Advance to frame 150 for a clear view of the globe. Deactivate the 3D Snap toggle if it is still active, activate the Select and Rotate tool (View Z-axis), and in the Top view, rotate the Globe object to its starting orientation (see Figure 10.8). Remember it is going to rotate (in the camera view) from the left to the right.

   You're ready to animate the rotation now.

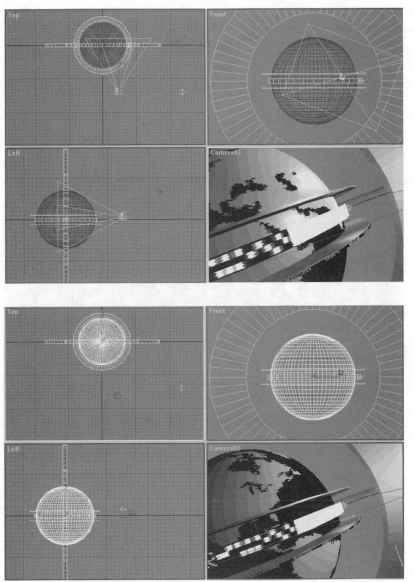

Figure 10.7
The continents are visible in the shaded Camera01 view.

Figure 10.8
The Globe object is rotated to the desired start orientation.

3. Advance to frame 210 and activate the Animate button. Using the Select and Rotate tool (View Z-axis) in the Top view, rotate the Globe object approximately 60 degrees (see Figure 10.9). Deactivate the Animate button.

It's time to animate the rotation of the wireframe frame of the globe. However, the frame is made of several circle shapes, and you don't want to have to animate each one separately. So group them into one unit.

4. Press the H key to open the Select Objects dialog. Select all the Circle shapes (as shown in Figure 10.10) and click Select to select them in the scene.

5. Choose Group > Group from the toolbar. In the Group dialog, enter the Group name: **wireframe** and click OK to group all the circle shapes together.

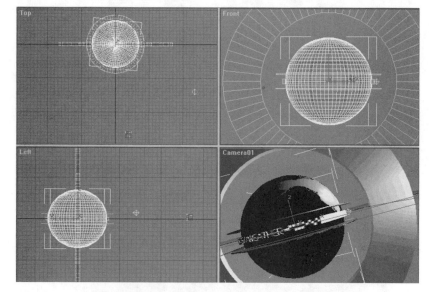

Figure 10.9
The Globe object is rotated approximately 60 degrees.

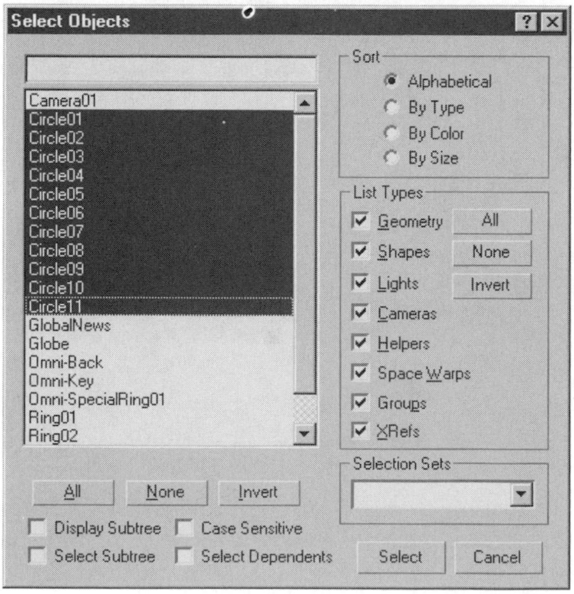

Figure 10.10
All 11 Circle shapes are selected.

Because the circle shapes are now grouped together, they will act as one object. Now you can animate the whole wireframe group.

6. Advance to frame 210 and activate the Animate button. Activate the Select and Rotate tool (View Z axis) and in the Top view rotate the wireframe group Z: –120 degrees (Figure 10.11). Deactivate the Animate button.

   The globe and the wireframe are animated correctly.

7. Save your work as **10TV02.max**.

   Looking at John's storyboard, you can clearly see the squares to the left of the global news type first, and then the type rotates around the globe from the right to the left. Taking that into account, orient the object into its start position.

8. Advance to Frame 120 for a good look at the globe. Select the GlobalNews object and activate the Select and Rotate tool (Local Z-axis). Rotate the GlobalNews object Z: **–80** degrees. You should just barely see the black of the image rounding the right side in the distance (as shown in Figure 10.12).

   Now you can animate the rotation of the GlobalNews object. You don't necessarily want to read all the type on the ring. The most important type is the "Global News" type; everything else is filler.

9. Advance to frame 210 and activate the Animate button. Using the Select and Rotate tool (Local Z-axis), rotate the GlobalNews object Z: **–180** degrees (as shown in Figure 10.13). Deactivate the Animate button.

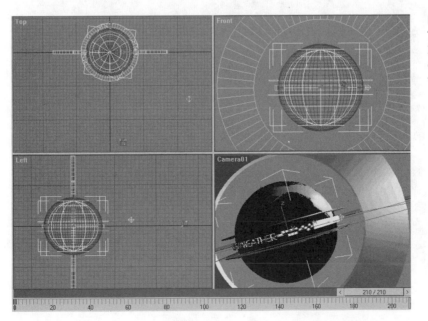

Figure 10.11
The wireframe group has been rotated –120 degrees in the Top view.

Figure 10.12
The GlobalNews object is rotated into its start orientation.

Figure 10.13
The GlobalNews object is rotated Z: –180 degrees at frame 210.

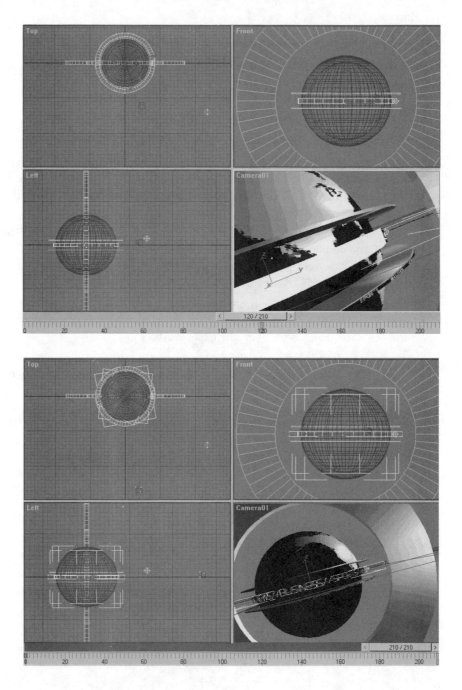

If you play the animation, you should see the Global News type rotate around the globe from the right to the left.

There is only one object left to animate: the RingLarge object. Its animation is just as simple as the others. It will sweep through the scene to add a little interest to the background. After you animate the RingLarge object, you will tweak the settings of the lights and perfect the rendered appearance of the scene.

10. Activate the Select and Rotate tool (View Z-axis), and in the Top view, rotate the RingLarge object Z: **60** degrees into its start orientation (see Figure 10.14).

Now you can animate the rotation of the RingLarge object into its end orientation.

11. Advance to frame 210 and activate the Animate button. Using the Select and Rotate tool (View Z-axis) in the Top view, rotate the RingLarge object Z: **–110** degrees to its end orientation (shown in Figure 10.15). Then deactivate the Animate button.

The animation for the objects in the scene is complete. Now you can turn your attention to making sure the scene is lit correctly.

12. Save your work as **10TV03.max**.

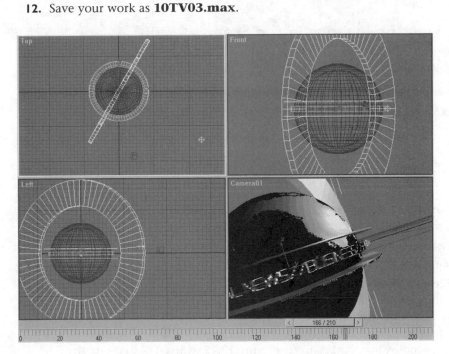

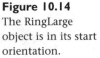

Figure 10.14
The RingLarge object is in its start orientation.

Figure 10.15
The RingLarge object
in its end orientation.

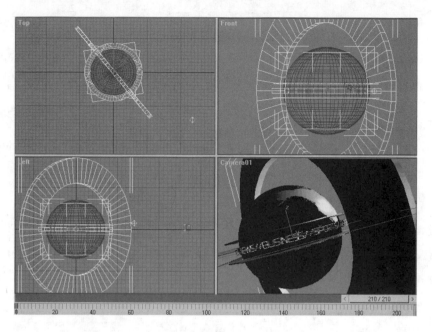

Checking the Lighting in the Scene

You are thrilled with the animation of the objects and the camera in your scene. However, you haven't really been rendering too many test frames to ensure the beauty of the rendered animation. Now that everything is in place, you can focus on checking the lights in your scene, and you can decide where you should add more.

Exercise 10.4   Tweaking the Lights in a Scene

Roll up your sleeves, render a test frame, and begin to artistically tweak the scene.

1. With **10TV03.**max open, advance to frame 180 and render it through the Camera01 view (as shown in Figure 10.16).

   The rendering looks good, but the RingLarge object is nearly in complete darkness. You should shed some light on it.

2. Create an Omni light in the Top view with the color RGB: **150, 150, 150** and move it to XYZ: **–700, –400, 100**. Name this light **OmniRingLFront** and click the Exclude button to open the Exclude/Include dialog. In the Exclude/Include dialog, choose Include, select RightLarge, and click the arrow pointing to the right (see Figure 10.17). Click OK to create the Include list.

Figure 10.16
The Camera01 view rendered at frame 180.

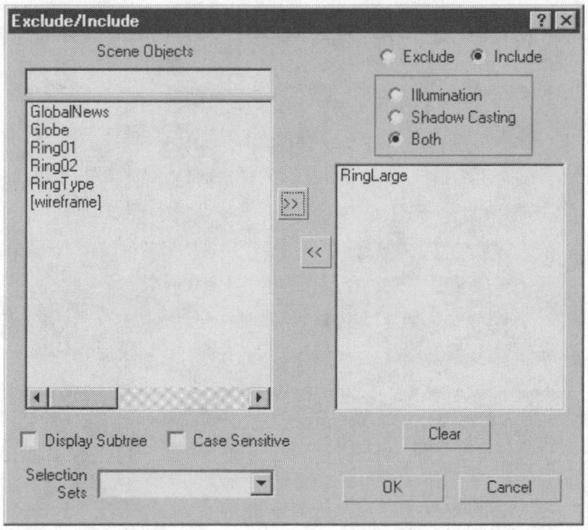

Figure 10.17
The correctly configured Include list for the OmniRingLFront light.

As you can see in Figure 10.18, the light is now correctly adjusted.

The OmniRingLFront light casts its light on only the RingLarge object.

3. Render frame 180 again through the Camera01 view (as shown in Figure 10.19).

Plenty of light is now cast on the RingLarge object throughout the animation.

Figure 10.18
The OmniRingLFront light is in the correct position with the correct parameters.

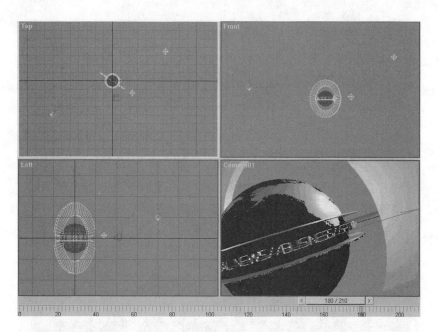

Figure 10.19
The RingLarge object now has ample light on it at frame 180.

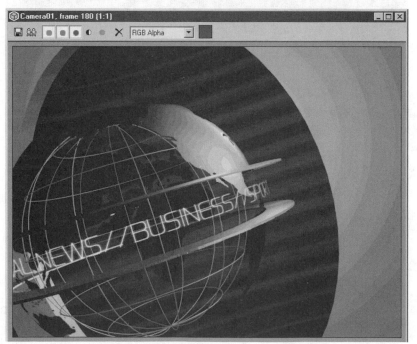

Exercise 10.5   Adding More Special Ring Lights

There is only one more area I think could be improved with more light: in-between the rings. There is only one light there currently, and the rest of the ring looks dull and boring. If you add two more lights inside the ring, you can animate them to travel within the rings, adding even more interest to the rendered animation.

If you select the Omni-SpecialRing01 light and move its pivot to XYZ: **0**, **0**, **0**, you can then instance the light twice along that pivot. After creating the instances, you can animate them along the pivot as well.

1. Select the Omni-SpecialRing01 light and open the Hierarchy panel. Activate the Affect Pivot Only button, and using the Select and Move tool, move the pivot to XYZ: **0**, **0**, **0** (see Figure 10.20). Deactivate the Affect Pivot Only button.

   The Omni-SpecialRing01's pivot is at the center of the globe. You can now create the two instances of the light.

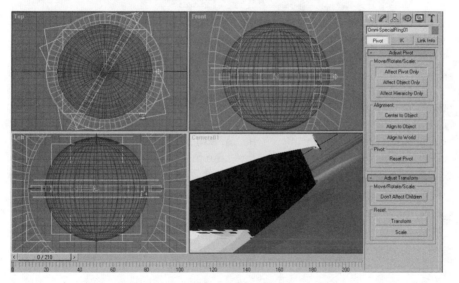

Figure 10.20
The Omni-SpecialRing01's pivot is now at XYZ: 0, 0, 0.

2. With Omni-SpecialRing01 selected, activate the Select and Rotate tool (View Z-axis). In the Top view, Shift+rotate the Omni light Z: **120** degrees, and then release the mouse button. In the Clone Options dialog, choose Instance and change the Number of Copies to **2** (as shown in Figure 10.21). Click OK to create the two instances (see Figure 10.22).

Figure 10.21
The Clone Options dialog with the correct settings.

Figure 10.22
The two instanced Omni lights are visible in the views.

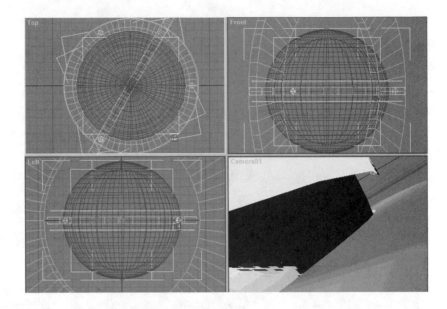

You can now animate the three lights to add a little more interest to the rendered animation. Before you can animate though, you need to rotate the lights into their start orientations. Looking down through the Top view, the lights will rotate clockwise around the globe. To make sure the original Omni-SpecialRing01 light illuminates the most important right side of the globe's rings in the beginning of the animation, you will rotate the lights counterclockwise a few degrees before animating them forward.

3. Select the three Omni-SpecialRing Omni lights (01, 02, and 03) and activate the Select and Rotate tool (View Z-axis—Use Selection Center). Activate the Selection Lock toggle, and in the Top view, rotate the three selected lights Z: **30** degrees (see Figure 10.23).

The Omni-SpecialRing lights are in the optimal start orientation for the scene now. You can advance to frame 210 and animate their rotation.

4. Advance to frame 210 and activate the Animate button. Using the Select and Rotate tool (View Z-axis), rotate the three Omni-SpecialRing lights Z: **–160** degrees in the Top view (as shown in Figure 10.24). Deactivate the Animate button and Selection Lock toggle.

5. The lights are all perfect now. Save your work as **10TV04.max**.

If you play the animation, you will see the effect of the lights traveling between the rings.

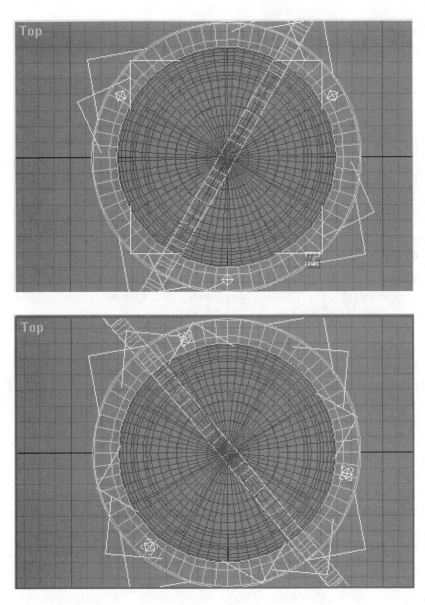

Figure 10.23
The Omni-SpecialRing lights are rotated Z:30 degrees in the Top view

Figure 10.24
The three Omni lights have been rotated Z: −160 degrees.

Adding the Lens Flare

It is not hard to notice the lens flares on John's storyboard (see Figure 10.25). The truth is that lens flares are a great graphic device that easily adds visual interest and realism to an image. If you have ever watched a news program on TV, you probably know that not too many minutes go by without a lens flare.

Figure 10.25
John's storyboard for
TV 3 News.

This animation is no exception. You will be adding two lens flares to the complete animation: one during the first section and one during the second section to punctuate the logo. John's storyboard clearly illustrates a flare that is centered between the two rings and that gets brighter as the scene progresses. You will actually use the flare as a transition device to help bring on the second scene smoothly. As the flare of the first shot brightens, the Venetian blinds will reveal themselves, completing the transition.

Exercise 10.6   Adding Lens Effects in Video Post

There are two ways to create lens flares in 3ds max: by using a Video Post filter or by using Render Effects. The Lens Flares option in Render Effects is good for creating less-complicated flares; the Video Post filter allows you to visually build lens flares quickly. The one thing both flares have in common is that both need a source. In this scene, you will create a point helper to be the source of the flare.

1. Make sure **10tv04.max** is open and select Create > Helpers. Click the Point button and create a point helper in the Top view. Move the point helper to XYZ: **130**, **166**, **0** (as shown in Figure 10.26).

   The Point01 helper will be the source of the lens flare in this scene. If you play the animation, you will see it always stays relatively snug in between the rings. You have to create a Video Post Queue in order to create the lens flare effect. You will need to create three basic events: the scene input event (the camera), the image filter event (the lens flare), and the image output event (saving the rendered image). It's as simple as that. Now start creating the queue.

2. Choose Rendering > Video Post to open the Video Post dialog. Click the Add Scene Event button. Click OK to accept the default settings.

   The Camera01 event is now in the queue (see Figure 10.27).

   Now add the flare event.

3. Click the Add Image Filter Event button. In the Add Image Filter Event dialog, change Adobe Photoshop Filter to Lens Effects Flare (see Figure 10.28), and then click OK to close the dialog.

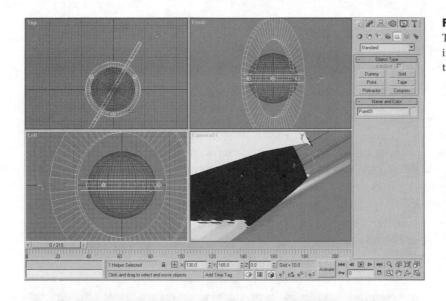

Figure 10.26
The Point01 helper is in the correct position.

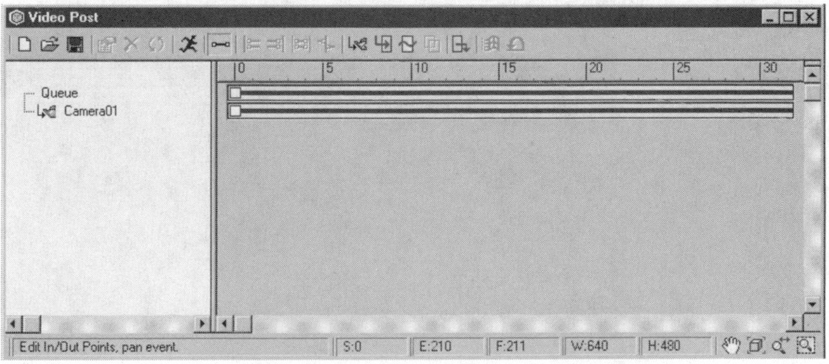

Figure 10.27
The Camera01 event is added to the Video Post Queue.

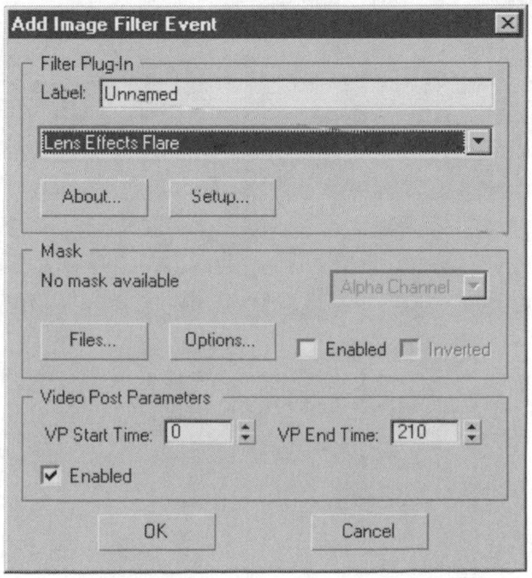

Figure 10.28
The Add Image Filter Event dialog with Lens Effects Flare selected.

The Lens Effects Flare event is added to the queue (see Figure 10.29).

To complete the queue, you will add the Image Output Event.

4. Click the Image Output Event button. In the Image Output Event dialog, click the Files button. In the Select Image File for Video Post Output folder, enter the desired filename. In my scene, I entered \3ds4-ma\project3\ images\shota.avi, and in the Video Compression setup, I chose Full Frames (Uncompressed) (as shown in Figure 10.30). Full Frames will allow me to save a playable avi file without sacrificing image quality. When I composite it into the second scene, the quality will be perfect (as compared to a compressed format). Click OK to add the Image Output Event to the queue (see Figure 10.31).

Great! The Video Post Queue is complete. But you still have to adjust the lens flare's settings.

5. Save your work as **10TV05.max**.

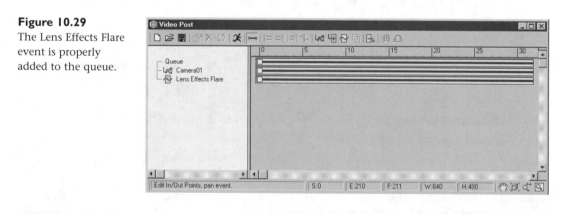

Figure 10.29
The Lens Effects Flare event is properly added to the queue.

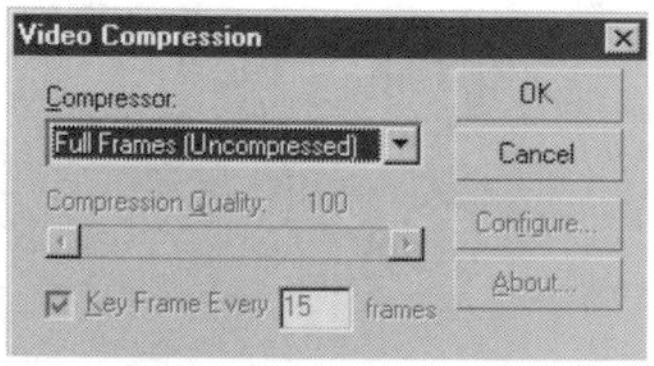

Figure 10.30
The Video Compression dialog with Full Frames (Uncompressed) selected.

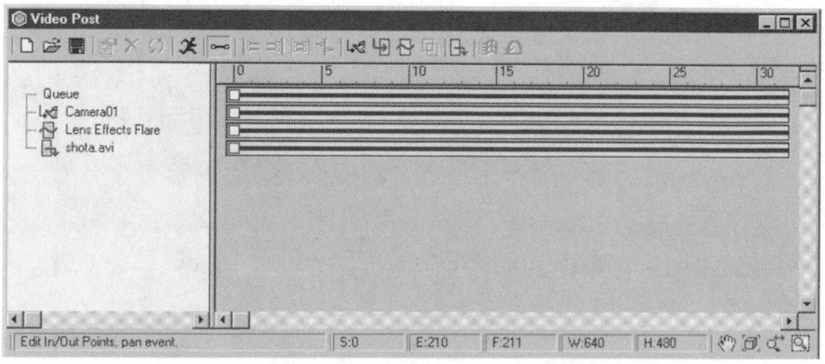

Figure 10.31
The finished Video Post Queue.

Exercise 10.7   Adjusting the Lens Flare's Parameters

You just finished the Video Post Queue that contains the Lens Effects Flare filter. Now you need to open the Lens Effect Flare's parameters and adjust them to design the desired flare effect.

1. Make sure **10TV05.max** is open and at frame 0. Open the Video Post Queue. Double-click the Lens Effects Flare event to open the Edit Filter Event dialog. Click the Setup button to open the lens flare's parameters. In the Lens Flare Properties group, click the Node Sources button to open the Select Flare Objects dialog. Select Point01 (as shown in Figure 10.32), and then click OK to exit the dialog. Click the VP Queue button (to use a frame rendered from the scene in the preview), and then click the Preview button. After a few moments, the frame appears in the preview window with the flare applied (see Figure 10.33).

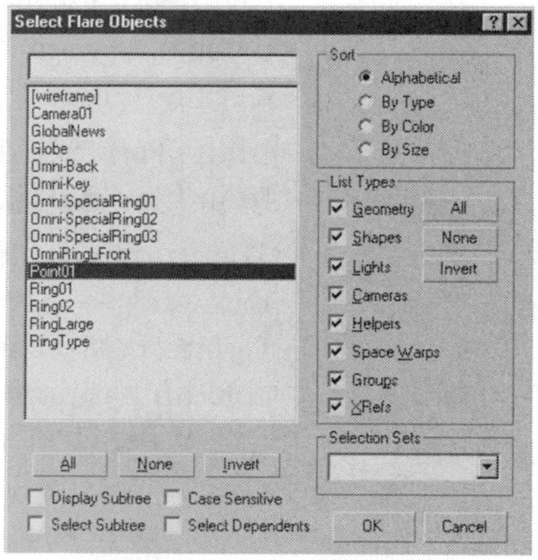

Figure 10.32
The Select Flare Objects dialog with Point01 selected.

Here you get your first glance at how the default lens flare looks on your objects. It looks like you are about to enter warp speed! That's not good. The first problem with the flare is that Squeeze is applied to all its elements. Squeeze is what makes ovals out of all the wonderful circle flare secondaries. You'd better turn off Squeeze.

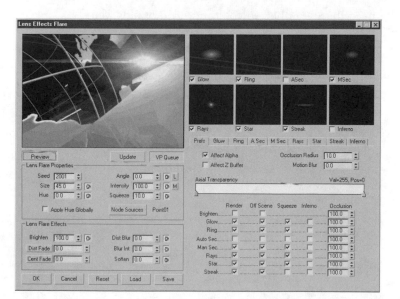

Figure 10.33
The Lens Effects Flare dialog with a VP Queue Preview active.

2. In the Prefs tab, remove every check mark in the Squeeze column (see Figure 10.34).

The next aspect of the flare that doesn't fit in to the image is the blue warp speed streak. Get rid of that.

3. In the Prefs tab, deselect Streak from the Render column.

The streak is removed from the flare preview (as shown in Figure 10.35). The Off Scene column has no effect on the flare if the element isn't checked in the Render column.

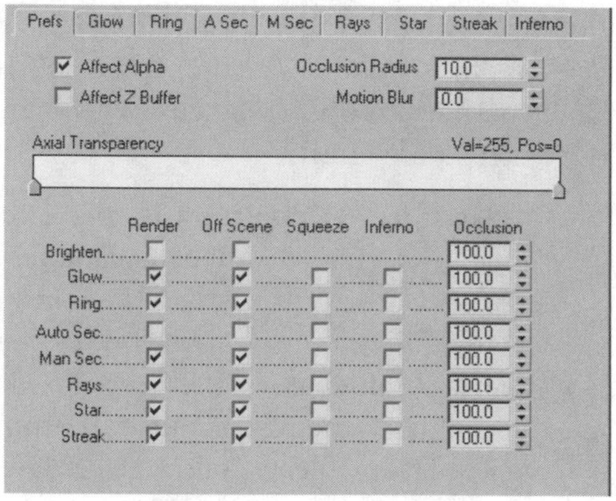

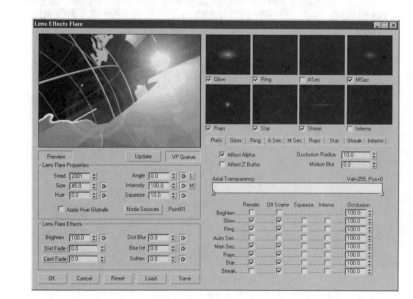

Figure 10.34

Remove all the check marks from the Lens Effects Flare dialog's Squeeze column.

If Off Scene is checked, the flare element renders even when the source is out of the camera view. Because you deselected Render for the Streak, it will not render at all.

You should be concerned with the Occlusion value as well. Currently all the elements are set to 100 percent occlusion. This means that the elements disappear as the source passes behind objects, and you don't want that to occur in this scene.

4. Lower all the Occlusion values to **0**.

You don't need the Star either, so you can get rid of it as well.

Figure 10.35

The Streak is removed from the flare.

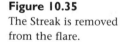

5. Deselect Star in the Render column (see Figure 10.36).

   John's storyboard shows the flare as more of an orange color, but right now it looks bluish. Adjust the Glow element's color gradient to add much more gold to the glow. Before you do that though, advance to a frame that will allow you to view the flare over the background.

6. Advance to frame 120 and click the Update button in the Lens Effects Flare dialog so that the image renders again and you can see the scene at frame 120. Then click the Glow tab (see Figure 10.37).

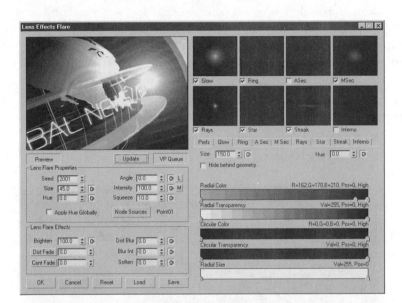

Figure 10.36
The Star element has been removed from the flare.

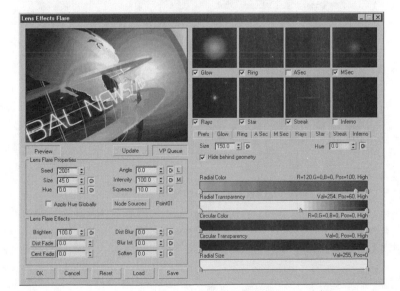

Figure 10.37
The Glow tab is open in the Lens Effects Flare dialog.

If you look at the Radial Color gradient, you can see why the glow is so bluish. Make it more gold.

7. Double-click the first gradient flag (the first one on the left) and change its color to RGB: **210, 150, 0**. Double-click the middle flag and change its color to RGB: **120, 0, 0**. Right-click the middle flag and choose Copy. Right-click the last flag and choose Paste. The result should be a gradient from orange to red. Also, check Hide Behind Geometry.

The Radial Color gradient is now good. When you clicked the Hide Behind Geometry option, the glow effect was applied only to the background environment; therefore, the glow effect hides behind the geometry. This creates a great backlit effect. However, the flare isn't as intense as it could be. By adjusting the Radial Transparency gradient, you can increase the intensity of the glow.

8. Click the pointer on the whitest pixels of the Radial Transparency gradient and drag right to create a new flag at Pos=60 (as shown in Figure 10.38).

The flare looks about perfect.

9. Save your work as **10TV06.max**.

Figure 10.38
The flare is more intense with a brighter Radial Transparency gradient.

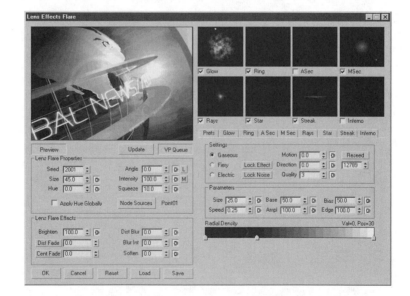

Exercise 10.8   Adding Inferno to the Glow Element

If you examine the flare on John's storyboard, you will notice the glow is smoky, and not a perfect graduated sphere like yours. By adding Inferno to the glow, you can accomplish this smoky effect.

1. Make sure **10TV06.max** is open. In the Lens Effects Flare dialog, click the Prefs tab and check Glow in the Inferno column (as shown in Figure 10.39).

   Well, that is certainly a dramatic effect! You will need to soften the Inferno effect a bit before you can stamp it with the seal of approval.

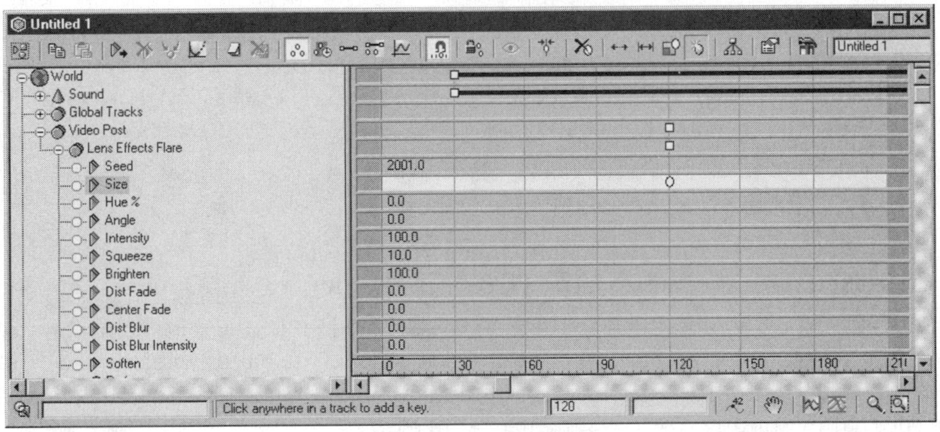

Figure 10.39
Glow is checked in the Inferno column.

2. Click the Inferno tab. In the Settings group, change the Motion value to **0**.

   You change the Motion value to **0** because Motion pans the noise effect through the scene, as if the wind were blowing. The Direction value assigns the direction the "wind" blows (0 being 12 o'clock, and the direction changing clockwise as the value increases). The value of 360 returns the direction to 12 o'clock). You do not want any "wind" in this scene.

3. In the Parameters group, change the Size to **25** and the Speed to **.25**.

   You are increasing the size of the effect to create larger, more realistic clouds. You are changing the Speed value to .25 (from 1) to slow down the undulation of the clouds. This will create a slow billowing cloud time-lapse effect. The Inferno effect allows for large gaps to form between the clouds. You always want the center of the glow effect to be a solid glow, which you can accomplish by adjusting the Radial Density gradient.

4. In the Inferno tab, double-click the left flag of the Radial Density gradient and change its color to black RGB: **0, 0, 0** to make the glow more solid toward the source. Then make it even a little more solid. Click the pointer over a black pixel in the gradient and drag to create a flag at Pos=30 (see Figure 10.40).

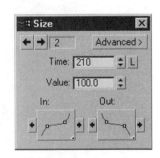

Figure 10.40
The finished Inferno effect.

Note

If the Inferno effect does not appear in the Glow sample slot, turn the check box for the Glow sample slot off and then back on to update it.

The flare is perfect now. Save it so you can use it over the second shot in the animation as well.

5. In the Lens Effects Flare dialog, click the Save button. In the Save Filter Settings dialog, choose a folder to save the flare to (**\3ds4-ma\project3**), enter the filename **flare01.lzf**, and click OK to save the flare effect.

6. Click OK to exit the Lens Effects Flare dialog, save your work as **10TV07.max**, and close the Video Post dialog.

Exercise 10.9   Animating the Flare and Rendering the Queue

To add even more movement to the scene, you will animate the flare to increase in size right before the Venetian blinds transition occurs. The blinds will animate in at around the start of the third measure of music, roughly frame 130. So you will precede that by starting growth of the flare at frame 120.

1. Make sure **10TV07.max** is open and open the Track View. Expand the Video Post > Lens Effects Flare tracks and click Zoom Horizontal Extents. Activate the Add Keys tool, and in the Size track, click to create a key at frame 120 (as shown in Figure 10.41).

   Now add another key at frame 210 and change its value to 100.

2. With the Add Keys tool still active, click at frame 210 to create another key in the Size track. Right-click to open the key's Size dialog and change the Value to **100** (see Figure 10.42). Close the Size dialog. The two keys in the

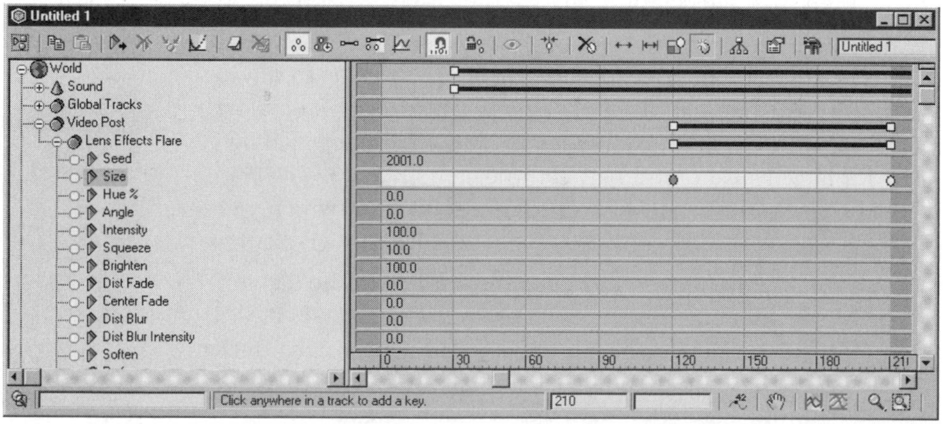

Figure 10.41

The Track View with a key at frame 120 in the Size track.

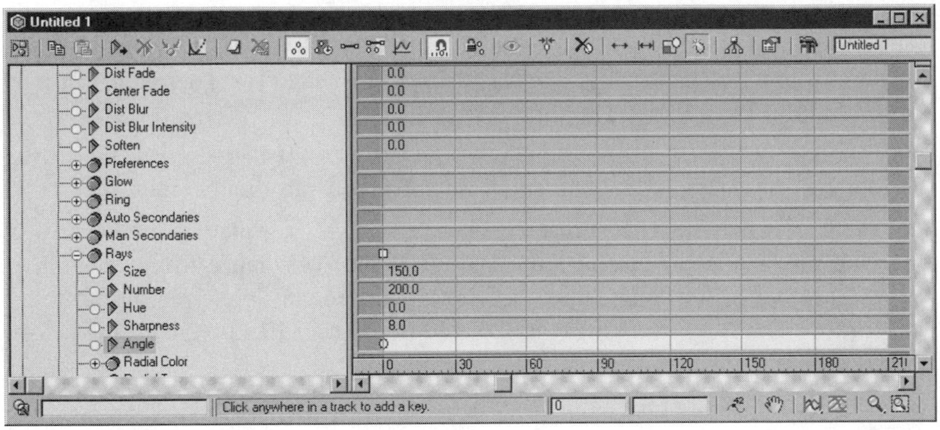

Figure 10.42

The Size dialog shows a Value of 100 at frame 210.

Size track will animate the overall size of the flare from 45 (the default value) to 100 between frames 120 and 210 (see Figure 10.43).

While you are in the Track View and editing the Lens Effects Flare settings, go ahead and add a little rotation to the rays of the flare.

3. Expand the Rays track of the Lens Effects Flare in the Track View. Activate the Add Keys tool—if it's not already active—and click on the Angle track at frame 0 to create a key (see Figure 10.44).

You can add a key to frame 210 and change its value to add rotation to the rays.

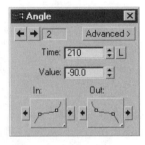

Figure 10.43

In the Track View, you see the Size track's keys at frames 120 and 210.

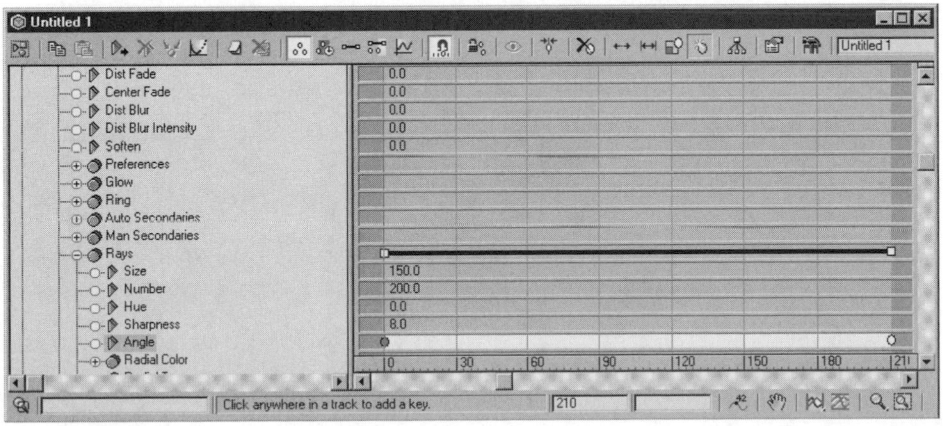

Figure 10.44

Create a key at frame 0 in the Angle track.

4. Create a second key at frame 210 on the Angle track and right-click it to open its Angle dialog. Change the Value to **–90** (as shown in Figure 10.45), and then close the dialog. The Angle track is finished (see Figure 10.46). Close the Track View.

The Rays will now slowly rotate counterclockwise 90 degrees over the course of the animation. The first scene is finished. You can finally render it.

5. Save your work as **10TV08.max,** open the Video Post dialog, and click the Execute Sequence button. In the Execute Video Post dialog, leave Range 0 To 210 active, and in the Output Size group, choose your preferred output resolution. The suggested setting is 320×240 (see Figure 10.47). Click Render to render the queue.

The queue will render frames 0 to 210.

Figure 10.45
The Angle dialog shows a Value of –90 at frame 210.

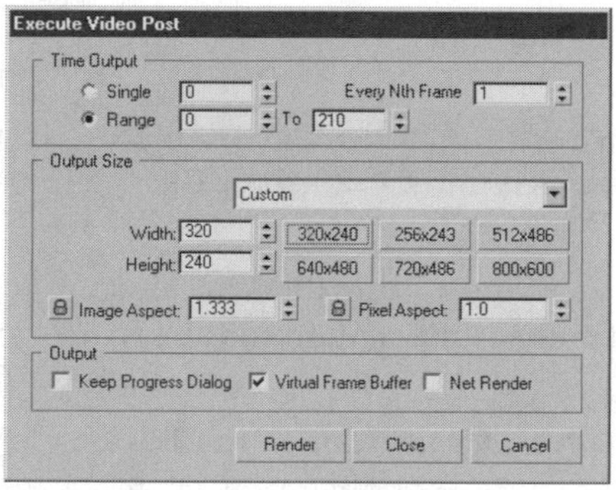

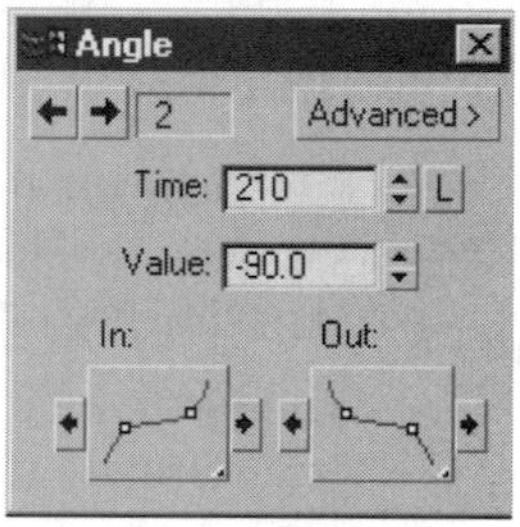

Figure 10.46
The Angle track has keys at frames 0 and 210.

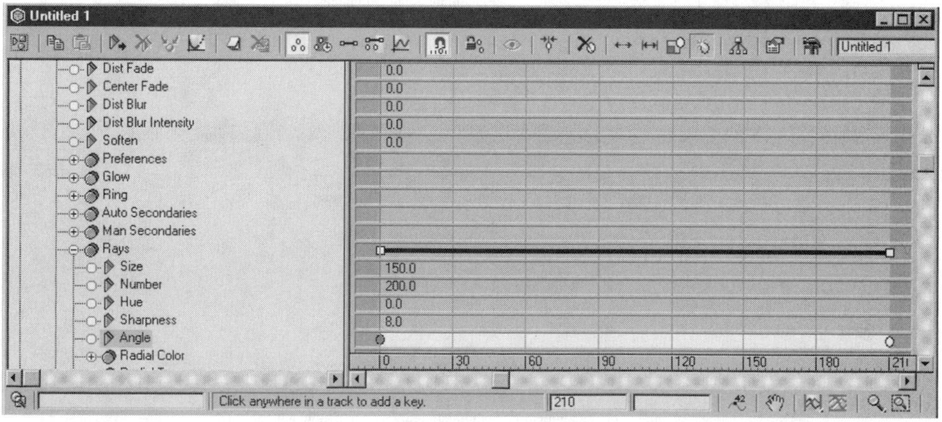

Figure 10.47
The Execute Video Post dialog with the suggested settings.

In Conclusion

The animation looks great. You have successfully finished the first half of the animation and are rendering it. I bet you can't wait to start the next section so you can complete the entire animation. Well, you'll need to wait a little while as the animation renders. Besides, it's good to get up, relax your eyes, and stretch a little. And while you're up and about, you can stop by Mr. Boss's office and brag about how well the animation is turning out!

Chapter 11

Finishing the TV 3 News Open Project

You now have the first half of the animation "in the bag," so to speak. The globe scene is rendered and looks great. To finish the TV 3 news opening, you need to create the second half of the animation: the TV 3 logo and the Venetian blinds. Looking at John's storyboard (shown in Figure 11.1), you think re-creating the animation will be fairly simple.

Figure 11.1
John's storyboard for the TV 3 news opening.

In this chapter, you gain experience in the following areas:

- Using the Refine tool to adjust long and narrow shapes for beveling
- Using the Place Highlight tool to accurately position lights
- Using an XForm modifier to perform sub-object animations
- Using multiple mapping coordinates in one material
- Creating complex animated gradient maps
- Using Color Map to adjust an image's output
- Creating a key using the Motion panel
- Tracing the logo with a flare using Path Constraints

Creating the TV 3 Logo Scene

Basically, you need to create the TV 3 logo, the Venetian blinds, a bar of text, and a lens flare. The camera motion is going to be a very linear dolly backward, revealing the objects as it passes by them. The finish line is in sight; keep up the stride.

Exercise 11.1   Adding the Sound and Background to a Scene

You will be choreographing the animation to Gordon's music in this scene, so you need to load the audio and offset it 30 frames. You will adjust your scene length to 390 frames (13 seconds) so you can hear the entire cut of audio.

1. Choose File > Reset 3dsS max. Open the Track View, select and right-click the Sound track, and choose Properties to open the Sound Options dialog. Click the Choose Sound button, choose **\3ds4-ma\project3\sounds\ GlobalNews3D.wav**, and click OK twice to load the audio into the

Track View. Use the Zoom tool until the time is shown in 10 frame intervals.
Drag the Sound track to move its start to frame 30 (see Figure 11.2). Close
the Track View.

The animation's length is currently 100 frames; you need to change it to 390
frames to match the length of the audio.

2. Click the Time Configuration button to open the Time Configuration dialog.
   Change the End Time to **390** (as shown in Figure 11.3) and click OK to close
   the dialog.

   If you were to play the animation, you would hear the music play in its
   entirety. The audio is correctly placed in the scene, and the scene is the right
   length. Now load the first half of the animation as the environment background image.

3. Choose Rendering > Environment to open the Environment dialog. Click
   the Environment Map button to open the Material/Map Browser, choose
   Bitmap, and click OK to open the Select Bitmap Image File for Import dialog.
   Locate the file you rendered in the last chapter and open it into the
   Environment dialog; in this case, the file is **\3ds4-ma\project3\images\
   shota.avi** (see Figure 11.4).

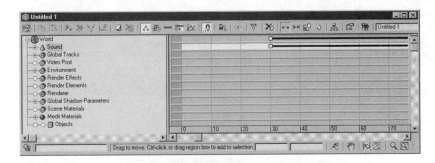

Figure 11.2
The sound track is
loaded and offset to
start at frame 30.

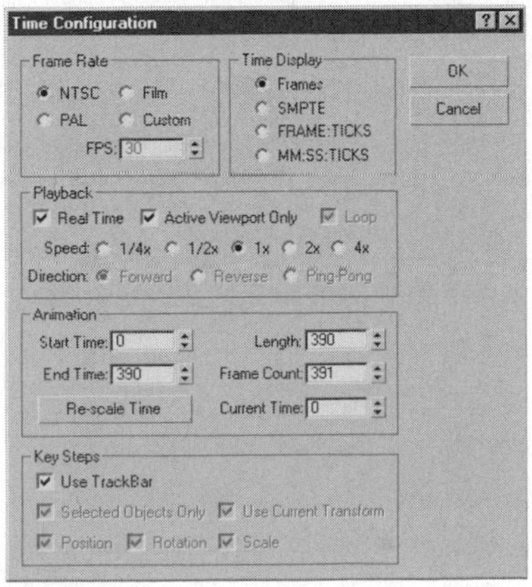

Figure 11.3
The Time
Configuration dialog
with an End Time of
390.

You will instance the environment map into the Material Editor, where you will animate it later.

4. Open the Material Editor. Drag the Environment Map button to the first material preview slot of the first row. In the Instance (Copy) Map dialog, choose Instance and click OK to create the instance. Name the map **Env** (as shown in Figure 11.5). Close the Environment dialog and the Material Editor.

The scene is ready; now you can do your magic.

5. Save your work as **11TV01.max**.

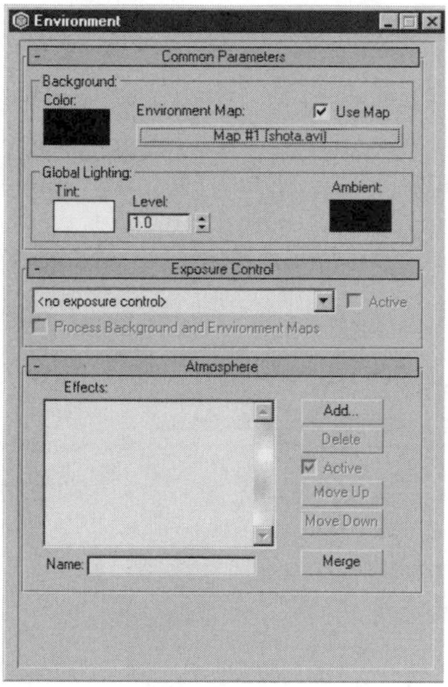

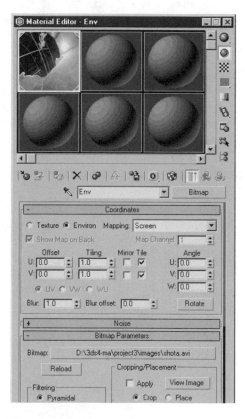

Figure 11.4
The Environment dialog with the rendered animation from the previous chapter loaded.

Figure 11.5
The Environment Map is instanced into the Material Editor.

Building the TV 3 Logo

John was nice enough to provide you with an Adobe Illustrator file of the TV 3 logo. As you learned working on Victor's 2002 Vote project, having an Illustrator file is often not as wonderful as it seems. Imported Illustrator files often need to be cleaned up. But having something that needs work is usually better than having to start from scratch.

Exercise 11.2   Importing and Editing the Logo Shape

You will import John's TV 3 logo file and copy it so you can use it as a template.

1. With **11TV01.max** open, choose File > Import to open the Select File to Import dialog. Change Files of Type to Adobe Illustrator (*.AI), choose **\3ds4-ma\project3\ai\tv3_logo.ai**, and click Open to open the AI Import dialog. Leave Merge Objects with Current Scene active, and click OK to open the Shape Import dialog. Choose Single Object and click OK to import the shape. Maximize the Top view and turn off the view's grid (see Figure 11.6).

   The TV 3 logo has been imported successfully. Examining the curve on the left side of the logo, you can plainly see that there are not enough steps to create a smooth curve. Add more steps now.

2. With the imported shape selected, open the Modify Panel and expand the Interpolation rollout. Change the Steps value to **20** and rename the shape **TV3** (see Figure 11.7).

   Create a copy of the TV 3 logo so you can use it as a template when you are editing the imported shape.

Figure 11.6
The TV 3 logo is imported from an Adobe Illustrator file.

Figure 11.7
The TV 3 logo has
enough steps to
smoothly curve.

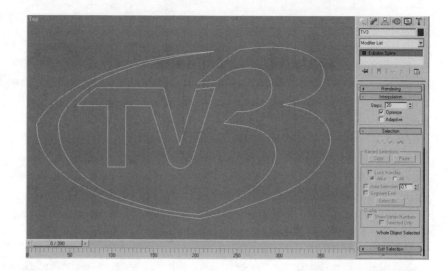

3. With TV3 selected, choose Edit > Clone to open the Clone Options dialog. In the Object group, leave Copy selected, change the name to **TV3-template** (see Figure 11.8), and click OK to create the clone. Use the Select Objects dialog to re-select the TV3 shape.

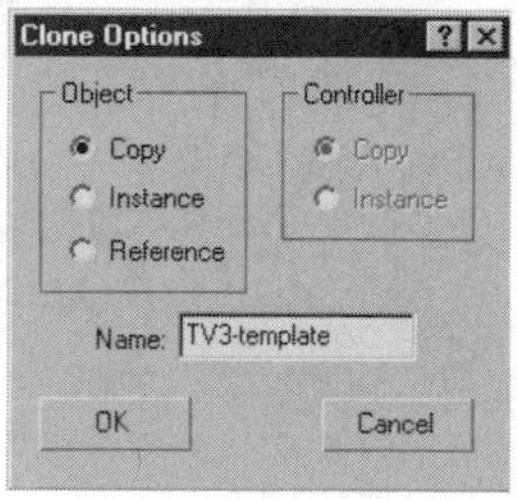

4. Work on the outline of the TV 3 logo using Figure 11.9 as a guide. (It shows the preferred layout for vertices and the adjustments of their tangent handles.)

Figure 11.8
The Clone Options dialog
with the correct settings.

If you completed the billboard in the first project and the vote machine in the second project, cleaning up an outline is old hat. If not, you'll want to use these tips:

- Beware of two or more vertices occupying the same space. To determine how many vertices are in a specific area, drag a rectangular selection around the area in question and check the Modify panel for the vertex count.

- If you need to change the vertex type, right-click the vertex and choose a different type from the quad menu.

- Use Shift+drag when you want to adjust one Bézier handle separately from its partner.

- Be sure to change the vertex back to Bézier type in order to ensure a smooth uniform texture when you bevel the shape.

5. When you are happy with the TV 3 logo shape, exit sub-object mode, delete the TV3-template object, and save your work as **11TV02.max**.

Figure 11.9
The correct configuration of vertices to optimally create the TV 3 logo.

Exercise 11.3   Beveling a Shape

You now have a clean logo shape to work with. But before you bevel it, you should apply an XForm modifier to the shape and increase the scale to better accommodate the bevel. After the shape is scaled correctly, you will collapse it back to an editable shape.

 1. With **11TV02.max** open, minimize the Top view. Add an XForm modifier to the TV3 shape. Using the Select and Uniform Scale tool, scale the XForm gizmo 3000 percent. Click Zoom Extents All Selected (see Figure 11.10).

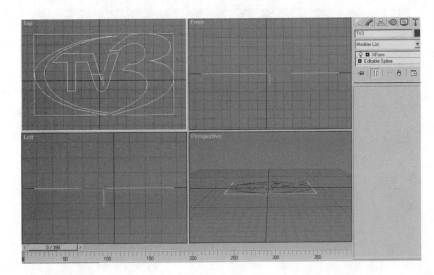 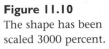

Figure 11.10
The shape has been scaled 3000 percent.

Even though the shape looks the same, you know that a bevel will more easily be applied to this larger shape (you learned *that* while working on the vote machine). Collapse the stack.

2. With the TV3 shape selected, right-click the TV3 shape and choose Convert To > Convert to Editable Spline.

Now you can apply the bevel to the shape.

3. In the Modify stack, apply a Bevel modifier to the TV3 shape and enter these settings:

Start Outline: **0**

Level 1: Height: **1** Outline: **1**

Level 2: Height: **8** Outline: **0**

Level 3: Height: **1** Outline: **–1**

As you can see in Figure 11.11, the TV 3 logo is now beveled.

The bevel looks good on the logo, but one thing distresses you. The top point of the left crescent is pointing through the number 3 now. Since the point of the shape is so long and narrow, the bevel needs to be extended into the number 3 in order for the bevel's outline to remain uniform. You can use the Refine tool to add more vertices to the point to smooth it out, rounding the point.

4. Maximize the Top view and return to the Editable Spline in the Modify stack. Zoom into the point of the left crescent and activate Vertex sub-object mode (see Figure 11.12). In the Geometry rollout, activate the Refine button and click on the point to create two new vertices (see Figure 11.13).

Figure 11.11
The correct bevel on the TV 3 logo.

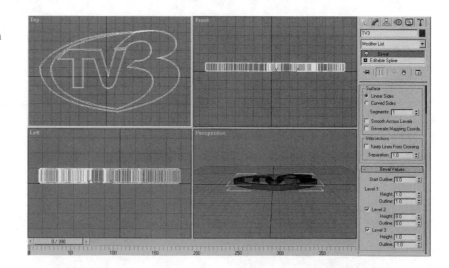

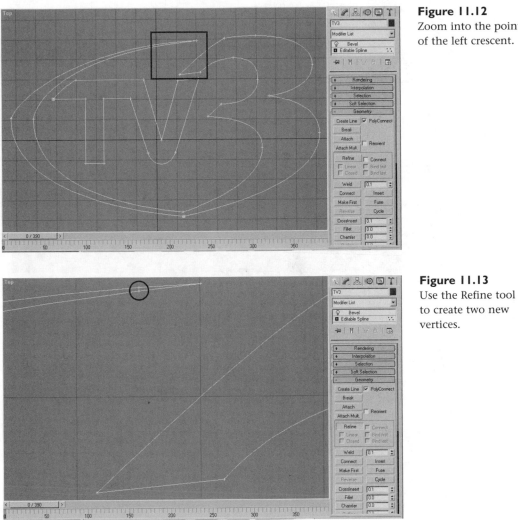

Figure 11.12
Zoom into the point
of the left crescent.

Figure 11.13
Use the Refine tool
to create two new
vertices.

5. Deactivate the Refine tool, select the vertex at the very point of the crescent, and delete it (see Figure 11.14).

   That should fix the problem you were having with the bevel. Take a look and see.

6. Minimize the Top view and click Zoom Extents All. Return to the root of the TV3 shape and activate the Bevel modifier in the stack.

   Ahh, much better (see Figure 11.15).

   Once the TV 3 logo is built, you can move it into its correct orientation.

Figure 11.14
The point vertex is
deleted.

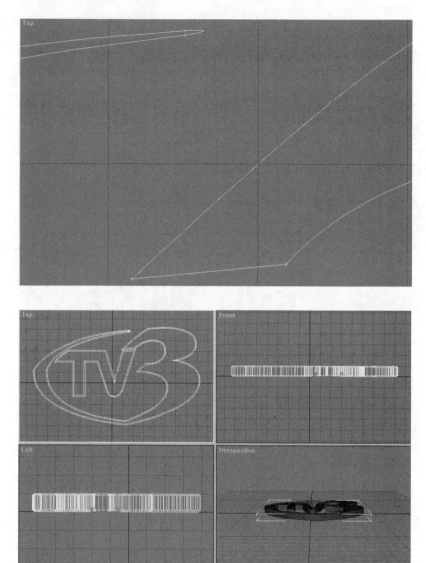

Figure 11.15
The bevel of the TV 3
logo is complete.

7. Open the Hierarchy panel and activate the Affect Pivot Only button. Click
   the Center to Object button and deactivate the Affect Pivot Only button.

   The TV 3 logo's pivot is centered to the object.

8. Activate the Select and Move tool and move the TV3 object to XYZ: **0, 0, 0**.
   Activate the Select and Rotate tool (Local X-axis) and rotate the TV3 object
   X: **90** degrees (as shown in Figure 11.16).

   The TV 3 logo is ready for its material.

9. Save your work as **11TV03.max**.

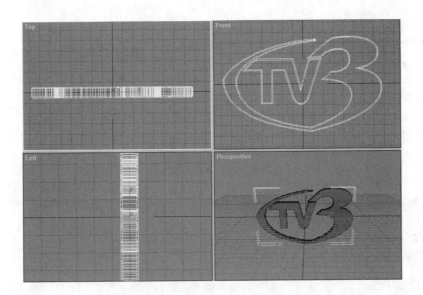

Figure 11.16
The TV3 object is oriented correctly in the scene.

Exercise 11.4 Adding a Camera and a Light

Before you create the gold material for the TV 3 logo, you need to add a camera and a light to the scene. For this scene, you will use only one light, which will illuminate the face of the TV 3 logo and will create a very dramatic effect as the logo turns into position during the animation.

1. Make sure **11TV03.max** is open and open the Create > Cameras panel. Click the Free button and create a camera with a 35mm lens in the Front view. Move the camera to XYZ: **0, –210, –3**. Change the Perspective view to the Camera01 view and click Zoom Extents All. Turn off the grid in the Camera01 view and activate Show Safe Frames (Figure 11.17).

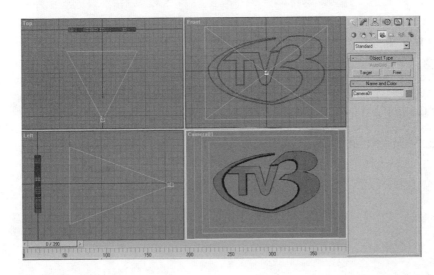

Figure 11.17
Camera01 is in the correct location in the scene.

This is where the logo will reside at the end of the animation. Now add an Omni light to the scene to illuminate the TV 3 logo.

2. Open the Create > Lights panel, click the Omni button, and create an Omni light in the Top view with a color of RGB: **180, 180, 180** (see Figure 11.18). Position the light as closely as possible to the position in Figure 11.18.

In the following step, you will use the Place Highlight tool that will position the highlight on the surface but keep the light the same distance from the surface. If the light is positioned closer or further than the light in Figure 11.18, the rest of the objects in the scene might be lit undesirably.

Figure 11.18

The Omni01 light is created in the Top view with a color of RGB: 180, 180, 180.

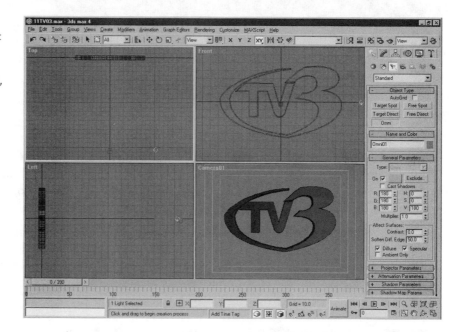

Now position the light to create a highlight where the letter "T" meets the letter "V".

3. Activate the Place Highlight tool (on the toolbar from the Align flyout). In the Camera01 view, drag the mouse in the area where the T meets the V so that the light will move, and then create a highlight in that precise area. Release the mouse button when the highlight is where the two letters join. Click Zoom Extents All (see Figure 11.19).

The light and the camera are in place for the scene.

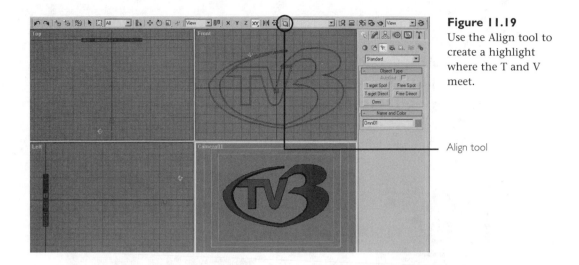

Figure 11.19
Use the Align tool to create a highlight where the T and V meet.

Align tool

Exercise 11.5   Adding the Gold Material to the TV3 Object

Now that the TV3 object is correctly lit, you can create and apply the gold material.

1. Select the TV 3 logo and open the Material Editor. Select the second preview slot of the first row. Name the material **Gold** and assign it to the TV3 object.

   In the Shader Basic Parameters rollout, change the shader from Blinn to Metal. In the Metal Basic Parameters rollout, click the Ambient swatch and change the color to RGB: **137, 71, 0**. To create a polished metal highlight, change the Specular Level to **200** and the Glossiness to **70** (as shown in Figure 11.20).

   The gold material looks great, but what is a polished metal material without a reflection map? Just add one now.

2. Expand the Maps rollout and click the Reflection button to open the Material/Map Browser. In the Material/Map Browser, choose Bitmap and click OK to open the Select Bitmap Image File dialog. Choose **\3ds4-ma\ project3\maps\ gold-ref.jpg** (a gold version of the reflection map we used on the vote machine) and click Open to load the image. Name the map **Gold-rfl** and in the Coordinates rollout, change the Blur offset to **.01** to soften the image (see Figure 11.21).

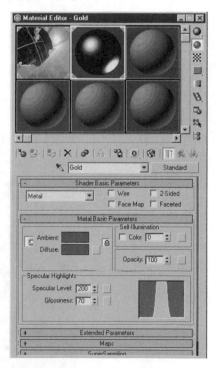

Figure 11.20
The Gold material with the correct settings so far.

The reflection is a little too intense; decrease its amount slightly.

3. Click Go to Parent to return to the root of the Gold material. In the Maps rollout, change the Reflection Amount to **60** (as shown in Figure 11.22).

The Gold material is finished.

4. Render the Camera01 view to see the gold material on the TV3 object (see Figure 11.23).

The TV 3 logo looks great. It's a keeper.

5. Save your work as **11TV04.max** and close the Material Editor.

Figure 11.21
The finished reflection map for the gold material.

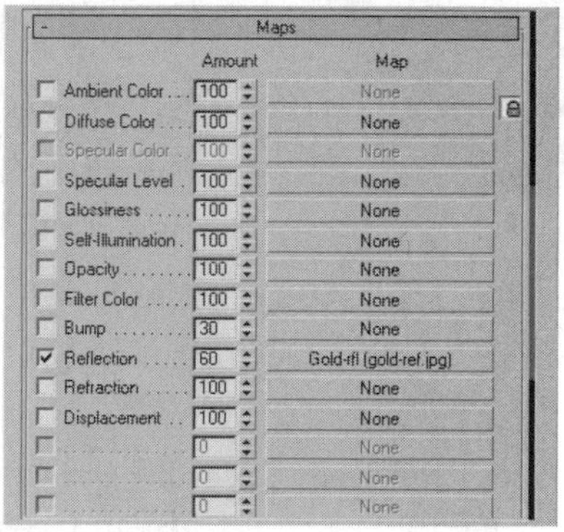

Figure 11.22
The Reflection amount is lowered to 60 to create a less-intense reflection.

Figure 11.23
The rendered TV 3 logo with the new Gold material.

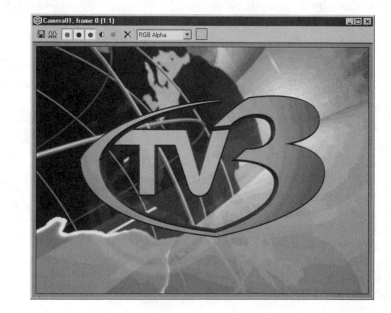

Creating Animatable Venetian Blinds

Now you need to create a set of animatable Venetian blinds. Each blind will be a plane, or a two-polygon rectangle. If you were to create multiple-plane objects and use them as your blinds, each one would carry its own keys for animation. However, you might prefer to come up with a solution that allows for only one set of keys to operate all the blinds uniformly.

The solution you arrived at was to use a vertex level XForm modifier on the lower two vertices of each blind. This way, all the blinds will be contained in one object and controlled by one XForm modifier, acting on selected vertices.

The blind material you will be creating will utilize the mapping coordinates on the individual blind objects and will also utilize screen mapping. You will add a linear gradient to the length of the blinds to give them dimension and separation from each other. Mapped in the color channels of the linear gradient, you will place screen mapped radial gradients to achieve the blue oval pattern on the storyboard.

Exercise 11.6   Using One XForm Modifier to Control Several Vertices

First, you'll build the blinds and apply their material.

1. With **11TV04.max** open, open the Create > Geometry panel and click the Plane button. Maximize the Front view and create a plane with a Length of **10** and a Width of **1000**. Change the Length Segs and Width Segs to **1**. Check Generate Mapping Coords so you can use the mapping coordinates when applying the blind texture to the object. Move the plane object to XYZ: **0, 150, 200** and name the plane object **Blind01**. Click Zoom Extents All (see Figure 11.24).

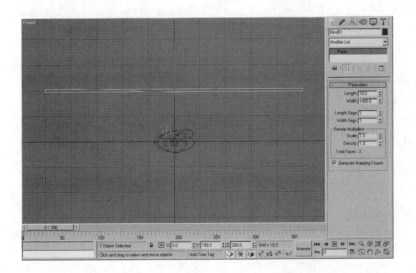

Figure 11.24
The Blind01 object in the correct location in the Front view.

You will copy the Blind01 object to create the remaining blinds. However, before you do that, collapse it into an Editable Poly and select the two bottom vertices.

2. Right-click the Blind01 object and choose Convert To > Convert to Editable Poly. Activate Vertex sub-object mode and drag a rectangular selection around the bottom two vertices to select them (as shown in Figure 11.25).

Figure 11.25

The two bottom vertices of the Blind01 object are selected.

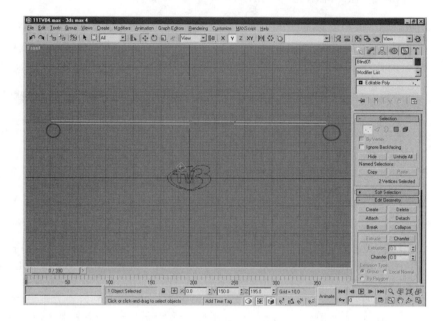

Now when you create copies of the Blind01 object, all of them will have the bottom two vertices selected in sub-object mode.

3. Deactivate Vertex sub-object mode and activate the 3D Snap toggle. Activate the Select and Move tool (View XY-axis), and then Shift+drag the Blind01 object down one grid line and release the mouse. In the Clone Options dialog, leave Copy selected and change the Number of copies to **40**. Click OK to create the copies and turn off the grid in the Front view (as shown in Figure 11.26). Deactivate the 3D Snap toggle.

You now have 41 individual blind objects that you can combine into one.

4. Select Blind01 and in the Edit Geometry rollout of the Modify panel, click the Attach List button. In the Attach List dialog, select Blind02 through Blind41 (see Figure 11.27). Click Attach to attach the 40 blind objects to the original.

Figure 11.26
Create 40 copies of the Blind01 object in the Front view.

There are now 41 "blind" objects attached together into one object. Because you selected the bottom two vertices of the first blind object before you copied it, the two bottom vertices of all the blind objects are selected.

5. Enter Vertex sub-object mode.

It appears that only the two very bottom vertices are selected and no others. Rest assured, all the bottom vertices are selected; the Selection rollout informs upi that 82 vertices are selected (see Figure 11.28).

You will now apply an XForm modifier to the selected vertices. Then, by animating the XForm gizmo, you will be able to animate the blinds uniformly with only one animation track.

6. With Vertex sub-object still active, apply an XForm modifier. Minimize the Front view and click Zoom Extents All. With the XForm gizmo still active, activate the Select and Move tool and move the gizmo to XYZ: **0, 140, 5** (as shown in Figure 11.29).

You now have the blinds all ready to animate.

7. Advance to frame 390 and activate the Animate button. Using the Select and Move tool, move the XForm gizmo to XYZ: **0, 140, –5** (as shown in Figure 11.30). Deactivate the Animate button and return to the top level of the XForm modifier.

Figure 11.27
The Attach List dialog with the 40 copied Blind objects selected.

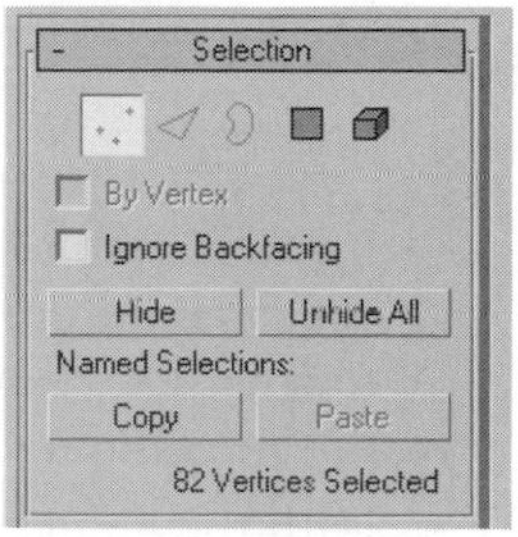

Figure 11.28
It appears that only the bottom two vertices are selected; however, the Selection rollout tells the truth.

Figure 11.29
By moving the XForm
gizmo, you can see
the individual blinds.

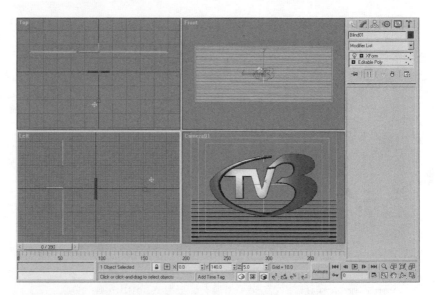

Figure 11.30
The blinds are in
their final, closed,
position.

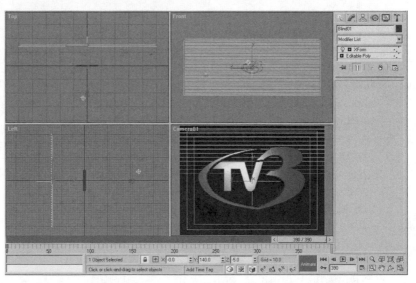

If you play the animation, you will see the blinds slowly close over the
course of the animation. Because you won't even see the blinds until
roughly 130, you should move the start key to frame 140 to get the most of
the animation.

8. With the Blind01 object selected, drag the key from frame 0 to frame 140 on
the track bar.

Right now the blinds are facing you straight on. John's storyboard shows the blinds at more of an angle to the camera. Make sure you orient the blinds correctly.

9. Activate the Select and Rotate tool (View Z-axis) and in the Top view, rotate the Blind01 object Z: **–30** degrees (as shown in Figure 11.31).

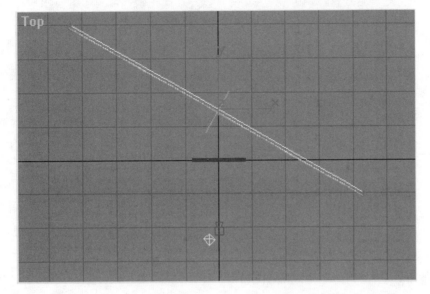

Figure 11.31
The Blind01 object is in its correct orientation.

The Blind01 object is animated and in the correct orientation. You'll need to save your work and then apply the material.

10. Save your work as **11TV05.max**.

Add the linear gradient to the blinds, and you will better understand what the material will do.

11. With **11TV05.max** open, advance to frame 320 and open the Material Editor. Select the third material preview slot in the first row, name the material **Blinds**, and assign the material to the Blind01 object. In the Blinn Basic Parameters rollout, change the Self-Illumination amount to **100**. Click the Diffuse map button to open the Material/Map Browser. Choose Gradient and click OK to load the gradient into the Diffuse map channel. Name the map **Blinds-dif** and render the Camera01 view (see Figure 11.32).

You can see how the linear gradient visually separates each individual blind from the next.

Figure 11.32
Camera01 rendered at
frame 320.

Animating the Environment Background

Before you add the screen mapped gradients to the blinds, animate the environment background image to fade to black so you can accurately view the blinds. Because the animation in the environment background ends by frame 210, you need to dissolve it out by then. To create the dissolve, you will use a Mix material and animate it to transition from the animation to black between frames 145 and 210.

Exercise 11.7   Creating a Dissolve

Here you'll set up the dissolve in the Env map so that the environment background fades to black.

1. In the Material Editor, select the Env map. Click the Bitmap button to open the Material/Map Browser. Choose Mix and click OK. In the Replace Map dialog, leave Keep Old Map As Sub-Map? selected and click OK. Drag the black color swatch from Color #1 to Color #2 and copy it (see Figure 11.33).

2. Advance to frame 210 and activate the Animate button. In the Material Editor, enter a Mix Amount of **100** and deactivate the Animate button.

    You've mixed from the animation to the black color. However, the animation occurs between frames 0 and 210, so you need to adjust it to animate between frames 145 and 210.

3. Right-click on the Mix Amount spinner edit box and select Show in Track View. In the MixAmount track, move the key from frame 0 to frame 145 (see Figure 11.34). Close the Track View.

The environment background is now correctly animated.

4. Save your work as **11VT06.max**.

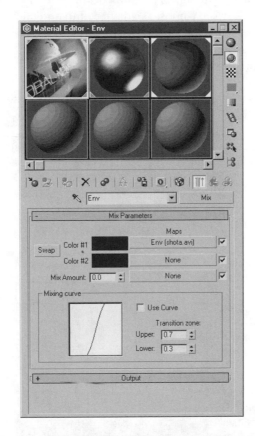

Figure 11.33
The Env map is in the Color #1 slot, and the black color is copied to Color #2.

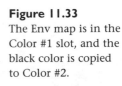

Figure 11.34
The Track View with the MixAmount keys in the correct locations.

Exercise 11.8   Adding the Radial Gradients to the Blind Material

You can now continue to create the blind's material. First, add the first screen mapped radial gradient.

1. With **11VT06.max** open, return to the Blinds-dif map in the Material Editor. In the Gradient Parameters rollout, click the Color #2 button to open the Material/Maps Browser. Choose Gradient Ramp and click OK to load the gradient ramp. In the Gradient Ramp Parameters rollout, change the Gradient Type to Radial and deactivate the Show End Result button (see Figure 11.35). Name this material **Blinds-blue**.

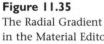

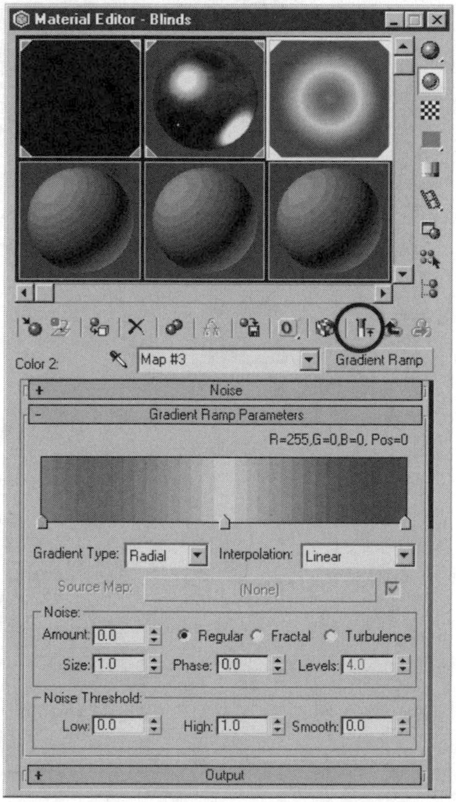

Figure 11.35
The Radial Gradient in the Material Editor with Show End Result deactivated.

Change the colors of the gradient to better reflect those on the storyboard.

2. Double-click the leftmost flag of the gradient (refer to Figure 11.35) and change its color to RGB: **50, 120, 255**. Click the middle flag and change its color to RGB: **30, 60, 190**. Finally, click the last flag and change its color to RGB: **0, 0, 0**.

The radial gradient better matches what John has illustrated on his storyboard. However, the gradient on the storyboard is brightest in the lower-left corner. Position the gradient into the correct spot.

3. In the Coordinates rollout, change the Mapping to Environ(ment) Mapping: Screen, locking the gradient to the screen so that no matter where the camera is, the gradient will always be the way it appears in the preview window. To prove the point, advance to frame 320 and render it through the Camera01 view

   It may be hard to see because the radial gradient is only the middle color of the linear gradient. But if you look hard enough, you can see the blue radial gradient in the center of the screen, mapped on the blinds.

   Okay, back to moving the gradient to match the storyboard.

4. In the Coordinates rollout, change the U Offset to **–.25** and V Offset to **–.35**. To make the gradient larger, change the U Tiling to **.4** and V Tiling to **.8** (as shown in Figure 11.36).

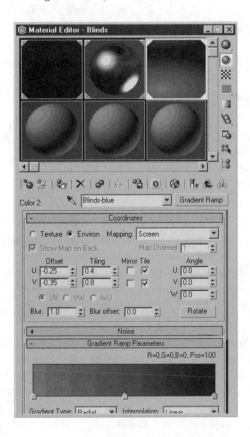

Figure 11.36
The gradient is now placed correctly.

The gradient is in the correct position. You should be able to see a little of the tiled gradient peaking in from the top. That's okay, it will add to the whole randomness of the material.

Speaking of randomness, add a little noise to the gradient.

5. In the Noise group of the Gradient Ramp Parameters rollout, change the Amount to **.5** and change the Size to **3.5** (see Figure 11.37).

The noise is a nice touch to the gradient; it provides a nice random feel. While you're at it, go ahead and animate it.

6. Advance to frame 390 and activate the Animate button. Change the Phase to **15** and deactivate the Animate button (see Figure 11.38). Click the Make Preview button and in the Create Material Preview dialog, click OK to create the preview. After the preview renders, it will play, showing the slow undulation of the noise.

The Blinds-blue map is finished. Copy it to the first color channel of the Blinds-dif map and change its parameters to make it darker.

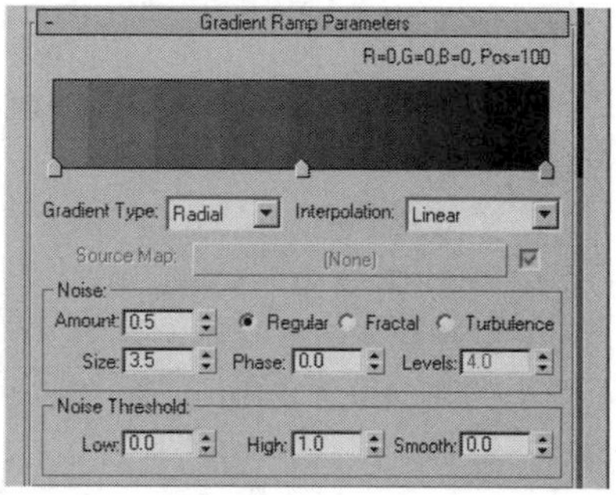

Figure 11.37
The gradient is more organic with noise applied.

Figure 11.38
The Blinds-blue map is now animated.

7. Click the Go to Parent button to return to the Blinds-dif map. In the Gradient Parameters rollout, copy the Blinds-blue map to the Color #1 button and open its parameters. Name the map **Blinds-purple**. In the Coordinates rollout, change the mapping to Environ Mapping: Screen (a pesky bug in the Material Editor doesn't copy the Mapping type). In the Gradient Ramp Parameters rollout, double-click the first flag and change its color to RGB: **120, 25, 190**. Click the second flag and change its color to RGB: **85, 15, 140.**

Because you copied this gradient, its animation copied as well. You don't want both gradients to have the same noise pattern. Therefore, to offset their patterns, you can simply change the Phase value. Currently the Phase of the Blinds-purple map animates from 0 to 15 between frames 0 and 390. If at frame 390 you changed the Phase value to 30 without activating the Animate button, the Phase value would animate from 15 to 30 between frames 0 and 390. Go ahead and do that.

8. Make sure you are still at frame 390, and in the Gradient Ramp Parameters rollout, change the Phase value to **30**.

   The Phase now animates from 15 to 30 between frames 0 and 390. Now instance the Blinds-purple map to the Color #3 slot of the Blinds-dif map.

9. Click Go to Parent to view the Blinds-dif map's parameters. In the Gradient Parameters rollout, drag the Blinds-purple map button over Color #3's map button and release the mouse. In the Copy (Instance) Map dialog, choose Instance and click OK.

   The Blinds-purple map is instanced into the Color #3 map. The Blinds material is finished. Render a frame and check it out.

10. Render frame 320 through the Camera01 view (as shown in Figure 11.39).

    The Blinds material looks fantastic.

11. Save your work as **11TV07.max** and close the Material Editor.

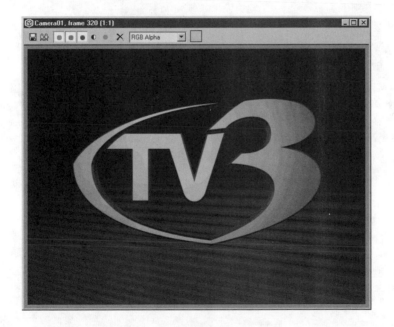

Figure 11.39
The finished Blinds material rendered through the Camera01 view at frame 320.

Adding a Strip of Text

You are now going to create the final object you need to complete this animation: a strip of type. John's storyboard shows one strip in the foreground and three in the background. In this animation, you will create only one behind the logo. If, after you add the first strip of text and animate it, you feel there should be more, you can add one or more on your own.

Exercise 11.9   Mapping Text on a Plane Object

To create the strip of text, you will opacity map the text on a plane object.

1. With **11TV07.max** open, open the Create > Geometry panel and click the Plane button. In the Front view, create a plane object with a Length of **30** and a Width of **1000**. Name the object **StripText** (as shown in Figure 11.40).

   Now move the object into the correct orientation.

2. Move the StripText object to XYZ: **320, –95, –41**. Using the Select and Rotate tool (View Z-axis) in the Top view, rotate the StripText object Z: **–30** (see Figure 11.41).

Figure 11.40
The StripText object was created in the Front view.

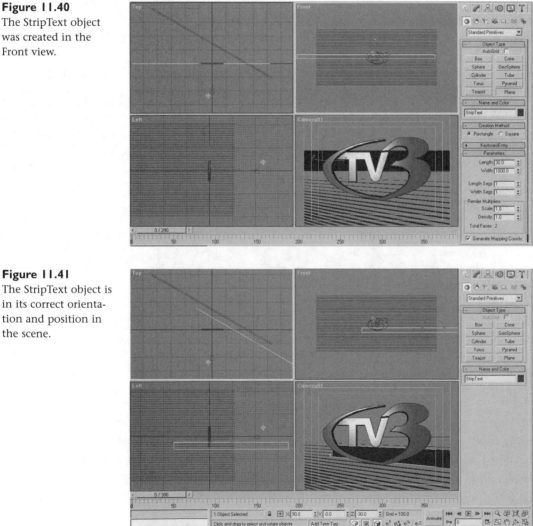

Figure 11.41
The StripText object is in its correct orientation and position in the scene.

Now you can apply the material to the StripText object.

3. Open the Material Editor and select the first preview slot of the second row. Name this material **StripText** and apply the material to the StripText object. In the Blinn Basic Parameters rollout, change the Self-Illumination value to **100**. Click the Diffuse color swatch and change its color to RGB: **255, 255, 255.**

Now you can add the opacity map to the material to cut out the type.

4. Click the Opacity map button to open the Material/Map Browser. Choose Bitmap and click OK to open the Select Bitmap Image File dialog. Choose **\3ds4-ma\project3\maps\GlobalNewsBlur.jpg** and click Open to open the image. Rename the map **StripText-opc** and click Show Map in Viewport. Render frame 320 through the Camera01 view (see Figure 11.42).

The type on the StripText object is a little too bright. You can adjust the output level of the GlobalNewsBlur.jpg image in the material to make the type more transparent.

5. In the Material Editor, expand the Output rollout. Check Enable Color Map, and the graph becomes active. Select the right graph point and move it to 1.0/.5 (as shown in Figure 11.43). Then close the Material Editor.

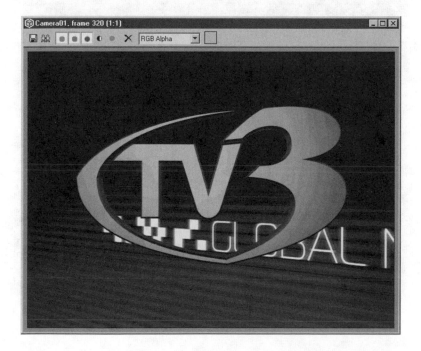

Figure 11.42
Frame 320 rendered through the Camera01 view.

By lowering the point from 1 to .5, you reduce the output of the map by half.

6. Render frame 320 again (see Figure 11.44).

The type looks like it belongs there now. You are finished creating all the objects and adding their materials. Cool!

7. Save your work as **11TV08.max**.

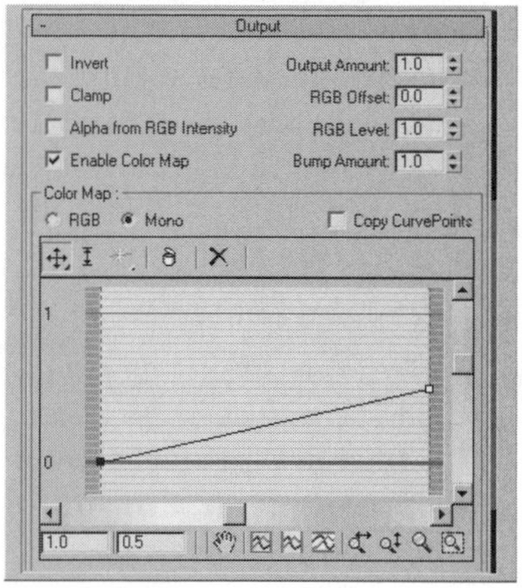

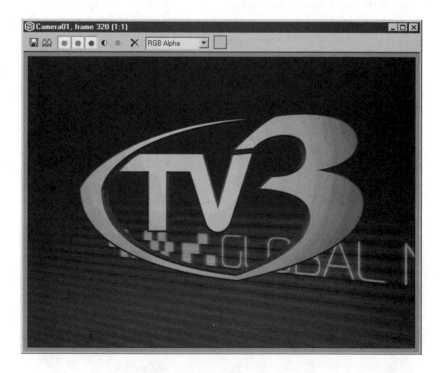

Figure 11.43
The Color Map's output is reduced by half.

Figure 11.44
Frame 320 rendered through the Camera01 view.

Animating the TV 3 Logo

Looking at John's storyboard, you can see that the TV 3 logo matches the perspective of the blinds when you first see it, and as the animation reaches its end, the TV 3 logo turns to face forward. Because the camera will be dollying backward through the scene, you will see the blinds first and then the TV 3 logo.

Exercise 11.10   Setting Up the Rotation of an Object

Earlier, when you analyzed the music, you decided you would see the logo at approximately frame 180 during the beginning of the fourth measure of music. Because you want the viewer to see the TV 3 logo in the canted perspective before it starts to turn, you will start its rotation at frame 200 and end it in its forward orientation at frame 300 as the music hits its final crescendo.

1. With **11TV08.max** open, select the TV3 object. Advance to frame 200 and activate the Animate button. Use the Select and Rotate tool (Local Y-axis) to rotate the TV3 object Y: **–30** degrees (as shown in Figure 11.45).

   You just created a key at frame 200, but 3ds max also created a key at frame 0 that you do not need. You can delete it.

2. On the track bar, right-click the key at frame 0 and choose Delete Key > TV3: Rotation.

   Now you're ready to animate the TV3 object into its end orientation.

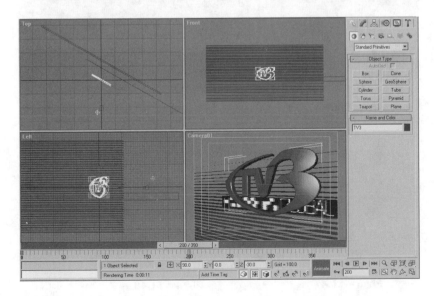

Figure 11.45
The TV3 object now matches the same cant as the blinds.

3. Advance to frame 300 and, using the Select and Rotate tool (Local Y-axis), rotate the TV3 object Y: **30** degrees to face forward again (as shown in Figure 11.46). Deactivate the Animate button.

The animation for the TV3 object is complete. Now pull out all the stops and ease the rotation in and out.

4. On the track bar, right-click the key at frame 200 and choose TV3: Rotation to open its dialog. Change the Ease From: value to **25** (as shown in Figure 11.47) and click the arrow pointing to the right to move to the next key. Change the Ease To: value of key 2 to **25** (as shown in Figure 11.48). Close the dialog.

The TV3 object's rotation now starts and ends smoothly. Nice touch!

Figure 11.46
The TV3 object faces the camera at frame 300.

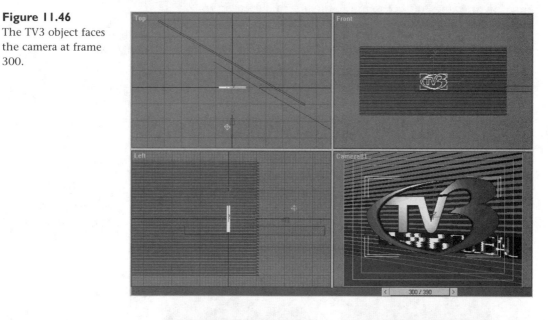

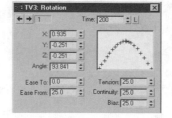

Figure 11.47
The Ease From value for key 1 is 25.

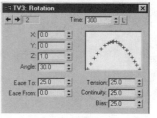

Figure 11.48
The Ease To value for key 2 is 25.

Exercise 11.11   Animating the StripText Object

Animating the StripText object is going to be simple. All you need to do is key the object's motion from right to left. Because the StripText object is layered closely to the blinds, you will see it much sooner than you do the TV 3 logo. You will need to start its motion at frame 150, and it will continue to the end of the animation at frame 390. Animate it now.

1. Select the StripText object and activate the Select and Move tool (Local X-axis). Advance to frame 390 and activate the Animate button. Move the StripText object roughly X: **–1000** units and deactivate the Animate button (see Figure 11.49).

The motion of the Strip text object is correct. However, it animates between frames 0 and 390. You need to move the key at frame 0 to frame 150.

2. In the track bar, move the key from frame 0 to frame 150.

The animation for the Strip Text object is complete.

3. Save your work as **11TV09.max**.

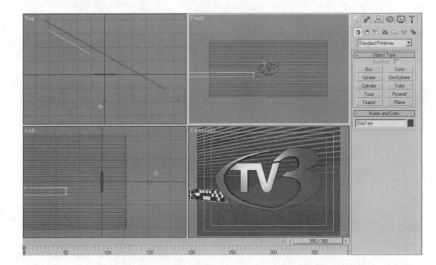

Figure 11.49
The StripText object's position at frame 390.

Exercise 11.12   Animating the Camera

Life couldn't be simpler; all you have left to do is create linear camera motion between frames 130 and 230. You will be dollying backward through the blinds and through the TV 3 logo, and then the camera will stop in its ending location. Go on and get started.

1. With **11TV09.max** open, select Camera01 and advance to frame 230. Because the camera is located where you want it to end, you need to create a key for it at frame 230. Open the Motion panel and in the PRS Parameters rollout, click Position in the Create Key group. The button becomes ghosted, indicating a key has been created (see Figure 11.50).

Now you need to create a start key for the camera.

2. Advance to frame 130 and activate the Animate button. Move the camera to XYZ: **33, 150, 0** (shown in Figure 11.51). Scrub through the animation to make sure the camera doesn't accidentally intersect with any objects. If it does, readjust the start position until it doesn't. Deactivate the Animate button.

When the camera path is correct, add an ease to the position key at frame 230 so the camera will slowly come to a halt.

Figure 11.50
The Position button becomes ghosted after you click it.

Figure 11.51
The camera is in its starting position.

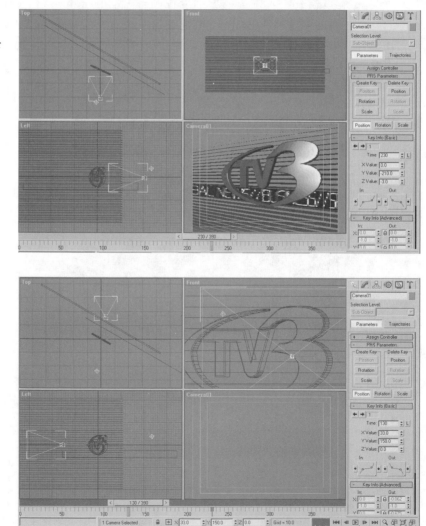

3. On the track bar, right-click the key at frame 230 and choose Camera01: Position to open its dialog. Change the In tangent to Slow (as shown in Figure 11.52) and close the dialog. Check the animation again for any accidental camera collisions and fix them if necessary.

4. Save your work as **11TV10.max**.

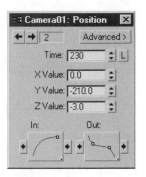

Figure 11.52
The Camera01: Position dialog with a Slow In tangent.

Setting Up the Lens Flare

The animation of the objects in the scene is complete. Now you will add one final touch: a lens flare. Instead of placing the flare high and to the left of the logo, as indicated on the storyboard, you will "trace" the upper half of the crescent shape on the logo.

Exercise 11.13   Creating a Segment of a Shape

Before you create the lens flare, you need to determine how you are going to animate the flare's trajectory around the perimeter of the crescent shape. To animate the flare's trajectory, you will animate the flare's source along a path. To create the path, you will copy the TV 3 logo object, delete the Bevel modifier, and delete most of the shape except for the area you want to trace with the flare.

1. With **11TV10.max** open, select the TV3 object. Choose Edit > Clone and create a copy of the object with the name **TV3-trace**. Advance to frame 330 and click Zoom Extents All Selected. Open the Modify panel and delete the Bevel modifier. Activate Segment sub-object level and select the upper-left crescent segment (see Figure 11.53).

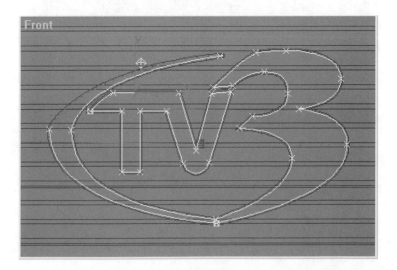

Figure 11.53
The upper-left crescent segment is selected.

2. Choose Edit > Select Invert to invert the selection (see Figure 11.54).

3. Press the Delete key to delete the selected segments, leaving only the upper-left crescent shape (as shown in Figure 11.55). Return to the Top-Level of the TV3-trace shape.

   If you look in the Top view at the selected TV3-trace shape, you can see that it's behind the logo. You need to move it in front of the logo.

4. Activate the Select and Move tool (View Y-axis) and in the Top view, move the TV3-trace shape in front of the TV3 object (see Figure 11.56).

   The TV3-trace shape is no longer obscured by the logo object. You can now add the Point helper that will act as the source of the flare to the scene.

Figure 11.54
The unneeded segments are selected now.

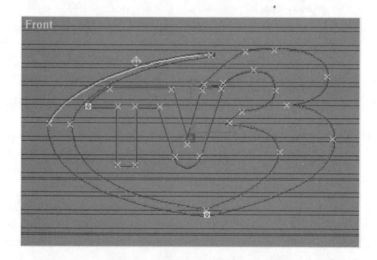

Figure 11.55
The upper-left segment will act as the path for the flare.

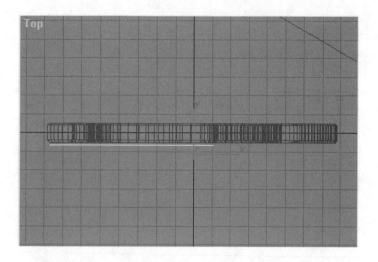

Figure 11.56
The TV3-trace shape is in front of the TV3 object.

Exercise 11.14   Adding an Animated Point Helper

In the first scene, you created a Point helper to act as the source for the flare. You need to create another Point helper in this scene for the same purpose. After you add the Point helper to the scene, you will animate it on a path constraint to the TV3-trace shape.

1. Open the Create > Helpers panel and click the Point button. Click to create a Point helper anywhere in the Top view and leave the name **Point01**.

   Now you will animate the Point helper along the TV3-trace shape.

2. With the Point01 helper selected, open the Motion panel. Expand the Assign Controller rollout, select the Position track, and click the Assign Controller button (see Figure 11.57). In the Assign Position Controller dialog, choose Path Constraint (see Figure 11.58) and click OK to add the constraint.

3. In the Path Parameters rollout, click the Add Path button and click the TV3-trace shape. Its name then appears in the Target column (as shown in Figure 11.59). Deactivate the Add Path button.

   The Point01 helper now animates along the path from frame 0 to 390. Feel free to play the animation and examine the motion. You will see the flare only between frames 220 and 330, so adjust the Point01 helper's keys accordingly.

Figure 11.57
Select the Position track and click the Assign Controller button.

4. With the Point01 object selected, drag the key on the track bar at frame 0 to frame 220. Drag the key on the track bar at frame 390 to frame 330 (see Figure 11.60).

If you play the animation again, you will see the Point01 helper tracing the edge of the upper-left crescent between frames 220 and 330. You are now ready to add the lens flare to scene.

Figure 11.58
Path Constraint is selected in the Assign Position Controller dialog.

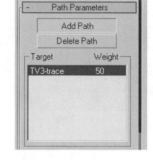

Figure 11.59
The TV3-trace shape has been added to the Target column.

Figure 11.60
The Point01 helper's keys are now in the correct locations.

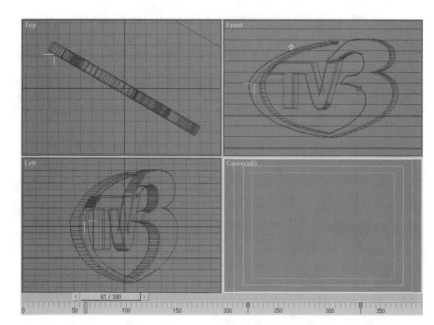

Exercise 11.15   Creating the Video Post Queue

You need to create a Video Post queue for this scene in order to add the lens flare. Because you've created one already (for the first scene), this should be a cinch.

1. Open the Video Post dialog. Click the Add Scene Event button and click OK to accept its default settings. Click the Add Image Filter Event button, choose Lens Effects Flare, and click OK to add it to the queue. Click the Add Image Output Event button and choose an output path and file name (I used \3ds4-ma\project3\images\TV-Done.mov). Then click OK to add it to the queue (see Figure 11.61).

2. Save your work as **11TV11.max**.

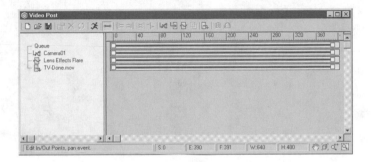

Figure 11.61
The complete Video Post queue.

Exercise 11.16   Loading and Adjusting the Lens Flare

You can now load the flare you created for the first scene and see how it looks with your logo.

1. With **11TV10.max** open, advance to frame 280. In the Video Post queue, double-click the Lens Effects Flare event to open the Edit Filter Event dialog. Click the Setup button to open the Lens Effects Flare dialog. Click the Load button and load the flare you created in the first scene (\3ds4-ma\project3\flare01.lzf). Activate the VP Queue and Preview buttons to render a test frame (see Figure 11.62).

Figure 11.62
The Lens Flare preview.

The logo looks like it's on fire—not a good thing. You'd better can the Inferno effect.

2. Click the Prefs tab and deselect Inferno in the Glow column.

That looks better, but the glow is far too large. Make it smaller.

3. Click the Glow tab and change the Size to **50**. Deselect Hide Behind Geometry so that the flare plays in front of the logo (see Figure 11.63).

The glow looks much better. However, it's a little too bright. To fix that, adjust the Radial Transparency.

4. Right-click the middle flag of the Radial Transparency gradient and click Delete to delete the flag. Double-click the left flag of the Radial Transparency gradient and change the color to RGB: **150, 150, 150** (see Figure 11.64).

The flare looks fantastic now. You're ready to animate it.

5. Click OK to close the Lens Effects Flare dialog.

Figure 11.63
The glow becomes smaller and appears in front of the logo object.

Figure 11.64
The finished flare.

Exercise 11.17   Animating the Lens Flare

Now that the flare is perfect, you can animate a few of its parameters to add a little spice to the effect. You will start by animating the intensity of the flare so it will appear at frame 220 and disappear at frame 330.

1. Open the Track View and expand the Video Post > Lens Effects Flare track. Activate the Add Keys tool and click in the Intensity track to create keys at frames 220, 245, and 330 (as shown in Figure 11.65).

Figure 11.65
In the Intensity track, create keys at frames 220, 245, and 330.

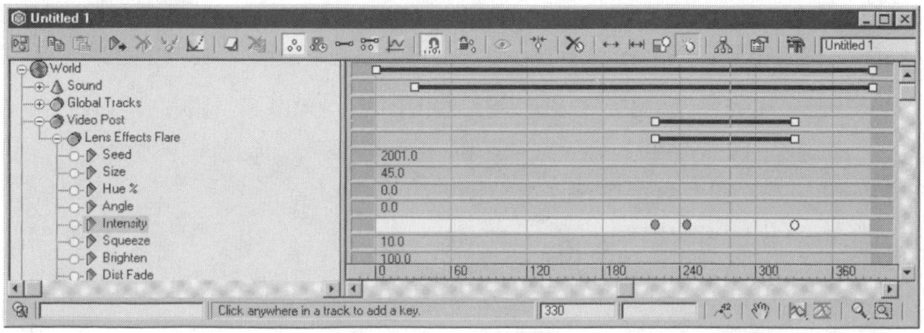

The Intensity should be 0 at frames 220 and 330.

2. Right-click the key at frame 220 to open the Intensity dialog. Change the Value to **0** and click the arrow pointing to the right twice to access key 3's parameters. Change its value to **0** (as shown in Figure 11.66). Close the dialog.

Figure 11.66
The intensity at frame 330 is 0.

The intensity is animated to be 0 at frame 220, 100 at frame 245, and 0 at frame 330. This will cause the flare to dissolve on and off between frames 220 and 330.

You will now make the flare's manual secondaries "burst" by animating their Plane Scale values. The plane is the line on which the secondaries are created. A plane value of 0 will put the secondaries at the source of the flare; a larger plane value will move the secondaries further from the source. When you animate the Plane Scale values, the secondaries travel from the source of the flare outward.

3. Expand the Man Secondaries track in the Track View. With the Add Keys tool active, add keys to the Plane Scale track at frames 220 and 330 (see Figure 11.67).

4. Right-click the key at frame 220 to open the Plane Scale dialog and change its Value to **0**. Click the arrow pointing to the right to advance to the second key at frame 330 and change its Value to **2**. Close the dialog.

The manual secondaries will now burst from the flare as it dissolves at frame 220 and will continue to grow until the flare disappears.

You need to animate one last parameter before you can stick a fork in this animation. You need to animate the Rays angle, just like you did in the first scene.

5. Expand the Rays track in the Track View and click to create keys at frames 220 and 330 in the Angle track (see Figure 11.68).

Now animate a slow counterclockwise rotation.

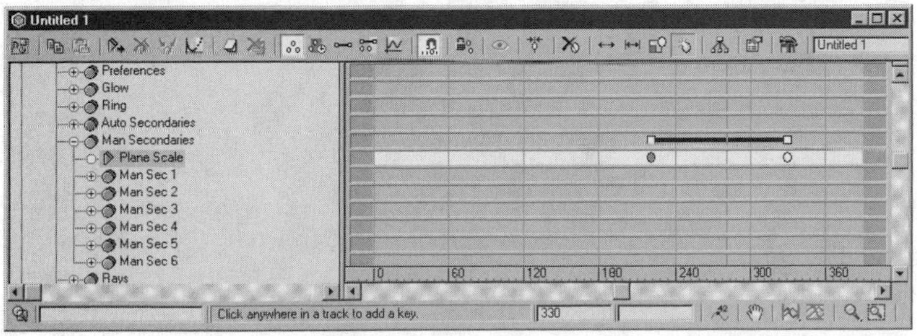

Figure 11.67
On the Plane Scale track, create keys at frames 220 and 330.

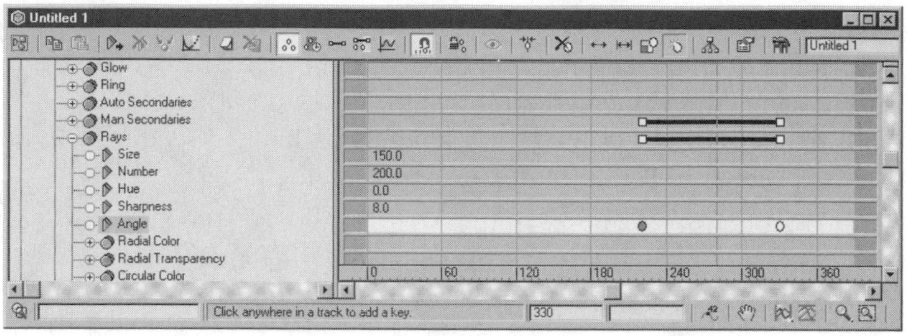

Figure 11.68

The Angle track has keys at frames 220 and 330.

6. Right-click the key at frame 330 to open the Angle dialog. Change the Value to **–90** and close the dialog and the Track View.

   That's it—the animation is finished!

7. Save your work as **11TV12.max**.

8. When you are ready to render your animation, click the Execute Sequence button in the Video Post dialog. In the Execute Video Post dialog, choose your preferred output size (320×240 is suggested) and click Render. Figure 11.69 shows the final result.

   When the animation finishes rendering, you call Mr. Boss and John over to see the result of all your hard work. They are thrilled with it. Feeling good about yourself, you lean back in your chair and allow yourself to be hypnotized by the looping animation. You certainly deserve a good trance after all the hard work you've put in.

Figure 11.69

The final render.

In Conclusion

It has been my pleasure to share in your journey through the exciting world of media animation. I hope you enjoyed the projects Vince, Victor, John, Gordon, and myself put together for this release. More important, I hope you've learned valuable information to help you perform and excel in your job as an animator. It has been wonderful sharing my time with you. Thank you for your continued support.

Part 4

Real World Case Studies

Over and over, I'm asked, "How'd you do it? How'd you create this or that animation to introduce an MSNBC segment?" Well, this part of the book walks you through the process used to come up with three real world animations for MSNBC—The Millennium, Decision 2000, and Newsfront (which has not yet aired).

In the pages that follow, you'll see the collaborative effort that went into creating each animation—from concept through rendering. Rather than step you through each phase, the chapters provide an overview of the entire process. My goal in sharing this information is to give you an understanding of the "big picture" of media animation, how it all fits together to produce projects that WOW your audience and please your client or boss.

Real World Case Study 1: The Millennium

We can all fondly look back to 1999 and
remember the excitement surrounding the
"historical" moment when the clock
struck twelve midnight, bringing us into

the year 2000. The months leading into the millennium left most people in the world questioning their computers' Y2K compliance. If that wasn't enough, the media heightened our awareness of terrorist plots and national safety and reminded us how much our lives depend on computers.

Although some people simply shrugged off the warnings and continued as normal, others took them seriously and stocked up on bottled water, flashlights, batteries, and franks 'n' beans. I am sure we can all remember exactly what went through our minds during those times. I will always remember exactly where I was during the days leading into the new century—staring at a computer screen wondering how I was going to get all my work finished.

The dawn of the new millennium didn't bring most of the world much of anything; however, it did provide me with some absolutely beautiful O.T. checks.

Ready, Set, Go!

In my opinion, there are two types of news: *expected* news and *unexpected* news. As you probably already figured out, *expected* news is an event like a football game. Unexpected news, on the other hand, is what the news industry thrives on. When something incredible catches the world off guard, they report it and rake in the ratings.

The millennium was a little bit of both though, because the unexpected eerily loomed over Y2K's head. We saw it coming; we all knew it was on December 31, 1999. You would think we would start making the graphics months in advance. Yeah, you would think that, wouldn't you?

The reality of life, work, and the world, however, held much more in store for me. Yes, anyone could see that the big day was getting closer and closer, but there was plenty of other work I needed to finish before I could start creating the graphics for the project. By the time I finished all my work and was ready to start the graphics for the millennium, I had three weeks until the big day.

Right around the time I was getting geared up to create the Millennium animation for MSNBC, NBC News was finishing up their title animation. I needed to see what they had produced before I could start creating the animation for MSNBC, because the two had to appear to be part of the same package.

The Creative Director, Sam Mandragona; the Assistant Creative Director, Joe Dettmore; and I examined what the graphics department for NBC News (New York) had cooked up for their look (see Figure RW1.1). We needed to incorporate into our animation the logo design that had been created at NBC News.

After looking at the logo, Joe, Sam, and I brainstormed ideas for the animation. What we came up with was, in a nutshell, clocks and globes.

I created more than thirty animations of the earth spinning, illustrating the individual time zones. Each time zone was highlighted with texture maps and volumetric beams. These took a great deal of organization, attention to detail, and time. When I finished the time zone animations, I moved on to creating the open.

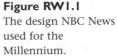

Figure RW1.1
The design NBC News used for the Millennium.

Creating the Animation

When it finally came time to concentrate on creating the title animation for MSNBC millennium coverage, I had about a week and a half to complete it. While I was generating visual ideas and blocking out basic objects, Joe Dettmore was in Sound Design with Gordon Miller, creating the score for the animation.

Joe had the very basic principals of the animation in his head. He wanted clocks, globes, and a strong NBC identity. The animation was designed to have particles expanding outwardly, like the universe, during the beginning of the animation. When the animation was complete, the particles would be brought together to form the "Millennium" type, bringing the whole concept together as well.

Joe and I decided that the animation should be broken up into four sections. Those four sections are described below. You can view realwld1\millennium.avi to see the completed animation.

Shot 1: The Clocks

The establishing shot of the animation contains three different colored clocks with rapidly changing faces (see Figure RW1.2). The purpose of this shot is to engage the viewers by introducing them to the time and space theme, which will play throughout the animation. This section concludes with a veil of particles.

Figure RW1.2
A frame of the clocks from the final animation.

This shot was the simplest shot for me, personally, to complete. Although it appears first, it was the third shot (of the four) that I completed for this animation. Joe completed most of the pre-production. Anna Kostyrko, a staff designer, captured the clock face images into the Quantel Paintbox Express (a proprietary video image processing tool). Joe loaded the still clock face images from the Paintbox into the Quantel Hal Express (a proprietary video compositing tool), color corrected them, and assembled the images into an animated sequence.

Joe then manipulated the resulting clock face animation to create three separate clock face animations: one red, one blue, and one gold. These animations were recorded to my DDR (Digital Disk Recorder) and were imported onto my hard drive as individual Targa files.

Once the three colored clock face images sequences were on my hard drive, I began to build some test scenes to illustrate some of the different ways the rendered output could appear. The first sample I created, realwld1\jclck01.avi (see Figure RW1.3), has all three clocks self-intersecting, which created a thick, layered and almost chaotic appearance.

The second sample, realwld1\jclck02.avi (shown in Figure RW1.4) shows the three clocks layered and parallel to each other. When they were fully rendered, I called Sam and Joe to examine these thumbnails and offer their creative criticism. We agreed that the first one was a little too confusing for an establishing shot, so we decided we should use something closer to the second one.

Figure RW1.3
The first test I created for the first shot, jclck01.avi.

Figure RW1.4
The second clock test I created, jclck02.avi.

Someone offered up the suggestion to put glass over the clock faces to give them more punch. The glass over the clock faces would not only create extra highlights and dimension, but also refract the clock faces beneath them, adding more depth.

In the next few sections, I quickly step you through how the clocks were created. To fully understand the process, you will want to load **realwld1\scenes\clock01.max** from the accompanying CD (see Figure RW1.5). Four objects are visible in the scene: the circular framework of the clock (Clock-In01 and Clock-Out01), the glass lens (Clock-Glass01), and the billboard for the clock face images (Clock-Map01).

You will notice four objects in the scene: a square, two tube primitives, and a squashed hemisphere. We will concentrate our attention on how to create the clock face map and the refractive clock lens. To do so, we will examine each object individually.

Figure RW1.5
Clock01.max.

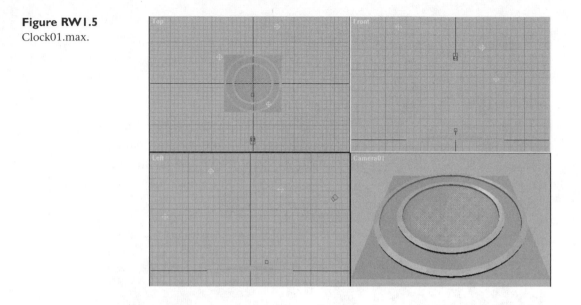

The Clock-Map01 Object

This object is the billboard in which the clock face texture map was applied. For this example, I substituted the clock face map with a checkerboard texture (see Figures RW1.6 and RW1.7).

Figure RW1.6
The Clock-Map01 object in all four views.

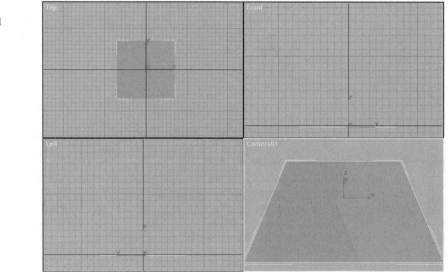

Figure RW1.7
The Clock-Map01
object rendered.

If you examine the Clock01.max file, you will notice that the Clock-Map01 object is simply a square shape with a Mesh Select and UVW Map modifier applied. How, then, does this rectangle render as a circle? The answer to this question is easily discovered in the Material Editor (see Figure RW1.8).

The Clock-Map01 object's material has a Gradient Ramp map in its Opacity slot. The Gradient Type is set to Radial, which creates the circular gradient that is visible in the material preview slot. Because of this radial gradient, the square Clock-Map01 object renders as a soft circle.

The Clock-Glass01 Object

This object, as you recall, is the clear glass lens that rests over the clock face. Its primary purpose in the scene is to catch highlights and refract the objects below it (see Figures RW1.9 and RW1.10).

The Clock-Glass01 object is a Sphere primitive with a Hemisphere setting of .5. The Hemisphere setting chopped the sphere precisely in half, and an XForm modifier was applied and scaled to flatten it.

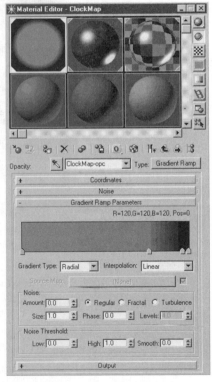

Figure RW1.8
The Material Editor displaying
Clock-Map01's opacity map.

Figure RW1.9
The Clock-Glass01 object resting above the Clock-Map01 object.

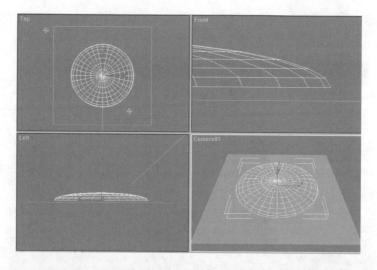

Figure RW1.10
The rendered scene with both the Clock-Glass01 and the Clock-Map01 object.

A Raytrace Refraction map was applied to the Clock-Glass01 object in the Material Editor. To create a more dramatic refraction, I also increased the Index of Refraction amount to 1.7 in the Extended Parameters rollout of the material.

The Clock-In01 object was intended to appear as though it were supporting the Clock-Glass01 object (see Figure RW1.11). This makes the clock seem to be a more solid and realistic fixture. In Figure RW1.12, you can see two of these clocks overlapping one another and how the lower clock is refracted in the higher clock. In Clock01.max, both clocks are included in the file; however, you need to unhide the second one.

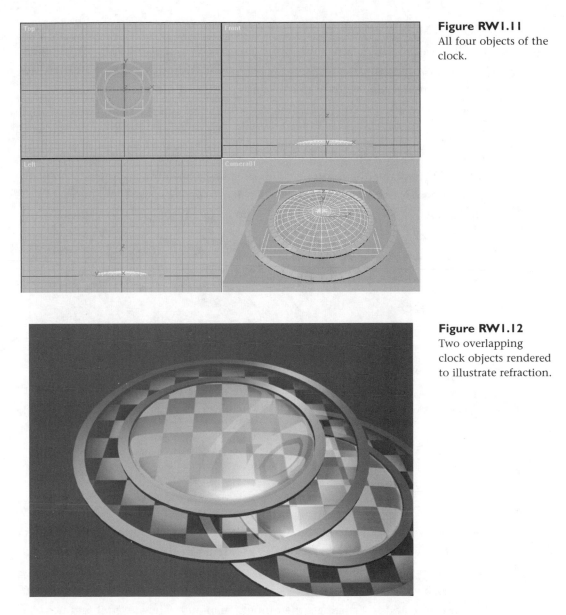

Figure RW1.11
All four objects of the clock.

Figure RW1.12
Two overlapping clock objects rendered to illustrate refraction.

These clocks perfectly demonstrate how a little ingenuity can build a simple scene with dramatic results. As mentioned above, the clock scene was the easiest of the scenes I created. Even though it was easy to complete, however, the actual rendered look is sophisticated. This animation (Shot 1) was created, rendered, and approved with no re-renders, all in one day.

Shot 2: The NBC Peacock

The shot of the NBC peacock inside the globe (shown in Figure RW1.13) is probably my favorite of the four shots in the animation. Although it wasn't the first section I created, it was the one that ultimately excited me about working on this project. This shot was actually the first shot completed and approved. It set the pace for the rest of the scenes.

Joe and I started by discussing ideas for new things we could do with the NBC peacock. During our discussion, I remembered that I had always wanted to build on the volumetric peacock I had created for CNBC's *Upfront Tonight*. I told Joe that I had an idea, and I asked him to give me a few hours to put something together.

Figure RW1.13
A frame from the NBC peacock scene of the Millennium animation.

I wanted to make smoke rings that traveled along the length of the volumetric beams of the peacock as they swept into position. The file realwld1\peakbeam.avi (shown in Figure RW1.14) shows my first complete test rendering of the volumetric peacock with smoke rings. When it finished rendering, I called Sam and Joe in to take a look at it so I could get their input. Thankfully, they loved it as much as I did. So I went to work creating the completed shot.

First, I created the volumetric light beams that would ultimately become the feathers of the NBC peacock. To make the colorful streaks of light in each beam, I applied a Gradient Ramp map in each light's Projector slot. You will examine that process shortly, when you look at how the smoke beams were created.

My first test of the
volumetric light
peacock.

When the light beams were created in position and a test had been rendered, I made
each light a child to its own personal Dummy helper. The rotation of the Dummy
helper is what causes the beams to sweep through the scene. When I was happy with
the way the scene was animated, I created clone of all the spotlights to use as the
smoke ring emitters.

In the next few sections, I quickly step you through how the smoke rings were
created. To fully understand the process, you will want to load **realwld1\scenes\
beam01.max** from the included CD (Figure RW1.15). The contents of the scene are
simply a target spot light and a target camera.

Volumetric lights are commonly used in 3D animations because of their simplicity.
Used correctly, volume lights add subtle accents that heighten the overall aesthetics
of an image. However, in some cases, a bold, bright volume light adds the brazen
punch the animation needs.

The controls 3ds max provides make it easy to create animated volume lights. Going
into this animation, I decided to build on a simple technique that was already in my
arsenal: animating the length (attenuation) of a volume light. The principle behind
this effect is to animate the Far Attenuation of the light, making the beam of light
appear to grow.

The Cross-Section

Load **realwld1\scenes\beam01.max** from the included CD (see Figure RW1.15).
The contents of the scene are simply a target spotlight and a target camera.

The first step in creating the smoke ring effect was to animate the Attenuation of
the light. As I mentioned previously, animating the Far Attenuation of the spotlight

Figure RW1.15
beam01.max.

animates the length of the beam (or where the beam ends). To make the light appear to be blowing smoke rings, the Near Attenuation of the light must also be animated in sync with the Far Attenuation. This will create a thin cross-section of light emanating from the light. If you were to select the Spot01 object in the Beam01.max scene and play the animation, you would notice that the Near Attenuation and Far Attenuation are slightly apart but move together (see Figures RW1.16 and RW1.17).

This animated cross-section creates the motion of the smoke ring the volume light will create.

Figure RW1.16
At frame 15, the Near Attenuation and Far Attenuation are near the source of light.

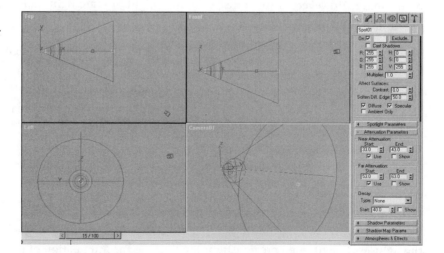

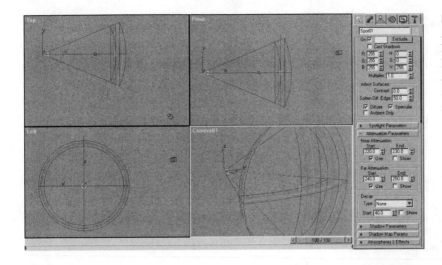

Figure RW1.17
At frame 100, the Near Attenuation and Far Attenuation are animated further away from the light source.

The Ring of Light

This effect is intended to look like a smoke ring, except it uses light instead of smoke. To that end, a special map had to be created in the Material Editor and used as the light's Projector Map (see Figure RW1.18).

The Projector map is simply a Gradient Ramp procedural map. Its type is set to Radial, and the start and end colors are set to black. Also, a touch of Noise is added to the gradient to add a more organic look. This Gradient Ramp is projected through the beam of light. The color black will not emit any light. Therefore, only the green circle will appear in the rendering when Volume Fog is activated on the light (see Figures RW1.19 and RW1.20).

To add a little more punch to the effect, I animated the phase of the Noise on the Radial Gradient Ramp. This created an undulating smoke/light effect that's visible in the rendered animation, beam01.avi. When applied to the growing beams of light that formed the peacock, this added the necessary punch to make the effect new and fresh.

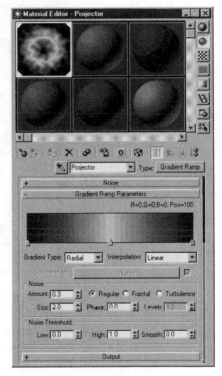

Figure RW1.18
The Material Editor with the spotlight's Projector Map active.

Figure RW1.19
The scene at frame 76.

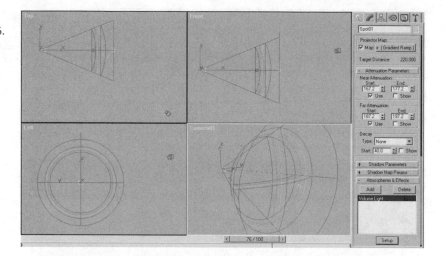

Figure RW1.20
The rendered smoke ring effect.

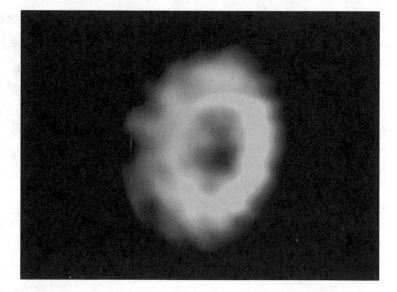

The Peacock Feathers

I created the six feathers of the NBC peacock with twelve volume lights. Six of the volume lights grew from the center and created the solid beams; the other six were the "smoke ring" volume lights you just learned about. I framed this volumetric peacock with a rounded framework of the peacock (see Figure RW1.21).

The peacock was placed inside a model of the earth's continents. The camera was animated to orbit from right to left through the inside of the globe (see Figure RW1.22).

Figure RW1.21
A frame from the final animation from the right side of the image clearly shows the rounded framework of the peacock.

Figure RW1.22
The four views of the rendered frame shown in Figure RW1.20.

One final volume light was placed in the rear of the scene to backlight the peacock as the shot reaches the end. This volume light helps transition this shot to the next shot, which shows the exterior of the globe with the clocks surrounding it.

The Peacock Particle Effect

As the peacock resolves, particles emit from the framework of the peacock. A Particle Array with a copy of the peacock shape as the Object-Based Emitter created this effect. Since the Particle Array cannot use shapes as an Object-Based Emitter, I simply applied a Mesh Select Modifier to the shape, which turns the shape into a mesh. If you load realwld01/scenes/peakpart.max, you will see the elements used for the particle effects from the original scene (shown in Figure RW1.23).

You will also notice a Motor Space Warp in the very center of the peacock. This Space Warp spins the particles around the peacock shortly after they are emitted (see Figure RW1.24). Otherwise, the particles would travel in a straight line and would lack dramatic impact.

Figure RW1.23
Frame 90 from peakpart.max.

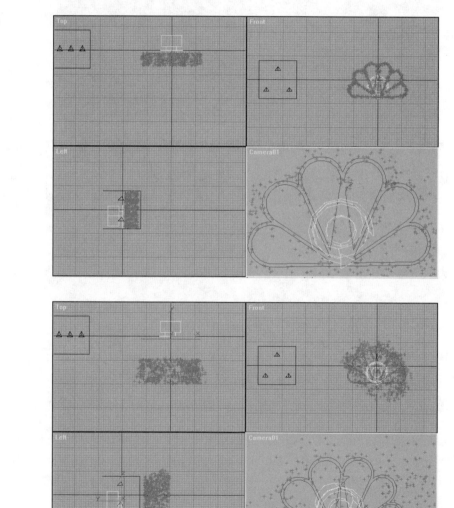

Figure RW1.24
Frame 117 from peakpart.max.

This completes the process for creating the second shot. The only other thing I should mention is that the stars in the background were added by using a bitmap of stars on a spherical environment background.

Shot 3: The Globe and the Clock

The third shot in this animation marks the first time you see the globe exterior and the clock apparatus surrounding it (see Figure RW1.25). A great deal of time was put into designing and creating the finished clock object. Figures RW1.26 through RW1.28 illustrate the evolution of the clock design throughout the creative process.

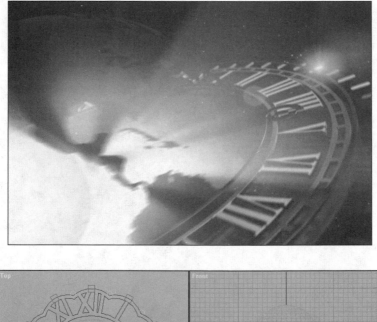

Figure RW1.25
An image from Shot 3 of the final animation.

Figure RW1.26
One of the very first basic designs for a clock created for the Millennium project. Notice how this clock makes the earth (sphere) to be more of a toy than the real earth.

Figure RW1.27
A more refined and polished version of the clock. However, it was not used because it was too visually complicated.

Figure RW1.28
The clock used in the final animation.

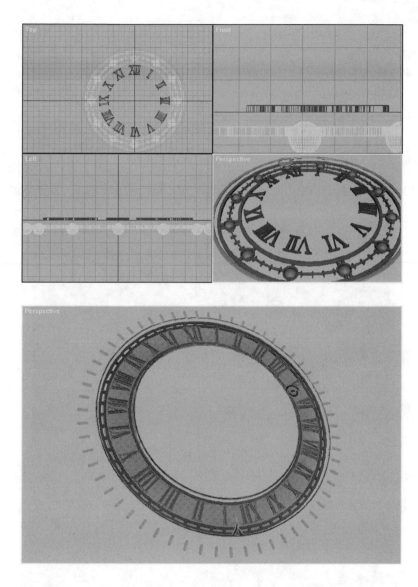

The Clock Face

Joe Dettmore and I agreed that we should create a clock with twenty-four hours on it. In the final design, the clock has the Roman numerals for one through twelve repeated on its face twice. After we decided on the design for the clock, I handed it off to Jonathan Burleson to create the spline of the clock face. Along with being a unique clock face, this clock appealed to me because of how huge it appears to be. By this I mean that when it wraps around the earth, the earth makes the clock look huge (see Figure RW1.29)—as opposed to the clock making the earth look like a toy.

When Jonathan finished his work on the clock face shape, I loaded it into 3ds max, beveled it, and added the materials. Because the clock was going to have a globe in the center, we needed to decide how the hands were going to be created. We certainly didn't want the hands of the clock to project from the center and extend through the earth's surface. To get around this problem, I created circular clock hands that surrounded the earth object (shown in Figure RW1.30).

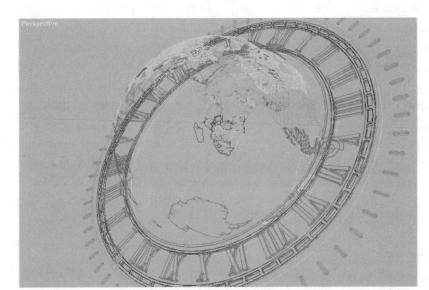

Figure RW1.29
The clock looks natural wrapping around the earth.

Figure RW1.30
A close-up wireframe detail of the hands of the Millennium clock.

The model of the globe was purchased from a popular 3D stock object company. The globe was then imported and transformed to occupy its designated place within the clock.

The Globe's Volumetric Beams

A Free Spot light, with a falloff of 85 degrees, created the volumetric light beams that emanate from the center of the globe. The Free Spot light was assigned a Look At Motion Controller with the Camera designated as its Target. The Look At controller kept the Free Spot light pointed directly at the camera, keeping the effect uniformly round no matter where the camera moved. I used a Free Spot instead of an Omni light because the Omni threw too many beams (in all directions). The Free Spot creates the illusion that light is shooting 360 degrees, but it is not so overwhelming. This is clearly illustrated in the example file realwld1\scenes\vollight.max on the CD (shown in Figure RW1.31). Figure RW1.32 shows a rendered frame from this scene. Both lights use the same attenuation and volume light settings; however, because the Free Spot (right) emits an 85-degree cone of light, its effect is subtler.

The Camera

With the geometry and effects of the scene created, I added a camera and animated the scene. The camera was very close to the clock object in the beginning of the animation and considerably further away at the end. To animate the camera's position smoothly, I roughly animated it until I was happy with where the camera was located at each position key during the animation.

Figure RW1.31
Vollight.max illustrates the difference between using an Omni light and a Free Spot light to generate the volume light effect.

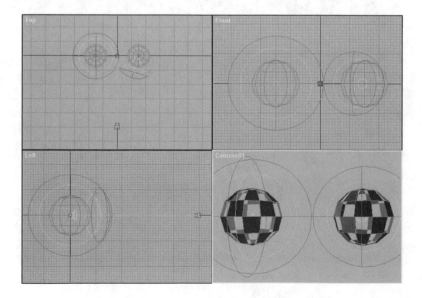

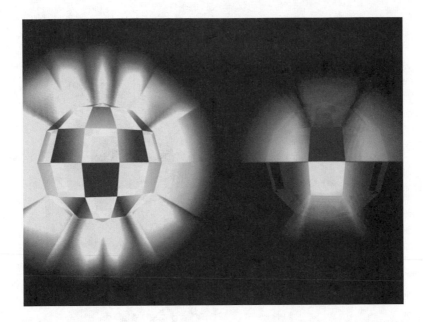

Figure RW1.32
A rendered frame
from vollight.max.

Because of the Bézier interpolation of the keys, the camera moved undesirably. To fix it, I entered the Motion panel, went to the Trajectories rollout, and clicked Convert To in the Spline Conversion group. This converted the camera's trajectory into an editable spline. A Path controller was then assigned to the camera, and the converted trajectory shape was assigned as the path. I then used the Bézier handles to smooth out the shape of the path to desirably animate the position of the camera.

Shot 4: The Millennium Logo

Figure RW1.33 shows the final shot I put together for the animation, and if I remember correctly, I had less than 24 hours to complete it. However, I had a reasonably clear idea of what I needed to do before I started animating. Because most of the background (the clock and globe) was already done, all I really needed to do was build the text, and then I was ready to start animating.

Joe and I had discussed this shot from the very beginning of production. We knew the general effects we wanted to see, such as the particles traveling backwards to create the Millennium type. Just to make sure Joe and I were on the same base, Joe quickly drew up storyboards on sticky notes; those storyboards are shown in Figures RW1.34 through RW1.37.

Figure RW1.33
A frame from the
fourth shot of the
Millennium
animation.

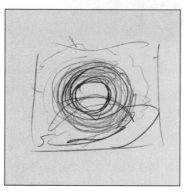

Figure RW1.34
Frame One of the sticky note storyboard.

Figure RW1.35
Frame Two.

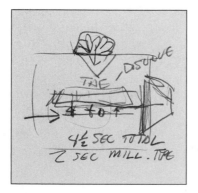

Figure RW1.36
Frame Three.

Figure RW1.37
Frame Four.

Frame One (Figure RW1.34) shows the camera looking straight down on the globe and surrounding clock. Frame Two of the storyboard (Figure RW1.35) illustrates the desired angle of clock/globe relationship. Notice the NBC peacock out of the frame above. Frame Three (Figure RW1.36) demonstrates the desired animation of the logo's elements. The trapezoid to the right is the Millennium type, and an arrow indicates its rotation into place. The arrow on the left specifies that the MSNBC type is to write on from the left. And once again the peacock is shown flying in from the top of the frame. Frame Four (Figure RW1.37) depicts all the elements in their final positions, completing the animation.

Although primitive, a storyboard such as the one above is an easy way to verify that all the minds working on a project are on the same track. In an ideal world, I would certainly have preferred to work with a beautifully illustrated storyboard. However, time usually doesn't afford us that luxury.

Building the Logo

Because I was able to recycle the clock and globe element from shot to shot, creating the background was simple. All I really had to do was animate the camera. When the motion of the globe and clock element was satisfactory, I sent it off to the render farm to render away.

Joe was compositing most of my elements in the Hal, so it was most convenient for both of us for me to create the logo elements as separate animations. This is because it is much easier to color-correct elements and offset their animation if they are all separate layers in the composite. Although the creation of these elements was fairly straightforward, I recall two things standing out.

When we were creating this shot, Joe and I were obsessed with two elements. The first was that we wanted to do something we had never done before with the MSNBC type, and the second related to the Millennium text particles. In the following sections, you will examine how each scene was created.

The MSNBC Type

View the file realwld1\msnbc.avi and the corresponding Max file realwld1\scenes\ mlmsnbc.max. The MSNBC type rotates onto the screen, letter by letter, in a flurry of fairy dust and lens flares (see Figure RW1.38). This scene could be broken down into four elements: the MSNBC objects, the particles, the MSNBC outline objects, and the lens flares. Even though the action passes very quickly, a lot happens.

Figure RW1.38
The MSNBC type
element.

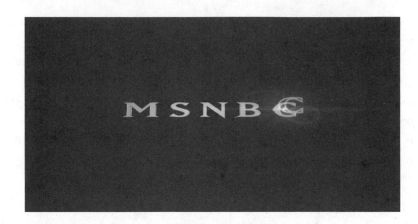

First, I animated the rotation of the MSNBC letters individually and experimented with their timing until I was satisfied. When their timing was correct, I animated their Visibility track to make each one appear as its rotation begins.

I created copies of each MSNBC letter shape and activated the Renderable check box in the General rollout. This allowed me to create the outlines of the MSNBC letters that emanate after they finish rotating into place. The Visibility tracks of the MSNBC outline objects were animated to make them appear and disappear.

One thing about the Visibility tracks in this scene is particularly noteworthy. For the MSNBC and the MSNBC outline objects, different animation Controllers are assigned to the tracks (see Figure RW1.39). The MSNBC (solid) objects have a simple On/Off controller, indicated by the blue line, which provides a simple on or off control. However, the MSNBC outline objects have a Linear Float controller that allows for the effect of being dissolved on and off.

Figure RW1.39
The Track View
with two different
Visibility tracks
expanded.

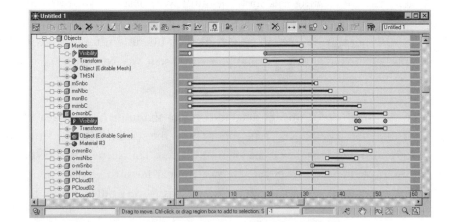

The fairy dust effect is created with multiple Particle Cloud emitters, each of which generates particles for only seven frames. The lens flares are added in Video Post; you can see their settings by accessing their individual dialogs.

The Millennium Particles

Joe had approached me early during this project and asked "Can we make particles go backward?" I thought to myself, "Even if they were going backward, they would have to be traveling forward." I answered, "Yes." Confused? I was too. Luckily it wasn't as hard as it seemed at first. Joe simply wanted the screen to be filled with random particles that were suddenly sucked back in space to spell the word "Millennium."

The easiest way to create the effect was to create the particles traveling forward and have Joe reverse the animation in the Hal. You can view realwld1\milparts.avi to see the particle animation I sent to Joe to reverse (see Figure RW1.40). Load real-wld1\ scenes\millprts.max as well to see the file that created this animation.

If you look at the realwld1\scenes\millprts.max scene, you may be overwhelmed by all the Space Warps that make up the scene (see Figure RW1.41). When it's broken down, it becomes quite simple.

The particles are emitted from a Particle Array particle system using the Millennium type as an Object-Based Emitter. The first Gravity Space Warp uses Spherical Force and pulls the particles together from frames 150–220, basically initiating the random motion of the particles. The second Gravity Space Warp acts as gravity as we

Figure RW1.40
The Millennium particles.

Figure RW1.41
Millprts.max.

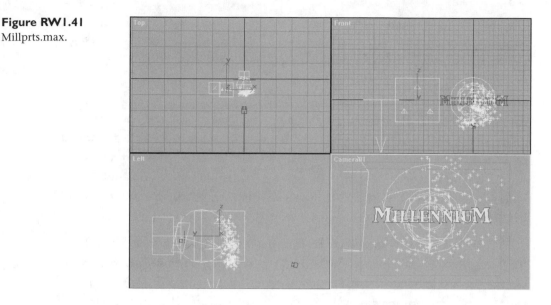

earthlings know it: It softly pulls the particles downward. The Wind Space Warp blows the particles toward the camera, starting at frame 200, and the Motor Space Warp gives the particles a nice twist, also starting at frame 200.

To give the appearance that the particles are streaks, I used two different types of Motion Blur on them. I used Object Motion Blur with a Duration of 1 frame, 16 Samples, and 16 Duration Subdivisions. The second motion blur I used is available only in Video Post; it's called Scene Motion Blur, and it's shown in Figure RW1.42.

Figure RW1.42
The Edit Scene Event dialog with Scene Motion Blur activated.

Scene Motion Blur renders each frame multiple times, as indicated in the Duration Subdivisions field, and then it dithers all the renderings for the frame together. So the combination of the Object and Scene Motion Blur created a very nice streaking effect.

Rendering the Final Composite

Joe color-corrected and composited the individual layers I had created and rendered. When each individual shot was finished, Joe created all the transitions from shot to shot. The final piece is right on the money—exactly what Joe and I had anticipated. Everyone was happy with the final product, and no changes were required, which was good because it was finished only hours before it was scheduled to air.

Real World Case Study 2: NBC News Decision 2000

I had worked in news graphics long enough to know that when the U.S. 2000 elections were right around the corner, it could mean only one thing: a whole lot of work. Turns out that none of us could have accurately foreseen the amount of work that lay on the road ahead. Knowing that the presidential race was close, something in the back of my head said, "Recount," but I didn't have time to think of what to do after Election Day; I needed to focus on creating what we knew we needed.

In the weeks leading up to our election coverage, I was working closely with Lori Neuhardt, MSNBC's Creative Director, and Vince Diga, designer, on the Newsfront project. We were working under tight schedules to wrap up the creation of Newsfront and then start the Decision 2000 animations. Sam Mandragona, NBC's Executive Creative Director, was kind enough to call me every two or three days to make sure I could start the project on time.

While I was working on Newsfront, Sam stopped by to chat about the Decision 2000 project. He brought a Xerox of a pencil sketch storyboard that had been drawn by Tony Franquera, NBC's Associate Creative Director, on the train during his commute to work. It looked pretty straightforward (see Figure RW2.1), but I had concerns about having enough action to fill the 20 seconds of animation in one camera shot. We decided to conquer that hurdle when it rose in front of us.

Before I started the animation, I asked Sam if he could have someone colorize the storyboards to give me a better idea of the desired feel. He assured me he was on it and headed back across the river to 30 Rock (NBC NY—30 Rockefeller Center).

Figure RW2.1
Tony's preliminary storyboard for Decision 2000 is on the right side. The sketches on the left were the result of my project planning session with Sam.

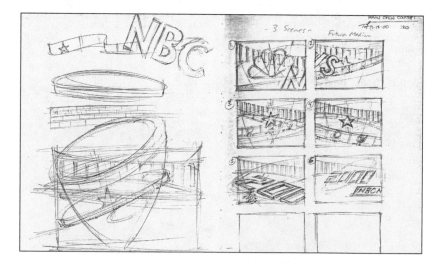

Making the Preliminary Studies

The day after I wrapped up the Newsfront animation, I started to sink my heels into Decision 2000. I examined the pencil sketch storyboard and began to collect my thoughts. Sam had told me they wanted the animation to have dark colors and glasslike materials. The pencil strokes told me one thing clearly: There were going to be glass rings. Two to three weeks before I needed to have the animation finished, I started to develop it.

RingsA01.max

To help me visualize the glass ring concept, I created my first scene in 3ds max 4, mostly to develop a mood for the scene and to begin creating the "glass" materials. The first scene I created was \3ds4-ma\realwld2\scenes\ringsA01.max (shown in Figure RW2.2).

RingsA01.max is a simple scene with a few colored Omni lights, a camera, and four Tube primitives linked in a hierarchy with Noise Rotation Controllers assigned to them. You can watch the rendered animation by viewing \3ds4-ma\realwld2\ringsA01.mov. Four glass rings rotate and refract through one another as they turn randomly.

The visual effect, although dark, is quite complex and interesting. It may or may not be a big surprise that this was an extremely simple scene to create. In the Material Editor, you can see the settings for the Material #1 material (see Figure RW2.3). (Bad John for not naming your materials!)

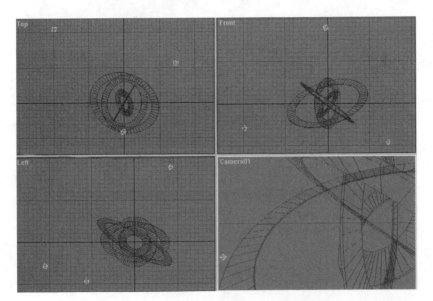

Figure RW2.2
RingsA01.max.

The material is 100% transparent (signified by the Opacity value of 0), so no color is derived from the Ambient or Diffuse channels of the material. The specular highlights are both white, and the First Specular Layer highlight has some Anisotropy applied for a more metallic look. The blue and orange color that appears on the rings as they rotate is obtained from the colored Omni lights in the scene.

The refraction is created with a Raytrace Refraction Map applied to the material. The default settings are applied. I did, however, change the Index of the Refraction: value to .75 in the Extended Parameters rollout of the material. To obtain the Index of Refraction setting, I generally refer to the list in the Help menu (shown in Figure RW2.4).

Glass is usually a setting of 1.5, but because my rings were flat objects, that setting didn't work quite as dramatically as I desired. Through trial and error, I found that .75 was a much better setting.

Figure RW2.3

The Material Editor settings for Material #1.

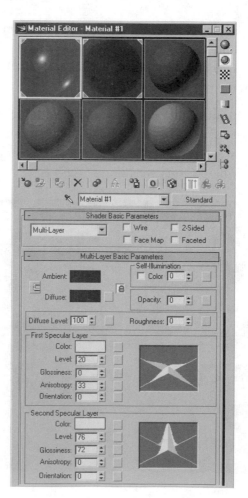

Tip

You can animate the Index of Refraction value from its lowest value 0 through 10 to see what value works best in your scene.

I was happy with the result of this scene, and I kept it in my back pocket in case I needed it. I still didn't have the color storyboards to work with, so I wasn't sure if it was what was desired; I knew it was close though.

RingsB01.max

Because I was happy with the rendered result of the ringsA01.max file, I decided to push it a little further. Tony's pencil storyboard shows the colonnade that surrounds the scene. I built the columns with as low a polygon count as I could and

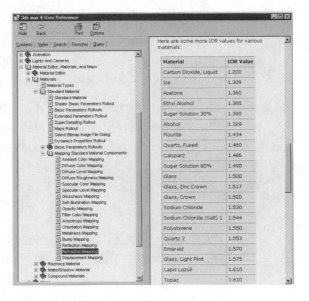

Figure RW2.4

The 3ds max 4 User Reference with the Refraction Mapping help open.

placed them in a scene similar to ringsA01.max. The result can be viewed in \3ds4-ma\realwld2\scenes\ringsB01.max (shown in Figure RW2.5). You can watch the rendered animation by viewing \3ds4-ma\realwld2\ringsB01.mov.

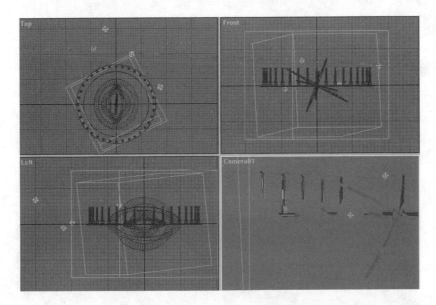

Figure RW2.5
RingsB01.max.

The ring's material is the same, but the Index of Refraction was changed to a more modest value of .9. The pillar objects in the scene have a very simple blue plastic material applied. The floor that the pillars are resting on has the same material as the pillars except a Flat Mirror reflection was added to reflect the pillars slightly.

When I finished this animation, I called Joe Dettmore, MSNBC's Assistant Creative Director, to have him view the results. Joe and I discussed the rendered animations and how we could use this refraction effect on an upcoming project if it wasn't used on Decision 2000. While I waited for the color storyboards, I started to familiarize myself with the Decision 2000 logo object that I had created a while back.

Working with the Storyboard

Two weeks before my deadline, Sam and Tony stopped by with a color storyboard of sorts (see Figure RW2.6).

From the beginning, we were planning for the animation to be three shots long, meaning there would be three scenes, and we would transition from one to the next with dissolves. Tony's storyboard was basically the first shot of this sequence. Along with this color storyboard, they brought along other backgrounds and preliminary images they had been working on at 30 Rock (see Figure RW2.7).

Looking at these images, I could see that I had the color scheme down fairly close. But the newer storyboard didn't contain as many rings as I had first predicted.

Sam, Toni, Joe, and I sat in my office and discussed what should happen with the animation. Finally, we had everyone in one room and ready to talk about the project in detail. We spoke a lot about the presidential ring that is symbolized by the gold ring on Tony's storyboard. This ring was going to have the picture of every

Figure RW2.6
The color storyboard for Decision 2000.

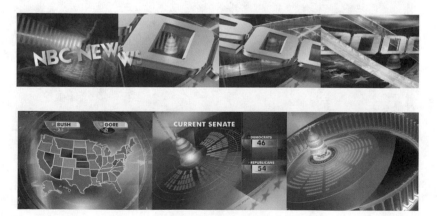

Figure RW2.7
Preliminary background images created at 30 Rock.

president chronologically texture mapped around it. As we progressed through the animation, we would see apparently random sections of the ring progressing to the more recent presidents.

Sam and Toni brought up the fact that they wanted to see the Presidential seal somewhere in the animation as well. Joe chimed in and asked me to play those ray-traced refracted tube object animations I created. As the animations looped out on my monitor, it was unanimous that these rings should become the Presidential seal. Now we all had a rough idea of what I needed to create. All that was left was for me to make sense of it all.

Before we wrapped up the meeting, we agreed that there should be four shots in the animation instead of three. The first shot would be the establishing shot that showcased the Presidential seal and colonnade; this would allow viewers to get a grasp on where they were. The second shot would be the presidential ring. The third shot would be the peacock and U.S. Capitol dome, and the fourth shot would be the Decision 2000 logo. It sounded simple. I was left to actually do it all in less than two weeks.

Creating Shot 1

I decided to work on the animation from start to finish. So I started with the first shot, the Presidential seal and colonnade (see Figure RW2.8). Before I could complete the shot, however, I needed to build a clean and appropriate Presidential seal.

Figure RW2.8
A frame from shot 1.

This proved to be one of the biggest hurdles of the project. But if I could just complete the Presidential seal, I could then build the rest of the scene around it.

The Presidential Seal

What was the quickest way to make a clean Presidential seal? That was the question. The text and stars were the easy part. What concerned me most were the eagle and shield. I scanned the seal from a cover of a book about the presidency. I tried to clean up the color artwork to make a black and white bump or displacement map. The moiré pattern of the scan made it nearly impossible to quickly create the map I needed. I then loaded the book cover scan as the Viewport background to try to build the object as a mesh. I didn't get far (see Figure RW2.9) before I realized it would take forever to do that as well.

After about a day or day and a half, I still hadn't accomplished anything. I was working over the weekend. It was Sunday afternoon, and I was anxious to have something finished for Monday morning. I decided to go for a walk.

When I left my room, I ran into Christo Manco, a designer on our team. He was working the weekend as well. It didn't take long before I was ferociously grumbling about my predicament. Because Christo is usually the person who traces the logos

Figure RW2.9
An attempt at modeling the eagle (those things are feathers).

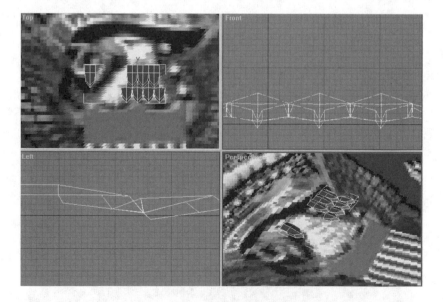

in Illustrator for use in 3D, I joked that he might have a lot of tracing on his hands. He glanced up at me and said, "Tsukasa has a CD with all those government seals on it."

Too bad Tsukasa had left MSNBC a few months back for a warmer job in Miami. But that got me thinking. "Was the CD really *his* or did we have one at MSNBC as well?" I raided the closet where we keep all our digital archives and came across a CD that I thought might have it. I put it into my workstation, but the CD wouldn't read on a PC. So I went to a Mac system and loaded the CD. Voilá! There was in fact an Illustrator file of the Presidential seal! Now all I had to do was load it into 3ds max, clean it up a bit, and extrude it.

Nah. It couldn't be that simple. After I imported the Illustrator file of the Presidential seal into 3ds max, I started to break it up into sections (head, wings, claws and so on) to be cleaned up. However, the 5,997 vertices of the seal shape intimidated me (see Figure RW2.10), and after creating only the head and beak, I gave up and opted for a much simpler solution.

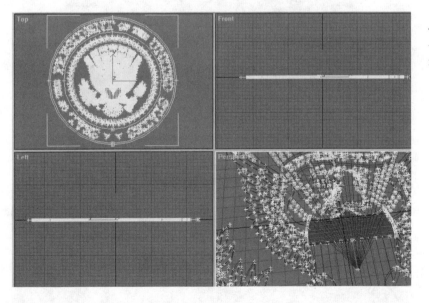

Figure RW2.10
The Illustrator file of the Presidential seal imported into max.

Finally, I realized I could use the Illustrator file of the seal to generate the bump map I wanted in the first place! Why didn't I think of that sooner? When I loaded the Illustrator file into Photoshop, it gave me the image I needed. I simply cropped out the eagle portion and saved it as a jpg (see Figure RW2.11). I named this image bird2good.jpg.

To give the seal a little life in the first shot, Joe, Sam, Toni, and I decided that the shield should have a little color. To apply it, I needed to generate two more texture maps using bird2good.jpg as the template; the texture maps were bird2good-color.jpg and bird2good-colormatte.jpg. They're shown in Figure RW2.12.

Figure RW2.11
Bird2good.jpg.

Figure RW2.12
Bird2good-color-matte.jpg (left) and bird2good-color.jpg (right).

Using the refraction material we discussed earlier as a base, I added the new maps I had created from the Illustrator file. Figure RW2.13 shows the RingBird material's settings. This material generated the precise result I wanted (see Figure RW2.14). You can't imagine how elated I was when this object and material was finished. From start to finish, it took me two and a half days to complete the objects and materials for the Presidential seal.

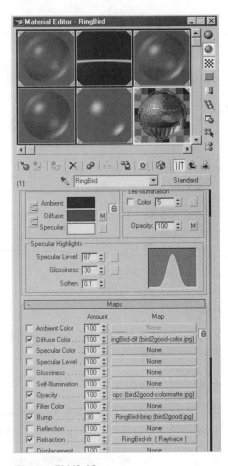

Figure RW2.13
The Material Editor showing the RingBird material settings (at lower right).

Figure RW2.14
The rendered object with the RingBird material applied.

The Colonnade and NBC NEWS Type

The construction of the colonnade and the NBC NEWS type (shown in Figure RW2.15) was very simple. As a tribute to the Decision 98 animation, I merged the NBC NEWS type from the Decision 98 animation into the scene. The type object is simply a beveled type shape with a Bend modifier applied to arch the type.

To create the colonnade, I box modeled the top and bottom of each pillar. The round pillar was built by creating a lathe. To apply the lengthwise grooves in each pillar, I collapsed the pillar lathe into an editable mesh, selected every other row of polygons, and extruded them inward.

As you can see in Figure RW2.15, every tenth pillar is not selected. This is because I grouped the pillar objects into two groups. This way I could hide the pillars selected in Figure RW2.15 but still have every tenth pillar visible as a reference when I was animating. This allowed the realtime views to play back more accurately. However, later in production, I think I just selected each pillar, right-clicked it, chose Properties, and activated Display as Box. This accomplished the same thing by reducing each pillar into a box shape in the view, and it reduced the number of polygons in the scene.

The Environment

The environment is generally one of the hardest things to get right when you're building "high profile" animations. Usually nobody, including myself, can make up

Figure RW2.15
The colonnade objects (left) and NBC NEWS object (right).

his or her mind as to what looks best. At the time, the only thing I knew for sure was what Tony had in mind. So I copied his storyboard and created a bright blue horizon line over a black background (see Figure RW2.16).

Figure RW2.16
Frame 60 of shotA01.max rendered from Video Post.

Included on the CD is the file \3ds4-ma\realwld2\scenes\shotA01.max. This file has all the elements I used to create the environment for the scene and the camera motion. Also in the scene is the PillarFloor object, which the colonnade stood on. This was added as a reference of perspective. To see a wireframe animation of the first shot with all the objects, view \3ds4-ma\realwld2\wire_shotA.avi.

To create the blue horizon line, I applied a Gradient Ramp to the Environment map channel. If you load \3ds4-ma\realwld2\scenes\shotA01.max and open the Material Editor in the second material preview slot, you will see the Env map (shown in Figure RW2.17).

Notice that the Gradient Ramp is in the Color #1 slot of a Mix map. This is because the beginning of the shot shows the scene in darkness. Then in frames 25 through 45, the blue horizon appears. To accomplish the transition from black to the horizon, I mixed between Color #2 (black) and Color #1 (the Gradient Ramp) between frames 25 and 45. If you scrub the time slider, you can watch the dissolve.

To examine the Gradient Ramp, you can click the Gradient Ramp button in the Mix map (see Figure RW2.18).

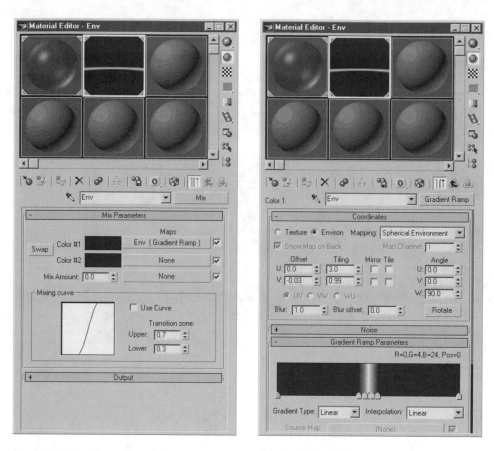

Figure RW2.17
The Material Editor with the Env map selected at frame 100.

Figure RW2.18
The Gradient Ramp for the blue horizon.

Because the Gradient Ramp uses the Spherical Environment mapping, the gradient is wrapped on an imaginary sphere around the scene. When the camera moves, the gradient will move appropriately.

I was getting anxious to see something rendered, but before I could render, I needed to add a flare to the horizon. I opened Video Post and applied a Lens Effects Flare (see Figure RW2.19). To my recollection, either I used the default flare, or I loaded one that came with 3ds max. I made some modifications and animated some of the parameters (as shown in Figure RW2.20).

The animated flare is also included with the \3ds4-ma\realwld2\scenes\shotA01.max file for your examination purposes. Also, the actual camera animation is included in this scene as well.

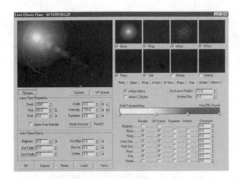

Figure RW2.19
The flare used on the blue horizon.

Figure RW2.20
Some of the animated tracks of the Lens
Effects Flare.

The NBC NEWS Shooters

The first shot was created in two passes. The first pass included the Presidential seal, the colonnade, the NBC NEWS type, and the environment—pretty much everything. In the second pass, I added the red, white, and blue shooters that pass above and below the NBC NEWS type. These two passes were then composited in Discreet Combustion. The reason I rendered it in two layers was that I was sure management liked everything except for the shooters. This way, if I needed to change the shooters, I wouldn't have to re-render everything.

The shooter file is included on the CD as well. You can find it at \3ds4-ma\real-wld2\scenes\shotA01shooter.max. Figure RW2.21 shows that file.

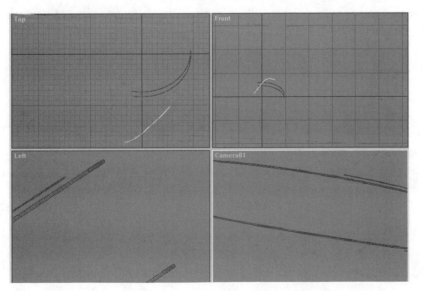

Figure RW2.21
ShotA01shooter.max.

The shooter objects are Torus primitives with an animated Slice value by which they "write on." At the tips of each shooter is a Point helper. This Point helper is the source for a Lens Effects Flare event in Video Post. The flare is basically just a red glow. The Lens Effects Flare settings are in Video Post of the shotA01shooter.max file for purposes of examination.

A Few Extra Thoughts

Sometimes projects this large and important go through very big changes relatively quickly. Often Sam will want to see my progress as often as once a day. Because Sam and I do not work in the same building (or state for that matter), I email tests back and forth to him. Four of these tests are on the CD: \3ds4-ma\realwld2\td2k1.mov through td2k4.mov.

I refer to these test animations again when discussing the other shots. However, right now I want you to view td2k1.mov. Notice that the eagle's shield doesn't have any red, white, and blue coloring and that a ring appears behind NBC NEWS. These two things don't appear that way in the final animation. This was the way the scene appeared when I first made it. It went through a few changes before it was considered final. If you view the other tests, you will see the final first pass of the first shot, but the shooter objects do not appear on any of them.

Creating Shot 2

Generally speaking, the second shot (see Figure RW2.22) of the animation was easy to create because most of the objects already existed. The only new object I needed to introduce to the scene was the ring with each president's face. By viewing the test animations \3ds4-ma\realwld2\td2k1.mov–td2k4.mov, you can see the iterations this object went through.

The Ring

At first I kept the appearance of the ring close to what Tony originally illustrated in his storyboard: a gold ring. As the production of the scene progressed though, we decided that blue was the best color for the ring. However, we were still debating about the appearance of the ring. The design we settled on is shown in Figure RW2.23.

Each facet of the ring had a flat front screen on which a president's head was to be textured. The back plate was arched to create interesting refractions as it moved

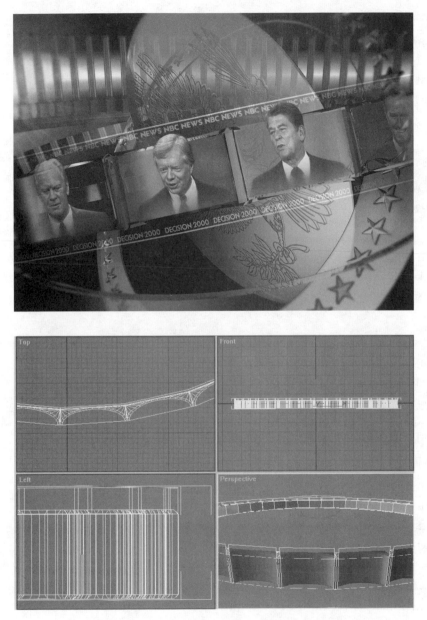

Figure RW2.22
Shot 2 of the Decision 2000 animation.

Figure RW2.23
The ring object used in the final anima-tion.

through the scene. Although this was the design we chose, we were unsure how to finish it. If you watch the test animations again you will see little red bars under-scoring and separating the president's heads. Those red bars were one of the design elements we were considering. In the end, we decided to go with the little NBC NEWS type and the simple stroked lines shown in Figure RW2.22.

The Presidents' Heads

When it came to acquiring the headshots of the presidents, I turned to Matt Wisner, the MSNBC Graphics Department's research point person. He was kind enough to round up at least one headshot for each president of this wonderful United States. I then started the long process of adding each image to a carefully measured strip in Photoshop (see Figure RW2.24).

Figure RW2.24
A portion of the presidents' heads strip.

Along with applying the headshots to this extremely long and narrow image, I needed to keep track of the alpha channel in order to key all the heads off the map. It is these still images of the presidents' heads that you see in the test animations on the CD.

Joe and I discussed the possibility of putting moving video on the foreground of the ring to add more drama to the animation. We decided hands down to make that a reality. Joe took on the daunting task of rotoscoping moving talking head video of the presidents. (The term *rotoscoped* refers to a matte that was hand drawn for each frame of video to key the head off the background.) Only five presidents needed to be rotoscoped. Joe spent a weekend accomplishing this on the Quantel Hal, a proprietary compositing system.

When Joe finished with his work to the presidents, I applied them to the object. The ring in the final animation still had the other presidents' heads as still images mapped on them, but because of the angle at which you see the ring in the final rendering, they can't be seen.

Finishing the Scene

This shot was finished a lot like the first shot was completed, in multiple passes. The first pass consisted of most all the objects; the second pass included the little rows of NBC NEWS type and the thin line scoring the top and bottom of the ring. You can see a wireframe of the first pass by viewing \3ds4-ma\realwld2\wire_shotB.avi.

The moving video president heads, however, were not rendered in the first pass. I was afraid that if something went wrong with the video and the matte, hours of rendering would be ruined. So I rendered the presidents separately as a third pass.

Speaking of hours of rendering, while I was working on this project, I kept 10 machines rendering around the clock. Certain shots in this animation took two days to render, using all 10 of those computers. As for the specs on those computers, well, it's a grab bag. Engineering hooked me up with anything available that resembled a speedy processor. So the computers ranged from single 600MHz machines to dual 800+ machines.

When all the passes had been rendered, I composited them in Combustion. To composite, I used an elliptical selection to select the perimeter of the image. I then used that selection to apply a slight blur to the perimeter of the image. It's very subtle, but it creates a nice blurred peripheral vision effect.

Creating Shot 3

Shot 3 didn't require as much attention as the first two shots did because, once again, most of the objects were already created. Shot 3, however, introduced two objects that have not yet been seen in this sequence: the peacock (see Figure RW2.25) and the U.S. Capitol dome (see Figure RW2.26).

Figure RW2.25
The NBC peacock from shot 3 of the Decision 2000 animation.

Figure RW2.26
The U.S. Capitol from
shot 3 of the Decision
2000 animation.

The NBC Peacock

The NBC peacock was an object I had used in other animations. I created it a few years back; I like it because everything is rounded, so it picks up great reflections and refractions. The color the peacock picks up is from the Specular color of the sub-materials. This means the only time the color is visible is when a light creates a specular highlight.

If you watch the test animations on the CD in file \3ds4-ma\realwld\ td2k1.mov–td2k4.mov, you can see the evolution of the peacock as I worked on the animation. Shot 3 in td2k1.mov was basically a place filler; I just needed something very rough to illustrate my intentions. In td2k3.mov, you will see a more refined peacock. Sam thought the peacock was too big in the picture and too thick, so I made those changes. When I re-rendered the scene, I just wrote over the old image files. In td2k3.mov, you can see the new changes I made (early part of the scene) and the old peacock (later part of the scene). At the time I constructed that test animation, the network had only rendered that many new frames. In td2k4.mov, you could see a version of the peacock much closer to the final.

The U.S. Capitol Dome

There isn't much of interest to point out about the dome. Basically I removed it from a complete capitol-building model that we purchased from a stock object company.

The Presidential Seal

In shot 3, we see the U.S. Capitol dome rise through a hole in the Presidential seal. As far as I know, it doesn't symbolize anything. It just looked cool, and we had to get the Capitol in somehow. If you watch \3ds4-ma\realwld\wire_shotC.avi, you can see the hole in the center of the Presidential seal open up, and the dome moves up through it. The following are the steps I used to animate the hole in the seal. Open \3ds4-ma\realwld2\scenes\shotC01.max (shown in Figure RW2.27) to see it.

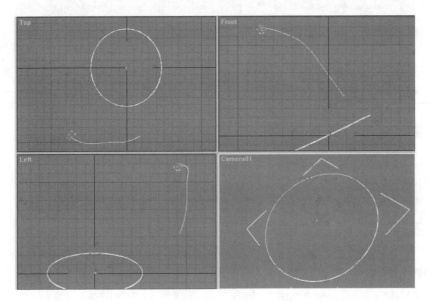

Figure RW2.27
ShotC01.max.

Looking at the Ring-Inner object, you can see that a small hole was beveled in the center of the object. I still needed to enlarge the hole. If I collapsed the stack and used a sub-object transform on the mesh to enlarge the hole, the size of the bevel would have been affected as well. To avoid this problem, I opted for a much cleaner process.

I applied a transform to the center circle of the shape before I applied the bevel modifier in the stack. If you were to select the Ring-Inner object and activate the Editable Spline object in the stack, you would see that the center vertices are selected and much further apart than they appear when all the modifiers are applied (see Figure RW2.28).

I left the vertex sub-object level active and applied an XForm modifier. I then animated the scale track of the XForm modifier between frames 90 and 160. On top of the XForm modifier (which was acting on the vertex sub-object level of the circle

Figure RW2.28
The Editable Spline
object in the stack is
selected.

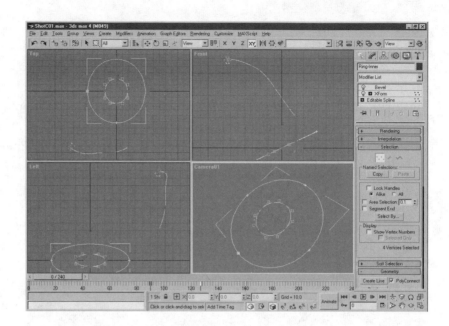

spline), I applied a bevel modifier. Therefore, the size of the hole was changed before
the Bevel modifier was applied; so the bevel will remain the same size throughout
the whole animation.

Creating Shot 4

Often when I am working on an animation this large, it seems there is very little
time to work on the most important part: the logo. I had only about two weeks to
create the entire animation from start to finish. However, one thing worked to my
advantage on this project: I had built the logo a few months back because the news
folks were already covering certain aspects of the story. Figure RW2.29 shows that
logo.

The Logo Resolve

If you examine the test animations I created (in \3ds4-ma\realwld2\
td2k2.mov–td2k4.mov), you will see many different variations of the logo resolve. I
tried very hard to animate the logo and the Presidential seal environment all in one
pass. I couldn't get a shot of the environment that I thought was interesting enough
and that, at the same time, allowed all the individual pieces of the logo to fly easily. The reason I wanted it to all be in one pass was that I wanted the refractions to
be accurately calculated.

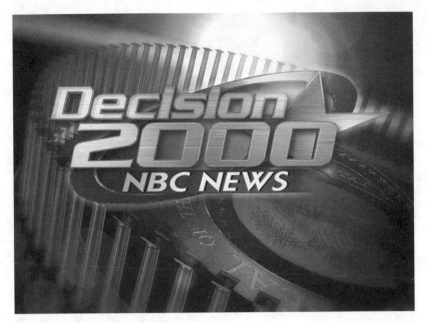

Figure RW2.29
Shot 4 from the Decision 2000 animation.

In the end, I decided to cheat and render the scene in multiple passes: the background pass and the individual logo element passes. If you view \3ds4-ma\realwld2\ wire_shotDb.avi, you will see a wireframe of the background animation. Notice that the hole in the Presidential seal closes up again.

The Materials

Rendering the logo in pieces has one great advantage: You have the ability to color correct, add effects, and apply 2D shadows to all the individual layers in Combustion (see Figure RW2.30). Generally, when I render my 3D animations, I immediately take the rendered output into Combustion and add contrast and saturation to the images. It adds a little extra punch.

Open \3ds4-ma\realwld2\scenes\shotDLogo01.max (see Figure RW2.31). If you play the animation, you should see the Decision 2000 type fly in as it does in the final animation. If you want to examine the materials on the type, open the Material Editor. You will notice that there are 10 materials with the name "decision." However, each one has a different capitalized letter (for example, Decision, dEcision, deCision, and so on). The capitalized letter signifies the object it is applied to. Each letter in the word "Decision" mixes from a clear glass refractive material to the gold-brushed glass material at a different time, which means each one needs individual materials.

Figure RW2.30
The brushed glass
material on the
Decision 2000 logo.

Figure RW2.31
ShotDLogo01.max.

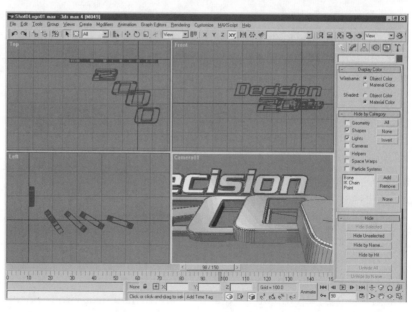

In this example, the renderer and the ray-traced refractions of the clear glass material use AshDback0000.ifl as the environment. This IFL simply points to AshDback.jpg, whereas originally it pointed to the full rendered background sequence. The "brushed" look is caused by the stretched Cellular map in the bump and specular map channels (it's stretched because of the low ".02" X: Tiling setting).

The type looks complex partly because of the number of bevels I managed to place onto the object. On top of that, there are two different sub-materials on the bevels alone (D2-eb and D2-fb). If you want to view the different sub-materials and see where they are placed on the objects, examine the 2000 material. You can uncheck the On/Off boxes and render only selected sub-materials on the 2000 type. Try rendering those tests at approximately frame 100.

Viewing the Final Animation

If you want to see the entire finished animation, view \3ds4-ma\realwld2\Decision2k.mov. This animation was supposed to air in its entirety twice and in shorter 3- to 10-second versions as well. Thanks to the recount situation, my animation received much more play than I ever imagined. I was very pleased with how the animation turned out, and I was very happy to hear that many people enjoyed it as well.

Real World Case
Study 3: Newsfront

Lori Neuhardt, the Creative Director of the

MSNBC Graphics Department, approached

me in mid-September 2000 and asked me

to look over some logo concepts Vince

Diga had been putting together from his

home workspace in Chicago. All the illustrations were flat 2D stylized images like the ones shown in Figure RW3.1. The images Lori and I were most interested in made generous use of the color red.

One of the first things I learned about making graphics for television was to *stay away from using lots of red*. The reason? The color red "bleeds" when it appears on a normal consumer television. By this I mean that the color red appears to streak or smear on most older television sets. If you have ever generously used the color red in an animation, you have probably experienced it firsthand.

That aside, I found it odd that we were actually considering making an animation based on a red palette because, working for news, we usually base everything on the color blue. I am not exactly sure why most of what we create at MSNBC is blue. But I do remember a conversation I once had with Joe Dettmore, the Assistant Creative

Figure RW3.1
Concept illustrations created for Newsfront.

Director, in which Joe said, "Blue just looks good." But, I digress. Let's get back to the Newsfront animation.

Looking at a frame of what would be the logo resolve of the animation (the lower-right frame in Figure RW3.1), I thought to myself, "This isn't even a 3D animation in the first place!" I was shocked because it was only a flat 2D logo on a 2D streaked background. As Lori, Francine Izzo (a 2D animator at MSNBC), and I discussed our intentions about the choreography of the animation, it quickly became apparent that this animation was going to be a fusion of both 2D and 3D.

Fran generated the idea of flying through the NBC peacock, and that sparked my imagination. When the meeting ended, I returned to my desk to start hashing out the idea.

Working Through the Pre-Production Phase

When I was back in my room sitting behind my workstation, I started to digest all the ideas that had been brought up in our meeting. All I really had to go on was the final frame image of the logo Vince had designed. The thought of flying the camera through the NBC peacock genuinely excited me. I started to experiment with the camera's journey through my familiar friend, the NBC peacock.

The First Attempt at a Flythrough

If you view the file \3ds4-ma\realwld3\peakflyA.mov on the CD, you will see the very first basic test I created to test the peacock idea. The thing that stands out the most is that the camera takes some extremely hard hits when it's going into and exiting the turn. The viewer might almost feel as though he would get whiplash watching it. To examine the source file that created this movie, open \3ds4-ma\realwld3\scenes\peakflyA.max (shown in Figure RW3.2).

If you examine peakflyA.max, you can clearly see my creative intention to fly the camera between the solid outline and the solid feathers of the peacock. Notice Line01, the upside-down fishhook shape in the Top view. This is the path the camera is constrained to. The whiplash we experience occurs when the camera passes from the straight to the curve or vice-versa. The camera is moving along the path at a constant velocity, and this creates the appearance of abrupt and choppy direction changes. I needed to figure out a way to rectify this problem.

Figure RW3.2

PeakflyA.max opened in 3ds max.

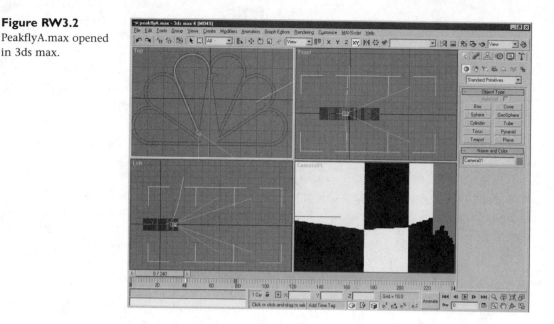

Another thing that really bothered me about using a motion path such as this one for the camera was that the camera needed to fly backward in order to view the peacock as it flew out and away from it. This posed an interesting problem for this animation. If at all possible, I did not want the viewer to be led backwards through an animation. In my opinion, the camera flying through backward would leave the viewer's eye feeling as though it had no control over what it was seeing. Basically, the backward motion was confusing to the eye, and that bothered me.

The Second Attempt at a Flythrough

Knowing that I didn't want to rapidly fly backward through the tight interior of the peacock, I turned my focus in another direction. In a meeting, I was told that this animation needed to be simple but have significant visual depth. They wanted to see layers of "stuff" going on in the far background as well as the foreground. In other words, they wanted to make it simple yet busy.

To add more depth, I decided to try to make a test in which the peacock's feathers were randomly traveling through space and slowly moved into position to create the famous peacock shape. You can view this test in the file \3ds4-ma\realwld3\ peakflyB.mov. You can also view the scene that created this by opening \3ds4-ma\ realwld3\scenes\peakflyB.max (see Figure RW3.3).

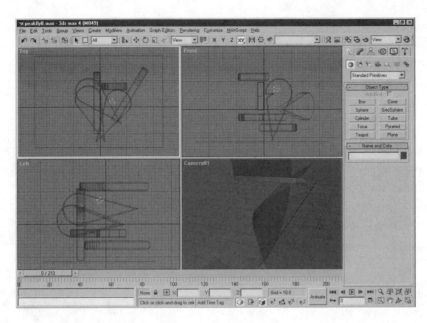

Figure RW3.3
PeakflyB.max opened
in 3ds max.

I created this scene as a contrast with the first test I had created. This scene has the peacock in pieces at the start of the animation, and the feel is random and layered. Technically, the scene is not very professionally created. For example, the feathers can clearly be seen intersecting one another at times. However, this scene was not intended to be the final product but the visualization of an idea.

Although this idea may be good for something in the future, it didn't have the pizzazz I wanted for this animation. The peacock feathers flew around randomly without purpose, and there didn't seem to be any underlying structure holding together in concept and in design. In a good animation, everything has a place and a meaning, whether it is in concept, design, or both. I couldn't figure out a way to turn this idea into what I needed it to be.

The Successful Flythrough

Vince and I constantly communicated back and forth over the phone. As I made tests, I would send them to Vince over the Web, he would watch them, and then we would discuss our options. In my head I could see an appealing flythrough inside the peacock, but I couldn't translate my thoughts into a camera path that made me happy. But during a conversation with Vince, it hit me: The camera had to be flying backward only when it was leaving the peacock. I immediately changed the way I was approaching the camera animation and started over.

I decided that I should try having the camera fly into the top of the peacock forward and out the bottom of the peacock backward. It sounded very simple, but remember the abrupt whiplash effect the camera had simply rounding a turn? How was I going to turn the camera around a full 180 degrees? The answer? Very slowly. You can view my very first test of this approach in \3ds4-ma\realwld3\peakflyC.mov. The file can be loaded from \3ds4-ma\realwld3\peakflyC.max (see Figure RW3.4).

I spent an hour or two tweaking the animated camera path for this test animation. For the most part, the camera travels rather smoothly throughout the duration of the animation. However, to keep the maximum amount of the peacock in the camera view during the turn, the back of the camera travels dangerously close to the wall behind it. In the case of this animation, the camera actually does back through the wall behind it. I had to use clipping planes in the camera's parameters to keep the viewer from seeing that during rendering.

To maintain accurate control, both visually and technically, I used two dummy objects to create a virtual camera jib. This gave me a great deal of control over the animation. The drawback was that all the smooth interpolation of the rotation overcompensated the rotation, and the camera tilted undesirably. If you have peakflyC.max loaded, you can see in the Camera01 view that the grid (which is basically a black line striking through the middle of the red wall from this angle) is crooked between frames 70 and 110 (as shown in Figure RW3.5).

Figure RW3.4
PeakflyC.max, the first successful camera test.

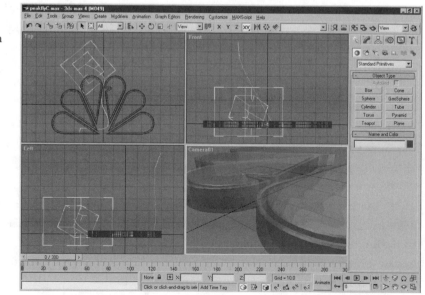

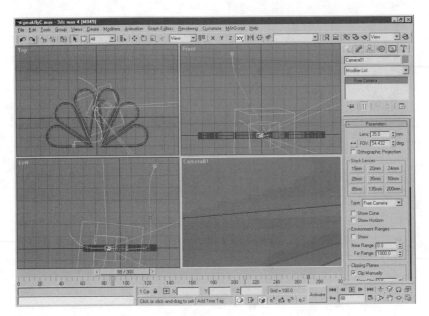

At the time I created it, I didn't even notice that the camera view was warped at such an angle. Not until Vince told me that it was lopsided did it become apparent to me. That aside, everyone was thrilled with this idea for a camera motion. So it was my duty to work all the kinks out of it. The Newsfront animation had officially begun.

The Final Camera Animation

With the concept for the camera move approved, I set about to make the move as perfect as possible. If I recall correctly, I worked on the camera move alone for almost two days. I kept watching it over and over again and tried to get every kink out until I was completely satisfied with the outcome. What I came up with was near perfect.

You can see the improved camera move by viewing \3ds4-ma\realwld3\peakflyD.mov. You can also load the scene that generated that movie from \3ds4-ma\realwld3\ peakflyD.max (see Figure RW3.6)

If you play the animation in the Camera01 view, you will see that the home grid (the black line from this angle) is perfectly level as the camera travels down the center of the peacock. To make a more stable camera path, I selected the camera (from a scene similar to the peakflyC.max file) and entered the Trajectories rollout of the

Figure RW3.6
PeakflyD.max contains the camera path used in the final animation.

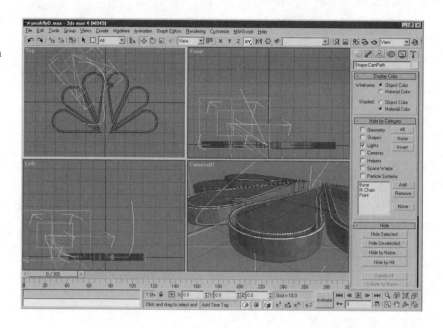

Motion panel (shown in Figure RW3.7). I then clicked the Convert To button to convert the current trajectory of the camera into a shape. This shape, in turn, was applied as a path constraint to the dummy object that is the parent of the camera.

The two dummy objects still acted as the virtual jib, rotating the camera to the desired locations. I was then able to smooth out the path shape that was generated in the Motion panel in the Modify panel. The rotation keys had to be adjusted as well to create an animation to my liking.

Creating the NBC Peacock Section

When I was finally satisfied with the camera animation, I made sure everyone involved with the project was pleased as well. I double- and triple-checked the smoothness of the move; it was critical that no further changes to the path occur because I knew that I was going to create the animation in multiple passes. Any change to the camera move would force me to re-render many layers.

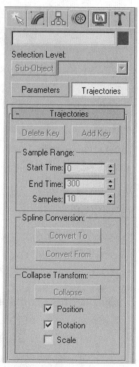

Figure RW3.7
The Trajectories rollout of the Motion panel.

I was going to execute the composite myself in Discreet Combustion. I wanted complete control of the composite, so I went as far as rendering the peacock objects out in four passes: the first and second feathers, the third feather, the fourth feather, and the fifth and sixth feathers. This allowed me to sandwich other layers between the feathers in the composite.

I do not usually make use of third-party plug-ins for my work at MSNBC. This is partly because when I was working on a high-profile project that would take a long time to render, our engineering department was kind enough to put together a makeshift render farm. I already had to install all the 3ds max software on each render server, and if I made use of any plug-ins, I would have had to install them as well. Usually I didn't have time install third-party plug-ins, especially on temporary machines. However, I now have a permanent rendering farm at work (that didn't come into place until after the completion of Newsfront), so my policy on third-party plug-ins may change.

Anyway, back to Newsfront. I did use a wonderful third-party Toon shader, Illustrate, to render a clean wireframe version of the peacock to use in the composite. If you view \3ds4-ma\realwld3\newsfront.mov, you will see how I utilized the wireframe version. The gold peacock wireframe dissolves over the animation approximately six seconds in and dissolves out with a blur at approximately nine seconds.

Putting Together the Environment

The environment the peacock lives in was created with basically three layers: the barcode, the mosaic, and the shooters. We will take a look at all three layers.

The Barcode

The very base layer of the environment could be described as a futuristic barcode (see Figure RW3.8). I created the environment by creating rectangular tics in a circular pattern and mapping a multi-colored tic pattern on a circular ribbon. You can see the background layer in \3ds4-ma\realwld3\P-Back.mov or \3ds4-ma\realwld3\P-Back.max.

The camera animation was merged into this scene to track the camera path perfectly. This layer was rendered as a sequence of targa files that were the bottom most layer in the composite created in Combustion. The remaining layers of the composite were placed on top of this layer.

Figure RW3.8
The rendered frame
200 of the futuristic
background.

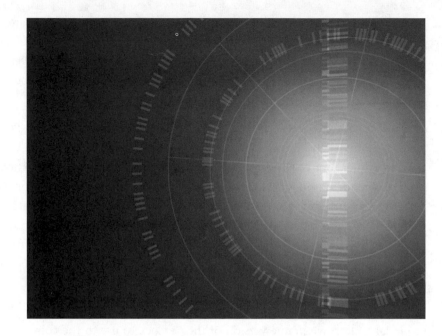

The Mosaic Lester Headshot

Because Lester Holt was going to be the host of the show, I decided I would try to incorporate his picture subliminally into the environment. Actually, I first tried to sneak in a picture of Colleen from *Survivor*, but I didn't want to risk someone figuring it out and having to change it. Anyway, I took a photo of Lester, and in Photoshop I applied a mosaic filter and drew a black grid on it (see Figure RW3.9).

I opacity-mapped this mosaic photo onto two yellow square shapes; one acted as the floor, the other acted as the ceiling (see Figure RW3.10). You can view the result of this layer by watching \3ds4-ma\realwld3\P-Lester.mov. The scene file is also available for examination \3ds4-ma\realwld3\scenes\P-Lester.max. This layer was applied additively to the barcode background in Combustion in the final composite.

The Shooters

My original plan contained only the barcode and the mosaic photo; but later in production, I decided to add the shooters. The beginning of the animation seemed a little stagnant, and I wanted to add a little more motion to the environment. I was working on a very tight schedule to wrap up this animation, so I turned to our archive footage. I found an animation that consisted of lines traveling in a criss-crossed grid pattern. I mapped this footage on a plane much like the mosaic picture of Lester. I then rendered it out, using the camera path so the footage tracked in the

Figure RW3.9
The mosaic photo of
Lester used to create
the environment.

Figure RW3.10
The rendered mosaic
photo grid layer at
frame 60.

scene. If you view \3ds4-ma\realwld3\newsfront.mov, you will see these shooting lines in the lower-left corner during the first second of the animation. They continue to travel through the peacock scene (as shown in Figure RW3.11).

Figure RW3.11
The grid line shooters are visible in the lower-left corner.

Finishing the Peacock

I mentioned earlier that I rendered the peacock in four layers: the first and second feathers, the third feather, the fourth feather, and the fifth and sixth feathers. Because the camera was facing the fourth feather for the majority of the animation, I focused most of my attention on the appearance of that feather.

The Textures of the Peacock

I applied seamless UVW Map coordinates around the perimeter of all the peacock feather objects. I then applied the textures I created to the specific areas of the peacock feather walls by adjusting the tile and offset values of the maps. This achieved the result I had desired; however, placing the textures on the feathers was time consuming.

Creating all the texture maps for the peacock feathers proved to be a daunting task. They needed to give the appearance of depth and suggest a hi-tech feel. The most noticeable texture on the peacock feathers is the scopes texture I created (see Figure RW3.12).

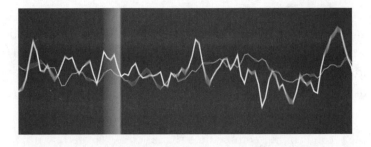

Figure RW3.12
The scopes texture that was used on the peacock feathers.

I created this texture inside 3ds max. To create the peaks and valley scopes, I created a straight line. In segment sub-object mode, I used the Divide tool to add 100 vertices on the line shape. I added that many vertices because the Noise modifier, which creates the peaks and valleys, acts only on the vertices. If there were only a start vertex and an end vertex, the Noise would have very little effect on the line. I added object motion blur to the lines to soften their rendered appearance.

You can see an animation of the scopes scene by viewing \3ds4-ma\realwld3\ scopes.mov. You can also examine the scene that created it by loading \3ds4-ma\ realwld3\scenes\scopes.max.

Another obvious texture map that's applied to the peacock feather is the meters texture (shown in Figure RW3.13). I created this texture in 3ds max as well. I started with a grid of squares that (from left to right) were colored red to bright yellow. Slightly in front of these squares, I created long black bands, one for each row. These black bands were then precisely animated to move left to right and reveal one square at a time.

To examine the resulting animation, view \3ds4-ma\realwld3\meters.mov. The 3ds max scene can be loaded from \3ds4-ma\realwld3\scenes\meters.max.

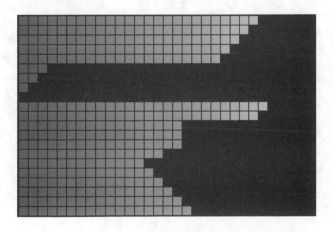

Figure RW3.13
The meters texture that was used on the peacock feathers.

The Peacock Composite

After I had all the peacock feathers textured, animated, and rendered I was able to start the composite for the scene. Because I had rendered the feathers separately, I was able to sandwich anything I wanted between them during the composite in Combustion. I mainly sandwiched other layers between the third and fourth feathers because that's where the camera focused.

In the first couple seconds of the animation, a digital clock (created by my fellow MSNBC 3D animator Jason Bube), a stock ticker, and the words "This just in to MSNBC" are wrapped around the curved part of the fourth peacock feather (the third from the left when you are facing the animation). These were all rendered as separate elements even though they were created in the same scene (see Figure RW3.14). I rendered them all separately so I would have maximum control of their appearance in the final composite.

The scene that contains these three objects is on the CD at \3ds4-ma\realwld3\ scenes\feath4misc.max. You can also view a rendered version of this file at \3ds4-ma\ Realwld3\feath4misc.mov. These layers, combined in Figure RW3.15, were sandwiched between the third and fourth feather of the peacock to give the appearance that they are part of the fourth peacock feather.

I tested several texture/composite ideas when I was working on this project. If you view \3ds4-ma\realwld3\testA.mov, you will see a preliminary test I created. Midway through the animation, you will see a wireframe globe animation that Vince

Figure RW3.14
A frame from the actual animation that shows the composited elements.

Figure RW3.15
A rendered frame from feath4misc.max; notice how the layers fit in with Figure RW3.14.

created for the project and I composited in. Unfortunately, this map didn't make it into the final piece.

I entertained myself while I was working on this project by adding inappropriate layers to the piece. If you view \3ds4-ma\realwld3\testB.mov, you will see a wireframe Harrier jet flying through the scene. I actually left this jet in until the very last time I composited the scene. If you view \3ds4-ma\realwld3\testC.mov, which was actually my first complete test of the animation, you will see the Harrier jet flying through the scene (it's underneath the white house). I recall management looking at the animation and saying, "That's not really going to be in there, is it?" Some of them actually liked it, though.

The Monitors

The video monitors proved to be one of the most tedious aspects of this project. The camera flew very quickly through the peacock, but the viewer needed enough time to view what was in the monitors. The most ideal time to see the monitors was when the camera was turning from shooting forward to backward. We knew that was where we wanted to see a large picture of Lester.

I was so wrapped up in the other aspects of the animation that I couldn't spend much time developing a style for the monitors. I tried, unsuccessfully, to design the monitors, but I didn't come up with anything that won me over. Therefore, I called on Vince's talent to help me put something together. I sent him a frame of the animation. The next day Vince returned my frame with beautiful monitors drawn in (see Figure RW3.16).

Figure RW3.16
The monitor illustration Vince created for the animation.

They were simple and practical and matched the style of the animation. Vince was even kind enough to provide me with Illustrator outlines of the different monitors that I could import into 3ds max and extrude into objects. When I had the monitors built, I sat with one of the directors of the show and we picked out shots to place into the monitors (see Figure RW3.17).

I have included the actual monitors from the animation on the CD. You can find this file at \3ds4-ma\realwld3\scenes\vid-monitorsA.max. (The materials have been removed because I could not include all the moving video clips from the animation.) I applied a simple material to the objects to avoid errors that might occur when I was loading it into 3ds max. If you'd like to see the rendered file, view \3ds4-ma\realwld3\vid-monitorsA.mov.

The stand-in image I placed in the video monitors (shown in Figure RW3.18) is a photograph I took while waiting in an airport for a plane. I loved all the reflections on the glass. I often take photos such as this one to inspire new ideas and designs. When I am out and about, I usually have a camera with me.

I also created a bank of monitors on the third peacock feather that you can see towards the end of the final Newsfront animation. This was rendered separately and composited in Combustion as well.

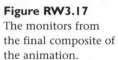

Figure RW3.17
The monitors from
the final composite of
the animation.

Figure RW3.18
Photographs such as
this one inspire new
ideas and designs.

Other Miscellaneous Layers

As I was building the final composite for the peacock scene, I realized that it didn't have enough depth. To give the illusion of depth in the composite, I created four plane objects in max, two on each side. One was further back than the other, so as the camera flew through the scene, it was unmistakable that there were two layers on each side. In Photoshop, I applied a mosaic filter to a group photograph from an Adventure Travel vacation (see Figure RW3.19). I then mirrored the image and applied it as an opacity map on the plane objects.

Figure RW3.19
This image was mapped to the four plane objects to add depth.

You can view this layer by watching \3ds4-ma\realwld3\digipanel.mov, and you can examine the scene by loading \3ds4-ma\realwld3\scenes\digipanel.max.

If you were paying close attention, you might have seen the particles flying through the file \3ds4-ma\realwld3\scenes\peakflyD.max. I added these particles, much like the Harrier jet, as a joke. But everyone really enjoyed the particles, so I decided to leave them in. They were rendered separately and composited in during the final peacock composite in Combustion.

Creating the Newsfront Logo Section

When I had completed the composite of the peacock section of the animation, I started to work on the creation of the final section of the animation, the logo. I needed a way to smoothly transition from the 3D NBC peacock section to the stylized 2D logo section. During a meeting, someone brought up using a Star Trek vortex effect. In my head, I could see this streaking back effect, but it was up to me to turn this front/back streaking into left/right streaking like on Vince's illustration. I needed to create the left/right streaking animation first, and then I could use that to create the vortex.

Creating the Streaking Animation

Vince's illustration called for a smooth and stylized swoosh pan background. At first, I tried to use stock footage of trains speeding by or time-lapse footage of cars' lights at night. These all created an effect that was far too choppy and distracting. I turned my attention to creating one of my own from scratch.

When I started to create the background, I asked myself, "What creates a streaking effect?" The answers were all similar: speeding objects passing the camera or quick camera movements.

To create the effect, I used two texture maps: streak2.jpg and streak2_a.jpg (shown in Figure RW3.20 and RW3.21, respectively). Both of these images were stretched to 100 times their normal aspect ratio along their X-axis (or in 3ds max UVW terms, the U-axis). This immediately created a streaking effect (see Figure RW3.22).

Figure RW3.20
Streak2.jpg, the image used to create the streak effect.

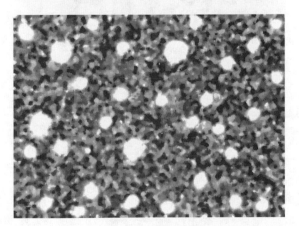

Figure RW3.21
Streak2_a.jpg, the matte image used to create the streak effect.

This is the principle that I used to create the background. If you view \3ds4-ma\real-wld3\back-streak.mov, you will see the background animation I created. If you load \3ds4-ma\realwld3\scenes\back-streak.max, you will see the scene that created this background. When you load the scene, you'll see that it contains no objects, lights, or camera. That's because I created the whole background as an Environment map in the Material Editor. You need to open the Material Editor to see the background (see Figure RW3.23).

Figure RW3.22
A cropped portion of streak2.jpg stretched 100 times along its X-axis.

Figure RW3.23
The streaks Environment map in the Material Editor.

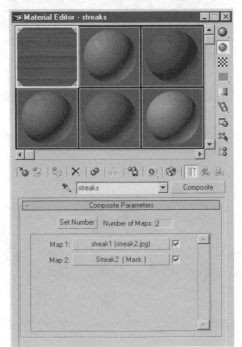

Notice the two maps in the Composite material. Map 1 is simply streak2.jpg with a U Tiling of .01 (to stretch it). Its U Offset is animated to change from 0 to –30 between frames 0 and 330. This creates the streaking motion as the image moves from right to left.

Map 2 is a Mask material. It consists of both streak2.jpg and streak2_a.jpg animated with the exact same parameters. Streak2_a.jpg is the mask in the material that instructs the Material Editor on how to apply the streak2.jpg to the composite. Both images have a U Tiling of .01 and have an animated U Offset from 0 to 15 between frames 0 and 330. The streaks created by Map 2 move from left to right, the opposite of Map 1, and they travel half as fast.

Building the Vortex

After I had created the streaking logo background, I started to build the Star Trek vortex effect. It took a couple of tries before I got it right, but I finally got it to fit perfectly into the animation. I used the streaking background as the texture for the vortex and applied it to a lathed shape I had created in 3ds max. You can examine the file I created for the vertex by loading \3ds4-ma\realwld3\scenes\vortex.max (shown in Figure RW3.24).

This scene solved the problem with transitioning from a front/back streaking image to a left/right streaking image. After I created the vortex object, I merged it with the

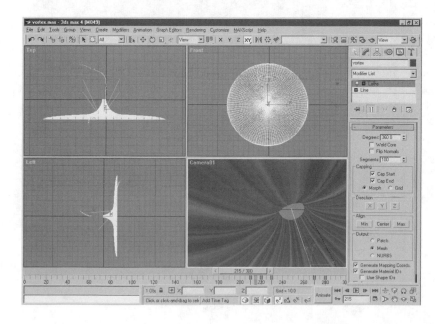

Figure RW3.24
Vortex.max was used to create the vortex transition in the Newsfront animation.

peacock scene's camera path. So as the camera flies through the front/back vortex, the vortex is animated to a new position, creating a left/right streaking image.

To soften the edge of the vortex when the camera first enters, I created an animated opacity map to reveal the vortex to the camera. The opacity map is a Gradient Ramp map type, and I animated the position and color of the flags over the duration of the animation (see Figures RW3.25 and RW3.26). You can see this layer rendered by viewing \3ds4-ma\realwld3\vortex.mov (it was rendered only from frame 200 to frame 300).

During the final composite of the Newsfront animation, I simply composited this layer over the peacock section and then dissolved the flat (left/right) streaking animation over the vortex. You can see this in the final animation now that you know what's happening. To view the final animation again, watch \3ds4-ma\realwld3\newsfront.mov.

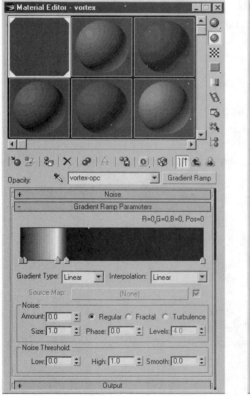

Figure RW3.25
The vortex-opc map at frame 220 is just in the beginning of the reveal.

Figure RW3.26
The vortex-opc map at frame 270 is at the end of the reveal.

Building the Newsfront Logo

Building the Newsfront logo animation was a lot of fun for me. I have a running joke that says this: "If you are a 3D animator working in news, you only need to know how to make gold, silver, and glass materials." This project, however, was none of those things: it was black, and actually, the letters themselves were nothing. The positive space of the black shapes created the letters with its negative space. We wanted to keep the sci-fi theme going, so I decided to add a few meteors to the futuristic animation.

In the final animation, the Newsfront logo flies into the animation as several squares. These squares randomly come together to form the Newsfront logo. To understand how I created this logo animation, you can load \3ds4-ma\realwld3\ scenes\logo.max (see Figure RW3.27). You can also view a rendered version of this scene at \3ds4-ma\realwld3\logo.mov.

For the logo, I created a plane primitive, added a grid of faces to it, and collapsed it into an editable mesh. I applied a planar UVW map coordinate to it and added the Newsfront type as an opacity map. I then broke that plane into eight random-looking pieces. Each of the eight random pieces has its own Bomb space warp with a detonation time and location that differs from the other bombs.

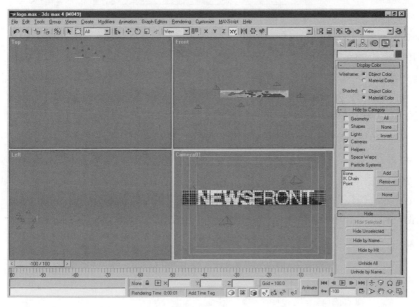

Figure RW3.27
The logo.max file contains the logo animation.

Bombs can only detonate forward, not backward, in 3ds max. If you play the animation scene in 3ds max, the pieces travel in reverse. This is because the animation is plays backward. Watch the time slider as the animation plays. To play a scene backward, you right-click the Play button to open the Time Configuration dialog. In the Time Configuration dialog, choose Reverse in the Playback group (see Figure RW3.28).

Figure RW3.28

The Time Configuration dialog, with Reverse selected in the Direction group.

The Reverse feature in the Time Configuration dialog only plays the animation backward in the views. When the scene renders, it still renders forward. That's why I keyed the animation between frames –100 and 0. When I rendered this animation forward, it labeled the targa files –100 to 0. When the images are loaded into the compositor, the compositor doesn't understand negative frame numbers, so essentially the frames were loaded from frame 0 to 100, reversing the frames.

With this completed, the Newsfront animation was ready to roll. In the corporate world, not everything turns out the way you expect. This animation is living proof of that. The long and short of it is that the parameters of the show are still in flux, and the animation will need further work. Stay tuned.

Appendix

What's on the CD-ROM

The accompanying CD-ROM is packed with all sorts of exercise files to help you work with this book and with 3ds max 4. The following sections contain detailed descriptions of the CD's contents.

For more information about the use of this CD, review the ReadMe.txt file in the root directory. That file includes important disclaimer information, as well as information about installation, system requirements, troubleshooting, and technical support.

Technical Support Issues

If you have any difficulties with this CD, you can access our web site at http://www.newriders.com.

System Requirements

This CD-ROM was configured for use on systems running Windows 9x or Windows NT.

Loading the CD Files

To load the files from the CD, insert the disc into your CD-ROM drive. If AutoPlay is enabled on your machine, the CD-ROM setup program starts automatically the first time you insert the disc. You can copy the files to your hard drive or use them right off the disc.

Note

This CD-ROM uses long filenames and mixed-case filenames, requiring the use of a protected mode CD-ROM driver.

Exercise Files

This CD contains all the files you'll need to complete the exercises in *3ds max 4 Media Animation*. These files can be found in the root directory of each Project or Real World folder within the \3ds4-ma\ folder.

Read This Before Opening the Software

By opening the CD package, you agree to be bound by the following agreement:

You may not copy or redistribute the entire CD-ROM as a whole. Copying and redistribution of individual software programs on the CD-ROM is governed by terms set by individual copyright holders.

This software is sold as-is, without warranty of any kind, either expressed or implied, including but not limited to the implied warranties of merchantability and fitness for a particular purpose. Neither the publisher nor its dealers or distributors assumes any liability for any alleged or actual damages arising from the use of this program. (Some states do not allow for the exclusion of implied warranties, so the exclusion may not apply to you.)

Index

Symbols

24-bit color information, 297
8-bit opacity information, 297

A

adding
    cameras to scenes, 447-448
    depth to NBC peacock scene, 552
    depth of field, 326-329, 338-339, 353, 357-358
    effects glows, 133-135
    faces to objects, 22
    flares to horizons, 522
    floors, 312-314
    globes and rings, 377-380
    glows, 133-135
    Inferno to glows, 430-432
    layers to composite environment maps, 121-126
    lens flares in video post, 424-426
    lighting to scenes, 447-448
    lightning, 174-178
    lights, 96-97, 421-422
    linear gradients, 455
    materials
        to lights, 98-99
        to objects, 64-65, 449-450
    materials to objects, 47-49
    music to scenes, 316-317
    music tracks to camera animation, 110-113
    Point helpers to scenes, 471-472
    radial gradients to Blind material, 458-461
    reflection maps, 449
    self-illumination to sub-materials, 144-145
    sound to scenes, 438-440
    soundtracks, 408-410
    special effects, 126
        effects glow, 133-135
        Video Post Lens Effects Glow, 136-138
        volume lights, 126-133
    sub-materials, 32-35
    texture to extrusions, 22-23
    UVW Map modifier, 39-41, 67
    vertices
        with Refine button, 29
        with Refine tool, 16-17
    Video Post Lens Effects Glow, 136-138
    Viewport Background to your
        workspace, 5-7
adjusting
    blur, 327
    camera animation, 117-118
    Glossiness and Specular Level settings, 387
    interpolation, 159-160
    Lens Effects Glow, 138-141
    Lens Flare's parameters, 427-430
    Material IDs, 40
    shapes, 210-213
    tangent handles, 207-208
        length, 211-212
    vertices, 199
Adobe Illustrator. *See* Illustrator
Align tool, 92, 449
    directing particle emissions, 168-171
aligning objects, 78-79
alpha, 297
Alpha Source group, 299
animatable Venetian blinds, creating, 451
animating
    armatures, 333-334
    cameras, 335-340, 343-346, 349-358, 467-469
        free cameras, 410-411
    environment backgrounds, 456-457
    flares, 432-434
    hands
        adjusting interpolation, 159-160
        synchronizing to sound tracks, 154-158
    heads, 148-152
    Index of Refraction, 513
    jibs, 113-116
    layers of composite material, 346-349
    lens flares, 474-476
    lights, flickering effect, 162-165
    objects, 412-417
    scenes, 323-326
    StripText objects, 467
animation
    creating for MSNBC Y2K coverage.
      See MSNBC Y2K coverage
    matching to audio, 439
    NBC News Decision 2000. *See* NBC News
      Decision 2000
    Newfront logo
        building, 557-558
        streaking animation, 553-555
    planning to music, 317-319
    rendering, 141-142, 178-179
    streaking animation, Newsfront logo, 553-555
    synchronizing to sound tracks, 154-158
    testing, 524
antialiasing, 391
applying
    Extrude modifier to shapes, 34
    mapping coordinates to screens, 293-297
    modifiers to multiple objects, 76-77
    UVW Map, 31
armatures, animating, 333-334
Assign Random Colors, 194
Attach List dialog, 275-280
audio. *See also* sound tracks
    adding to scenes, 408-410
    matching to animation length, 439

Auto Grid, creating cylinder primitives, 230-234
Auto Smooth, 254

B

back lights, 383
backdrops
    adding Viewport Background, 5-7
    creating, 5
backgrounds
    environment backgrounds
        animating, 456-457
        composite environment maps, 119-126
    horizons, creating, 521
    white backgrounds, template images, 7
barcodes, creating environment for NBC
    peacock, 543
Bend modifier, 84-88
Bevel modifier, parameters, 226-229
beveled type, NBC NEWS type, 520
beveling shapes, 237-241, 443-446
Bezier vertices, 54
Blind material, adding radial gradients to,
    458-461
blinds, creating, 451
blue, 536
blue metallic material, creating with Phong
    shaders, 375-376
blur, adjusting, 327
bobbing heads, 148-152
body objects, detaching splines from, 217-221
body templates, tracing, 27-30
Boolean subtraction, 12
Boolean technique, 46
Boolean Union, uniting splines, 15
Booleans,
    creating fire from circle shapes, 11-12
    object-level booleans, 244-250
brightening colors, 142-144
building
    jibs, 108-110
    vortex, Newfront logo, 555-556
bump maps, creating, 99-100
    from Illustrator files, 517-519
Burleson, Jonathon, 498
buttons
    Quick Render button, 19, 34
    Tube button, 378

C

camera animation, 108
    adding music tracks, 110-113
    adjusting, 117-118
    flying through NBC peacock, 537-541
    jibs
        animating, 113-116
        building, 108-110

camera jibs
    copying, 322
    creating, 320-322
    hiding, 341
    positioning, 330-332
cameras
    adding to scenes, 447-448
    animating, 335-340, 343-346, 349-358, 467-469
        free cameras, 410-411
    creating, 72-73
    graphics for MSNBC Y2K coverage, 500-501
    positioning, 341-342
    setting values, 74
centering shape's pivots, 222-225, 237-241
changing
    density in volume lights, 131
    mapping coordinates, 21-22
    Material IDs, 40, 48
    sub-object levels, 13
    vertex types, 29
circle shapes, creating illusion of
    wireframe objects, 370-374
circle star ceilings, 304-309
circles, creating
    from scratch, 8
    from squares, 487
circus silhouettes, adding to composite
    environment maps, 123-126
clocks, animation for MSNBC Y2K coverage,
    484-485
    creating, 486-487
        clock faces, 498-499
        glass faces, 487-489
Clone to Element option, 304-309
cloning
    Clone to Element option, 304-309
    objects, 194
clouds, adding to composite
    environment maps, 121-123
clowns
    adding sub-materials, 32-35
    extruding shapes, 30-31
    hands
        creating, 35
        mirroring objects, 42-45
        Modify tab, 38-39
        tracing, 36-37
    heads
        adding materials to, 47-49
        animating, 148-152
        creating, 45-47
    tracing body templates, 27-30
colonnade, 520
colors
    blue, 536
    brightening, 142-144
    Object Color dialog, 194
    red, 536
    spotlights, 95
combustion, 527

composite
environment maps
adding layers to, 121-126
creating, 119-121
maps, creating, 297-300
material, animating layers of, 346-349
of NBC peacock, 548-549

controlling vertices with XForm modifier, 451-455

converting shapes into objects, 61-63

copying
camera jibs, 322
instead of instancing, 256-260
objects, 101-103

Corner type vertices, 46

correcting size of imported Illustrator files, 186-193

creating
animatable Venetian blinds, 451
animation for MSNBC Y2K coverage, 483-484
clocks, 484-485
globe and clock, 497-498
millennium logo, 501-503
NBC peacock, 490-491
backdrops. *See* backdrops
backgrounds. *See* backgrounds
blue metallic material with Phong shaders, 375-376
bump maps, 99-100
from Illustrator files, 517-519
cameras, 72-73
animation. See camera animation
jibs, 320-322
circle star ceilings, 304-309
circles, 8
clocks (graphics for MSNBC), 486-487
glasses faces, 487-489
clown hands, 35
colonnade, 520
composite maps, 297-300
environment maps, 119-121
cylinder primitives with Auto Grid, 230-234
cylinders, 103-104
dissolves, 456-457
environments, NBC News Decision 2000, 520-522
fire, pointy fire tongues, 11-12
glass rings, 511-514
heads, 45-47
helpers, 108
hierarchies
Attach List dialog, 275-280
to hold objects together, 235-237
horizons, 521
IFLs, 174-178
lamps by lathing, 81-84
leg objects, 222
lens flares, 424-426
lighting fixtures, 81
lights, omni lights, 310-312
logos, Newfront logo, 557-558
materials
with lighting, 381-384
sub-materials, 66-67

matte finishes with Phong shader, 283-286
millennium logo for MSNBC Y2K coverage, 503-507
multi/sub-object materials, 290-293
NBC peacock for Newsfront. *See* Newsfront, creating NBC peacock
oceans with opacity maps, 385-392
plateaus, 253
Point helpers, 471-472
Presidential seal, 516-519
rack focus, 358-359
reflective gold materials, 392-394
rings for NBC News Decision 2000, 524-525
segments of shapes, 469-470
shapes in sub-object mode, 267-272
spotlights, 92-95
sub-materials, 66-67
type with opacity maps, 396-401
vertices, 29
Video Post queues, 359-363, 473
volume lights, 126-133
Wire material, 369
wireframe objects with circle shapes, 370-374

Curved Sides parameter, Bevel modifier, 229

cylinder objects
as rods, 272-274
modifying in sub-object mode, 251-256

cylinder primitives
creating with Auto Grid, 230-234
practicing with, 265-266

cylinders, creating, 103-104

D

DDR (Digital Disk Recorder), 484

Decision 2000. *See* NBC News Decision 2000

default interpolation, 33

defocus, 358-359

deleting vertices, 13-15, 29, 58

density, changing in volume lights, 131

depth, adding to NBC peacock scene, 552

depth of field, adding, 326-329, 338-339, 353, 357-358

detaching splines from shapes, 217-221

Dettmore, Joe, 482, 514

Diga, Vince, 510, 535

Digital Disk Recorder (DDR), 484

directing particle emissions with Align tool, 168-171

dissolves, creating, 456-457

Dolly Camera tool, 73

E

editing
IFLs, 177
imported objects, 441-442
objects, 83

effects glows, adding, 133-135

elements, 330. *See also* objects
hiding unwanted elements, 319, 322

End caps, failure to appear, 63

Environment Screen mapping, 120

environments
    backgrounds, animating, 456-457
    creating for NBC News Decision 2000, 520-522
    Gradient Ramps, 521-522
    for NBC peacock, 543-546

Extrude modifier, 32, 187-189
    applying to shapes, 34

extruding
    objects, 17-20
    shapes, 30-31, 242-244

extrusions, adding texture to, 22-23

F

faces, adding to objects, 22

failure of End caps to appear, 63

feathers, creating for NBC peacock with volume lights, 494-495

files, Illustrator files
    importing, 185-186
    problems with. *See* Illustrator, problems with imported files

filters
    Lens Effects Glow filter, 137
    Perimeter Alpha filter, 138

Filters dialog, 157

finessing lamps, 89-91

finishing touches to NBC peacock, 546
    adding depth to scene, 552
    composite, 548-549
    textures, 546-547
    video monitors, 549-550

fire, creating pointy fire tongues, 11-12

flares
    adding to horizons, 522
    animating, 432-434

Flat Mirror reflection, 514

flickering effect, animating lights, 162-165

floors, raytraced shadows, 312-314

flying through NBC peacock, 537
    attempt #1, 537-538
    attempt #2, 538-539
    successful attempt, 539-541

frame rates, 112
    RAM Player, 142

frames
    rendering, 19
    testing, 79

Franquera, Tony, 510

free cameras, animating, 410-411

G

Geometry rollout, 29

glass
    creating reflective glass particles, 171-174
    faces of clocks, creating, 487-489

shattering effects, 165-167
    directing particle emissions with Align tool, 168-171
    particle systems, 167-168

glass rings, creating, 511-514

globe and clock, animation for MSNBC Y2K coverage, 497-498
    cameras, 500-501
    creating clock face, 498-499
    globe's volumetric light beams, 500-501

globes
    adding to objects, 377-380
    graphics for MSNBC Y2K coverage, creating volumetric light beams, 500-501

Glossiness map, 387

glossy material, opacity mapping text from, 401-405

glows. *See also* light
    adding, 133-135
    Inferno to, 430-432
    Video Post Lens Effects, 136-138
    adjusting, 138-141

gold material, 449

Gradient Ramps, horizons, 521-522

graphics for MSNBC Y2K. *See* MSNBC Y2K coverage

H

hands
    animating, adjusting interpolation, 159-160
    mirroring objects, 42-45
    Modify tab, 38-39
    synchronizing animation to sound tracks, 154-158
    tracing, 36-37

heads
    adding materials to, 47-49
    animating, 148-152
    creating, 45-47

headshots of presidents, for NBC News Decision 2000, 526

helpers, creating, 108

hiding
    objects, 341
    unwanted elements, 319, 322

hierarchies
    creating with Attach List dialog, 275-280
    holding objects together, 235-237
    linking objects in hierarchies, 68, 301-302

highlighting, objects, 104-105

highlights, specular highlights, 386, 390

holding objects together with hierarchies, 235-237

Holt, Lester, 544

horizons, 521-522

I

IFLs (Image File Lists), 174-178

illustrations, matching objects to, 73-75

Illustrator
  correcting size of imported Illustrator files,
    186-193
  files, importing, 185-186
  Newsfront, 543
  problems with imported files, 186
    removing extra vertices, 195-198
    removing splines with Weld tool, 199-203
    removing unwanted vertices, 203-213
    scaling, 186
  touching up imported Illustrator files, 193-195
  using files from Illustrator to create bump
    maps, 517-519
Image Alpha, 299
Image File Lists (IFLs), 174-178
**image maps, offsetting to improve their
  position, 394-395**
**images, putting rendered images to music,
  359-363**
importing
  Illustrator files, 185-186
  objects, 441-442
Index of Refraction, animating, 513
Inferno, adding to glows, 430-432
instancing objects with Shift+Rotate, 302-304
interpolation
  adjusting, 159-160
  default interpolation, 33
Interpolation rollout, 13
Isolate tool, 287-288
Izzo, Francine, 537

J-K

jibs
  animating, 113-116
  building, 108-110
**joining shapes with sub-object boolean
  operations, 260-264**
keys, matching to sound tracks, 160-162
Kostyrko, Anna, 484

L

lamps
  adding a glow to, 133-135
  creating by lathing, 81-84
  finessing, 89-91
Lathe modifier, 91
lathing to create lamps, 81-84
layers
  adding to composite environment maps,
    121-126
  animating layers of composite material,
    346-349
leg objects, creating, 222
length of tangent handles, adjusting, 211-212
Lens Effects Flare, 524
Lens Effects Glow
  adding, 136-138
  adjusting, 138-141

lens flares, 423-424
  adding in Video Post, 424-426
  animating, 474-476
  loading, 473-474
  parameters, adjusting, 427-430
light bulbs
  creating shattering effects, 165-167
  shattering effects
    creating particle systems, 167-168
    creating reflective glass particles, 171-174
light fixtures,
  creating, 81
  copying, 101-103
lightning
  adding to your scenes, 174-178
  looping, 178
lights. *See also* **glows**
  adding, 96-97
    materials to, 98-99
    more, 421-422
    to scenes, 447-448
  aiding in the creation of materials, 381-384
  animating flickering effect, 162-165
  back lights, 383
  glows
    adding, 133-135
    adjusting Video Post Lens Effects, 138-141
    Video Post Lens Effects Glow, 136-138
  Multiplier values, 164
  Omni lights, 381
    creating, 310-312
  OmniBack light, 96
  rings of, 493
  spotlights, creating, 92-95
  tweaking, 418-419
  volume lights
    creating, 126-133
    creating feathers for NBC peacock, 494-495
    creating light beams, 500-501
linear gradients, adding, 455
linking objects
  with Bend modifier, 84-88
  in hierarchies, 68, 301-302
loading lens flares, 473-474
Lock Zoom/Pan, 6
logos
  NBC News Decision 2000, 530-531
  Newfront, 552
    creating, 557-558
    streaking animation, 553-555
    vortex, 555-556
  rendering, 531-533
looping lightning, 178

M

Manco, Christo, 516
Mandragona, Sam, 482, 510
mapping
  coordinates
    applying to screens, 293-297
    changing, 21-22
  text on plane objects, 462-464

maps
  bump maps, creating, 99-100
  Raytrace Refraction map, 488
matching
  animation length to audio, 439
  keys to sound tracks, 160-162
  objects to illustrations, 73-75
Material Editor, creating clocks, 487
Material IDs
  adjusting, 40
  changing, 40, 48
material maps, preparing objects for, 286-290
materials
  adding
    to lights, 98-99
    to objects, 47-49, 64-65, 449-450
  Blind material, adding radial gradients to,
    458-461
  blue metallic material, creating with Phong
    shaders, 375-376
  creating with lighting, 381-384
  glass rings, creating, 511-514
  glossy material, opacity mapping text from,
    401-405
  gold material, 449
  metals, creating matte finishes, 283-286
  multi/sub-object materials, creating, 290-293
  NBC News Decision 2000, 531-533
  organizing, 24-27
  raytrace materials, 392
  reflective gold material, creating, 392-394
  sub-materials, creating, 66-67
  Wire material, creating, 369
matte finishes, creating with Phong shader,
  283-286
Metal shader, 283
metals, creating matte finishes, 283-286
millennium logo, animation for MSNBC Y2K
  coverage, 501-503
  creating, 503-507
Mirror tool, 378
Mirror: World Coordinates dialog, 256
mirroring objects, 42-45
modifiers
  Bend modifier, 84-88
  Bevel modifier, parameters, 226-229
  Extrude modifier, 32, 187-189
    applying to shapes, 34
  Lathe modifier, 91
  using on multiple objects, 76-77
  UVW Map modifier, 21
    adding, 39-41, 67
  XForm modifier
    beveling shapes, 443
    controlling vertices, 451-455
    rotating objects, 42-43
Modify tab, 38-39
modifying
  cylinder objects in sub-object mode, 251-256
  shapes, Modify tab, 38-39
monitors, NBC peacock, 549-550

moons, adding to scenes, 119-121
mosaics, creating environment for NBC
  peacock, 544
motion, 151-152
Motor Space warp, 496
moving
  objects, 10, 149
  type, 76
MSNBC Y2K coverage
  clocks, creating, 486-489
  creating animation for, 483-484
    clocks, 484-485
    globe and clock, 497-498
    millennium logo, 501-503
    NBC peacock, 490-491
  graphics for Y2K, 482-483
multi/sub-object materials, creating, 290-293
Multiplier values, 164
music. See also soundtracks
  adding
    to camera animation, 110-113
    to scenes, 316-317
  planning animation to, 317-319
  putting rendered images to, 359-363

N

National Television Standards Committee
  (NTSC), 112
NBC News Decision 2000, 509-510
  final animation, viewing, 533
  glass rings, 511-514
  shot 1, 515
    colonnade and NBC NEWS type, 520
    environment, 520-522
    Presidential seal, 516-519
    shooters, 523-524
    testing, 524
  shot 2, 524-527
  shot 3, 527-530
  shot 4, 530-533
  working with storyboards, 514-515
NBC peacock, NBC News Decision 2000
  animation for MSNBC Y2K coverage, 490-491
    creating feathers with volume lights, 494-495
    creating particle effects, 495-497
    smoke rings, 491-493
  creating for Newsfront, 542-543
  environments, 543-546
  finishing touches, 546
    adding depth to scene, 552
    composite, 548-549
    textures, 546-547
    video monitors, 549-550
  flying through, 537-541
Neuhardt, Lori, 510, 535
Newsfront, 535-536
  creating logo, 552
    streaking animation, 553-555
    vortex, 555-556
  creating NBC peacock, 542-543, 546
    adding depth to scene, 552

composite, 548-549
environments, 543-546
textures, 546-547
video monitors, 549-550
flying through NBC peacock, 537-541
Illustrator, 543
NTSC (National Television Standards
Committee), 112

O

Object Color dialog, 194
object-level Booleans, 244-250
objects. *See also* elements
adding
depth to, 552
faces to, 22
layers to composite environment maps,
121-126
materials to, 47-49, 64-65, 98-99, 449-450
rings to, 377-380
UVW Map modifier, 39-41
aligning, 78-79
animating, 412-417
armatures, animating, 333-334
cameras, animating, 335-340, 343-346, 349-358
cloning, 194
with Clone to Element option, 304-309
converting from shapes, 61-63
copying, 101-103
cylinder objects
creating, 103-104
modifying in sub-object mode, 251-256
as rods, 272-274
detaching splines from shapes, 217-221
editing, 83
imported objects, 441-442
extruding, 17-20
globes, adding, 377-380
hands. *See* hands
heads, animating, 148-152
hiding, 341
highlighting, 104-105
holding together with hierarchies, 235-237
importing, 441-442
instancing with Shift+Rotate, 302-304
lathing, 81-84
legs, creating, 222
linking
with Bend modifier, 84-88
linking in hierarchies, 68, 301-302
matching to illustrations, 73-75
mirroring objects, 42-45
moving, 10, 149
plane objects, mapping text to, 462-464
preparing for material maps, 286-290
rings, adding to objects, 377-380
rising through holes in other objects, 529-530
rods, 272-274
rotating, 86, 412-417
with XForm modifier, 42-43
rotation of, setting up, 465-466
scaling, 74-76
standing up in world space, 69-72

StripText objects, animating, 467
synchronizing to sound tracks, 154-158
touching up, 89-91
unhiding, 330-332, 341
using modifiers on multiple objects, 76-77
wireframe objects, creating with circle shapes,
370-374
oceans, creating with opacity maps, 385-392
offsetting image maps to improve their
position, 394-395
Omni lights, 381
creating, 310-312
OmniBack light, 96
opacity maps
creating
oceans, 385-392
type, 396-401
mapping text
from glossy material, 401-405
to plane objects, 462-464
options, Clone to Element option, 304-309
organizing materials, 24-27
Outline tool, 57-61

P

pad, 111
parameters
of Bevel modifier, 226-229
Lens Flare, adjusting, 427-430
particle effects, creating for NBC peacock,
495-497
particle emissions
creating reflective glass particles, 171-174
directing with Align tool, 168-171
particle systems
creating shattering effects, 167-168
directing emissions with Align tool,
168-171
in millennium logo for MSNBC Y2K coverage,
505-507
Perimeter Alpha filter, 138
Phong shader
creating blue metallic material, 375-376
creating matte finishes, 283-286
ping pong motions, 152
pinning, definition of, 74
pivots, centering shape's pivots, 222-225, 237-
241
pixel information, right-click pixel
information, 66
Place Highlight tool, 448
plane objects, mapping text to, 462-464
planning animation to storyboards and music,
317-319
plateaus, creating, 253
Point helpers, creating, 471-472
pointy fire tongues, creating, 11-12

positioning
camera jibs, 330-332
cameras, 341-342
practicing with cylinder primitives, 265-266
pre-roll, 111
Premultiplied Alpha, 299
preparing objects for material maps, 286-290
Presidential seal
creating, 516-519
NBC News Decision 2000, 529-530
problems with imported Illustrator files, 186
correcting size of imported files, 186-193
removing
extra vertices, 195-198
splines with Weld tool, 199-203
unwanted vertices, 195-198, 203-210
scaling, 186
touching up, 193-195

Q-R

Queues, rendering, 432-434
Quick Render button, 19, 34

rack focus, creating, 358-359
Radial Color gradient, 430
radial gradients, adding to Blind material, 458-461
RAM Player, 142-144
Ray Traced shadows, 312-314
raytrace maps, 392
raytrace materials, 392
Raytrace Refraction map, 488
raytraced reflections, 391
real world examples
MSNBC Y2K coverage. *See* MSNBC Y2K
coverage
NBC News Decision 2000. *See* NBC News
Decision 2000
Newsfront. *See* Newsfront
rectangle shapes, 7-9
red, 536
Refine button, adding vertices, 29
Refine tool, 227, 445
adding vertices, 16-17
reflection maps, adding, 449
reflections, Flat Mirror reflection, 514
reflective gold materials, creating, 392-394
Region Zoom, 36
removing. *See also* **deleting**
splines with Weld tool, 199-203
vertices, 195-198, 203-210
rendered images, putting to music, 359-363
rendering
animations, 141-142, 178-179
logos, 531-533
NBC News Decision 2000, 526-527
queues, 432-434
test frames, 19, 34

right-click pixel information, 66
rings
adding to objects, 377-380
creating for NBC News Decision 2000, 524-525
of light, 493
of smoke, creating for NBC peacock, 491-493
**rising objects through holes in other objects,
529-530**
rods, cylinder objects, 272-274
rotating
objects, 86, 412-417
setting up, 465-466
XForm modifier, 42-43
text, 503-505
rotoscoping, 526

S

scaling
imported Illustrator files, 186
objects, 74-76
scenes, animating, 323-326
screen splines, 195
**screens, applying mapping coordinates to, 293-
297**
segments of shapes, creating, 469-470
Select and Move tool, 76
switching with Select and Uniform tool, 10
Select and Non-Uniform Scale tool, 74-76
Select and Rotate tool, 43
Select and Uniform Scale tool, 188
switching with Select and Move tool, 10
Select Object tool, 71
**self-illumination, adding to sub-materials, 144-
145**
shaders
Metal shader, 283
Phong shader, 283-286
shadows, raytraced shadows, 312-314
shapes
adjusting, 210-213
applying Extrude modifier to, 34
beveling, 237-241, 443-446
body templates, tracing, 27-30
centering pivots, 222-225
centering shape's pivots, 237-241
circles, creating, 8
converting into objects, 61-63
creating in sub-object mode, 267-272
detaching splines from, 217-221
extruding, 30-31, 242-244
fire, pointy fire tongues, 11
hands, tracing, 36-37
joining with sub-object Boolean operations,
260-264
mirroring objects, 42-45
modifying, 38-39
rectangle shapes, 7-9
segments of, creating, 469-470
working with, 45-47

shattering effects, 165-167
    creating
        particle systems, 167-168
        reflective glass particles, 171-174
    directing particle emissions with Align tool,
        168-171

Shift+Rotate, instancing objects, 302-304

shooters
    creating environment for NBC peacock,
        544-546
    NBC News Decision 2000, 523-524

Show End Result on/off toggle, 83

size of imported Illustrator files, correcting,
    186-193

smoke rings, creating for NBC peacock,
    491-493

smoothing motion, 151

SMPTE (Society of Motion Picture and
    Television Engineers), 112

sound, adding to scenes, 438-440

sound tracks
    matching to keys, 160-162
    setting up, 153-154
    synchronizing animation to, 154-158

soundtracks, 316. *See also* music
    adding to scenes, 408-410

space warps, Motor space warps, 496

special effects, 126
    adding effects glow, 133-135
    Video Post Lens Effects Glow, 136-138
    volume lights, creating, 126-133

specular highlights, 386, 390

splines. *See also* vertices
    creating new points, 58
    detaching from shapes, 217-221
    removing with Weld tool, 199-203
    screen splines, 195
    subtracting, 248
    uniting, 15

spotlights, creating, 92-95

squares, appearing as circles, 487

standard shapes, rectangle shapes, 7-9

standing objects up in world space, 69-72

Star Trek Vortex effect, Newsfront logo, 555-
    556

Status Panel, 334

Step Interpolation, 13

stepping, 371

Steps values, 13

storyboards, NBC News Decision 2000, 514-515

streaking animation, Newfront logo, 553-555

StripText objects, animating, 467

sub-materials
    adding, 32-35
        self-illumination to, 144-145
    creating, 66-67
    organizing, 24-27

sub-object Boolean operations, joining shapes,
    260-264

sub-object levels, changing, 13

sub-object mode
    creating shapes, 267-272
    modifying cylinder objects, 251-256

sub-objects, working with, 10-12

subtacting splines, 248

switching between Select and Move and Select
    and Uniform tools, 10

synchronizing
    animation to sound tracks, 154-158
    music and animation, 317-319

T

tangent handles, 202
    adjusting, 207-208
        length, 211-212

template images, white backgrounds, 7

templates, tracing body templates, 27-30

test frames, rendering, 19, 34

testing
    animation, 524
    frames, 79

text
    beveling, 520
    creating with opacity maps, 396-401
    mapping on plane objects, 462-464
    moving, 76
    opacity mapping from glossy material, 401-
        405
    tracing, 53-56

text rotating, 503-505

texture
    adding to extrusions, 22-23
    on NBC peacock, 546-547

tiling, 25-27

tips for editing objects, 442

tools
    Align tool, 92, 449
        directing particle emissions, 168-171
    Dolly Camera tool, 73
    Isolate tool, 287-288
    Mirror tool, 378
    Outline tool, 57-61
    Place Highlight tool, 448
    Refine tool, 227, 445
    Select and Move tool, 76
    Select and Non-Uniform Scale tool, 74-76
    Select and Rotate tool, 43
    Select and Uniform Scale tool, 188
    Select Object tool, 71
    switching between Select and Move and Select
        and Uniform tools, 10
    Weld tool, removing splines, 199-203
    Zoom tool, 388

touching up
    imported Illustrator files, 193-195
    objects, 89-91

tracing
    hands, 36-37
    Outline tool, 57-61

shapes to be mirrored, 36-37
with standard shapes, 7
templates, body templates, 27-30
type, 53-56
troubleshooting End caps, 63
Tube button, 378
tweaking lights, 418-419
type. *See* text

U

unhiding objects, 330-332, 341
uniting splines, 15
unwanted elements, hiding, 319, 322
U.S. Capitol Dome
    NBC News Decision 2000, 528
    rising through hole in Presidential seal, 529-530
Use Transform Coordinate Center, 378
UVW coordinates, 121
UVW Map modifier
    adding, 39-41, 67
    applying, 31
UVW Mapping gizmo, 31
UVW Mapping modifier, 21

V

values for camera settings, 74
Venetian blinds, creating, 451
vertex types, changing, 29
vertices. *See also* splines
    adding, 16-17, 29
    adjusting, 199
    Bezier vertices, 54
    controlling with XForm modifier, 451-455
    Corner type vertices, 46
    creating, 29
    deleting, 13-15, 29, 58
    removing, 195-198, 203-210
    tangent handles, 202
video monitors, NBC peacock, 549-550
Video Post, adding lens flares, 424-426
Video Post Lens Effects Glow
    adding, 136-138
    adjusting, 138-141
Video Post queues, creating, 359-363, 473
viewing NBC News Decision 2000 final
    animation, 533
Viewport Background
    adding to your workspace, 5-7
    zooming, 6
volume lights, creating, 126-133
    feathers for NBC peacock, 494-495
    volumetric light beams, 500-501
vortex, Newfront logo, 555-556

W

Weld tool, removing splines, 199-203
white backgrounds and template images, 7
Wire material, creating, 369
wireframe objects, creating with circle shapes, 370-374
Wisner, Matt, 526
working with sub-objects, 10-12
World Coordinate system, 379
world space, standing objects in, 69-72

X-Y-Z

XForm modifier
    beveling shapes, 443
    controlling vertices, 451-455
    rotating objects, 42-43
Y2K, graphics for MSNBC Y2K coverage, 482-483
Zoom tool, 388
zooming, Viewport Background, 6

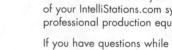

Solutions from experts you know and trust.

www.informit.com

OPERATING SYSTEMS

WEB DEVELOPMENT

PROGRAMMING

NETWORKING

CERTIFICATION

AND MORE...

**Expert Access.
Free Content.**

New Riders has partnered with **InformIT.com** to bring technical information to your desktop. Drawing on New Riders authors and reviewers to provide additional information on topics you're interested in, **InformIT.com** has free, in-depth information you won't find anywhere else.

- **Master the skills you need, when you need them**

- **Call on resources from some of the best minds in the industry**

- **Get answers when you need them, using InformIT's comprehensive library or live experts online**

- **Go above and beyond what you find in New Riders books, extending your knowledge**

As an **InformIT** partner, **New Riders** has shared the wisdom and knowledge of our authors with you online. Visit **InformIT.com** to see what you're missing.

www.informit.com ▪ www.newriders.com

New Riders

The 3ds max 4 Media Animation CD

The CD that accompanies this book contains the project and Real World files. All the example files provided by the author enable you to work through the step-by-step projects.

Accessing the Project Files from the CD

The majority of projects in this book use pre-built *3ds max 4* files that contain preset parameters, artwork, audio, or other important information you need to work through and build the final project.

All the project files are conveniently located in the root directory of each Project or Real World folder within the \3ds4-ma\ folder. To access the project files for the Funhouse project (Project 1), for example, locate the following directory on the accompanying CD: the \3ds4-ma\Project 1.

We recommend that you copy the files on the CD to your hard drive. The playing of the .avi or .mov files is dependent on your system configuration; older systems may not play the files smoothly.

> For a complete list of the CD-ROM contents, please see the appendix, "What's on the CD-ROM."

Colophon: *3ds max 4 Media Animation* was laid out and produced with the help of Microsoft Word, Adobe Acrobat, Adobe Photoshop, Collage Complete, and QuarkXpress on a variety of systems, including a Macintosh G4. With the exception of pages that were printed out for proofreading, all files—text, images, and project files—were transferred via email or ftp and edited on-screen.

All body text was set in the Bergamo family. All headings, figure captions, and cover text were set in the Imago family. The Symbol and Sean's Symbol typefaces were used throughout for special symbols and bullets.

3ds max 4 Media Animation was printed on 50# Husky Offset Smooth paper at R.R. Donnelley & Sons in Crawfordsville, Indiana. Prepress consisted of PostScript computer-to-plate technology (filmless process). The cover was printed at Moore Langen Printing in Terre Haute, Indiana, on Carolina, coated on one side.